Managing Electronic Media
Making, Marketing, and Moving Digital Content

Joan Van Tassel

Lisa Poe-Howfield

AMSTERDAM • BOSTON • HEIDELBERG • LONDON
NEW YORK • OXFORD • PARIS • SAN DIEGO
SAN FRANCISCO • SINGAPORE • SYDNEY • TOKYO

Focal Press is an imprint of Elsevier

Focal Press is an imprint of Elsevier
30 Corporate Drive, Suite 400, Burlington, MA 01803, USA
The Boulevard, Langford Lane, Kidlington, Oxford, OX5 1GB, UK

Notices
Knowledge and best practice in this field are constantly changing. As new research and experience broaden our understanding, changes in research methods, professional practices, or medical treatment may become necessary.

Practitioners and researchers must always rely on their own experience and knowledge in evaluating and using any information, methods, compounds, or experiments described herein. In using such information or methods they should be mindful of their own safety and the safety of others, including parties for whom they have a professional responsibility.

To the fullest extent of the law, neither the Publisher nor the authors, contributors, or editors, assume any liability for any injury and/or damage to persons or property as a matter of products liability, negligence or otherwise, or from any use or operation of any methods, products, instructions, or ideas contained in the material herein.

Library of Congress Cataloging-in-Publication Data
Van Tassel, Joan M.
Managing electronic media : making, marketing, and moving digital content / Joan Van Tassel, Lisa Poe-Howfield.
   p. cm.
Includes bibliographical references and index.
ISBN 978-0-240-81020-1 (pbk. : alk. paper) 1. Mass media—Management. I. Poe-Howfield, Lisa. II. Title.
P96.M34V36 2010
302.23—dc22

                              2009052491

British Library Cataloguing-in-Publication Data
A catalogue record for this book is available from the British Library.

ISBN: 978-0-240-81020-1

For information on all Focal Press publications
visit our website at *www.elsevierdirect.com*

10 11 12 13 14 5 4 3 2 1

Printed in the United States of America

Typeset by: diacriTech, Chennai, India

Contents

Introduction and Acknowledgments

For almost 15 years, I wrote for the Special Issues section of the *Hollywood Reporter*, writing about the effects of digital technologies on the media industries. In the course of that reporting, I interviewed virtually all of the executives who were guiding the major media and entertainment companies through the choppy waters of a new media landscape. They were called upon to address the changes brought about by the introduction of digital content creation technologies – cameras, nonlinear editing, computer-generated imagery for animation and special effects, the Internet and peer-to-peer networks, and the proliferation of channels and media players, such as mobile, game consoles, DVRs, HDTV, Blu-ray, and all the other rapidly changing consumer electronics devices.

Not surprisingly, the ripples of changes in technology soon reached the public, which eagerly adopted many of the new ways to consume media, changing their media uses and habits. They also sent unceasing tides of change through the media industry itself, with which managers at every company and every level had to deal. It was a truly chaotic business environment – a sneeze in Chicago may not cause a tsunami in Beijing, but computer processors in San Jose certainly caused a tsunami in the media industry that has lasted for longer than two decades.

Digital content creation changed the speed, flexibility, and cost of content production, making it cheaper for consumers, but sometimes more expensive for blockbusters loaded with special effects, such as *Titanic*. Networked distribution enabled media companies to employ skilled creators from around the world, opened up global market for content products, and greatly lowered the cost of sending media to all corners of the globe. It also enabled consumers to send media files to all those same corners, undercutting existing business practices and valuable sources of revenue.

The speed and scope of change continue. The media industry is still coping with the effects of the Internet – Internet 1. But Internet 2 is coming, and it will arrive during the careers *and* lives of today's generation of college students. Internet 2 is in development around the world. The universities and governments of many countries are connected to it, and scientists and engineers are hard at work building the technologies needed for its introduction and public adoption.

The purpose of this book is to lay a foundation for understanding and participating in the ongoing evolution of the media industry. It provides the concepts and vocabulary that managers have devised to meet the challenges of today's market and to position their organizations to succeed in a dynamic future business environment. At the same time, managers rely on many traditional ideas and processes to guide their actions. In some ways, media businesses are not so different from how they were in the past, or isolated from the practices that govern modern businesses everywhere.

The book tries to keep one foot in the recent past, another in the near future, without losing sight of the present, which demands knowledge of both past and future dimensions:

- Chapter 1 introduces students to the media industries – their size, structure, segments, and role in society.
- Chapter 2 looks at media organizations, what they do, and how they create value to be successful and profitable.
- Chapter 3 examines leadership and management techniques, with brief bios of the business accomplishments of media industry managers.
- Chapter 4 details how media companies handle human resources, in industries that are highly dependent on skilled creative people.
- Chapter 5 shows students how to follow the money, giving them insight into the pervasive importance in media industry organization of financial planning, budgeting, and management.
- Chapter 6 explores the new paradigm of media consumers, who may be customers, viewers, listeners, readers, users, players, friends, and followers, depending on which media segment an executive manages.
- Chapter 7 discusses the revolution in media content, including traditional and new means of production, content acquisition, and user-generated content.
- Chapter 8 presents the Big Picture strategies for marketing media content, at the heart of organizational growth and profitability.
- Chapter 9 gets into the detail of marketing – readying content products and shaping them to succeed in the marketplace.
- Chapter 10 covers sales management, a key function in any organization, where the revenues flow into the cash register.
- Chapter 11 lays out the new world of content distribution as companies maintain the traditional means of delivering content to consumers, even as they try to seize the opportunities offered by digital channels.
- Chapter 12 considers the language of conducting media business, showing how every part of the industry creates value in the marketplace, allowing organizations to bring in revenue.

- Chapter 13 presents ever-evolving media industry business models that serve as a shorthand way of describing the products the business will bring to market and how it will attract consumers. The business model also includes how the organization will deliver the product or service and derive revenue from it.
- Chapter 14 provides an overview of the legal and regulatory issues that affect media enterprises that operate in both U.S. and international markets, including the new frontier of the Internet.
- Chapter 15 asks some of the most difficult questions the media industries face: the ethical considerations brought up by their influential role in the public sphere and private consciousness of individuals.

Some readers may want to know why there is no chapter – perhaps even several chapters – specifically looking at communication technologies. To some extent, these topics are covered in Chapter 11, in the discussion of distributing content. The distribution infrastructure – wired and wireless networks – figure so large in all our lives that such a topic deserves its own book to estimate the likely future growth and capacity. Such projections are more or less impossible for consumer devices. There are probably college students at work in their garages and dorms right now figuring out some new fabulous way to consume content that no one has ever thought of before and will turn some part of the media industry upside down. I look forward to their products and the enchanting creations that will follow, but I will not attempt to guess what they might produce! Indeed, if I could, I would be out in my own garage.

ACKNOWLEDGMENTS

Joan Van Tassel

I want to thank so many people for their help, guidance, and patience as I wrote this book. First and foremost, Elinor Actipis and Michele Cronin at Focal Press deserve medals for their forbearance and kindness to me as I wrote this book. I admire them and cannot express entirely my gratitude to them, except to say a heartfelt "Thank you." I am also indebted to the skilled copy editing of Nancy Kotary.

To my co-author Lisa Poe-Howfield, I extend my appreciation for her knowledge, willingness, and creativity. She has been a stalwart companion in this process. I am also grateful to contributors Augie Grant (a veteran co-conspirator/grad student with me at the Annenberg School at USC) who has gone on to great success, and his student, Chris Roberts, who provided such knowledge and skill for Chapters 14 and 15. Reviewers played a key role with their comments and observations, delivered honestly and constructively. Truly, Robert B. Affe,

Todd Chambers, John Allen Hendricks, and a reviewer who wished to be anonymous have improved the book far beyond what it would have been without their generous assistance.

An author's family always pays a price, including my siblings, Elaine Baer and Nancy, Gordon, Karen, Bailey, Emmy, and Lucille Van Tassel. Robert and Irene Newton, Mona Nasir, and my personal coach, star journalist Mary Murphy. Have always been huge supporters, too. I love them, each and every one.

National University colleagues have given me time, encouragement, and support in the writing of this book. I must mention members of the administration, Debra Bean, Patricia Potter, and Karla Berry. I would not want to leave out my wonderful faculty colleagues: Cynthia Chandler, Louis Rumpf, Scott Campbell, Sara Ellen Amster, Sara Kelly, Roger Gunn, John Banks, Maureen O'Hara, and Ismail Sebetan.

Finally, Peter Clarke and Susan Evans at the University of Southern California were my mentors at the Annenberg School for Communication and continue to inspire, encourage, and help me to this day. I remember Everett Rogers, a member of my dissertation committee when I was a graduate student, and always regret his passing. The world without Ev is a lesser place. To Ron Rice, I will always be grateful for his direction given to me on the day I defended my dissertation: "Go forth and communicate." With this book, I hope I have.

Lisa Poe-Howfield

First and foremost! In my maiden voyage as coauthor, I send out my eternal gratitude, respect and thanks to Joan Marie Van Tassel for providing me with this incredible opportunity. Your dedication to share your knowledge, not to mention your patience in walking me through the process, serves as a great inspiration to all…thank you!

Thank you to Elinor Actipis and Michele Cronin at Focal Press Media for keeping me on track and providing just the right guidance.

Professionally, I have been blessed with great role models in my life including Jim and Beverly Rogers (Owners of Sunbelt Communications); Ralph Toddre (President and COO of Sunbelt Communications); Desiree Long (Executive Assistant, KVBC TV 3) and my dear friend and former colleague, Judy Reich-Milby. You have all inspired me to greater heights- thank you.

Sincere appreciation to those who contributed to our "Day in the Life" segments: Elliott Grove, Bob Kaplitz, Vivi Zigler, Valerie Geller, Craig Robinson, Brad Williams, Richard Conlon, Sam Bush, Wendy Shelton, Anne-Marie Gillen, Dorothy Hui, Lloyd Kaufman, and Debbie Carter. Also, much thanks to Terry King from Clear Channel who provided great insight to the world of radio.

Thank you all for taking time from your busy schedules to share your real life experiences.

On a personal note, I give thanks to my parents, Allen and Peggy Poe, who sacrificed much and worked diligently to provide me with the means to obtain my college education at Pepperdine University and to my Mother-in-law, Margaret Howfield, who lost her battle with leukemia while this book was being written, but left a legacy of true strength. A very special thank you and much love to my husband, Ian Howfield, and son, Kyle Root, who continually demonstrate incredible support with their kind words, witty humor and powerful hugs – making all things possible.

DAY IN THE LIFE FEATURES

Day in the Life section feature top media executives and highlight their everyday routines, showcasing some of their key concerns and perspectives on today's media. Each section includes a brief essay and a daily rundown.

Craig Robinson – President and General Manager, KNBC/TV-Los Angeles, California (Chapter 1)

Lloyd Kaufman – Co-Founder and President of Troma Entertainment; Chairman of the Independent Film & Television Alliance (IFTA); author of *Direct Your Own Damn Movie, Produce Your Own Damn Movie*, and *Make Your Own Damn Movie* (Chapter 2)

Sam Bush – Senior Vice President and Chief Financial Officer of Saga Communications, Inc. (Chapter 5)

Debbie Carter – Vice President and Director of Sales for Blair Television (Chapter 6)

Ann Marie Gillen – CEO and Founder of the Gillen Group, LLC; Film Producer & Entertainment Industry Consultant (Chapter 7)

Dorothy Hui – Vice President, Partnership Marketing & Sales, Wind-up Records (Chapter 8)

Elliot Grove – Director and Founder of the Raindance Film Festival and the British Independent Film Awards; author of *Raindance Writers' Lab* and *Raindance Producers' Lab* (Chapter 9)

Wendy Y. Shelton – Sales Manager, KVBC TV-3 (NBC), Las Vegas, Nevada (Chapter 10)

Valerie Geller – President, Geller Media International; Broadcast Consultant; author of *Creating Powerful Radio* (Chapter 11)

Richard Conlon – Vice President, New Media & Strategic Development - Broadcast Music, Inc. (BMI) (Chapter 12)

Bob Kaplitz – Principal and Senior Station Strategies for AR&D, author of *Creating Execution Superstars with Budgets Cut to the Bone* (Chapter 13)

Vivi Zigler – President of NBC Digital Entertainment (Chapter 13)

Brad Williams – Vice President, Member Benefits and Developments – NAB (National Association of Broadcasters) (Chapter 14)

CHAPTER 1

The Media Industries: Segments, Structures, and Similarities

Don't hate the media. Be the media.

Jello Biafra

CHAPTER OBJECTIVES

The objective of this chapter is to provide you with information about:
- The structure and characteristics of the content industries
- The segments that make up the content industries
- The wide range of businesses within the segments of the content industries
- The changing cultural, social, political, and economic conditions that establish the business context of the content industries

CONTENTS

INTRODUCTION

Movies, music, games, magazines, books, newspapers, Internet, comedy, drama, news – this media content constitutes the exciting visible face of the media world that thrills and enthralls audiences around the world. Many people have fantasies of being in the public eye as actors, singers, writers, and journalists, and a few of us go on to perform. But behind the scenes, there are many rewarding careers in the media industries to discover, promote, support, and manage all the activities that must be completed to bring these wonderful works to life and to audiences.

The history of electronic mass media is short. The precursors, books and newspapers, have been around for several hundred years, but the phenomenon of mass media is less than 150 years old. Electricity-based technologies have their roots in the nineteenth century, but all emerge as media platforms in the twentieth century, as shown in Figure 1-1.

DOI: 10.1016/B978-0-240-81020-1.00001-4

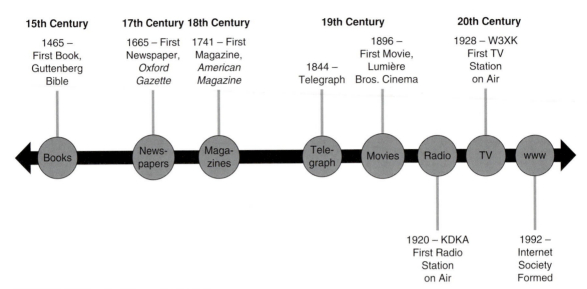

FIGURE 1-1 Timeline of mass media platforms

The short lifetime of electronic media means that the structure of media companies evolved somewhat differently from businesses in older, industrial enterprises. They standardized products and processes, seeking greater production efficiencies. Once developed, manufacturing may not change for several years. But each content product has at least some unique properties, such as episodes of television series, and others are entirely unique, including motion pictures and music albums. It is only at the point of distribution that content products are standardized for delivery and consumption.

At the same time, there are also many similarities between companies in the media industry and those in other sectors. Most of the work in media organizations is initiated and supported by managers – executives who have responsibility for directing, controlling, and supervising the affairs of the enterprise. To carry out the work, they draw on all the human, financial, technological, and environmental resources available to them.[1]

For example, in television, when a show's popularity begins to slip, network executives begin to think about developing a new product, a new show to air in that time period. They will ask producers and writers to submit ideas that would appeal to the audience, sift through those ideas, develop a few of them, produce a couple of pilots, test the pilots with a panel of people who would be in the audience, and order episodes of the show they think will succeed. Similarly, music executives are always on the lookout for new talent, but they might think a performer in a particular genre – country, hip-hop, ethnic – might be more successful than an equally talented jazz musician or Romanian gypsy band.

Managers work in every kind of organization, industry, geography, nation, and society. Their responsibilities have a great deal in common, whether the task is managing a chemical company, a large farm, a not-for-profit social service agency, or a music label. Yet each business enterprise and environment has its own characteristics that affect how managers conceptualize problems and solutions and how they carry out their duties.

The glamorous media industries are no exception – even routine, predictable work carries the patina of the power and visibility that surrounds these enterprises. Human resources hire personnel – sometimes performers like Sean Penn. Legal departments negotiate and approve contracts – sometimes for albums like *OK Computer* by Radiohead. Business development units establish partnerships, finance and accounting departments handle payables and receivables and impose organizational cost-reduction programs, and marketing teams traverse the complex wholesale and retail channels that finally put products in the hands of consumers, for all produced content – even a compelling hit TV series like *House.*

STRUCTURE AND CHARACTERISTICS OF THE MEDIA INDUSTRIES

It is a given that managers will know a great deal about the industry in which they work. They get that information from many sources. Some media enterprises gather and analyze information about their consumers and customers from direct contact. If they don't have internal information, companies receive research reports that tell executives about their audience, product performance, and markets. There is a lot of public information as well, as the media are frequent subjects of journalistic coverage that report on financial, technological, and cultural aspects of the industry. Managers also gain valuable information from their own personal experiences with buying and consuming content.

Another factor that influences how managers make decisions is the importance of the media in people's lives. Many spend more time watching, listening, and reading the media than they do anything else, except breathing. Adding up all of the time they engage with media – waking to the sound of the clock radio/ CD player and television set, checking and responding to email throughout the day, listening to a car radio and an iPod, watching a portable DVD, playing games on mobile phones, surfing the Net, and watching television before bed – the average person in the United States spends more than 9.5 hours per day with the media and will spend $936.75 per year on media consumption.[2] Nine and a half hours is more time than most people spend sleeping!

Given the amount of time devoted to media use, it is no surprise that the media exert profound cultural, economic, political, and psychological influences.

Indeed, the media constitute a pervasive, virtual environment whose impact sometimes seems to transcend even the physical world. Managers find that their business can be affected by the content they provide – remember Janet Jackson's "wardrobe malfunction"? It upset many viewers, resulting in fines for the network and electronic banishment for Jackson.

Industry Size and Composition

In 2011, the global media industries will account for nearly $2.0 trillion in revenue.[3] However, they are part of a larger commercial complex, called the *copyright industries*. The organizations that make up the copyright industries engage in the "generation, production and dissemination of new copyrighted material."[4] The specific content may differ, but the management of these activities is strikingly similar, regardless of the specific industry segment or enterprise in which they take place.

Four components make up the copyright industries:

- **Core industries:** Industries whose primary purpose is to create, produce, distribute, or exhibit copyrighted materials, including broadcast, music, motion pictures, entertainment software, newspapers, and magazines, as shown in Figure 1-2.
- **Partial copyright industries:** Industries for which only some aspect or portion of the products qualify for copyright protection, such as the Ford Motor Company, whose cars may be patented, but not copyrighted. However, the brochures, TV spots, and other promotional materials the company produces are copyright-protected.
- **Nondedicated support industries:** Industries that provide distribution, marketing, and sales support to the copyrighted content economy, including transportation services, telecommunications services, wholesalers, and retail establishments. Examples of nondedicated support industries are telephone companies and Internet infrastructures that provide the transport networks for content.
- **Interdependent industries:** Industries that manufacture and sell products that enable the creation, production, distribution, or consumption of copyrighted material. Such industries include manufacturers of consumer electronics products and media – televisions, DVD players, game consoles, cameras, microphones, lighting equipment, discs and tape, headphones, and so forth – the technologies that depend on the copyright industries for content that drive consumers to buy playback devices.

Media companies make up the largest component of the core copyright industries. The primary purpose of these enterprises is to create, produce, market, and distribute books, newspapers, magazines, advertising, music and music media (records, CDs, and prerecorded tapes), motion pictures, television and

Motion Pictures	Radio & Television (Cable, Broadcast, and Satellite)	Music Recording, CDs, Downloads	Entertainment and Business Software	Newspapers, Periodicals, and Books

FIGURE 1-2 The core copyright industries

COPYRIGHT

A legal framework that applies to original works that reserves the right of copying to the creator. Different countries have different legal frameworks that define these rights in different ways with respect to duration, enforcement mechanisms, and penalties for violation. In the United States, copyright is constitutionally protected.

radio programs, and computer software (including videogames). As shown in Figure 1-2, the copyright industries are an important part of the U.S. economy and copyrighted products are the largest U.S. export.

In Europe, the copyright industries are equally important. In 2000, they contributed more than a trillion euros (€1,200 billion) to the EU economy – about 5.3 percent of its total value. And they employed more than 5 million people in the European Union, constituting 3.1 percent of the total EU workforce.[5] In the United Kingdom, the importance of the creation of copyrighted material is even greater: creative industries account for 8 percent of the economy.[6]

Although there are many management jobs in the core industries, they also exist in large numbers in the support and interdependent industries. The partial copyright category is an interesting one for today's job seekers. This category covers the media needs of enterprises that offer products and services in other industries: automobiles, clothing, cosmetics, fishing gear, restaurants, and car washing establishments. All these companies need material to communicate to consumers, investors, and employees. Increasingly, these communications include video and audio, which require more expertise and management supervision than print media.[7]

Industry Segments

People who work in one of the copyright industry segments usually think of themselves as being in the music business, television business, or movie business. In other words, they identify with the specific segment they work for. Even so, they often know quite a bit about other segments, particularly those that are closely related, perhaps drawing on the same content or talent pool.

Analysts break down the media industries into segments in several ways. For the purposes of this chapter, segments of the media industries include filmed

CAGR

In business, compound annual growth rate describes changes in value over time, taking into account year-to-year changes. In media and entertainment industries, CAGR normally refers to revenues, but the formula applies to any asset. It is a more accurate measurement than simply saying, "revenues are expected to double over the next five years." (When an industry is shrinking, the CAGR will be a negative value.) The formula to calculate CAGR is:

$$CAGR = \left(\frac{Ending\ Value}{Beginning\ Value} \right)^{\left(\frac{1}{\#\ Years} \right)} - 1$$

entertainment, broadcast and cable television networks, television distribution, recorded music, radio, Internet advertising, Internet access, videogames, book, newspaper, magazine and other print publishing, and corporate media. The next sections will look at the size and structure of each of the segments.

Managers within each segment of the creative industries need to consider the particulars of their organization and the markets they face. Typically, the markets are large, often global in scope. In some the growth rate (CAGR, for compound annual growth rate – see the box on this term) is high, in others more moderate. Table 1-1 describes some of the differences between creative industry segments. In the table, notice that all these segments face a similar formidable challenge: the ease of copying and large-scale piracy in the digital environment.

Filmed Entertainment

Los Angeles, New York, London, Paris, Mumbai, and Hong Kong are the global centers of filmed entertainment. The category includes revenues received from motion pictures, theater box offices, rental income from video stores, sales in retail establishments, and online subscriptions (including downloaded films and TV programs and DVDs sent through the mail). This category does not include revenues received from distribution via cable, satellite, telephone companies – all covered in the TV distribution segment.

Filmed entertainment occupies a special place in the media industry, because it drives revenues beyond the box office to many different businesses in the media industries. For example, when a motion picture is successful at the box office, it is likely to attract DVD purchases and rentals as well. It may spawn a sequel, prequel, or TV series. Its characters may be spun off to other properties. If the movie appeals to children, there may be lucrative downstream licensing opportunities for everything from calendars to bedsheets and keychain fobs. A hit TV show opens up some of the same opportunities and has the added advantage of running over a period of years.

Table 1-1 Comparing Media Industry Segments. Based on PricewaterhouseCoopers Media & Entertainment Markets, 2008–2013

Industry Segment	Est. 2009 Global Market Size (in billions)/ 2008–2011 CAGR (percent)	Growth Drivers	Challenges to Growth
Filmed Entertainment	92.6/4.9	Digital direct-to-consumer distribution: downloads and subscriptions Digital cinema High-definition DVDs	Ease of digital copying and piracy
Television Networks	204.6/5.8	Growth of high-definition TV Growth of digital households and rise in multichannel advertising	Ease of digital copying and piracy
Television Distribution	206.7/9.3	Growth of digital households, by cable and telephone companies, particularly in the Asia Pacific region	—
Recorded Music	37.7/2.3	Digital distribution Wireless, mobile digital distribution	Ease of digital copying and piracy Lackluster content
Radio	80.7/5.2	High-definition radio Satellite radio	Stale formats Lackluster content
Internet Advertising & Access Spending	272.6/5.2	Expansion of number of broadband households Rise of Internet as center for social networking and media and entertainment center	Dependent on network accessibility for and band-width to consumers
Videogames	44.2/9.1	Expansion of number of broadband households Introduction of new games Introduction of more advanced devices Expansion of wireless subscribers Expansion of broadband wireless subscribers	Ease of digital copying and piracy
Magazine Publishing	110/3.1	Rising incomes in emerging markets	Reader and advertising migration to the Internet
Newspaper Publishing	191.1/2.1	Free papers are source of most growth	Reader and advertising migration to the Internet
Book Publishing	135/3.6	e-Readers and other electronic devices will stimulate growth Growth in textbooks and professional books	Electronic sales may cut into print sales Reader migration to the Internet
Business Information	100.2/5.8	Growth of global economic activity Growth of international investment Interest in high-growth emerging markets	

Filmed entertainment is a fairly large segment of the media industries, but not nearly as big as the market for television networks and television distribution.[8] Forecasts of worldwide revenues anticipate growth at a modest 4.9 percent (CAGR) over the next 5 years. The United States and Europe are the largest markets, but they are also relatively slow-growing. The Asia Pacific and Latin America regions are the world's fastest growing markets.

Filmed entertainment brings in significant revenue, but it is also expensive to create. High costs impose a significant barrier to entry for many producers, although with the transition to digital production tools and distribution, there is some cost reduction. Nevertheless, the reality remains that big blockbusters come from big studios. With the exception of only a few independent studios and producers, large studios that are business units of huge multinational media corporations produce and distribute most globally successful motion pictures.

Forecasting revenues for this segment is difficult, because filmed entertainment is a hit-driven business – income depends on the release of compelling content. However, they will continue to grow through 2010, stimulated by new technologies such as digital cinema, modernized theatrical auditoriums, high-definition television screens and DVDs, subscription and on-demand Internet downloading services, mobile players and receivers, and the expansion of the number of broadband households. According to copyright owners, one inhibitor of growth is the copying and distribution of content without permission from (and usually without payment to) the copyright holder. Professional counterfeiters and casual copying through peer-to-peer networking both contribute to some loss of profits by media companies, although there is disagreement about exactly how much money is involved.

Broadcast and Cable Television Networks

Economists base the size of the market for broadcast and cable television networks on the income these networks attract from advertisers as well as revenue from carriers, such as cable and satellite operators. The geographical centers of television networks mirror those of filmed entertainment, and they are usually operated by the same media giants. In the United States, this category includes local television stations and cable operators. In Europe and Asia, it includes monies from public license fees. Estimates of global revenues for this segment predict it will grow from about $181.4 billion in 2007 to $228.3 in 2011, a CAGR of 4.8 percent.[9] The fastest-growing regions are Latin America and Europe, which are likely to experience a modest growth rate due to networks in the regions relying on stagnant government-collected license fees.

A rising standard of living in many countries around the world, increased advertising, and the penetration of high-definition television will stimulate growth in broadcast and cable television networks. In the United States,

The Nielsen company, which provides television viewing data for the industry, defines ratings and shares:

Rating: A *rating* is a percent of the universe that is being measured, most commonly discussed as a percent of all television households.[*]

Share: A *share* is the percent of households or persons using television at the time the program is airing and who are watching a particular program [...]. Shares can be useful as a gauge of competitive standing.[10]

---

[*] NOTE: All households are counted, whether they have the TV set on or not.

Internet video and the growth of video-on-demand platforms will also drive increased revenue at 6.5 percent CAGR. Revenue from the release of seasons of TV programming on DVDs adds incrementally to income, although piracy is a concern as this market grows.

In the past, U.S. broadcast television networks created hit shows that had broad appeal. Many years ago, when there were only three networks, a hit show might attain a share of 70 percent of the viewing audience. (Nielsen Media Research measures the popularity of television shows for the industry by reporting *rating points* and *shares*. These terms will be covered more fully in Chapter 6, which examines audiences and programming.)

Today there are hundreds of networks and the mass audience has splintered under the onslaught of cable networks with niche appeal. In the first week of October 2009, Nielsen data showed that the four largest broadcast networks were a shadow of their former 30 percent or more selves: CBS averaged 11.3 million viewers (7.2 rating, 12 share). ABC had 9.6 million viewers (6.2, 10), NBC had 7.8 million (4.9, 8), and Fox had 7.6 million (4.5, 7). Even the most popular shows fare little better. In the fall of 2009, *House* began the new season with a 6.5 rating (6.5 percent of all TV households) and a 16 share (16 percent of all TV households watching a television show at the time).

Even though the number of people watching any particular television show went down, the cost of buying television advertising time actually went up. Broadcast networks actually charge a premium for commercial time. The reason? There are only a few places where advertisers can reach a mass audience. There may be a point of diminishing returns, but it is nowhere in sight. Any medium that can aggregate a large audience will attract advertisers who market products that have broad appeal, and television still does that job better than any other medium.

A steady rise in the number of digital households, which will bring in more advertising and high-definition television channels, will stimulate the growth in this segment. In addition, the rental and sale of DVDs that hold an entire season of shows is a growing source of revenue for television networks that have created hit shows. Both classic and contemporary TV shows can sell well. As with other content distributed on DVDs, piracy could threaten this new revenue stream.

However, the audience continues to fragment across multiple media venues. Broadband Internet access is growing rapidly. More than 54 million households have access to video-on-demand services.[11] More than 35 million have DVRs (digital video recorders).[12] On April 9, 2007, Apple announced that it had sold 220 million iPods.[13]

Television Distribution

Television distribution includes the amount consumers spend on subscriptions and premium channel access, such as pay-per-view and video-on-demand access. It also includes revenues for TV programming distributed on mobile phones in Asia, where consumers pay subscription fees for this service. Growth for television distribution will be high: 9.3 percent CAGR between 2007 and 2011.[14] However, this overall figure hides the large discrepancy in regional growth: TV distribution will grow 18.1 percent CAGR in Asia, with especially big increases in the Asia Pacific region, 12.3 percent in Latin America, and 12.3 percent in Europe, the Middle East, and Africa.

However, in the United States, growth will be a modest 5.4 percent, because consumers can already choose cable or satellite television delivery, and the market is saturated – subscription penetration is at nearly 90 percent. Viewers in other regions have fewer choices, and many have only satellite subscription service as a multichannel provider. As telephone companies begin to offer high-speed Internet access services, they are likely to market bundled offers of television subscription and Internet access both in all regions of the world, but in the United States, they are likely to take market share away from cable and satellite, rather than increasing the overall market very much.

Recorded Music

Music is recorded around the globe, in most major cities of the world. The equipment is essentially the same, whether the gig takes place in Los Angeles or Lima. In the United States, most music labels and much music recording takes place in New York, Nashville, and Los Angeles.

Executives in the recorded music segment have faced angry, skeptical, disdainful, and disbelieving audiences over the past decade and a half – audiences that include consumers, performers and musicians, and managers from other media industries. They point to poor planning and lazy marketing, inept talent spotting and development, and lately, consumer-hostile responses to the threat posed by the Internet. Within the industry, managers have been divided over strategies to ensure profitability.

Ringtones: The sounds your mobile phone makes when it rings
Ringtunes: Sounds based on recognized songs that mobile phones make when they ring
Ringbacks: The sounds you hear in your mobile phone when the telephone you are calling is ringing

By any measure, it has not been a good 15 years for this industry segment. The market for recorded music encompasses physical media – albums, single recordings, and music video – and paid digital distribution via both wired and wireless networks. In addition to songs and albums, the category also includes revenue from the sales of ringtones, ringtunes, and ringbacks. The global market is growing very slowly, from $36.1 billion in 2006 to about $40.4 billion in 2011, a 2.3 percent CAGR. Even in fast-growing regions like Asia Pacific and Latin America, the market will grow only at 5.4 percent CAGR. Forecasts call for the United States, the largest market in this category, to decline by 0.4 percent CAGR.

The decline of the market for recorded music seems to be accelerating. In mid-2007, reported sales of the top-selling CD albums were down 30 percent, compared to the same period the year before. Some analysts attribute the lowering revenues to piracy, and both professional counterfeiting and peer-to-peer file sharing have probably played a role in the decline of sales. However, others point to poor market leadership on the part of large music companies, or *music labels*, as they are often called.

"The mighty music business is in a free fall – it has lost control of radio; retail outlets like Tower Records have shut down; MTV rarely broadcasts music videos; and the once lucrative album market has been overshadowed by downloaded singles, which mainly benefits Apple," writes Hirschberg (2007) in the *New York Times Magazine*.[15] Commenting in the article, David Geffen, the legendary music mogul, said, "The music business, as a whole, has lost its faith in content. Only ten years ago, companies wanted to make records, presumably good records, and see if they sold. But panic has set in, and now it's no longer about making music, it's all about how to sell music. And there's no clear answer about how to fix that problem. But I still believe that the top priority at any record company has to be coming up with great music." One blogger offered the following explanation of the industry's woes: "Free music downloading; suing your customers; alienating your customers by spying on them; inexpensive single downloads; low or no quality product; overpriced medium; greedy industry."

The industry is in the midst of a rapid transition from physical distribution to digital distribution. Between 2006 and 2011, global physical distribution will decline by 9.6 percent CAGR. This change in the business environment means that labels that hope to be successful will need to find methods of doing business based on digital distribution.[16]

However, digital files are vulnerable to easy copying, so they have engaged in many efforts to reduce casual copying and file sharing by consumers. Between 2003 and 2007, the music labels' trade group, the Recording Industry Association of America, initiated or threatened legal action against more than 20,000 people.[17] They have also adopted technological barriers such as proprietary file formats that require special players or software that restricts copying. These technologies are often called *digital rights management* or *DRM*.

Radio

The radio segment includes advertising revenue spending, local over-the-air free broadcast radio stations, and advertising spending and consumer subscription spending for satellite radio. Companies that own radio companies are usually in financial centers of the country where they operate; however, transmitters can be anywhere or, as with satellite delivery, everywhere. Like the music industry, broadcast radio is experiencing a difficult business environment. Overall global revenues are projected to grow at 5.2 CAGR.[18] In Europe, increases in radio ad revenue are unlikely to top 3 percent between 2007 and 2011. In the United States, advertising on radio has been flat for 3 years and forecasters predict that 2007 levels will range between 2 percent up and 2 percent down.[19] Despite the stagnant revenues, the sale of radio stations has not slowed, because investors continue to find radio stations very profitable businesses, particularly in medium and large markets.

There are several explanations for the industry's lack of growth in mature markets, such as the United States and Europe. Some analysts cite concern with business processes, such as the complexity advertisers face when buying time on multiple stations, lack of electronic invoicing, and audience measurement. Other observers believe that formats and programming practices are a problem.

"Radio is a stale medium," says Steve Kalb, senior VP and director of broadcast media for Mullen's mediaHUB, who notes that he keeps a close eye on declining listening levels. "Every town has the same kind of format. It's the same music. It's very generic and white-bread. The homogenization of radio is frightening."[20]

In the United States, consolidation is often blamed for the death of programming that would attract new viewers. Throughout the 1990s, large national media companies bought up many local stations that were formerly "mom and pops," individual- or family-owned stations with ties to the locality. For example, Clear Channel, the largest radio group in the United States, owned more than 1,150 stations. However, there appears to be some deconsolidation occurring in 2007, as Clear Channel announced it was selling more than 362 of its stations, mostly in small, rural markets. By mid-2009, many analysts predicted the largest U.S. radio conglomerate would have to declare bankruptcy, and later in the year, Citadel had filed for bankruptcy and several other terrestrial broadcasters were on the brink.[21]

In the United States, consolidation occurred as a result of changes in regulations by the Federal Communication Commission (FCC), which eliminated barriers to the number of stations companies could own. The FCC also lowered the requirements for local programming, so that many stations run simply as automated computer servers, transmitting content produced elsewhere. In this way, consolidation has reduced the number of jobs in the radio industry, so that a very small number of managers run a very large number of stations. The loss of individual stations has also caused station diversity to decline, so that stations (and their managers) appear to speak with one voice.

Analysts expect radio format audiences to shift in the next few years, with country music listenership growing by 24 percent, news/talk formats by 20 percent, urban stations by 15 percent, and Spanish radio 14 percent. All other formats, such as oldies, adult contemporary, rock, jazz, and adult hits, are projected to decline.[22] Independent music labels suffer the most from the near-monopoly on commercial radio by major labels – their *pay-for-play* domination of radio makes it impossible for independent musicians to get airplay, confining independent artists to the margins. Now file sharing and CD burning have created the first real opportunity to break the major label cartel, and independents have the most to gain. Many independents are no longer pounding on the doors of radio stations, because they believe that the link between radio play and music sales is now broken.[23] In their view, the Internet provides a much more flexible, discovery-oriented medium for fans to find new music.

Internet Advertising and Access Spending

Internet advertising is the fastest growing ad medium. It is a segment where job seekers just out of college may be able to find a job and be able to grow a career as the industry matures. Much of the job of Internet managers is educating those not intimately involved with the industry about what the Net can do for them and their companies.

Internet companies are everywhere, but they are thick on the ground in technological centers. They are likely to be near universities that offer sophisticated computer science and other communications engineering programs and confer master's and doctoral degrees. In the United States, these locations are Silicon Valley in California; Austin, Texas; and Boston, Massachusetts. In Asia, Tokyo, Seoul, and Singapore are major centers of Internet activity. In Europe, London, Paris, Rome, and other capital cities dominate. In Australia, Auckland and Sydney are centers of Internet innovation.

In 2003, Internet advertising and access spending made up 3 percent of global advertising; by 2011, it will rise to 14 percent. PricewaterhouseCoopers estimates that the global Internet advertising market will grow from $22.9 billion in 2007 to $73 billion in 2011, a CAGR of 18.3 percent. All global regions will experience double-digit increases. During the same period, revenues from the global Internet access market will rise from $169.5 billion to $298.4, a 12.2 percent CAGR. The access market differs across regions, because some territories already have a large number of subscribers. The U.S. Internet access market will grow at a 7.1 percent CAGR; Asia Pacific will expand at a 16.9 percent CAGR.[24]

In 2004, Internet advertising revenues surpassed those of out of home advertising (outdoor boards and signs). In 2007, the Net overtook radio. In 2010, it will bring in more ad dollars than magazines. However, as of 2007, Internet ad income ($49.6 billion) is far behind the remaining mass media – television ($196.9 billion) and newspapers ($117,878).

Globally, Internet advertising is growing at a double-digit rate, about 18.3 CAGR. As fast as this category is expanding, it is still limited by overall rates of connectivity. In the United States, where advertising is a long-established part of media environments, the Internet advertising market is well developed. In 2007, almost 40.3 percent of advertisers' budgets went toward keyword search – about three-quarters of this spending went to Google. Classified ads received 25.6 percent of ad money, video brought in 3.3 percent, and other forms of advertising such as banner ads and display ads accounted for 30.8 percent of all money spent on Internet advertising. Forecasts call for keyword search advertising to increase over the next 5 years. Spending on banner ads and other static formats will decline as broadband usage expands, allowing advertisers to use more video content.

Managers of Internet companies agree that one barrier to faster ad revenue growth in this media segment has been the absence of agreed-upon methods of measuring effectiveness, or *metrics*. Advertising managers use metrics to convince their supervisors to spend part of their budgets on Web sites. They also use metrics after the campaign to show the effectiveness of the ad spend.

The universal language of advertising, irrespective of medium, is *impressions*. The Internet Advertising Bureau (IAB), a trade group, has been working on establishing industry-wide metrics for impressions. Two companies dominate the measurement of Internet advertising, ComScore and Nielsen/NetRatings. Advertisers are concerned with discrepancies between the measurements of each firm of the same sites as well as differences between what the measurement companies report and the records maintained on the advertisers' servers.

In April 2007, IAB president and CEO Randall Rothenberg wrote to ComScore and Nielsen/NetRatings, asking them to hold a summit meeting to resolve measurement issues: "We are seeking your agreement to a near-term timetable for independent audits and accreditations of your companies' interactive-audience measurement processes. We also hope to open a dialogue with you

IMPRESSION

Exposure of a person or household to an advertising message. Sometimes advertisers pay for the services of an ad agency, based on a particular number of impressions by specific demographic groups, such as "men 18–35," "women 25–49," or even more narrowly targeted groups. As the focus narrows, the cost per impression goes up.

about assuring the integrity of audience measurement systems and processes as interactive technologies continue to evolve."[25] In 2008, the IAB issued guidelines for audience reach measurement. The group hoped to establish consistent definitions of metrics and to set measurement standards. However, some of these issues were still not resolved by mid-2009, particularly for rich media, such as video.[26]

Internet advertising will become prominent when the industry reaches a consensus about how to collect, aggregate, mine, and apply specific metrics – and position themselves to supply them. This is the work of the today's managers and executives in the Internet, and they are actively engaged in it. The use of Google Analytics is widespread, but does not provide a neutral measurement service, as Nielsen does for the television industry.

Once the metrics issues are more fully worked out, the Internet will offer a powerful complement to the mass giants, because it offers advertisers the ability to reach individuals with offers tailored to their needs and desires. In a world where there are few information sources, advertisers must present general offers to an aggregated buying public. The Internet brings an almost infinite number of information sources that changes advertising and marketing strategy to one of applying data to individual customers.

Internet advertising depends on the number of people who are connected, so managers in Internet companies support broadband subscription as much as they can. People with broadband spend more time online. The greater bandwidth allows advertisers to use graphics, animation, audio, and even video to communicate their commercial messages. In 2007, the United States accounted for 52 percent of Internet advertising revenues, but only 19.6 percent of Internet access spending. Asia Pacific spent the most on access, making up 39 percent of the global total, and Europe was the second largest market, paying out 35.8 percent of all spending.[27]

People around the world are trading in their dialup service for broadband access. Table 1-2 shows the percentage of the population that has broadband connectivity, compared to dialup access to the Internet in some regions of the world.

Table 1-2 Internet Household Connectivity, by Access Type and Region[28]

Territory	Connected to Internet (percent)	Connect Using Broadband (percent)	Connect Using Dialup (percent)
United States	76.6	51.9	24.7
Western Europe	65	49.3	15.7
Eastern Europe	26.7	12.8	13.9
Asia Pacific	28.9	15.7	13.2
Latin America	10.6	6	4.6

Videogames

Videogames are popular. In 2003, the industry surpassed the motion picture industry in revenue. The market for videogames includes consumer spending on the games themselves, rather than the hardware platform on which to play them. (The game platforms – computers, consoles, and handhelds – are all part of the consumer electronics industry, not the media industries.) Games are purchased individually or by subscription, as retail boxed games or downloaded digital products. The types of games are console games, personal computer games, online games, streamed on-demand games, and wireless mobile games. In the United States, advertising spending for messages within games is included as well.

As in many other media segments, videogames are hit-driven. Sales can be volatile, changing from month to month. As of September 2009, the most popular console games were Halo 3 (Xbox 360), Sports Resort (Wii), and Professor Layton and the Diabolical Box (Nintendo DS). The most popular online games in mid-2009 were World of Warcraft, Habbo Hotel, and RuneScape.

The market for console games is cyclical: a cycle starts with the introduction of a new console. Then designers build games that take advantage of the more advanced features the new console offers. When one of the new games generates buzz and becomes increasingly popular, gamers must buy the new console if they want to play the new hit game. Competitors introduce their own versions of the upgraded consoles, developers create more games, and the market solidifies for awhile as the games and machines penetrate the market. Then a company introduces a new console with enhanced features – and the cycle begins again.

There is an ongoing competition between console and PC-based games. Consoles are dedicated to gaming and can provide fast play and rich graphics at a lower price point than computers. However, computers are general-purpose machines that can emulate any game console. The chameleon-like characteristics of computers mean that gamers can play a game created for any platform on their computers, not just the console for which developers designed the game. In 2007, Microsoft introduced the Vista operating system. It shows how important videogames are in today's marketplace that the purpose of many of Vista's features was to enrich gaming by providing for faster graphics handling and game play.

The design of some games limits them to play by a single person; others allow small groups or teams to play. If the means of playing the game – console or PC – provides online connectivity, then the game may allow many people to play, sometimes numbering in the thousands. Such games are called *MMOGs*, which stands for *massive multiplayer online games*. Games fit into one or more *genres*, based on the design of the play, the theme, or the underlying reality that the game references. The most popular genres are action (including shooter games), adventure, fighting, role-playing, simulation, sports, and strategy games. Other genres are adult, arcade, advergame, artillery, education, music, party, pinball, puzzle, stealth, survival, horror, traditional, and vehicular combat games.

The growth of the videogame market reflects advances in rich, realistic, fast-changing graphics and the speed of game play. These characteristics depend on the processing speed of the hardware it runs on – console, computer, or handheld, so advances in processing precede sales and profits. The expansion

BANDWIDTH

The size of an information channel. One way to picture a communication channel is as a pipe that carries liquid. The bigger the pipe, the more liquid it will carry.

A water pipe carries a given amount of water in a given amount of time. For example, a pump might have the capacity to move 50,000 gallons of water per hour. Similarly, although the technical measure of bandwidth is the number of frequencies it includes, the more oft-used measurement is the data rate, or the amount of information bits carried, usually in seconds. For example, cable companies routinely deliver 3 megabits per seconds (3 mbps) of information to their computer companies. This measurement means that the channel permits the transmission of 3 million bits of information every second.

Communication channels are bundles of frequencies, which are waves of energy that move through the air. Like water, they flow. The greater the number of frequencies that a channel accommodates, the more information the channel can carry.

The word *bandwidth* is very descriptive. A *band* is a set of frequencies. Frequencies are the number of cycles associated with a wave of energy that moves through the air and even buildings. (Your cell phone works in your house, for example.) The *width* is the number of frequencies that, taken together, compose the channel.

A technique called *modulation* involves modifying the frequencies of the waves that reflects the information to be transmitted. When the transmitter pushes out the waves, the receiver looks at the modifications and retrieves the information from the waves, one bit at a time.

of broadband network access, both wired and wireless, will also stimulate the growth of this segment.[29] Near real-time knowledge of other players' actions and the ability to launch immediate responses make for satisfying fast game action. This real-time *tele-presence*, accompanied by information about how the moves of hundreds (even thousands) of other players affect the environment, is a function of how much information can be provided to all the players in a given amount of time – the available *bandwidth*.

Bandwidth is a two-edged sword. It makes it possible for gamers to play with many people live over the Internet. The popularity of MMOGs like World of Warcraft, Habbo Hotel, and RuneScape, each with millions of monthly subscribers, testifies to the increasing appeal of online gaming. Media giants have taken notice of this trend and both Warner Bros. and MTV have developed game-like online environments to promote their brands.[30] But plentiful bandwidth also allows users to download large files very quickly, enabling the piracy of game software – just as it facilitates downloading of music, movies and television programming.

A DAY IN THE LIFE OF CRAIG ROBINSON

**Craig Robinson, President and GM,
KNBC TV/Los Angeles, California**

Craig Robinson is the President and General Manager of KNBC-TV in Los Angeles, California, the second largest television market in the United States. In his own words, Craig describes his climb to the top: "Through the years I've had the good fortune to hold many key jobs within a television station, including executive assistant, sales trainee, salesperson, sales manager and vice president of sales. Working at all levels of the organization has given me an appreciation for some of the positions that aren't high profile, but that are integral to the success of the business."

When asked to describe a "typical" day in this high-profile and fast-paced position, Craig provides a quick snapshot: "Every day involves some revenue forecasting and expense pacing. On an average day, there will also be meetings with news, engineering and the web staff internally. I also meet with city leaders and community groups on a regular basis."

How does a typical day begin for the President and GM of one of the top TV markets in the country? "Checking last night's ratings performance on my BlackBerry." Meaning that Craig's day starts well before he sets foot into the television station. He first looks at his agenda upon arriving at the KNBC office, which will set the pace for the upcoming day. "After returning urgent emails and calls, I schedule the more complex meetings for the morning, while everyone is fresh."

We've all heard that old adage, "It ain't easy at the top." So, tell us what are some of the most challenging issues you face?

"Keeping a motivated and healthy workforce is always the most challenging issue, particularly in a tough economic environment."

It's well known that you sincerely enjoy your position. Can you describe the highlights of your workday?

"Talking to the people who make it happen every day, acknowledging their successes. I meet on a regular basis with the heads of each department, but it's always energizing to hear from the people on the front lines."

After a full day at the office, which is typically longer than eight hours, how do you end your day?

"Often with a community event or client dinner."

At the end of the day, what advice would you offer those who are looking to follow in your footsteps?

"Concentrate on the job at hand. It's important to have long-term goals, but if you spend all of your time looking at the next job, you won't give your full attention to your current one. Excel at your current assignment and the other opportunities will find you."

Wise words from a man who is keeping his eye on the future, one day at a time.

Daily Planner

vertex42

Date: 8/17/2009   Craig Robinson

17 August, 2009
Monday

July 2009								August 2009								September 2009						
Su	M	Tu	W	Th	F	Sa		Su	M	Tu	W	Th	F	Sa		Su	M	Tu	W	Th	F	Sa
			1	2	3	4								1				1	2	3	4	5
5	6	7	8	9	10	11		2	3	4	5	6	7	8		6	7	8	9	10	11	12
12	13	14	15	16	17	18		9	10	11	12	13	14	15		13	14	15	16	17	18	19
19	20	21	22	23	24	25		16	17	18	19	20	21	22		20	21	22	23	24	25	26
26	27	28	29	30	31			23	24	25	26	27	28	29		27	28	29	30			
								30	31													

Remember
Sarah Birthday

Confirm November trip

☑ ABC Prioritized Task List

Time People to Call

$Amt Expenses

Appointments

7	:00	
	:30	
8	:00	Syndicated Programming
	:15	Presentation
	:30	
	:45	
9	:00	
	:15	
	:30	
	:45	
10	:00	Marketing Meeting
	:15	
	:30	News Meeting
	:45	
11	:00	
	:15	
	:30	Digital Channel Discussion
	:45	
12	:00	Web Team Lunch
	:15	
	:30	
	:45	
1	:00	
	:15	
	:30	
	:45	
2	:00	
	:15	
	:30	Expense Review
	:45	
3	:00	
	:15	
	:30	
	:45	
4	:00	Sales Estimate Meeting
	:15	
	:30	
	:45	
5	:00	
	:30	
6	:00	Presentation to Broadcast Students
	:30	
7	:00	
	:30	
8	:00	
	:30	
9	:00	
	:30	

Notes

> ### BUSINESS MODEL
>
> A business model is part of an overall business plan that describes how a company plans to make money from the mix of products and services it offers in the commercial marketplace. Chapter 13 describes media and entertainment business models in detail.

The rapid global expansion of number of broadband households, the introduction of new games and ever more advanced devices, the increasing popularity of MMOGs, and the rise in the number of narrowband and broadband wireless subscribers are all driving the growth of the videogames market. For the console segment of the industry, the introduction of games based on a new console marks the beginning of a high cycle. At the beginning and end of a cycle, the market drags. Jobs follow activity, so there is no better time to look for work in the videogame industry than when new games come that are tailored to the latest generation of consoles. The huge revenues of this segment has encouraged many educational institutions to offer curricula that lead to certificates and degrees in videogames.

Publishing

This category includes business information, magazine, newspaper, and book publishing, most of which are growing quite slowly – only business information is growing at a compound annual growth rate of more than 5 percent. These are mature industries that all face some degree of threat from the Internet, particularly newspapers and business information. The sale of print books may decrease because of the rise of e-readers, but these will act to stimulate books modestly.

COMMON CHARACTERISTICS OF THE SEGMENTS OF THE MEDIA INDUSTRIES

Despite the personal identification that people who work in a particular media industry have with it, there are striking similarities between the segments: they are sensitive to changes in technology, popular in both global and local environments, and involved in the creation of both information and entertainment products. They help create and are vulnerable to cultural, social, and political trends. They also face a long list of similar economic challenges and opportunities.

Sensitivity to Changes in Technology

All media employ technology to create and deliver content and, in modern life, most entertainment reaches consumers through one or more media.

The continuing appearance of new technologies means that there is a constant shuffling of content and media platforms, as companies respond to the changed environment. The harnessing of technology to information and entertainment provides many opportunities to media enterprises, but changes in technology may also disrupt specific business models.

Today's media managers need to understand about the technologies that affect their business. If they are not engineers, they need to find a way to learn about technology so that they are not intimidated by the many discussions that include such considerations. Earning the respect of colleagues, partners, co-workers, and subordinates depends on having a good grasp of key technologies that can affect the business and industry.

The Global Internet and the Broadband Explosion

Distribution over the Internet brings content owners and distributors enor-mous business opportunities and challenges. It offers the potential for world-wide, *friction-free* distribution, a term that describes the ease, speed, and lower cost of distributing digital products across the Internet, as compared to physi-cally moving them across geographies. It provides an infrastructure for imme-diate payment. And, most importantly, it allows the identification of individual consumers.

Consider broadcast networks. A television or radio station transmits a program and an audience tunes in to it. The company does not know who received the programming, which program elements and ads they responded to, or how long they viewed or listened. They can get ratings from the Nielsen service, measurements of a tiny sample that – no matter how carefully selected – can-not rival the accuracy of the precise measurement of each and every content consumer transaction that Internet data provides.

The Internet is a universal data carrier. It transports any kind of data, leaving it to the receiving device to decode the stream of information as text, sound, and image. Given sufficient bandwidth, it carries with equal facility written mate-rial, audio, graphics, and video. This flexibility is very different from traditional distribution systems: TV transmitters transmit video and audio; radio transmit-ters transmit sound; newspapers and magazines circulate text and photos; and so forth.

More bandwidth means more data, more content to the consumer. Globally, more than 400 million people have broadband service. Global broadband quadrupled during 2008, growing from 0.01 percent of broadband per capita in the first quarter to 0.04 percent in the fourth quarter.[31] In the United States, it is available to 85 percent of U.S. residents and about 63 percent subscribe, as of March 2009. By 2011, the number of broadband subscribers is expected to rise to more than 90 percent.[32] In 2009, European countries held eight of the top ten places for adoption of broadband Internet access The United States was in the eleventh position.[33]

From Push to Pull

Do you ask for content, or does somebody give it to you, whether you like it or not? Social systems and their related communication systems have a center and an edge, the periphery. Think of the organization of cities and towns with a central business district and suburbs. Different societies have different structures, so that one may be more centralized or dispersed than another; one may feature frequent communication between members and another leave people in greater isolation. In top-down hierarchical social systems, command communication moves from the center to the periphery – from the boss to the janitor. In flatter systems, some command communication may flow from the bottom up, so that the leaders are informed by the experience of the followers.

When information originates from the center and radiates outward toward the members at the edges of a communication network, it is called *push*.[34] A broadcast network, cable system, or satellite system is a good example of a push network. The originator decides whether to push information, what to push, when to push it, at what cost, and to whom. The audience has the choice to tune in or not under conditions set mainly by the entity at the center of the network.

The Internet is a system with two-way communication flow that allows users to request content, to *pull* information from the network. In a computer network, this distinction is captured in the phrase "server push, user pull." When information is pulled (or requested) by the receiver, it is the receiver who decides when to make the request and defines what is to be received. The relationship between center and periphery may not be equal, but pull systems give more control to the periphery of the network than do push systems.

Digital, Downloadable Formats Are Replacing Physical Formats

In 2006, digital spending streams contributed more to global entertainment and media revenues than did the sales of physical media.[35] Downloading text, graphics, and audio is possible over dialup connections and fast and easy over broadband. Some people are even downloading motion pictures and television shows, although many more watch in theaters, on DVDs, or over the air or cable. However, as bandwidth increases and downloads become faster and more convenient, the number of downloads will grow.

Mobile devices, especially when they are connected to the network at broadband speeds, accelerate the move to digital, downloadable formats by increasing the opportunities and occasions subscribers have to download and pay for content. Narrowband mobile applications, like texting, playing games, and downloading and paying for games and ringtones, demonstrate the attractiveness and convenience of untethered communication and entertainment services to consumers on the go.

The Move to Mobile

Cutting the cord is a global phenomenon. The number of wireless broadband-capable mobile devices continues to grow, including cell phones, PDAs, and notebook and palmtop computers. With broadband functionality, these devices are able to send, receive, and display music, video broadcasts, and videogames, as well as voice and data. The number of wireless subscribers will expand from 2.3 billion in 2006 to 3.4 billion in 2011.[36]

According to a study by Juniper Research, 204 million mobile phone customers will generate $22 billion in mobile payments by 2011. In 2007, there continued to be unresolved revenue sharing issues between sellers and mobile service operators and payment-processing service providers.[37] However, the technology exists to enable such payments once the market participants reach agreement about their business arrangements.

Global Distribution, Local Diversity

Global communication systems extend the reach of media to almost everyone, everywhere, nearly instantaneously. At the same time, global economic growth is raising revenues in many regions, allowing people to pay for connectivity, access, and content. The immense profitability of global hits makes it tempting for companies to develop properties that can transcend cultural differences. However, the level of investment required to create and distribute such properties is a large barrier to entry to small and medium-sized enterprises.[38]

Although there are obvious benefits to creating and distributing global blockbusters, the vast majority of media is created and consumed locally. For example, some U.S. consumers may love Japanese anime, but in the domestic market, *South Park* and *The Simpsons* will garner the greater revenue. Not all properties translate across cultures or even national boundaries. Comedy is notoriously difficult to move from one culture to another, but drama, news, music, and other content may also be limited to their geography of origin. It is likely that the penetration of the Internet will accelerate the transportability of commercially successful media content, but complete cultural compatibility is still in the future.

The Great Content Divide

Most of the media industry segments divide the content they produce into one of two broad categories: information or entertainment. Most media giants create both types.[39] In filmed entertainment, there are fictional motion pictures and there are documentaries and reality-based movies. In television, radio, and print, the separation between information and entertainment is fairly clear, although reality TV and comedy shows such as *The Daily Show*, *The Colbert Report*, and *Countdown with Keith Olbermann* have blurred the boundaries between the two genres. Some critics believe that this blending began with network television news, with its use of flashy graphics, sensationalized stories, and glamorous anchors.

Motion pictures, music, and videogames are primarily entertainment media. Newspapers favor information-based content, with side trips to entertainment in the comic section. In the other industry segments, such as television, radio, magazines, and the Internet, content is more equally divided between the two types.

For managers, the distinction is important, because each type of material comes with its own set of standards. Entertainment content must attract viewers and users; information content must inform them without alienating them. On the whole, the creation and distribution of entertainment products do not entail liability, although there may be criminal penalties for engagement with pornographic, treasonous, or other societally prohibited material.

There is greater liability associated with information content. Standards of trustworthiness apply, as do strictures against fraud, libel, false light, and other representations deemed harmful to society as a whole or individuals. Moreover, many violations of taste in entertainment material may be greeted with a wink and a nod; such violations in informational material may have more serious consequences.

Sensitivity to Cultural, Social, Economic, and Political Trends

Cultural, social, and political ideas shape the way the media must approach its audience. In the creation of content, achieving popularity entails either giving people something they need (uses) or want (gratifications), which vary depending on the society in which a media organization is operating.[40] In both cases, the material has to address users and consumers within their cultural, social, and political milieu. On the other hand, the media produce compelling material that sets the agenda for what people think and talk about, so content can become very controversial.[41]

Societies go to great lengths to manage and regulate content. In Chapter 14, the book will address legal issues that affect media operation and content. Chapter 15 will cover media ethics, as social norms also limit how media companies operate.

The media industries also share the economics of creativity. Within these industries, the general perception is that companies will succeed or fail based on the quality of creative work, as defined by commercial hits and blockbusters. The management of creativity is an essential skill in these organizations. In media segments such as motion pictures, television, and music, some executives exert influence because they are able to interact well with talented content creators and performers. In addition, the economics of creativity affects budgets and profits, subjects which will be covered more fully in Chapter 5.

SUMMARY

This chapter described what media managers and executives need to know about their industry, including its size, scope, and characteristics. It provided information about industry segments, including size, drivers of and barriers to growth, and challenges. It looked at some contextual similarities faced by the segments, the different growth drivers between, and the external environments they face.

WHAT'S AHEAD

The next chapter examines in detail the organizations that participate in the M&E industry segments. It distinguishes between organizations that produce content, distribute it, market it, and transport it, as well as those that engage in most or all of these activities. The chapter covers organizational structures, processes, information flows, workflows, and the economics of industries that are based on creative activities, including the media industries. The organizations covered in Chapter 2 include studios, TV networks and stations, radio stations, production companies, music labels, and other corporations, such as nonprofit groups, and government agencies that produce and distribute content.

CASE STUDY 1.1 MEDIA EXPANSION

Alpha Broadcast Group owns 28 TV stations (6 ABC, 14 NBC, and 8 CBS affiliates) and 61 radio stations. The company executives are putting together a strategic plan to chart the future of the company. The three objectives are:

- To position the company for the future
- To attain greater profitability
- To reach young people aged 12–25 years

The executives have decided to expand operations into other media. What properties or mix of properties would you recommend for investment: newspapers, Internet sites and services, or mobile services? Explain your recommendation.

CASE STUDY 1.2 PLANNING AHEAD FOR SUCCESS

Media and Entertainment (M&E): Industries, Segments, Businesses, and Environment

Robert Burns may have said it best in his poem "To a Mouse" when he eloquently stated in his native Scottish brogue that "even the best-laid plans of mice and men oft go awry." This inspired the title of the book most students read in high school, *Of Mice and Men*. Of course, this is the loosely translated English version, but the message is very clear: It is a reminder that even a well-thought-out strategy has the potential to fail.

So how can you reduce the risk of a plan going awry? The quick answer is research. In fact, many reality shows (such as *The Apprentice*) begin with this basic strategy to place you on the path to success. Ask yourself, who is the best target customer for the product? How do you effectively reach out and appeal to this market?

It is critical in the preplanning stages that one researches the market conditions thoroughly and fully understand cultural variances, such as heritage, language, religion, population, politics, and sociocultural and economic conditions.

Fully understanding these variables will ultimately lead to the success or failure of a product or service.

No pressure, right?

Assignment

As the product manager for a videogame company, you have been assigned to market a game that involves bicycle racing. You have been asked to release the game in the United States and also in France.

1. Get creative and name the game in both English and French. Can it be the same or should it be different?
2. Define your target market. Research videogames that would appeal to bicycling enthusiasts. What are the common traits? Would it be the same in both countries?
3. Identify at least three appealing components for your product. Determine how they might differ from one another.
4. How would your marketing strategy differ in the United States from in France and why?

REFERENCES

1. Management. Dictionary.com. *Dictionary.com Unabridged (v 1.1)*. Random House, Inc. Accessed August 18, 2007, at http://dictionary.reference.com/browse/management.

2. U.S. Census Bureau (2006). *Media usage and consumer spending: 2000 to 2009*. Washington, DC: U.S. Government Printing Office.

3. PricewaterhouseCoopers (2007). *Global entertainment and media outlook 2007–2011 – Television networks: Broadcast and cable*. New York: PwC.

4. Siwek, S. (2006). *Copyright industries in the U.S. economy: The 2006 report*. Economists Incorporated. Accessed September 6, 2009 at http://www.iipa.com.

5. Internal Market and Services Directorate General (DG MARKT) (n.d.). *Internal market – copyright and neighbouring rights – index*. Accessed August 8, 2007, at http://ec.europa.eu/internal_market/copyright/index_en.htm.

6. National Endowment for Science, Technology and the Arts (NESTA). (2006). *Creating growth: How the UK can develop world class creative businesses*. London: Nesta.

7. —— (January 31, 2008). Corporate video spend on TV and branded sites jumps in 2007. *The NewsMarket*. Accessed August 28, 2009, at http://www.marketwire.com/press-release/The-Newsmarket-816090.html.

8. PricewaterhouseCoopers (2007). *Global entertainment and media outlook 2007–2011 – Filmed entertainment*. New York: PwC.

9. PricewaterhouseCoopers (2007). *Global entertainment and media outlook 2007–2011 – Television distribution*. New York: PwC.

10. Information about ratings and shares is available at the Nielsen web site, http://www.nielsenmedia.com/FAQ/ratings.html, and the Television Bureau of Advertising (TVB), http://www.tvb.org.

11. This information is provided by measurement service Rentrak, as reported in by Media Biz. Accessed September 9, 2009, at: http://www.mediabiz.com/news/articles/?publication_id=4&release_id=125.

12. These figures appeared in a press release from the Leichtman Research Group, available at http://www.leichtmanresearch.com/press/091009release.html.

13. Drake, J. (April 9, 2007). 100 millionth Apple iPod sold. Accessed June 26, 2009, at http://www.associatedcontent.com/article/208934/100_millionth_apple_ipod_sold.html.

14. PricewaterhouseCoopers (2007). *Global entertainment and media outlook 2007–2011 – Television distribution*. New York: PwC.

15. Hirschberg, L. (September 2, 2007). The music man. *New York Times Magazine*. Accessed November 6, 2008, at http://www.nytimes.com/2007/09/02/magazine/02rubin.t.html?_r=1&oref=slogin.

16. PricewaterhouseCoopers (2007). *Global entertainment and media outlook 2007–2011 – Recorded music*. New York: PwC.

17. Electronic Frontier Foundation (2007). *RIAA v. The People: Four years later*. Accessed September 1, 2007, at http://www.eff.org/IP/P2P/riaa_at_four.pdf.

18. PricewaterhouseCoopers (2007). *Global entertainment and media outlook 2007–2011 – Radio and out-of-home advertising*. New York: PwC.

19. Bachman, K. (January 1, 2007). Forecast 2007: Radio. *Media Week*. http://www.mediaweek.com/mw/news/tvstations/article_display.jsp?vnu_content_id=1003526034.

20. Ibid.

21. ——— (July 1, 2009). Radio One, Citadel outlooks look grim, Clear Channel eases closer to bankruptcy. Accessed September 10, 2009, at http://www.mediabuyerplanner.com/entry/43795/radio-one-citadel-outlooks-look-grim-clear-channel-eases-closer-to-bankrupt/.

22. Podmetrics (April 11, 2007). Radio format trends. Accessed August 15, 2007, http://podmetrics.wordpress.com/2007/04/12/radio-format-trends-2012-4112007.

23. Hirschberg, op. cit.

24. PricewaterhouseCoopers (2007). *Global entertainment and media outlook 2007–2011 – Internet advertising and access spending*. New York: PwC.

25. ClickZ (2007). *IAB takes ComScore and NetRatings to Task*. Accessed July 15, 2007, at http://blog.clickz.com/070420-124318.html.

26. Acquah, V. (May 15, 2009). Comscore MediaMetrix vs. Nielsen Netratings: Round X. Accessed September 15, 2009, at http://test.blueanalytics.com/index.php/blog/article/comscore_mediametrix_vs._nielsen_netratings_round_x.

27. PricewaterhouseCoopers (2007). *Global entertainment and media outlook 2007–2011 – Internet advertising and access spending*. New York: PwC.

28. Ibid.

29. PricewaterhouseCoopers (2007). *Global entertainment and media outlook 2007–2011 – Video games*. New York: PwC.

30. Terdiman, D. (2007). *Online gaming hits its groove*. CNET News. Accessed September 12, 2009, at http://news.cnet.com/Online-gaming-hits-its-groove/2100-1043_3-6206970.html.

31. Blenford, A. (September 15, 2009). *New Africa broadband ready*. BBC News. Accessed September 28, 2009, at http://news.bbc.co.uk/2/hi/technology/8257038.stm.

32. Horrigan, J. (June, 2009). *Home broadband adoption*. Pew Internet. Accessed August 19, 2009, at http://www.pewinternet.org/Reports/2009/10-Home-Broadband-Adoption-2009.aspx.

33. ——— (April 6, 2009). *Europe tops broadband penetration poll*. Accessed August 4, 2009, at http://www.netimperative.com/news/2009/april/europe-tops-broadband-penetration-poll.

34. Hagel, J. & Brown, J. S. (2005). *From push to pull: Emerging models for mobilizing resources.* Accessed September 14, 2007, at http://www.johnseelybrown.com/pushmepullyou4.72.pdf.

35. PricewaterhouseCoopers (2007). *Global entertainment and media outlook 2007–2011 – Global overview.* New York: PwC.

36. PricewaterhouseCoopers (2007). *Global entertainment and media outlook 2007–2011 – Global overview.* New York: PwC.

37. Goode, A. (May 18, 2007). Press release: Mobile payments to generate almost $22bn of transactions by 2011 and be adopted by 204m mobile phone users. Accessed September 12, 2007, at http://www.juniperresearch.com/shop/viewpressrelease.php?id=88&pr=52>.

38. ——— (2002). *That's entertainment: Media conglomerates go global.* Accessed September 14, 2007, at http://knowledge.wharton.upenn.edu/article.cfm?articleid=518&CFID=37203086& CFTOKEN=91529408&jsessionid=9a30405ca182336b1322.

39. Cooper-Chen, A. (2005). The world of television. *Global Entertainment Media: Content, Audiences, Issues.* Mahwah, NJ: Lawrence Erlbaum & Associates.

40. Blumler, J. G. & Katz, E. (1974). *The uses of mass communication.* Newbury Park, CA: Sage.

41. McCombs, M. & Shaw, D. (Summer 1972). The agenda-setting function of mass media. *The Public Opinion Quarterly* 36:2, 176–187.

INTERNET RESOURCES

1. Forecast 2007: Radio. http://www.mediaweek.com/mw/news/tvstations/article_display.jsp?vnu_content_id=1003526034.

2. Courtney Love Does the Math (wherein CL, writing on Salon.com, explains how an album could make $11 million and the band is still flippin' burgers for a day job). http://archive.salon.com/tech/feature/2000/06/14/love/print.html.

3. Impact of Radio Play on Music Sales, preliminary version of econometric study by Stan Liebowitz. http://www.ftc.gov/be/seminardocs/060928liebowitzimpactradioplay.pdf.

4. Podmetrics. *Radio Format Trends.* http://podmetrics.wordpress.com/2007/04/12/radio-format-trends-2012-4112007.

5. Video Games as Art. http://crave.cnet.com/8301-1_105-9769761-1.html?tag=nl.e501.

CHAPTER 2

Media Organizations

Six conglomerates – Viacom, Time Warner, NBC-Universal, Sony, Fox, and Disney ... control 98% of the programs that carry commercial advertising during prime time television (including commercial network and cable programming) and 96% of total U.S. film rentals. They control 75% of commercial television in non-prime-time slots, 80% of subscribers to Pay TV, and 65% of advertising revenues in commercial radio.

S. Christopherson[1]

CHAPTER OBJECTIVES

The objective of this chapter is to provide you with information about:
- Defining an organization
- The types, structure, and characteristics of the media industries and businesses
- Media industry segments
- Media industries, organizational processes, work flows, and information flows
- The economic characteristics of media industry enterprises
- The content value chain and distribution chain
- The changing cultural, social, political, and economic conditions of the media industries

INTRODUCTION

The development, production, marketing, and distribution of large-scale creative products most often take place within organizations. They include companies whose sole activities involve media and entertainment, business units of larger enterprises, artists' collectives, nonprofit organizations, and

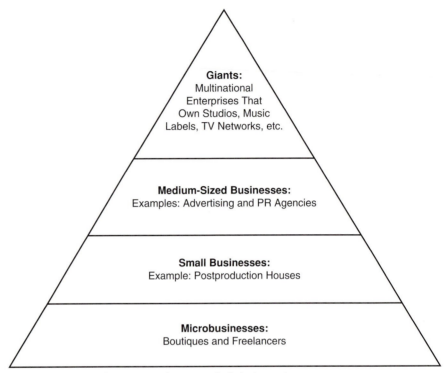

FIGURE 2-1 Pyramid structure of many media industry sectors

government agencies. In all these cases, an organization must be large enough to carry out the many tasks associated with bringing content to a public sphere. See Figure 2-1.

Digital technologies and networks make it possible for individuals and small groups – not just networks, studios, and large production companies – to produce, market, and distribute media and entertainment products. Many of these small and perhaps amateur efforts are not large-scale, long-term businesses. Mark Cuban, although he is more well known as the fiery owner of the Dallas Mavericks, also owns the HDNet cable network. Drawing on his experience as a content creator and marketer, he distinguishes between individual efforts, which are "labors of love," and business ventures, which produce a "product for profit."

When small-scale producers move to enter a larger market, perhaps marketing content products to a larger audience or to distributing a sequel to a first successful product, they find that they require an organization to manage the now more complex initiatives. Many segments of the media industries have a few large multinational corporations that are responsible for many of the content products and a large base of individual creative people.

DEFINING AN ORGANIZATION

There are many ways to define an organization. Most definitions include something about members and relationships, goals or objectives, and structured activity. Some descriptions include concepts of structure, specialization, and coordination, as well. A few examples will illustrate these points:

- A structured process in which individuals interact for objectives[2]
- A dynamic social system of cooperative interactions with the purpose of satisfying individual needs[3]
- A system consisting generally of inputs, process, outputs, feedback, and environment[4]
- Every organized human activity – from the making of pots to the placing of a man on the moon – gives rise to two fundamental and opposing requirements: the *division of labor* by function that assigns workers to perform diverse tasks and the *coordination* of these tasks to accomplish organizational goals[5]

Organizations also have boundaries.[6,7] Boundaries are always somewhat permeable, because organizations exist in an environment that entails interaction with economic, governmental, and social forces that give rise to market opportunities and constraints. Organizations adapt to these various conditions by adopting strategies, technologies, and structures that will better enable them to reach their goals.

Taken together, media industries typically form a pyramid structure. At the bottom are many freelancers and microbusinesses, including individual service providers and small boutiques, such as photography studios. Moving up the pyramid are small businesses like postproduction houses, prop suppliers, and casting agencies. Medium-sized enterprises include such businesses as advertising and PR agencies and production companies. And at the top are multinational giants like Viacom, Disney, and Warner Bros.

Structure is one way that organizations manage the division of labor and the coordination of tasks. Some organizational theorists conceptualize structure as communication, so that to the extent that one individual reports to another and receives a response, it defines the structure of the organization.[8] There are many kinds of organizational structures, but two forms predominate: *hierarchy* and *heterarchy*. Hierarchy means the vertical ranking of workers, where the higher-ranked employees (superiors) exercise authority over lower-ranked employees (subordinates). Heterarchy means that the members of a group have equal power and authority. Hierarchy describes a top-to-bottom vertical structure of authority; heterarchy describes a horizontal, lateral structure of authority. Other elements of organizational structures include size, formalization, specialization, hierarchy, centralization, professionalism, and percentage of workforce involved in core activities.[9]

Building on the concept of the division of labor, Mintzberg[10] noted that organizations are composed of five elements, which are usually present to some degree:

- **Strategic apex:** The people who have the overall responsibility for managing the organization, including boards of directors and top management
- **Operating core:** The people who have responsibility for producing the output of the organization – motion pictures, TV programs, CD albums, radio shows, press releases, marketing plans, etc.
- **Line:** Middle managers who are responsible for implementing and tracking the plans, policies, and procedures promulgated by top management in the strategic apex
- **Technostructure:** Staff people responsible for direct support, such as technology, analysis, and planning
- **Support staff:** Staff responsible for indirect functions, including legal counsel, accounting, and facilities operation and maintenance

In the media industries, there is a traditional division between management, the *suits*, and content creators, the *creatives*. These terms are heard throughout media businesses, including filmed entertainment, news operations, advertising, and videogames. It is easy to overemphasize the opposition between these two groups; in most instances, they work together smoothly to produce and market successful products. Nevertheless, there are important differences between the two groups. Managers are usually employees, working for a salary, performance-based bonuses, and advancement in the corporate structure. Creative people may be employees, but the most highly skilled and paid are often engaged as independent contractors. Managers must coordinate and control in an environment where there is considerable uncertainty, potentially bringing them into conflict with content creators who must invent and develop products whose ultimate success is not amenable to precise prediction. In the motivations for work of love and money, money is more of an incentive for managers; creative people also find intrinsic rewards in the work itself.[11] Chapter 4 will look at these differences more closely.

When an enterprise requires many workers to work together to accomplish goals, it requires coordination to schedule and combine the diverse efforts into a unified workflow. The type of coordination employed by an organization provides a more detailed expression of its structure, characterized as entrepreneurial, machine, professional, diversified, missionary, and innovative,[12,13] as shown in Table 2-1.

ORGANIZATIONAL INFORMATION FLOWS

Information flow describes how messages move from one person or group to another. Communication may follow formal or informal pathways. Formal pathways are the organizationally defined and authorized links by which

Table 2-1 Coordination in Media Businesses

Dominant Form of Coordination	Type of Organizational Structure	Examples of Media Businesses
Direct supervision	Entrepreneurial	Individual creators, such as photographers, retouchers, negative cutters, actors
Standardization of work	Machine	CD/DVD duplication houses
Standardization of skills	Professional	Crafts professions: gaffers, grips, editors; news, directors
Standardization of outputs	Diversified	Animation houses; postproduction facilities; TV production companies
Standardization of norms	Missionary	Partisan publications, documentaries, etc.
Mutual adjustment	Innovative	Music labels, motion picture studios

members send, receive, and record information required by tasks and functions. Typically, formal paths come from management at higher levels of the organization, going to lower levels. Informal pathways are usually person-to-person communications that may deal with work-related or outside issues. People often use informal channels to learn how the organization actually functions and to convey opinions and attitudes.[14]

Downward information flows from the top down. Upward information moves from the bottom up. Communication between unequal members of an organization is sometimes called *superior–subordinate communication*. By contrast, horizontal communication occurs between peers and departments. Finally, there are information flows across organizational boundaries, in and out of the enterprise.

In contemporary organizations, much communication occurs over computer networks. Most large companies also use *enterprise applications software* to manage essential information and to support management decision making. The enterprise system integrates previously separate computerized domains – accounting and financial data, management information, supply chain management, and human resources systems. Common enterprise applications software systems include Oracle/PeopleSoft, SAP, Microsoft, and others. Organizations offer middle-level and entry-level managers training on such systems and expect these executives to use them to gather information and provide reports.[15]

Organizations also operate an internal email system, intended for organizational messages. However, almost all workers also use it for informal and personal messages. One study found that 23 percent of corporate users' email was personal.[16] A survey of 526 U.S. businesses revealed that 36 percent of employers track the content, keystrokes, and time spent at the keyboard by their employees; 55 percent retain and review employees' messages. Workers should exercise care in their use of email: 25 percent of the surveyed companies terminated employees for email misuse.[17]

Increasingly, employees also use instant messaging (IM) in the workplace; they find it a useful way to determine whether a colleague is in the office or available for synchronous two-way communication. According to a 2006 survey, 50 percent of workers download IM tools from the Internet and 35 percent of use it at work. Thirty-one percent of the companies said they had policies for IM use, but only 13 percent retain records of employee IMs.[18]

Types of Organizations in the Media Industries

Media companies describe such a diverse array of organizations, practitioners, activities, products, and consumers that it is difficult to classify them. A songwriting banjo player, picking and strumming on a front porch in West Virginia, and the Boston Pops Orchestra both perform as part of the music industry. A writer penning a first novel in a threadbare garret and J. K. Rowling are authors seeking publishers in the book industry. *Titanic* and *Blair Witch Project* are both successful films. *Blair Witch* cost about $22,000 to make; the budget for *Titanic* was about $280 million. In order to make a profit, the film had to bring in $500 million in revenue; however, it ultimately set the record for box office revenue at $1.83 billion.[19]

The vast differences between participants in the same industry go beyond mere size and scale. They vary along such dimensions as types of organization, activities, and content products, the value of those products, methods of production, markets, distribution processes and channels, revenue sources, and customer relationships. The next sections cover the types of organizations that exist in the media industries: content-producing organizations, content marketing and distribution, content transport, and conglomerates and media ecologies. Conglomerates and media ecologies fit in more than one category, because they have business units engaged in activities that span multiple sectors.

Content-Producing Organizations

These enterprises make content. In some content-producing companies, content is the main activity and the primary product. In others, a business unit produces content to support the company's principal activity. For example, Ford Motor Company's advertising, PR, and corporate communications departments produce a great deal of content, although the principal line of business is the manufacture, distribution, and sale of automotive vehicles.

Companies that make content production their main activity include motion picture studios, television networks, production companies, many Web sites, and publishers of newspapers, magazines, and books. The size of content-producing entities ranges from multibillion-dollar multinationals to single individuals working as niche creative service providers under contract. For example, a studio may contract with an individual film editor, several special effects facilities, a visual postproduction house, an audio postproduction company, an accounting service, and hundreds, perhaps thousands, of other workers to handle the postproduction work on a single motion picture. Some of these entities will be small companies; others may even be individual freelancers.

Corporations, nonprofit organizations, and governmental agencies may all engage in substantial production of content to support their principal activity. Any large enterprise that has direct contact with ("touches") consumers, publics, or users is likely to produce or commission the production of content. Materials may include brochures, product sheets, catalogs, videos, podcasts, and Web sites. Increasingly, corporations are also moving into creating and distributing editorial content for free distribution to media outlets, not just materials specific to a marketing effort.

According to some industry studies, corporate spending on editorial projects in 2007 was estimated to fall between $28 and $55 billion and was predicted to grow at more than 20 percent per year.[20] The U.S. Government Printing Office spent nearly $851.5 million in printing and digital publishing alone.[21] A 2005 Committee on Governmental Reform (Minority Report), published by the U.S. House of Representatives, found that the Bush administration spent $88 billion on public relations, some of it financing video that was disseminated to news outlets. When the total spending for production of informational, training, and educational media is compiled, it must reach billions of dollars. Finally, a 2005 study found that nonprofit organizations spent $9 billion on marketing communications, which does not count purely educational materials.[22] The reasons for the explosion of content production on the part of non-media organizations include changes in the information and communication landscape over the past decade, including consumer behavior, so people search the Internet rather than look in the newspaper, encyclopedia, or library, technology that allows lower-cost production, and digital networks that reduce distribution costs.

Content Marketing, Distribution, and Exhibition Organizations

These organizations market and distribute it to consumers. They may commission or acquire the content, or they may undertake the activities on behalf of the content owner. These commercial operations include TV and radio stations, cable and satellite networks, cable and satellite programming services,

TV and movie syndicators and middlemen, and Internet aggregators and content providers. Some content-producing companies, such as HBO, Showtime, and network-affiliated television stations, also market and distribute content produced by others, as well as producing their own material. And to the extent that marketers create and produce marketing materials, they may also be considered content producers.

Some analysts looking at the future of the entertainment industry have suggested that movie studios and TV programming networks should commission content, but leave its production to creative people working in production companies. Sometimes this is called the "bank with a sales force" model. Once the content was finished, studios would market and distribute it. Similarly, music labels would locate and finance talent and then promote the finished works. The argument is that the "banker" sacrifices some control but lowers staffing and coordination costs, while still deriving revenues from creative work.[23]

Content Transport Organizations

These companies own the infrastructures that carry content to markets – either directly to consumers or to redistributors, who also use content-transport organizations to move it to the end-consumer. They are some of the world's largest enterprises, including telephone companies, fiber optic, and satellite system owners and operators. Of course, the Internet itself runs over these networks. In addition, there are other distribution network technologies, such as Wi-Fi and line-of-sight microwave technologies that carry media, including multipoint, multichannel distribution services (MMDS).[24]

Conglomerates and Media Ecologies

Multinational media giants span countries and even continents. The list of such corporations includes Bertelsmann, Disney, GE (NBC Universal), News Corporation, Sony, Viacom, Vivendi SA, and Time Warner. In the past decade, the list also includes Internet content aggregators and providers, Yahoo!, Google, and Microsoft.[25] Media conglomerates may own some or all of the necessary business units to create, produce, package, market, and distribute content. These companies own all or part of hundreds of companies, and ownership changes frequently due to mergers, acquisitions, divestments, and spinoffs. A list of some of the major holdings of the world's largest media conglomerates is shown in Table 2-2.

In addition to operating their own large enterprises, media conglomerates support an entire ecology of service providers that engage in specific projects, activities, and points in time, as shown in Table 2-3. Sometimes large media companies call on smaller ones because it is cheaper or faster to outsource the product or service; in other cases, the studio may want the skill of a particular group or individual.

Table 2-2 Major Holdings of Media Conglomerates

Big Eight	TV	Film	Publishing	Online Holdings	Other Media Holdings
Bertelsmann (Germany)	Europe's biggest TV company: RTL; Channel 5 (UK); Stakes in 22 TV channels	—	Random House, Knopf, Pantheon, Vintage, Modern Library, Bantam Doubleday, Bertelsmann/Springer; daily newspapers in Europe; 80 magazines worldwide	Lycos (Europe), MusicNet, AOL Europe (partial with AOL)	200 music labels – Arista, BMG Classics, RCA, Windham Hill Group; large music publisher and distributor; Majority owner, CLT-UFA; RTL Radio
General Electric (U.S.)	NBC, Bravo, Sci-Fi Channel, Telemundo, USA, Oxygen, Weather Plus, 25% A&E Networks, Biography Channel, part Weather Channel; International channels	NBC Universal (80% ownership), Universal Pictures, Focus Features, Rogue Pictures, Tribeca Films, Jersey Films, Kennedy/Mars Hall Company, Playtone Strike	*Sci-Fi* magazine	Film- & TV-related Web sites; Hulu .com, iVillage.com, newsvine.com	Music: Geffen, Motown Music, Polygram, Interscope; Theaters: Cineplex Odeon (partial), United Cinemas International
The Walt Disney Co.	ABC, ESPN, Touchstone TV, History Channel, A&E, Lifetime Television	Walt Disney Pictures, Touchstone Pictures, Miramax Films, Pixar Animation, Hollywood Pictures, Buena Vista International, A&E Indie Films	Hyperion Books, Disney properties	Disney-related Web sites	Majority ownership of Citadel Broadcasting (about 277 radio stations), ESPN Radio, Lifetime Radio, ABC radio; parks & resorts; Baby Einstein
News Corp. (Australia, UK, U.S.)	Fox Broadcasting, Fox News Channel, Fox Sports Channel, Fox Movie Channel, Fox College Sports, National Geographic Channel, other international, regional, and local channels	Fox Film Entertainment, Twentieth Century Fox Film Corp., Searchlight Pictures, Blue Sky Studios	*Wall Street Journal*, *New York Post*, Dow Jones, *The Times*, *Barron's*, *Weekly Standard*, many newspapers worldwide; books: HarperCollins	Fox Interactive Media – show, publishing, and channel-related Web sites; myspace.com	Satellite: 120 channels – BskyB, SKY Italia, LAPTV, STAR Channels, TATA Sky Outdoor advertising companies

Continued...

Table 2-2 Major Holdings of Media Conglomerates   *Continued*

Big Eight	TV	Film	Publishing	Online Holdings	Other Media Holdings
Time Warner (U.S.)	CNN, HBO, Cinemax, Cartoon Network, TBS, TNT, TruTV; international, regional, and local channels	Warner Bros. Pictures, Castle Rock, New Line Cinema, Telepictures, Cartoon Network Studios; Hanna-Barbera	Little, Brown & Co.; many magazines, including *Time, Sports Illustrated, Entertainment Weekly, Fortune, People, MAD*	Mapquest.com, America Online, DCComics.com, Netscape, Truveo .com TMZ.com, Bebo.com, NASCAR.com, PGA .com, many others	CBS Radio (140 stations), MTV Radio, BET Radio, Imagine Radio, Ltd.; Six Flags Entertainment
Sony (Japan)	Sony Pictures Entertainment, Columbia Tri-Star, Screen Gems	Sony Pictures Television, GSN (partial), Jim Henson Prods. (partial), Mandalay Entertainment (partial), Phoenix Pictures (partial); many international channels and holdings		Everquest	BMG Music, Sony Music, Columbia Records, Epic Records; Sony/ Loew's theaters, Metron, Magic Johnson Theaters; PlayStation and many videogames; consumer electronics
Viacom (U.S.)	CBS, MTV, Showtime, Smithsonian Channel, Movie Channel, Flix, Nickelodeon, TV Land, VH1, Spike TV, CMT, Noggin, Comedy Central, BET, UPN, King World, Spelling TV	Paramount Pictures, MTV Films, Nickelodeon Movies, Paramount Home Entertainment, Viacom 18 (50% India)	Simon & Schuster, Extreme Music Library, Director's Cuts Production Music, *Nickelodeon Magazine*	Ifilm.com, jokes.com, Xfire, GameSpot .com, MP3.com, Last.com, TheShowBuzz.com, Marketwatch.com, other movie-, show-, and channel-related Web sites	Infinity Broadcasting, Westwood One; Blockbuster Video; Famous Players cinemas
Vivendi (France)	Canal + Group, 20% NBC-Universal			GVT (Brazil) telecom & online services	Universal Music Group; Activision Blizzard (videogames); stakes in telecom companies

Table 2-3 Components of the Media Ecology

Business Category/Niche	Examples
Studios	**Majors:** Fox Entertainment Group (New Corp), Paramount Motion Pictures Group (Viacom), Sony Pictures Entertainment (Sony), NBC Universal (GE), Warner Bros. (Time Warner), Buena Vista Motion Pictures Group (Disney)
	Mini-Majors: Lions Gate Entertainment, The Weinstein Company, Dreamworks
Production companies	**U.S.:** Amblin Entertainment, American Zoetrope, Interscope, Lucasfilm, Ltd., Mandalay Pictures, Morgan Creek Productions, Plan B Entertainment, Revolution Studios, RKO Pictures, Spyglass Entertainment, Trimark Pictures, Village Roadshow Pictures
	Canada: Goliath 2 Production Studios, Porchlight Entertainment
	Europe: BBC Films, Channel Four Films, EMI Films, GaumontITC Entertainment, Pathe, StudioCanal, UGC, UFA
	Asia: Golden Harvest
	India: UTV
Crafts, guilds, and unions (includes writers, directors, producers, actors and performers, cinematographers, sound specialists, technicians, and crafts services workers, such as electricians, grips, locations, props, sets, wardrobe, makeup, catering)	IATSE NABET AFTRA SAG WGA DGA
Animation	Pixar Animation Studios, Disney Animation Studios, Imagi Animation Studio, Studio Ghibli
Special effects	Digital Domain, Cinesite, Industrial Light & Magic, Mac Guff, The Mill, Rhythm & Hues
Postproduction facilities: film, video, audio	Deluxe Entertainment Services Group, TVB, ITFC (UK), Soundfirm (Australia)
Independent contractors	Creative workers in any of the above categories may be contracted to work on a project.
Media replication services	Ever-changing group of service providers, contracted to mostly offshore companies that offer the lowest bid.
Distributors (motion pictures) and syndicators (television programs)	All major studios and networks own their own distribution business units. In addition, Telepictures, TVA Films, Domino Film and TV, PeaceArch
Theater exhibition	Regal, AMC, Cinemark, Carmike
Retail rental and sales outlets	Blockbusters, Wal-Mart, Netflix
Entertainment programs and publications	*Entertainment Weekly, People, TV Guide, Blender*
Consumer electronics	Sony, Panasonic, Sharp, Philips

A DAY IN THE LIFE OF LLOYD KAUFMAN

FIGURE 2-2 Lloyd Kaufman

FIGURE 2-3 Stuart Linver, intern for Lloyd Kaufman

Lloyd Kaufman, Co-Founder and President of Troma Entertainment; Chairman of the Independent Film & Television Alliance (IFTA)

Hi, my name is Stuart Linver. I'm a 15-year-old sophomore in high school who is currently interning at Troma Entertainment. Lloyd recently tripped and fell into a vat of toxic waste and unfortunately did not turn into a hideously deformed creature of superhuman size and strength, but instead is now in a coma, so I am here to give the truth about what Lloyd does every day at the lovely Troma building in New York City instead of him. Yes, Lloyd does everything,

from creating strategy for the Independent Film and Television Alliance Trade Association (IFTA) to whipping the Troma employees who make mistakes, to writing and directing iconic movies that influence a generation of directors. I have observed what he does through the span of a normal day. So here I am to tell you what the head of the legendary and last living, truly independent film studio goes through to keep the studio running.

8:45 a.m.

In the early morning, it is very quiet in the Troma office; everybody is doing his or her or its own work, keeping to themselves. Every now and then the phone rings and a short conversation would go on, but that never gets the attention of the employees. Everything is calm until I look out the window and see a 63-year-old man, staggering (he calls it jogging) across the 59th Street Bridge in 97-degree heat, drenched in sweat, looking like he's about to have a heart attack. The door bursts open finally, and Lloyd Kaufman flows through to his desk, right across from his Troma co-founder Michael Herz.

After a whole 5 seconds of resting, he walks over to some of the employees in the editing room who are putting together the Behind the Scenes footage from *Poultrygeist*. Lloyd has been shooting and editing with 35 mm film for almost 40 years and doesn't have a clue on how to work Troma's Final Cut Pro software used today. Getting a specific vision across to another person who is editing it for you can be incredibly frustrating, so from there on, we can all hear the muffled sound of Lloyd blowing steam in the editing room while every now and then being able to make out some of the words coming from the room (usually they include "*I'm going to blow my brains out!*").

10:00 a.m.

That's just the start of him going around to everybody working in the office, seeing what they're working on, stirring up some crap, and making sure they're doing it right, until it's time for the first appointment of the day. Lloyd meets with a 500-pound man who is willing to dress up as a Shirley Temple/Pollyanna-type character and perform a dance number in the next film about Toxie (try to find that in your $100,000,000 Michael Bay buddy cop epics). After that goes on for about an hour, the postage truck arrives with the mail, including a vast amount of fan mail from people around the world. Lloyd takes the time to personally respond to each and every one of them, unlike most companies and celebrities, who could give two shakes about the people who look up to them and send back an automated response or just don't respond at all, leaving the fans broken down and depressed.

12:15 p.m.
Lloyd carries a BlackBerry (he calls it his "crack fairy") and Twitters about five times a week. The Twittering is interrupted by a 16-year-old aspiring filmmaker buzzing at the front door of the Troma Building to talk to Lloyd about having him do a cameo appearance in his film that's currently in preproduction written and directed by this boy. Many scripts are sent in with small parts written for Lloyd, from small, no-budget films like *Bloodbath in the House of Knives* and *Knight of the Living Dead* to big-studio films like *Crank: High Voltage* and *Slither*. After talking to the young filmmaker, it's time for Lloyd to put on his serious hat. He makes some phone calls for IFTA to lobby a congressional committee in Washington about how the greedy media conglomerates are crushing the independent film industry. (For more information, watch "Lloyd Kaufman Defines Media Consolidation" at http://www.youtube.com/user/troma.)

1:00 p.m.
Lloyd now works on his MySpace and Facebook profiles, which have thousands of friends, while he scarfs down a nutritious lunch. What's better than a nice big bag of Cheez Doodles®? Then there's nothing better to go with the Cheez Doodles but a nice bag of Twizzlers®, and to polish that off, a two-liter bottle of Diet Coca-Cola®. It's the perfect quick meal that fits in between any amount of work.

That quick and hearty lunch gives Lloyd enough energy to start talking to his assistant about the upcoming San Diego Comic-Con at which he will be making an appearance. Not only that, but during the time in San Diego there will be a roast of Lloyd. Spider-Man creator Stan Lee is one of the roasters, so Lloyd needs to search the Internet for more insulting info about Stan Lee for the roast rebuttal.

1:30 p.m.
It would not be Troma if there were not at least one major thing that goes wrong. Today the amount of inventory being sent to some Best Buy stores is botched again and Best Buy cancels a huge order. So again, I can hear the Lloyd raging, screaming stuff such as, "*I am going to blow my brains*

out!" until the door buzzes again and it's time for another appointment.

2:30 p.m.
The door opens, and it is the 15-year-old Internet blogger sensation known as "Coolduder." He walks through the door ready to talk about his appearance in Lloyd's upcoming music video for the band *Not the Government*. Yes, this continues for another hour before all the information is sorted out for shooting and it's back to going through the mail until he comes upon a script submitted to Lloyd for his next feature-length film and, after wasting his time reading some of the horrid piece of crap, writes a response letter telling the writer it did not pass, while the script is thrown into the garbage bin next to old intern body parts.

3:30 p.m.
Two wannabe Tromettes (gynos [women] with small clothing and big … brains) come to the office. One has guns the size of bowling balls. The other has fun pillows the size of bowling balls. I believe in God again. So the remaining mail is gone through and then there is an evening meet and greet at *The Toxic Avenger Musical* now playing in an NYC theatre that Lloyd needs to prepare for.

4:45 p.m.
Lloyd receives word that Showtime cable TV network has "passed" on *Poultrygeist*. Even though it has played in over 300 screens, gotten great reviews from the *New York Times*, *Entertainment Weekly*, etc., and sold a kabillion DVDs, *Poultrygeist*, like *Citizen Toxie* and Trey Parker's *Cannibal the Musical*, will never play North American TV. "It's economic blacklisting," says Lloyd. "*I am going to blow my brains out!*"

6:30 p.m.
It's finally time to leave Troma, and Lloyd has a public appearance to make at the showing of *The Toxic Avenger Musical*. Of course he can't go in his ripe jogging clothes. So Lloyd changes into his suit and trademark bow tie that hangs on the ladder to the Troma building's roof hatch. Now it's time to call it a day at the Troma office and to head on out.

7:00 p.m.
Lloyd takes me for a quick Popov martini while he works his BlackBerry. An Australian newspaper calls to interview Lloyd. Now on his second martini, Lloyd gives a very unusual and hilarious interview.

Continued…

Daily Planner

vertex42

Date: 8/17/2009

Lloyd Kaufman

17 August, 2009
Monday

July 2009

Su	M	Tu	W	Th	F	Sa
			1	2	3	4
5	6	7	8	9	10	11
12	13	14	15	16	17	18
19	20	21	22	23	24	25
26	27	28	29	30	31	

August 2009

Su	M	Tu	W	Th	F	Sa
						1
2	3	4	5	6	7	8
9	10	11	12	13	14	15
16	17	18	19	20	21	22
23	24	25	26	27	28	29
30	31					

September 2009

Su	M	Tu	W	Th	F	Sa
		1	2	3	4	5
6	7	8	9	10	11	12
13	14	15	16	17	18	19
20	21	22	23	24	25	26
27	28	29	30			

Remember

Appointments

7	:00	Hangover - Take 4 Excedrin
	:30	Breakfast: Diet Mountain Dew
8	:00	Call Durban (So. Africa) re IFTA
	:15	
	:30	
	:45	Arrive at Troma
9	:00	Give interns advice
	:15	Check in editing room with Travis and Teresa
	:30	
	:45	Twitter
10	:00	Auditions for 500 lb. men
	:15	
	:30	
	:45	
11	:00	Make Phone calls answer fan mail
	:15	
	:30	
	:45	
12	:00	Talk to Michael Herz about Mother's Day remake
	:15	
	:30	Check up on Troma trailers edited for Netflix
	:45	IFTA Conference Calls
1	:00	MySpace & Facebook updates
	:15	Lunch (Twizzlers and Soda)
	:30	
	:45	
2	:00	
	:15	
	:30	Cool Duder appointment
	:45	
3	:00	Phone calls with Producer of
	:15	Toxic Avenger Musical
	:30	Tromette Appt.
	:45	
4	:00	Change into bow tie and suit
	:15	
	:30	
	:45	
5	:00	Call IFTA in California -
	:30	discuss campaign
6	:00	
	:30	Leave for Musical - Looking Sharp!
7	:00	Mentor High School Intern at Rudy's
	:30	Phone interview for Austrilia newspaper
8	:00	
	:15	Toxic Avenger Musical Meet & Greet
	:30	Toxic Avenger Musical Starts
9	:00	
	:30	Non-stop party Troma style to 5 a.m.

Notes

☑	ABC	**Prioritized Task List**

Time	**People to Call**

$Amt	**Expenses**

8:15 p.m.

Lloyd greets the audience at *The Toxic Avenger Musical.* People really seem to like him. *The Toxic Avenger Musical* has gone on, the crowd loved it, and the fans are swarming toward Lloyd and the stars of *The Toxic Avenger Musical.* What is a better way to celebrate than to go to the bar across the street and have a few drinks? So Lloyd and the cast/crew and some fans go to have a beer (Lloyd has a "stinger"), which then turns into two beers, then four or five, then turns into a few rounds of shots and so on. Lloyd stays with the "stingers."

11:00 p.m.

… More drinks …

12:30 a.m.

So after having some fun at the bar, Lloyd and the rest of the gang of new BFFs get together and decide to see what else is in town! James Gunn texts Lloyd about his friend Mia playing at a club in Park Slope. Lloyd's diminished posse smokes some grass, and gets on the "N" train while the night is young.

1:00 a.m.

Mia's concert in Park Slope is great!

2:00 a.m.

The group is smaller now.

… Still having fun …

5:00 a.m.

It is now 5 a.m., and I have no clue where the hell I am. I see Lloyd drunk, pissing on a lamppost, and singing drunken *Poultrygeist* songs. Like hell Lloyd is taking the subway back to New York in that condition, so I call a cab. I help Lloyd into the cab, as he can barely walk, and then wonder what the hell I am going to do. It's 5:00 a.m., I'm in Brooklyn, and I live in Connecticut! So I decide to take the train back to Long Island City to the Troma office and sleep there for the next few hours.

I will have a lot to tell my eleventh-grade classmates about how I spent my summer.

So now you see that between traveling to another convention every week and getting more wasted than Colin Farrell, Lloyd does do a lot of work for the IFTA and Troma. He helps keep independent cinema alive, keeps it so that we can all get our cheap shots on MiniDV with crappy sound and lighting out there for people to see. So appreciate Lloyd, because with all the parties, booze, and Twizzlers, he won't be here forever, and there is always the chance that he may really actually blow his brains out!

ORGANIZATIONAL PROCESSES AND WORKFLOWS

The traditional steps for bringing a creative product to market include development, preproduction, production, postproduction, marketing, and distribution. In the past, these activities took place in *silos*, where each phase of work proceeded in some isolation from the other phases. Today, work on a creative product is much more integrated through network connections, which has altered the organizational processes to manage, coordinate, and control the efforts. See Table 2-4.

The earlier section on communication flows in modern organizations mentioned enterprise resource planning as part of the overall move to computer communication. Now that the enormous scope of operations and range of activities is clear, the importance of enterprise resource planning (ERP) software to coordinate and manage global media companies is obvious. In one study of the introduction of ERP,[26] researchers found that managers pointed to positive effects of improved efficiency and control. They particularly liked the increased

Table 2-4

Phase	Traditional Process, Pre-1990	Digital Process, Evolving Since 1990
Development	Silo, computer-assisted (word processing)	No change. It's still a computer-assisted (word processing) silo
Preproduction	Computer-assisted (word processing, spreadsheet, project management software); coordinated within production organization	Computerized and networked; integrated within production organization (enterprise software)
Production	Silo, analog acquisition	Integrated, analog acquisition, converted to digital for postproduction
Postproduction	Silo, analog workflow and processing	Integrated (networked) through partnership arrangements; digital workflow and processing
Marketing	Silo, mostly analog workflow and processing	Integrated (networked) through partnership arrangements; mostly digital workflow and processing
Distribution	Silo, mostly analog workflow, processing, and distribution	Integrated (networked) through partnership arrangements; mostly digital workflow, processing, and distribution

ability to standardize policies and procedures across business units in such areas as finance and accounting, purchasing, and product distribution. Not all responses were positive. Some middle managers objected to the constraints that ERP systems placed on their independent decision making, excessive procedural rigidity, and a resulting loss of adaptive capability. These managers said that ERP made their work more difficult and complex because they had to duplicate the work of the ERP in more adaptable "shadow systems."

ERP systems may eliminate the jobs of some middle managers, increasing the workload of the remaining layers.[27] The managers whose work consists largely of collecting, analyzing, and reporting information and acting as information brokers between management levels are most vulnerable to having their jobs eliminated.[28]

The Digital Assembly Line

When content is in digital form, it is easy to transport, copy, and revise. Transferring the material over computer networks facilitates the transfer of work between team members, departments, vendors, and partners. The handover is virtually instantaneous compared with older modes of delivery such as hand-carrying, office mail, messenger, overnight and delivery service, which might take several minutes, hours, or even days. The increased velocity makes possible a much higher level of coordination of work.

One way to think about creating and distributing content in the digital environment is as a virtual *digital assembly line*. Technological change over the past decade has developed so that nearly all the pieces of this virtual digital assembly line to create and deliver commercial content have been put in place. Figure 2-4 shows the elements of an end-to-end global electronic content industry.

It is instructive to examine the evolution of the original assembly line in manufacturing that occurred in the early part of the twentieth century. The assembly line required about 100 years to emerge as an established workflow process that could support mass production. Although mass production techniques are

---

ELEMENTS OF AN END-TO-END E-INDUSTRY

1. Creation: The Digital Assembly Line

	Development	*Preproduction*	*Production*	*Postproduction*
Platform:	Word processing software	Project management & pre-visualization software	Digital camera	Editing software

2. Distribution

	Marketing	*Transport*	*Delivery*	*Consumption*
Platform:	Office/productivity software	Digital network	Digital network	Digital player

3. Monetization

	Consumer payment	*Financial settlement*	*Royalties to copyright holders*	*Profit Participants*
Platform:	Electronic banking via network	Accounting software	Royalty mgmt. system	Word processing software: contracts

→ → → →

FIGURE 2-4 Elements of a virtual content industry

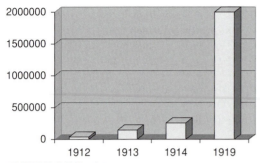

FIGURE 2-5 Number of cars manufactured by Ford Motor Company, 1912–1919

widely attributed to Henry Ford, he built on earlier technologies to create the sophisticated assembly line that revolutionized the automobile manufacturing industry.

One technology that enabled the assembly line a century later was developed by gun manufacturers – precision measurement and machining so that parts were interchangeable. In 1913, Henry Ford introduced the assembly line into his manufacturing operation.[29]

Ford's assembly line as a method of realizing mass production was wildly successful. Sales of the Model T rose from a few thousand in 1912 to 2 million in 1919, as shown in Figure 2-5.

The assembly line put Ford miles ahead of his competitors. By mid-1914, workers could assemble a car in 1 hour and 33 minutes of a single worker's time, compared to the fastest time for stationary assembly, 12 hours and 28 minutes. That year, 13,000 workers at Ford made 260,720 cars, while the rest of the industry required 66,350 workers to make 286,770.

Other sectors quickly adopted the mass production techniques. Today, the influence of mass production techniques extends to industries as diverse as agriculture, transportation, computer processing chip production, and fast food operations. Assembly line methods of mass production in manufacturing do not lend themselves to content production, although they do appear to be compatible with automated distribution and payment processes:

1. Break down the work process into simple, repetitive tasks
2. Simplify and standardize parts and processes
3. Use specialized equipment, materials, parts, and processes to reduce human input and increase output
4. Systematize total process

In the years following the introduction of mass production, the media and entertainment industries adopted elements of the industrial assembly line paradigm when it was possible. However, each content property is unique. More, its popularity depends on creators finding the subtle and elusive balance between innovation and convention, between excitement and expectations. As a result, many of the most essential, expensive, and capital-intensive processes in creating content retain a tie to artistry and craftsmanship.

In the creation phase, content products cannot just be stamped out like cars and other manufactured products. Most forms of content, especially motion pictures, are developed with an eye toward an array of ancillary and downstream markets, including licensing, productization, and a long series of release windows. Increasingly, a property that achieves success in one medium is recreated for other media, such as a film, TV series, music CD, book, stage musical, the Internet, a videogame, or even a comic book or an amusement park attraction.

Although a big hit in one arena bolsters the probability of success in other venues by providing a fan base for marketing efforts, it does not guarantee it. Few properties will cross media boundaries without a substantial creative and production effort to tailor it for consumption in the new environment. Indeed, royalties to talent, who are now well aware of the value of their creations, are likely to offset any efficiencies that might have been gained from reworking known material, and may even make product extensions much more costly than the film that generated them.

In the distribution phase, the equation turns around: Content products can be reproduced at a very low cost – much lower than reproduction costs of manufactured goods. To make media extensions profitable and available to consumers at prices they are willing to pay, it is necessary to mass-produce content products. At the same time, in interactive environments, people want material customized to their wants and needs. This leads to a seemingly contradictory goal for producers and providers: the production of mass customized content.[30] The popularity of skins for Internet browsers and computer media players is a good example of such personalized material. One way content sellers are addressing this issue is through specialized servers and software, content management systems. They permit the on-the-fly recreation of content products, based on individual requests. For example, music services could offer songs in different versions, such as with vocals, karaoke without vocals, and as ringtones. Consumers could even specify the part of the music they want for the ringtones.

Digital Workflow

The path of a project as it undergoes a process or set of processes is called *workflow*. Work in the digital domain has many differences from an analog process. One of the most important is that of location: proximity (closeness of workers to one another) is no longer a factor. In the analog world, work on content is hand-carried, sent by messenger, or shipped. In the digital world, it is emailed or posted on a server and retrieved in Paris, Hong Kong, or wherever the next worker happens to be.

The digital workflow makes distributed work teams faster and easier than ever before. However, despite the advantages, it introduces some difficulties as well. For example, it may take some time for an organization to implement the technological and management changes that a new digital workflow requires. It raises issues of security. And it is not always as easy to express creative and artistic concepts over a network as it might be in person.

One study of the introduction of digital workflow to academic publishing provides insight into the rewards and costs of moving to a digital workflow, which are likely to be similar throughout publishing enterprises and perhaps other content producing and distributing organizations as well. According to the study,

> The differences introduced with a digital workflow transform the publishing process and even the products significantly. The more fully they integrate a digital workflow, the more changes publishers will see. The process changes, schedules are compressed, and quality improves. Ultimately, the publisher may achieve financial rewards as well.[31]

The authors concluded that digital workflow introduced substantial changes in their publishers' business routines. It requires greater planning, quality control, staff training, and coordination and communication between those involved in the workflow. Finally, publishers must rely more on partners and suppliers than they did when they used an analog workflow.

Similar issues of cost, coordination, efficiency, and time savings arise in the feature film industry with the digital intermediate (DI) process – part of the postproduction phase of creating a motion picture. After a film is edited, a number of tasks remain, such as cutting the original negative to conform to the new edited version. The process requires the assembly of work by many separate entities, such as a negative cutter, one or more special effects artists or studios, sound facilities, and so forth.

DIGITAL WORKFLOW (FILMED ENTERTAINMENT)

Film Shoot: Film is shot on 16 mm or 35 mm
Transfer: Dailies transferred to digital tape format
Negative Cut: Using the offline EDL, the negative is cut in overlength, i.e., with handles
Digital Intermediate (DI) process begins:
  Scanning: Film is scanned to digital format, placed on disc
  Grading: Color correction in very high resolution
  Transfer: Graded material is transferred to editing workstation
  Assembly: Material is edited in workstation, using basic techniques
  Add Effects: Compositing, effects, image manipulation, and enhancement
  Cleanup: Removal of production artifacts (camera scratches, dust removal, etc.)
  Titles and credits are added
  Add Digital Effects: 3D, high-resolution animation, other prepared digital effects
  Recording & Developing: Project is recorded back to film
Mute Print, Answer Print, Release Prints:
  Mastering: Copying final project to release formats: DVD, HDTV, NTSC, etc.
  Interpositive Recording: Copy used as basis for mass replication
  Archiving: Film and digital formats archived for use in distribution in future format

This phase of postproduction in the analog world takes several weeks – sometimes even months. In the digital realm, it generally takes about 4 weeks. However, on some projects, there may be little or no savings of time. The real advantages of the digital process lie in the technical quality of the finished product and the flexibility that the digital intermediate process offers the director and producers to shape and mold a creative work. For example, filmmakers are able to see optical and digital effects immediately and to make changes at a workstation, instead of waiting for days for the effects to be sent out, added, and returned to the postproduction facility.[32]

The Content Value Chain

One distinguishing factor between enterprises in the creative industries is where in the *value chain* their activities take place, as shown in Figure 2-6. Companies that create content, aggregate content, and distribute content are all creative industry companies, but a particular organization may participate in only one, a few, or all of these activities. For example, News Corp. business units act in several parts of the content value chain. Several News Corp. companies create original content, such as Fox Studios, Fox Television, and Fox Sports. The corporation's cable networks also acquire and aggregate content produced by others. Finally, News Corp. distributes audiovisual content through its owned-and-operated television station group, cable networks, cable systems, and global satellite services. Similarly, ABC, NBC, and CBS television networks create original content and acquire and aggregate content produced by others. They distribute programming over the air via the television stations they own and operate, as well as through local affiliate stations owned by other broadcast groups with which they have agreements. By contrast, a small production company may only produce documentaries for cable channels.

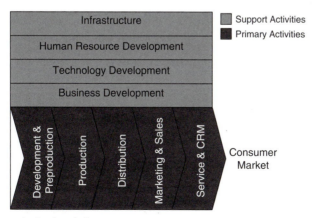

FIGURE 2-6 The content value chain

VALUE CHAIN

The term *value chain* was first coined by Michael Porter in his 1985 book *Competitive Advantage: Creating and Sustaining Superior Performance.*[33] The value chain categorizes the activities of an organization to create and add value as it develops, creates, markets, sells, and distributes a product or product line. Consider how a movie studio adds value to blank DVDs, which are worth less than $1 each. The studio develops and produces a motion picture, markets it, and replicates it on a DVD. The DVD, now encoded with a movie, sells for $15–$30 at retail.

Value chains are also used to describe the way various enterprises add value to an industrial process that spans many companies. Some of the activities in Figure 2-6 are called by different terms in the media industries:

- Inbound logistics = Development and preproduction
- Operations = Production
- Outbound logistics = Distribution
- Marketing and sales = Marketing and sales
- Services = Services

The Content Distribution Chain

The *distribution chain* (Figure 2-7) describes how finished content moves from the content creator or provider to the consumer. Content resides in storage, as tapes, DVDs, and files. The content provider authorizes the server to call up material from storage and to deliver it. A transport system stands between providers and consumers. Long-haul transport takes place over fiber optic and satellite networks; short-haul transport may include wireless and local cable and telephone networks as well.

Media companies differ in how they arrange their distribution chain, depending on which pieces they own. ABC, CBS, and NBC produce content. They pay both satellite and fiber optic transport providers to deliver the material to their owned-and-operated and affiliated television stations. Today's stations are often part of a broadcast group centralized network, so the programs may be transported again via fiber optic cable, satellite, or other wireless network to station transmitters; material may also go to cable headends. To reach consumers, the stations own their own transmitters and deliver programs directly to households.

By contrast, the parent of Fox Broadcasting, News Corp., owns its own satellite system. The broadcasting subsidiary pays the parent-owned satellite company, so there is no savings to the network. But for News Corp. as a whole, this distribution arrangement is less expensive than it is for the other broadcast networks, as News Corp. pockets the profits from the transport rather than paying it out.

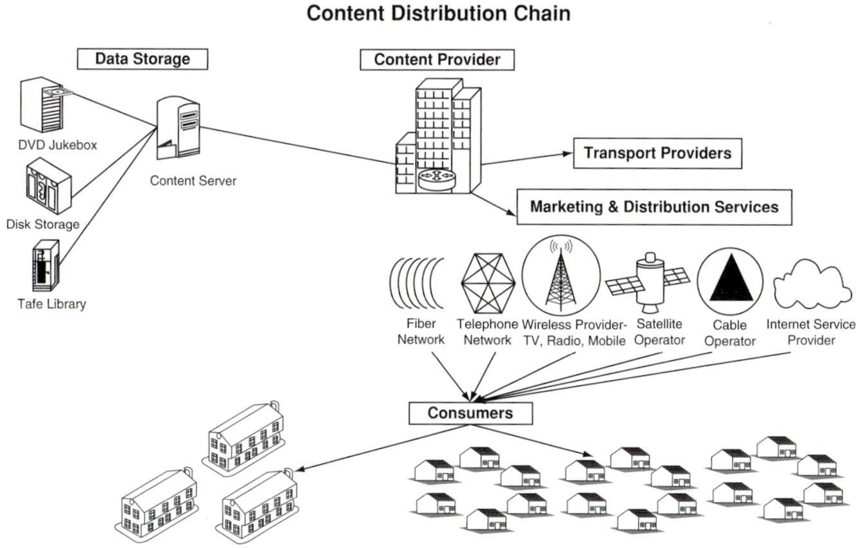

FIGURE 2-7 The content distribution chain

The Revenue Chain

"Follow the money" – this phrase describes the *revenue chain*. It shows how revenues flow to the participants in the content value and distribution chains. It is the only part of the business process that starts at the endpoint where the consumer pays, moving back to the content creator. The consumer pays for the content, often with a credit card, PayPal, or other payment mechanism. If it is other than cash, then there is a financial settlement that takes place within the banking industry. The money is then distributed to participants, based on royalty agreements and contracts between the participants, such as content creators, copyright owners and licensees, aggregators, and distributors. Needless to say, with so many players, they are often very complex.

ECONOMIC FACTORS THAT AFFECT ENTERPRISES IN THE CREATIVE INDUSTRIES

The field of economics seeks to answer three key questions: How much of a product (in economic terms, *goods*) should be produced for a given market? How will the products be produced? And who will consume the products?[34] Every organization must answer these questions for the markets it addresses and the products it produces. And, as in other industries, classic economic microeconomic principles apply, such as supply and demand. Disposable income also affects the amount of the household budget that can be spent on content, and the amount of leisure time is also a major factor.[35]

The size, scope, markets, products, and consumers vary greatly between creative industry sectors and between enterprises within sectors. Nevertheless, they do share some economic commonalities:[36]

- Most entertainment markets are *differentiated markets*, in which enterprises produce many different varieties (titles) of the same types of products (films, TV programs, books, magazines, etc.).
- They find it costly to produce information goods but inexpensive to reproduce them. (In economic terms, information products have *high fixed costs* and *low marginal costs*.)
- The goods they produce are *experience goods*, which means that potential customers cannot know the nature of the product because they have not yet experienced it and must rely on the experience of others in order to make decisions about using or buying it.
- They participate in an economy of attention: the sale of information goods depends on buyers having the time, energy, and desire to consume them.
- They are dependent on technologies and entire systems of technologies: an audience cannot see a movie without mechanisms for marketing communication, payment, product distribution, and display.
- Many segments of the creative industries are hit-driven, seeking products that will have wide appeal.
- Even though organizations seek hits, it is very difficult (if not impossible) for them to predict the factors will make a particular product a hit, business environments characterized by Caves as "nobody knows."[37]

Because organizations that seek success in the creative industries depend on creativity and innovation, they benefit from the skillful management of people with creative skills and the organizational structure that underlies the work. Typically, organizations hire individuals who have the relationship skills needed to "handle" creative people and processes. A good example of how powerfully entertainment executives are rewarded for such abilities is the career of Jamie Tarses. At NBC, she shepherded the development and production of *Friends*, guiding it to become a key part of the network's Thursday night powerhouse. Hoping to harness Tarses's ability to connect with a then-new generation of creatives, ABC hired her from NBC, making her the first female president of ABC Entertainment Network at 32 years old, a position she held until 1999.

THE ORGANIZATIONAL CONTEXT: ECONOMIC AND SOCIAL FACTORS

All businesses operate within larger cultural, social, political, and economic contexts. This situation means that although the classic economic principles of supply and demand are often the primary determinants of the success of a business, they are not the only ones. And sometimes there are conditions other than the economic arena that have enormous impacts on business as usual. Historically, many participants in creative industries believe that macro-economic business cycles, which affect the entire economic landscape, are less important in the profitability of content industries than in some others, such as home building or automobile purchases. In economic parlance, media and entertainment are called *counter-cyclic* segments.

However, when the overall economy experiences a downturn, it inevitably has some effect. In 2009, Waxman (2010) reported how the recession had affected Hollywood in 2009, in spite of successes such as *Paranormal Activity* and *Avatar*: "The dark news came all year as production companies closed, independent movie studios floundered and studios and networks cut hundreds of jobs. People were eliminated at Warner Brothers (800), News Corp (400 at MySpace), Disney (1,900), Sony (300) and Lionsgate (45). DreamWorks sat idle for months as it struggled to close its funding from a reluctant Indian partner. That, after giving up its dreams of being an independent studio. MGM began its downward slide toward a still-unresolved end game. Universal and Disney both underwent clean sweeps of their top executive ranks, and brought in younger and – in Disney's case – more aggressive change agents. Both Hollywood news trades went through serial cutbacks. Senator films sunk. Weinstein shrunk. The indie world sat there and shivered, as a whole."[38]

The creative industries are not monolithic, and some segments are affected more than others. For example, industry analyst Anthony Noto, speaking at the Reuters Media Summit in late 2007, said that lower ad revenue would affect those companies that depend on advertising spending, such as broadcast television networks. However, he also observed that companies that operate globally and over the Internet may be able to avoid the worst effects of the downturn.

As Strauss Zelnick, chairman of Take-Two Interactive Inc., creator of *Grand Theft Auto*, sums up the caution that creative industry companies should exercise: "No entertainment business is truly counter-cyclical," he said. "People try to tell you that, but it's just not the truth. Think about it – you've just lost your home. No, you're not going to pay $50 on a videogame – you're just not, even though it's Christmas time."[39]

The creative industries are particularly sensitive to changes in cultural, social, and political conditions. The firing of Don Imus is testimony to the strong emotional response groups and individuals may have to material that appears in the public sphere. Issues of appropriateness, fairness, accuracy, and indecency are a continual source of commentary, conversation, and even legislation.

Content purveyors may find that changes in any one of these contexts result in new freedoms or new constraints on their product offerings. On the business side, one example from the 1980s arose from the political ascendancy of the Reagan administration, which propelled deregulation to the forefront. The result was massive consolidation of the media and entertainment industries, which continues to extend its influence into the new century.

In 2004, Janet Jackson's "wardrobe malfunction" during her halftime Super Bowl XXXVIII performance created a firestorm. The result was a decision by the FCC to increase fines on broadcasters for failing to prevent such incidents. Since then, the climate for what may be deemed inappropriate material has become much harsher than it was before the 2004 controversy.

Indeed, one can point out that the major events that affect a society, such as 9/11 and the subsequent war in Iraq, have consequences far beyond the actual occurrence. More gradual changes, including political movements and changes in social attitudes, will also move the contextual conditions under which content enterprises operate. The creative industries serve as both crystal ball and mirror to society as a whole. Playing these sensitive roles in the social fabric as they do, perhaps it is not surprising that their content is noticed and responded to in ways that can have an effect on such enterprises.

SUMMARY

Organizations develop structures to manage the division of labor and the coordination of tasks to achieve their goals. The two most common forms of structure are hierarchy and heterarchy. Other structural characteristics are size, formalization, specialization, centralization, percentage, and percentage of the workforce involved in core activities. Organizations also have boundaries that are more or less permeable.

Organizations are composed of five elements: the strategic apex, operating core, line, technostructure, and support staff. They adopt some form of coordination, which is accomplished through communication. Information flows up, down, and laterally. Downward flows tend to be formal communications; upward and lateral flows may be both formal and informal. Electronic communication systems have had tremendous effects on organizational functioning.

The types of organizations within the creative industries are:

■   Content producing organizations
■   Content marketing and distribution organizations

- Content transport organizations
- Media conglomerates and media ecologies

In the creative industries, there are six key processes to bring a content product to market:

- Development
- Preproduction
- Production
- Postproduction
- Marketing
- Distribution

Technology is fundamental to the creative industries. As a long-term trend, all of the key processes in which they engage are moving to the online environment to create an end-to-end virtual industry. This trend includes all the elements of the content and distribution value chains and the revenue chain. It is not yet clear how the industry will be affected by the gradual evolution of an all-digital workflow.

The content value chain describes where the participation of each player adds to the eventual price the product can command from the consumer. The content distribution chain describes how finished content moves from the content provider to the consumer. The revenue chain describes how the money the consumer pays for the content reaches the distributors, copyright owners, and creators of the content.

As with all businesses, economics has an enormous influence. One problem with creative enterprises is that they are unable to predict the answers to the key economic questions of how much of a product should be produced, how will they be produced, and who will consume them. The key economic principles governing the answers to these questions are supply and demand, amount of disposable income, and, for content products, the amount of leisure time consumers have, because content requires consumer attention. Most entertainment markets are hit-driven differentiated markets. Content products are experience goods that have high fixed costs and low marginal costs.

Creative industries are less vulnerable than some other industries to overall downturns in the economy. However, they are particularly sensitive to larger cultural, social, and political conditions, including social attitudes and regulation.

WHAT'S AHEAD

The next chapter covers leadership and management, two fascinating and complex topics. There are few industries where the ability to lead is more important, because media and content both involve continuous, rapid change. Chapter 3 examines some of the classic approaches, then turns to contemporary ideas, as there are a variety of leadership and management styles throughout the media industries – sometimes within the same organization. Finally, the chapter looks at how media companies manage two of the most important and challenging aspects of their operations – technology and creative people.

CASE STUDY 2.1 MEDIA ORGANIZATIONS

The president of your TV station is looking seriously at a merger between your news department and a 24/7 Internet news organization. You have been assigned the task of researching the two entities and developing a game plan that integrates the two. Your news director, John Tatum, has been in the business for 35 years and knows the TV business inside and out. He prides himself on not using the Internet and prefers faxes to emails. Lucky for him, his assistant is capable of retrieving his email and keeps him up to speed. He has been in the market for a long time and has developed some long-standing relationships that come in handy for enterprising news stories.

Some of the newer reporters grumble that John isn't keeping up with the times and often feel frustrated when presenting new technology ideas that they feel would improve the look of the newscast. More often, they find themselves talking with the assistant news director, Eric Cane, who came up through the ranks as a general assignment reporter to producer and on to his new position about 5 years ago. He too understands the frustration and works with the executive producers to integrate some of the ideas into the newscasts and presents the information to John.

Your next step involves meeting with the 24/7 Internet organization and drawing some conclusions about the operation. Most of the online reporters possess a newspaper background and don't seem to be very happy about being joined in with a broadcast group. There is a sense that many of the reporters may quit to search for print positions as opposed to working for a TV station. The director of digital services has a background in developing Internet sites and is extremely creative. He gets along well with this staff, but appears to be more of a peer than a manager. He shares an office with his executive producer and the video journalists casually pop in a few times to talk and laugh about the events of the day.

The atmosphere is clearly more casual. The breaking stories were posted to the site as completed, but no rush to hit any deadlines. The atmosphere was a vast difference from the newsroom, where reporters, photographers, and editors work hastily toward completing their packages in time for their assigned newscasts. It was very clear that merging these two very different departments into one cohesive group was going to be interesting.

Assignment

1. Begin by developing a full assessment of a television newsroom. Feel free to contact a local newsroom in your hometown to understand the organizational structure. More importantly, be sure to gain an understanding of how the work is distributed daily:

    - The normal work hours
    - Positions and titles
    - Deadlines for each newscast

2. Do the same for an Internet company that develops news or entertainment content. Looking at the previous example, expand upon how the operations of this Web Co. might operate. Again, contact a Web site company and develop the organizational chart. As with the TV news division, find out about copy deadlines, breaking stories, etc.

3. After fully analyzing these two very different divisions, begin to devise a plan on how you could successfully merge. Which positions would be eliminated, be revised, or survive? Be sure to provide some logic on how and why.

4. In the final paragraph, explain how this merger would benefit the company while also including information on challenges of the merger.

CASE STUDY 2.2 THE MEANING OF MEDIA CONVERGENCE

Encyclopaedia Britannica defines *media convergence* as a phenomenon involving the interlocking of computing and information technology companies, telecommunications networks, and content providers from the publishing worlds of newspapers, magazines, music, radio, television, films, and entertainment software. Media convergence brings together the "three Cs"—computing, communications, and content. In this case study, you will analyze and learn about two media companies that have already merged and then come up with an idea for a media convergence plan in today's market.

Assignment
Part I
Conduct research on a media convergence that has occurred in the past 10 years. Write a brief summary about the convergence. Answer these questions as you conduct your findings:

- Why did the two companies merge?
- How did this convergence benefit each company?
- Were there any negative effects of the convergence?

Part II
Create your own converged company. Take a look around for two entertainment/media-based companies and develop a convergence plan.

- Begin with a full analysis of both companies.
- Identify the strengths and weaknesses of each.
- Name the new company.
- Are there departments that could be merged and are there any that must remain intact?
- What is the benefit to the consumer?
- How would you market the new company?
- Write a press release announcing the merger.

REFERENCES

1. Christopherson, S. (2006). Behind the scenes: How transnational firms are constructing a new international division of labor in media work. In T. Miller, *The Contemporary Hollywood Reader* (185–204). New York: Routledge.

2. Hicks, H. G. (1972). *Management of organizations*. New York: McGraw-Hill, 23.

3. Barnard, C. I. (1948). *Organization and Management: Selected Papers*, Cambridge, MA: Harvard University Press.

4. Wiener, N. (1965). *Cybernetics or control and communication in the animal and the machine*, 2nd ed. Cambridge, MA: MIT Press.

5. Mintzberg, H. (1983). Organization design: Fashion or fit? *Harvard Business Review* 59:1, 103–116.

6. Santos, F. M. & Eisenhardt, K. M. (2005). Organizational boundaries and theories of organization. *Organization Science* 16:5, 491–508.

7. Aldrich, H. E. (1979). *Organizations and environments*. Englewood Cliffs, NJ: Prentice-Hall.

8. Weick, K. E. (1979). *The social psychology of organizing*. New York: McGraw-Hill.

9. Mintzberg, op. cit.

10. Mintzberg, H. (1979). *Structuring of organizations*. Englewood Cliffs, NJ: Prentice Hall.

11. Caves, R. E. (2000). *Creative industries*. Cambridge, MA: Harvard University Press.

12. Ibid.

13. Martinez, J. I. & Jarillo, C. (1989). The evolution of research on coordination mechanisms in multinational corporations. *Journal of International Business Studies* 20:3, 489–514.

14. Karathanos, P. & Auriemmo, A. (March 1999). Care and feeding of the organizational grapevine. *Industrial Management*, 41(2), 26–30. Accessed October 11, 2009, from ABI/INFORM Global. (Document ID: 42563486.)

15. Ross, J. W., Vitale, M. R. & Willcocks, L. P. (2003). The continuing ERP revolution: Sustainable lessons, new modes of delivery. In G. Shanks, P. B. Seddon & L. P. Willcocks (Eds.), *Second wave enterprise resource planning systems* (102–132). Cambridge, UK: Cambridge University Press.

16. Loechner, J. (December 17, 2005). Good intentions notwithstanding, half of office email not work related. *Media Post.* Accessed June 18, 2008, at http://www.mediapost.com/publications/ index.cfm?fa=Articles.showArticle&art_aid=37878.

17. American Management Association & the ePolicy Institute (2006). *2006 Workplace e-mail, instant messaging & blog survey: Bosses battle risk by firing e-mail, IM & blog violators.* Accessed June 20, 2008, at http://www.amanet.org/press/amanews/2006blogs_2006.htm.

18. Ibid.

19. ——— (September 8, 2009). All time box office: *Titanic.* Accessed September 20, 2009, at http://www.celebritywonder.com/movie/0110.html.

20. Pulizzi, J. (2007). Are corporations the new kings of content? *Folio Magazine.* Accessed on February 19, 2008, at http://www.foliomag.com/2007/are-corporations-new-kings-content.

21. U.S. Government Printing Office (2005). *Voices of Change 2005 Annual Report.* Washington, DC: U.S. Government Printing Office, 15.

22. Watson, T. (2006). Special Report. Consumer philanthropy: Nonprofits spend billions to reach consumers: Changing our world pegs marketing spending at $7.6 billion annually. Accessed February 19, 2008, at http://www.onphilanthropy.com/site/News2?page= NewsArticle&id=6863.

23. Lichtenberg, J. (September 1999). The studio model: Should publishing follow Hollywood's approach to the creative process? *Publishing Research Quarterly* 15:3, 46–54.

24. Van Tassel, J. (2003). *Digital TV over broadband.* Woburn, MA: Focal Press.

25. Klinenberg, E. (2007). Breaking the news. *Mother Jones.* Accessed February 22, 2008, at http:// www.motherjones.com/news/feature/2007/03/and_then_there_were_eight.pdf.

26. Harley, B., Wright, C., Hall, R., & Dery, K. (2006). Management reactions to technological change: The example of enterprise resource planning. *The Journal of Applied Behavioral Science* 42:1, 58–74.

27. Kidd, J. & Richter, F.-J. (2001). The hollowing out of the workforce: What potential for organizational learning? *Human Systems Management* 20, 7–18.

28. Hall, R. (2002). Enterprise resource planning systems and organizational change: Transforming work organization? *Strategic Change* 11, 263–270.

29. White, J. B. (January 11, 1999). The line starts here. *Wall Street Journal.*

30. Barret, V. (June 17, 2009). Shutterfly's reinvention strategy. *Forbes.* Accessed August 21, 2009, at http://www.forbes.com/2009/06/17/shutterfly-digital-photos-intelligent-technology-housenbold.html.

31. Beebe, L. & Meyers, B. (2000). Digital workflow: Managing the process. *Journal of Electronic Publishing* 5:4. Accessed March 14, 2008, at http://hdl.handle.net/2027/spo.3336451.0005.403.

32. Ohanian, T. A. & Phillips, M. E. (2000). *Digital filmmaking: The changing art and craft of making motion pictures.* Woburn, MA: Focal Press.

33. Porter, M.E. (1985). *Competitive advantage: Creating and sustaining superior performance.* New York: Simon & Schuster.

34. Albarran, A. B. (2002). *Media economics,* 2nd Edition. Ames, IA: Iowa State Press.

35. Vogel, H. L. (2001). *Entertainment industry economics,* 5th Edition. New York: Cambridge University Press.

36. Shapiro, C. & Varian, H. (1998). *Information rules.* Boston: HBS Press.

37. Caves, R. E. (2005). *Switching channels*. Cambridge, MA: Harvard University Press.

38. Waxman, Sharon. (January 3, 2010). Hollywood cuts, retools and looks to the future. Accessed January 9, 2010, at http://www.thewrap.com/ind-column/hollywood-cuts-back-readjusts-and-looks-future-12452.

39. Li, K. (2007). U.S. slump casts pall over media, entertainment. *Reuters*. Accessed 4/28/08 at: http://www.reuters.com/article/MediaandCommunications07/idUSN2921008520071130.

CHAPTER 3

Leadership and Management

The difference between managers and leaders is fundamental. The manager administers, the leader innovates. The manager maintains, the leader develops. The manager relies on systems, the leader relies on people. The manager counts on control, the leader counts on trust. The manager does things right, the leader does the right things.

Warren Bennis[1]

CHAPTER OBJECTIVES

The objectives of this chapter are to provide you with information about:
- Defining leadership
- Approaches to leadership
- Defining managing
- Theories of management
- Management functions
- Managing structures and processes
- Managing technology and change
- Management in the creative industries

CONTENTS

INTRODUCTION

These are hard jobs, but somebody has to do them. Someone in management has to take pitches and green-light projects, negotiate contracts with Sean Penn and Eva Longoria, and arrange with the U.S. Interior Department to use a space on Mt. Rainier to recreate Everest base camp for a new blockbuster. Other "someones" have to plan the presentation for the biannual Television Press Tour, monitor the budget for James Cameron's in-production movie, and meet with the president of a production company in Shanghai to plan an upcoming Chinese-language co-production.

DOI: 10.1016/B978-0-240-81020-1.00003-8

In media companies, executives need to exercise both leadership and management. Leadership is a key element in creative enterprises, where many workers must develop original ideas and products. At the same time, media companies fail without good management, because it is possible to spend ("burn," as it is sometimes called) a lot of money developing entertainment devices and content.

This chapter introduces some well-known industry leaders and managers, often called *moguls*. It presents alternative theories of people who lead and manage and how they do it. It looks at the functions and processes of management and then turns to managing in creative industries, which are characterized by technology dependence and change.

As the quote from Warren Bennis that begins this chapter points out, leadership and management are related activities, but they are not the same. However, scholars differ in how to describe the relationship between them. For some, leadership and management skills are so dissimilar that they rarely appear in the same individual. For others, leadership is one facet among others of management. One difference between the two activities is that leadership inevitably involves human beings – a person cannot lead without followers. By contrast, management may or may not involve others: it is possible to manage objects, such as an investment portfolio, an estate, or a fleet of vehicles.

DEFINING LEADERSHIP: DOING THE RIGHT THING

Leadership has fascinated people for centuries. In the years between 58 and 52 BC, Julius Caesar appeared before the Roman Senate, enthralling both the legislators and the public, with his dramatic accounts of leadership. In his *Commentaries on the Gallic War and on the Civil War*, Caesar wrote a timeless description of a leader at work, referring to himself in the third person:

> The situation was critical and as no reserves were available, Caesar seized a shield from a soldier in the rear and made his way to the front line. He addressed each centurion by name and shouted encouragement to the rest of the troops, ordering them to push forward and open out their ranks so they could use their swords more easily. His coming gave them fresh heart and hope. Each man wanted to do his best under the eyes of his commander despite the peril.[2]

Caesar's description provides an essential key to leadership: being out in front of followers. Leaders provide a vision of a goal and a path for attaining it. And they motivate, inspire, and direct others to achieve those goals, even those who may not have the desire or intention of moving in the direction the leader wishes them to go.

APPROACHES TO LEADERSHIP

Are leaders born or made? Is leadership innate or can it be learned? The need for leadership in setting and attaining goals is crucial to many organizations, yet there is little clarity or agreement about these questions. Yet there has been an enormous amount of theorizing and research to learn about leadership, summarized in Table 3-1. Leadership is approached in terms of:

- Individual traits or attributes
- Specific, observable behaviors
- Properties of a position within an organization or group
- Features of a particular situation
- The nature of the relationships between the leader and followers within a group or organization

Table 3-1 Approaches to Leadership

Thinking About Leadership		
Source of Leadership	**Question**	**Answer**
Traits/attributes of an individual	What personal qualities do leaders have in common?	Single traits: drive, cognitive ability, etc. Combination of traits
Specific, observable behaviors	How do leaders act? Task orientation? Human dimension?	Decisively, thoughtfully, carefully, etc. (See Figure 3-3.)
Properties of a position in a group or organization	What position does the leader hold?	Legitimate role Task, social, and informal leaders
Features of a particular situation (contingency)	How can leaders get followers to do what they want in a given situation?	Adopt a leadership style appropriate to the situation: directive, supportive, participative, achievement-oriented, networking, values-based
Relationships between leader and followers	What are the patterns of behavior between leaders and followers?	If they share values and view of environment, outcomes will be effective. Positive exchanges Leader adjusts style to motivate followers: telling, selling, participating, and delegating
Meta – the bigger picture	How is the larger environmental context of leadership invoked?	Styles that draw on a bigger view: Charismatic Transactional Transformational Service-oriented Wisdom

There are adherents who provide good arguments for each of these approaches. Some of them are not mutually exclusive. Most people believe leadership is important, but it has not been possible to reach agreement among researchers and practitioners on which approach is best or when to apply a given approach to a particular leader or situation.

Leadership as Individual Traits or Attributes

The notion that individual character traits define leaders is not currently a dominant view, although few researchers would argue that they are not somehow important. Kirkpatrick and Locke identified six traits they believe differentiate leaders from other people: drive, motivation, honesty and integrity, self-confidence, cognitive ability, and knowledge of business.[3] Although it is easy to see that a person might be able to change his or her levels of motivation, honesty and integrity, and knowledge of business, it is difficult to imagine someone altering cognitive ability. So this view implies that, to some extent, leaders are born, not made. In addition, it is possible to find people who have this admirable mix of traits who are not leaders; similarly, one can find people in leadership positions who have these qualities, but do not prove to be particularly good leaders.

VIDEOGAME MOGUL: NOLAN BUSHNELL

Nolan Bushnell, shown in Figure 3-1, is often called the father of electronic gaming. He invented a game called *Pong* in 1972, which became an enormously successful paddle game. When he made a deal with Sears, he used television sets as the display, drawing the ubiquitous TV into the interactive domain. He founded a company called Atari to market the game, which he sold in 1976 to Warner Communications. In 1974, he developed a robotic character named Chuck E. Cheese and made it the basis of the Pizza Time Theaters.

Bushnell is more of an innovator and a leader than a manager. He saw the possibilities in videogames and packaged them for personal, in-home entertainment. He used the videogame and robotics to establish public entertainment venues with the Pizza Time Theaters. His experience demonstrates the tension that exists when creative innovation and management expertise compete within the same individual.

FIGURE 3-1 Nolan Bushnell. *Reproduced by permission of Kenn Stearns.*

More sophisticated views of leadership traits have emerged in recent years that consider traits as complex groups of abilities,[4] as shown in Figure 3-2.

Describing the traits that go into the clusters shown in the model, Zacarro notes:

> Cognitive capacities include general intelligence, cognitive complexity, and creativity. Dispositional attributes include adaptability, extroversion, risk propensity, and openness. Motives and values include need for socialized power, need for achievement, and motivation to lead. Social capacities include social and emotional intelligence as well as persuasion and negotiation skills. Problem-solving skills include meta-cognition, problem construction and solution generation, and self-regulation skills. Moreover, these clusters of traits are not taken in isolation. Rather, leaders rely on a complex interaction of the clusters of abilities to carry out nuanced actions.

Leadership as Specific Observable Behaviors

Traits are personal characteristics of leaders – decisive, thoughtful, careful, caring, visionary, and so forth. Just as some researchers think that if people have the appropriate traits they will be leaders, behaviorist researchers believe that if individuals exhibit the appropriate behaviors, they could be leaders.

Behavioral studies of leadership have looked at task orientation and the human dimension. When leaders consider the task, they focus on who does it, when they do it, how they do it, and so forth. When they consider the needs, expectations, and desires of their followers, they focus on the human dimension. There are many different ways of referring to these two dimensions, including behavior/task, concern for people/concern for

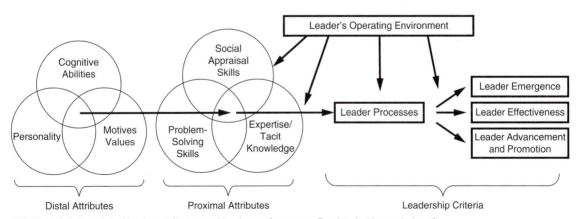

FIGURE 3-2 A model of leader attributes and leader performance. *Reprinted with permission of Stephen J. Zaccaro.*

production, employee-centered/task-centered, and consideration/initiating structure.[5] Consideration refers to considering others' wants and needs; initiating means concentrating on the task by directing, controlling, and monitoring performance.

Blake and Mouton published a classic work that established the behavioral approach to leadership.[6] They developed a questionnaire for managers, whose answers placed them on the *managerial* grid (or leadership grid), as shown in Figure 3-3, which places concern for people on the vertical axis and the concern for production on the horizontal axis. Leaders who score:

- High on concern for people, high on concern for production = *team management*
- High on concern for people, low on concern for production = *country-club management*
- Low on concern for people, high on concern for production = *task management*
- Low on concern for people, low on concern for production = *impoverished management*
- In the middle of both concern for people and production = *middle of the road management*

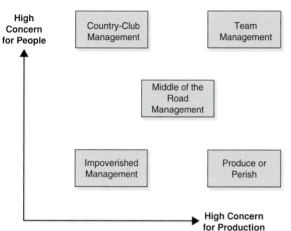

FIGURE 3-3 Blake and Mouton's leadership grid

MOVIE MOGUL: WALT DISNEY

Walt Disney, shown in Figure 3-4, founded the Disney Company in 1923 and ran the studio until his death in 1966.

FIGURE 3-4 Walt Disney. *Source: National Aeronautics and Space Administration.*

Throughout his career, he was known as a moral, thoughtful, and caring individual. A creative person himself, he invented the Mickey Mouse character and voiced it for many years. He knew every employee at the studio by name and wanted all of them to call him Walt. He instituted a policy of paying for education for his employees, and many of the animators who worked at the company took advantage of it.

Disney established and built a market for full-length animation motion pictures. The company innovated an animation "assembly line," organizing the system of key cell illustrations supplemented by lower-level animators fleshing out the motion sequence by creating individual cells. Disney also invented the studio-owned theme park. Concerned about the waste involved in destroying expensively created back lot movie sets, he drew on the abandoned sets to create Disneyland in Anaheim, California.

Leadership as Properties of a Position within an Organization or Group

So far, we have considered theories that locate the capacity for leadership within the person of the leader, either through traits or behaviors. However, other theories look toward characteristics of the situation or the environment to explain what makes leaders able to motivate others.

Leaders often have a position within an organization from which to express a vision and influence its acceptance. When leadership is conferred by virtue of an executive's position within an organizational hierarchical structure as a publicly appointed leader, it is called a *legitimate leadership* role.[7] Some social, task, and macro leaders do not hold formal leadership positions within the hierarchy, exercising influence informally. Social leaders take responsibility for the relationships between colleagues and co-workers, establishing and maintaining personal ties between them. Task leaders are usually appointed by the legitimate leader and guide and monitor the group's tasks so that they are on target, on budget, and on time. Macro leaders usually occupy senior positions that give them a broad view of the organization and place the task into the wider perspective of the overall organizational mission and objectives.

It is possible for one person to play all these roles or for them to be distributed among members of a work team or department, particularly if the individuals have complementary skills.[8]

Holding a position within the hierarchy provides a leader with *authority*, the ability to require that others carry out tasks and to specify how they do them. However, such power is substantially reduced in creative organizations, which

TV MOGUL: BRANDON TARTIKOFF

At NBC in 1980, Brandon Tartikoff became the youngest head of a network entertainment division, at 31 years old. The network was last in the ratings, and he and his mentor, Grant Tinker, turned the network around. Tartikoff is revered for his support of TV shows that became part of the "second Golden Age of television." Between 1980 and 1991, he supervised the creation of such TV programs as *The Cosby Show*, *Cheers*, *L.A. Law*, *Family Ties*, *Hill Street Blues*, *Miami Vice*, *Golden Girls*, and *Seinfeld*. Tartikoff was credited with supporting high-quality shows despite initial low ratings, allowing them the time to find an audience. He exerted great personal influence through his intellect, superb taste, and force of personality. He helped the careers of Rob Reiner, Jerry Seinfeld, Ted Danson, and Danny DeVito

and mentored a generation of television executives and producers.

One story about him concerns the casting of Michael J. Fox in *Family Ties*, maintaining that Fox did not have the kind of face that kids would want on a lunchbox. After Fox's success in the series and subsequent motion pictures, he sent Tartikoff a lunchbox with Fox's picture on it. The accompanying note read: "To Brandon: This is for you to put your crow in. Love and kisses, Michael J. Fox."[9] After he received it, Tartikoff kept the lunchbox in his office. Another anecdote claims that when Aaron Spelling, whose production company created the successful series *Dallas*, stepped off the elevator for a meeting with Tartikoff, a band hired by the NBC exec played *The Yellow Rose of Texas*.[10]

are often characterized by antiauthoritarian cultural values. Moreover, creative people may have levels of expertise not possessed by the leader. Working with creative and intellectually active workers, leaders must generally cultivate non-authoritarian methods of interacting with subordinates – persuasion, intellectual prowess, and personal influence.[11]

Leadership That Arises from a Particular Situation

Situational theories say that leadership, the ability to motivate followers to act in ways that fulfill organizational goals, depends on the leader understanding the nature of the particular conditions at a given point in time. Path–goal theory is the most studied of the contingency theories.[12,13,14] It says that workers have goals – money and other tangible rewards and intangible rewards like satisfaction and prestige. Leaders will succeed if they are able to align the worker's goals with those of the organization, providing a path for the worker to act in ways that will move toward achieving both personal and organizational goals. The function of the leader is to provide the support and resources the employee needs to do an effective job.

Path–goal theory identifies six leadership styles that leaders can use, depending on the nature of the employee and environmental conditions, as shown in Table 3-2. The characteristics of the employee include knowledge, skills,

Table 3-2 Leadership Styles of Path–Goal Theory	
Leadership Style	**Description**
Relational-Level Styles	
Directive	Directive managers specify the goals and the means to reach them. They monitor employees carefully and correct their activities through rewards and punishments.
Supportive	Supportive managers strive to help employees reach their personal goals. They concentrate on providing needed resources and creating an employee-centered workplace.
Participative	Participative leaders encourage people to work as a team, with all members contributing to the effort.
Achievement-oriented	Achievement-oriented managers emphasize excellence. They expect employees to commit themselves to the highest performance possible.
Environmental-Level Styles	
Networking[15]	Networking managers are oriented to the environment. They work within the broader organization to increase budgets, snag "good" assignments, and enhance the reputation of the work group.
Values-based[16]	Values-based leaders have a vision of the role of the work group in the organization that they share with followers. Employees are expected to adopt the vision and the values that underlie it.

experience, motivation, and psychological makeup; the characteristics of the situation include the type of task, the team, and the organization.

Leadership That Arises from the Nature of Relationships between Leader and Followers

An early formulation of the relationship between leaders and followers is the Leader–Member Exchange, or LMX.[17] The LMX looks at interdependent patterns of behavior between them that arise from shared goals and commitment to successful outcomes. Over time, if the exchange produces similar values and views of the environment, then there is a strong likelihood that the relationship will produce effective outcomes.[18]

Tierney et al. examined leader–subordinate relationships who were involved in creative work (a category that includes scientists and researchers).[19] The study looked at 191 employees engaged in research and development (R&D) for a large chemical company. The study found that two employee characteristics – intrinsic motivation and cognitive style – and positive leader–member exchanges increased the creativity of workers.

A more dynamic approach to the leader–follower interaction is the Situational Leadership Model.[20] Similar to path–goal theory, leaders motivate and inspire followers by adjusting their style to employee readiness. In this view, the readiness of workers to carry out tasks effectively is composed of ability to

MOVIE MOGUL: IRVING THALBERG

Irving Thalberg, shown in Figure 3-5, was called the "Boy Wonder," because he ran Universal Pictures at 20 years old and MGM studios at 23! Between 1924 and 1936, he oversaw more than 400 films at MGM. He was famous for his aesthetic ability to select stories and to make movie stars, including Greta Garbo, Clark Gable, Jean Harlow, Helen Hayes, and Joan Crawford. (If you don't know about these movie stars, ask your grandmother.)

He was a business whiz kid; he turned around a money-losing MGM to bring in $8 million in the middle of the Great Depression. He was a founding member of the Academy of Motion Pictures, source of Hollywood's coveted Academy Awards, which serves as an excellent marketing vehicle for the studios. Thalberg was also an innovator in the process of managing and harnessing creativity in the service of business. He established story conferences to detail production processes before shooting could begin. He invented the practice of showing audiences sneak previews and recut films based on the results. He also introduced a genre that is a movie mainstay to this day: the horror film.

FIGURE 3-5 Irving Thalberg. *Licensed under Creative Commons license, from the Library of Congress.*

undertake the work and the willingness or confidence to do it. Leaders draw on four styles: telling, selling, participating, and delegating. Depending on the interaction of a particular leader–worker relationship, the leader will adopt a style to motivate the worker to act in ways that fulfill organizational goals.

NEW META APPROACHES TO LEADERSHIP

Meta has several meanings. One of them is "more comprehensive," "beyond," or "transcendent," such as *metalinguistic*, which means beyond language use. In recent years, the research on leadership styles has moved beyond leader–individual and leader–team interactions to look at the how leaders relate to followers, based on their understanding of a larger social or organizational context. These styles are charismatic, transactional, transformational, and service-oriented.

Charismatic Leaders

We are all familiar with charismatic leaders – Mahatma Gandhi, Winston Churchill, Franklin Delano Roosevelt, John F. Kennedy, Ronald Reagan, and, many say, Barack Obama. These individuals have a stirring vision and communicate it in such a way as to inspire and excite others to overcome their differences to work with others and to lend their time, money, and energies to realize that vision as manifest reality. This distinction is generally the purview of religious, social, and political leaders who head movements and sweeping political coalitions.

Charisma may motivate workers for a short time. Inspirational efforts like rock bands, garage entrepreneurs, and the "let's put on a show!" groups can sustain their work for only a relatively short period of time. However, sustained enterprises require the consistent, detailed work of organization and business building.

Thus, although some leaders of organizations have charisma, they are rarely charismatic leaders per se. When considering such visionary – even flamboyant business leaders as Walt Disney, of the Walt Disney Company, Lee Iacocca of the Ford Motor Company, Jack Welch of General Electric, and mogul Barry Diller – we must look to how they merged it with other leadership styles.

Recall the influence of the behavioral school, with its two dimensions: concern for production and concern for people. To some extent, this duality is also reflected in these meta approaches. Just as the best managers are high in both task and people orientation, recent theorists have proposed the idea of full-range leadership, displayed by leaders who exercise both transactional and transformational characteristics.[22]

DIGITAL MOGUL: STEVE JOBS

Steve Jobs, shown in Figure 3-6, founded Apple. Then he left – and the company stumbled and nearly failed. So he came back to Apple and saved the company, turning it around. Then he took over the music business with iTunes and the iPod. And revolutionized the mobile phone business with iPhone. And while he was doing that, he established a full-length animation picture studio and probably would have dominated the full-length animated motion picture market or taken over Disney, if Disney hadn't bought Pixar Studios first.

Steve Jobs has accomplished all this because he has understood and anticipated the role of design in creating digital products and platforms. He senses the future before anyone else, interprets what mainstream consumers want and need, and delivers it. He is considered a demanding manager and is famous for holding long meetings every Monday. Says Jobs: "So what we do every Monday is we review the whole business. We look at what we sold the week before. We look at every single product under development, products we're having trouble with, products where the demand is larger than we can make. All the stuff in development, we review. And we do it every single week. I put out an agenda – 80 percent is the same as it was the last week, and we just walk down it every single week."[21]

FIGURE 3-6 Steve Jobs. *Credit: Matthew Lohe. Reproduced under Creative Commons License.*

Transactional Leaders

Transactional leaders operate in much the same fashion as the task-oriented leader. They are concerned with resources, schedules, and output. They set the parameters of tasks, benchmarks, and standards, form teams and work groups to carry them out, and monitor and reward performance. *Transaction* in this context means a system of rewards in which the relationship between leaders and followers is characterized by the striking of bargains: "If the follower performs, the leader rewards."[23] Rewards are the traditional job benefits of bonuses, merit pay, recognition, and promotion.

When the bargains between leaders and followers are well understood and consistent, transactional leadership can lead to employee satisfaction and adequate performance. However, performance may not exceed the levels negotiated in the bargain. Often transactional leaders have a relatively hands-off approach, giving subordinates responsibility and allowing them to carry out tasks. Only when there are mistakes or low performances does this type of transactional leader step in and intervene.

Transformational Leaders

If transactional leaders rely more on the power of their positions, transformational leaders rely more on persuasion. Thus, transformational leadership is similar to the people-oriented dimension posited by behavioral theorists, with one important difference: These leaders emphasize innovation, flexibility, and positive response to change. They share a visionary outlook and inspirational style with charismatic leaders, but they also tend to the resources and organizational structures that foster or inhibit employees' work.

As the term implies, transformational leaders are identified with periods of organizational change. Appelbaum et al. examined the findings of six studies of organizations undergoing large-scale change.[24] The analysis found that while leaders play a large role, the attitudes of employees make the difference between success and failure. Moreover, leaders must engage employees before the transition takes place.

The advantage conferred by the transformational leadership style is that leaders who engage employees and solicit their ideas and support are better able to persuade them to accept the need for change and the transition. According to the authors,

TV MOGUL: TED TURNER

Ted Turner, shown in Figure 3-7, probably did more than any other single individual to bring cable television into U.S. households. As part of merging a family-owned company with Rice Broadcasting, he acquired a money-losing Atlanta TV station, WTCG. He changed the programming and the call letters (to WTBS) and sent the signal to distant cable systems via a then-cutting-edge technology – satellite. This move made WTCG cable's first *superstation* and invented free-to-view basic cable.

More importantly, he launched CNN in 1980. The scrappy new channel achieved journalistic scoops, making it a major attraction for basic cable TV delivery. Fifteen years later, CNN had expanded into more than 150 million households in 140 countries and spawned a litter of me-too channels. In 1985, Ted Turner bought the MGM library as well as the pre-1950 Warner Bros. catalog, the library of an older movie studio, RKO, and many United Artists films. The library purchase was decried at the time as a foolish extravagance, but Turner proved the critics wrong and launched three more basic cable channels – TBS, TNT, and Turner Classic Movies – using many of the properties from those libraries. Turner also founded the Cartoon Network and owned many other media properties.

FIGURE 3-7 Ted Turner. *Source: Luke Ford, licensed under Creative Commons.*

Transformational leadership appears to have an advantage over coercive or directive-only leadership because employees perceive that they are being both considered and included in the change decision, ultimately leading to higher employee support of the change. The difference in the research points towards the ability of transformational leadership to effectively establish higher levels of communication, participation, and trust from their employees than other leadership styles.[25]

Service-Oriented Leadership

Rapid technological change is leading some scholars to think that the conceptions of leadership must change as well. The business environment in which organizations operate is increasingly turbulent. Markets are becoming more competitive and consumers can access information about price and features of a wide range of goods, giving them greater leverage in exercising purchase choice. In addition, the workforce in the creative industries is ever more educated and technically skilled, often beyond the ability of leaders to guide or even understand. In light of these realities, theorists have developed approaches to leadership, including leaders as servants of followers and coaches. Some modern theories have even suggested that leadership might not be necessary or can be dispersed among workers.

Boje and Dennehy proposed a servant model of leadership that is similar in many ways to that of the transformational model.[26] As the name of the model implies, this perspective views leaders as the servants of those they would lead. It goes beyond the idea of transformational leadership in that it emphasizes empowering followers and explicitly recognizes diversity. It also points to the cultural role of leaders as they recount the narratives about the foundational elements of the organization: its founding, heroes, hard times, and triumphs. The theorists use the word *servant* itself as an acronym to explain their construct of leaders as servants:

S – Serves
E – Empowers
R – Recounter of stories about the organization
V – Visionary
A – Androgynous, speaking in both male and female voices
N – Networker, representing the work team to organizational and
     extraorganizational constituencies
T – Team builder

Recent formulations also point to the leader as coach or mentor.[27] Coaching differs from leaders and managers, in that coaches help others develop and grow, while leaders and managers provide vision, direction, and, sometimes, control. Other perspectives argue that leadership can be replaced by technology through the routinization of tasks and digitization of workflow processes.[28]

And some theorists believe that when work teams are composed of highly skilled knowledge workers, they may even be self-managing, with leadership devolving on the individuals who should lead in a particular area or without the need for formal leaders at all.[29]

The idea of leaders as authentic and wise is also beginning to come to the forefront. Authentic leaders[30] seek the positive growth and development of their followers, the organization, themselves, and others affected by their actions. In their search for solutions that benefit as many people as possible, they apply ethical and moral values to their decisions, as well as principles of efficiency and cost-cutting. Such leadership requires mature individuals who have psychological and moral stability and substance – character that is perhaps beyond the reach of many.

A related theory is that of leadership wisdom.[31] In this view, the theorists pay tribute to the Greek tradition that says that the highest wisdom is to realize that no one really knows the nature of reality, the heart of a person, the right decision. In this acknowledgment comes wisdom, because it initiates a search for greater knowledge. Thus, leaders should take their time making difficult decisions, perhaps doing nothing at all, until they have sought out as much information as they can collect.

LINKING LEADERSHIP AND MANAGEMENT: MOTIVATION

Without followers, there are no leaders; without workers, there are no managers. Both leaders and managers must motivate people to perform in ways that fulfill organizational goals. To motivate others means understanding them – what makes them tick – and how to appeal to them. Most people are motivated to take actions on their own behalf, to make their own dreams come true.

Getting others to perform to satisfy the goals of their bosses or to fulfill the goals of an organization is not always an easy task. Leaders and managers think hard about their strategies to motivate the other people who they put to work. Table 3-3 shows some of the theories that examine motivation.

There are two types of motivation: extrinsic and intrinsic. *Extrinsic motivation* identifies the ways to motivate individuals as external to them, such as money, titles, status, perquisites, and power. *Intrinsic motivation* identifies the source of motivating another as inside the person, such as satisfaction, self-esteem, feelings of importance, and mastery. Most people are motivated by some combination of both types.

Maslow's Hierarchy of Needs

Maslow says that people have multiple needs that require both extrinsic and intrinsic rewards.[32] In this theory, some needs must be satisfied before the

Table 3-3 Theories of Motivation

Motivational Theories		
Source of Motivation	**Question**	**Answer**
Maslow: Needs	What do human beings need and what is their relative priority?	Hierarchy of needs (see Figure 3-3)
McGregor: Human nature	What is the nature of workers?	Theory X: Lazy, work-avoidant Theory Y: Seek fulfillment and meaning through work
Motivation as a process	How can leaders and managers motivate workers?	Reward desired behaviors, punish unwanted behaviors Manage expectations Make sure workers have sense of equity

individual can act to fulfill other, higher needs, as shown in Figure 3-8. For example, the basic physiological needs, such as food and shelter, are extrinsic to the individual and must be taken care of or the person cannot survive. Once people can eat and find shelter, they must concern themselves with safety needs, protecting themselves against illness, other animals, and other people. After satisfying these basic extrinsic needs, then people turn to social and relational needs, the intrinsic needs for esteem and self-actualization.

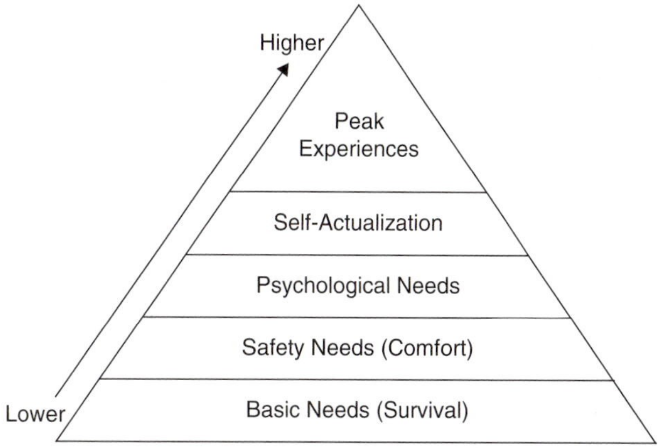

FIGURE 3-8 Maslow's hierarchy of needs

In this view, leaders and managers should realize that once the people who work for them have taken care of their basic and safety needs, other rewards will have to come into play. An executive who has earned an excellent salary for a few years will probably want increased responsibility, a more impressive title and office, a bigger expense account, and a key to the executive washroom, all in addition to the excellent salary. He or she may also want more authority, the opportunity to speak at industry trade shows and conventions, and the ability to influence the direction of the organization. Managers may also realize that they themselves seek different kinds of rewards as their career progresses.

Theory X and Y

If the hierarchy of needs seems to have a rarified view of people in the workplace, Theory X/Theory Y takes a much more down-to-earth approach.[34] It describes two extreme views of human beings as workers. Theory X comes from

DIGITAL MOGUL: MARK CUBAN

FIGURE 3-9 Mark Cuban. *Reproduced with permission from: James Duncan Davidson/O'Reilly Media, Inc., under Creative Commons License.*

Mark Cuban, shown in Figure 3-9, is a work in progress. He is owner of the Dallas Mavericks basketball team – and he is also chairman and co-owner of the high-definition programming channel HDNet, Landmark Theaters, and Magnolia Pictures. He is majority owner of Rysher Entertainment and holds a large stake of Lions Gate Entertainment.

Cuban made his first fortune by founding MicroSolutions and building the company into a national system integrator and IT reseller. Then he made even more money providing digital content to a Web site he developed, Audionet.com, which streamed sports events and music over the Internet. He understands the crucial connections between technology and entertainment. He is an iconoclast with the bigger-than-life personality of the great movie moguls, and he has established the foundation for a media conglomerate with properties in television, motion pictures, and distribution. He plans to make Landmark Theaters as the first all-digital theater chain.[33]

the nineteenth century and the first half of the twentieth century, when most managers viewed their employees as inherently lazy and work-avoidant. They believed that workers wanted and needed direction, control, and monitoring, and that the motivation for working was almost exclusively money. From the perspective of leaders and managers, workers are just another resource. As you will see later in the chapter, this perspective is congruent with the management theory of Taylor,[35] which dominated the first half of twentieth-century management thinking.

Theory Y provides a sharp contrast. In this approach, people seek fulfillment and meaning through their work. They prefer self-direction, autonomy, and flexible leadership that takes workers' knowledge and needs into consideration. They are motivated by opportunities to learn and lead, career advancement, and increased responsibilities. Leaders and managers see the people who work for them as valuable assets, not just costs and resources, whose talents lead to the accumulation of intellectual capital and property and significant business advantages.

Process Theories: Expectancy, Equity, and Self-determination

More recent approaches to motivation approach the subject as a process.[36] People in organizations learn what they can expect, and they behave according to those *expectancies*.[37] They also need a sense of *equity*, which they perceive by looking at others and seeing what they get, compared to themselves. For example, if a young woman sees that only men are promoted, she will either stop performing or leave the company. Similarly, if a manager in a family-owned business sees family members rewarded more than their competence and effort would suggest, he or she will become dissatisfied.[38]

So, everyone is fired up, ready to go … well, at least ready to go. Leaders and managers are more likely to achieve their goals if everyone is motivated, but they will also need to work hard to manage the effort over time if it is to succeed. The next section looks at management and the activities and processes it entails.

DEFINING MANAGEMENT: DOING THINGS RIGHT

What do managers do? As Table 3-4 indicates, theories of management ask different questions and come up with different solutions. However, they are

Table 3-4 Theories of Management

Thinking about Management		
Management Theory	**Question**	**Answer**
Taylor: Scientific management	How can work be made more efficient?	1. Observe work 2. Train employees 3. Match workers to tasks 4. Establish collaboration between managers and workers
Fayol: Principles of authority structures	What are the functions of management and how can they be implemented in structure?	1. Planning, organizing, commanding, coordinating, controlling 2. Centralization, authority, etc.
Mayo: Human relations school	How can psychological principles be applied to management?	1. Make workers feel valued 2. Attend to informal structures and communication
Barnard: Theories of authority and incentives	How can the best principles of both of scientific management and the human relations school be combined?	Answer lies in communication: explicit channels, short and direct lines, universal knowledge and access to communication, etc.
Ouchi: Theory Z	How can the best principles of Theories X and Y be applied to the organization as a whole?	1. Adapt Japanese management collectivist styles to American individualistic styles 2. Focus on organizational culture 3. Create culture that emphasizes: long-term employment, consensual decision making, individual responsibility 4. Evaluate and promote people slowly 5. Informal control, formal evaluation 6. Concern for organization as a whole

Some definitions of management:

■ Organizational process that includes planning, setting objectives and goals, managing resources (people, finances, technology, raw materials), deploying assets, and measuring results
■ Executing plans, coordinating activities and resources, fostering cooperation among organizational units, and supervising operations
■ Accomplishing goals in organizations through others
■ Process of achieving goals and objectives of organizations by bringing together human, physical, and financial resources, taking into account the operating environment
■ Efficient allocation of scarce resources to fulfill business objectives

consistent with some of the ideas considered earlier in the chapter in the discussion of leadership.

Some of the earliest writings about management set out functions that are still in the forefront today: planning, organizing, leading, coordinating, and controlling.[39] Other writers have pointed to directing, resourcing, and monitoring as well. Common definitions of management make it clear why these functions occupy prominent places in the descriptions of what managers do.

Classic Theories of Management

There are many theories of management that deal with specific contexts. The management of people includes managing individuals, teams, and organizational cultures. Managing organizational practices includes decision making, operations research, consideration of power and politics, use of technologies, management of knowledge and learning, innovation and change, and business ethics. Managing organizational structures must account for existing administration and bureaucracies, as well as designing structures that will address critical elements of the business environment, including regulation, technology, economic cycles, and globalization.

In spite of the seemingly endless supply of theories of management, there are two overarching schools of thought. Just as leadership studies point to Theory X and Theory Y, one perspective more task-centered and the other more people-centered, management theories display a similar duality of points of view. These two views emerged in the late nineteenth and early twentieth centuries with scientific theories of management versus human relations theories. The scientific theories came first.

Scientific Theories of Management

In the late nineteenth century, Frederick W. Taylor formally synthesized ideas that had been practiced in the United States since much earlier in the century.[40] An engineer, Taylor called his theory *scientific management*, although strictly speaking, it incorporated observation and measurement more than the principles of science, per se. Taylor observed and timed workers as they went about tasks, a process called *work-study* and then redesigned the way they carried them out to achieve greater efficiency. (The father in the book and film *Cheaper by the Dozen* is a Taylor-inspired character.) Scientific management envisioned refashioning workers to function more like the parts of a smoothly running machine, particularly manual laborers.

Taylor laid out four principles of scientific management:

1. Establish a science of work: Observe and time the result of work (number of tons lifted, number of parts finished, etc.) and use the results to redesign the workplace and tools of work. Once work productivity is increased, the pay of workers will rise.
2. Select and train employees: By giving objective tests to workers for aptitudes, managers can identify people most suited to a particular type of work – a scientific method of matching employees to tasks. Once identified, workers can be trained to reach their highest levels of efficiency.
3. Combine the sciences of work and employee selection and training: Obtain additional efficiencies by matching trained workers to scientifically designed tasks.
4. Establish close collaboration between managers and workers: Managers carry out mental work; workers carry out manual tasks. If each type of employee restricts attention to the task to which he or she is assigned, then they can collaborate to maximize efficiency.

Taylor was so identified with his theory that it also became known as *Taylorism*. It was a widely adopted management style in the first half of the twentieth century, particularly in stable environments, such as assembly-line production. It fostered hierarchical, centralized organizational structures that emphasized top-down communication and control, exercised along clear lines of authority.

In Europe, Henri Fayol was writing at about the same time as Taylor.[41] Also an engineer, he developed principles of authority structures. Fayol's formulations were not as concerned with the design of tasks as with defining the work of management. He developed 14 principles, such as centralization, a clear line of authority, one supervisor for an employee, fairness, equity, job security, order, and others. Fayol emphasized the functions of management – planning, organizing, commanding, coordinating, and controlling – and put management training at the center of his ideas.[42] Fayol's work was not published in the United States until the 1940s, and therefore exercised an earlier, stronger influence in Europe than in the United States.

Human Relations School Theory of Management

Australian theorist Elton Mayo had a background in psychology and psychiatry that shaped his perception of workplace management; thus, he looked at conflict as a form of psychosocial dysfunction that required treatment and favored the use of the *therapeutic interview* to resolve conflicts between parties.[43] Not surprisingly, he considered an engineering perspective to be inappropriate for managing people. He acknowledged the need for managers to have technical expertise, but argued that managers also needed social skills to maximize the motivation and satisfaction of subordinates.

Mayo believed that work was a central life interest for most people, from which they sought meaning and satisfaction. He also brought a group-level perspective to management theory. He observed that people work in teams or groups, so the workplace would be properly viewed as a social system with interdependent members. Mayo drew a distinction between the formal organizational hierarchy and informal group processes and communication, a valuable contribution to the study of organizations. He argued that informal social networks play a profound role in employee attitudes that the wise manager should recognize. Indeed, as people have fundamental needs for social connection, informal groups play a major role in fostering satisfaction in the workplace.

WORKING AT GOOGLE

Benefits Way Beyond the Basics

Food
Hungry? Check out our free lunch and dinner – our gourmet chefs create a wide variety of healthy and delicious meals every day. Got the munchies? Google also offers snacks to help satisfy you in between meals.

On-Site Doctor
At Google headquarters in Mountain View, California, you have the convenience of seeing a doctor on-site.

Shuttle Service
Google is pleased to provide its Mountain View employees with free shuttles to several San Francisco, East Bay, and South Bay locations.

Financial Planning Classes
Google provides objective and conflict-free financial education classes. The courses are comprehensive and cover a variety of financial topics.

Other On-Site Services
At Google headquarters in Mountain View, there's on-site oil change, car wash, dry cleaning, massage therapy, gym, hair stylist, fitness classes, and bike repair.

Other Great Benefits
Halloween and holiday party, health fair, credit union, sauna, roller hockey, outdoor volleyball court, discounts for products and local attractions.[44]

Mayo formulated his ideas partly from his participation in the Hawthorne studies. These were a series of experiments conducted at the Western Electric plant in Hawthorne, Illinois, between 1924 and 1927. The experiments tested various physical arrangements, including cleanliness, seating, and increased illumination. Each change resulted in a short increase in productivity, a phenomenon known as the *Hawthorne effect*, which occurs when people in the workplace are put under overt scrutiny. The Hawthorne effect makes it difficult to account for whether changes in productivity result from the experimental stimulus, or the special attention of being studied.

Mayo examined this unexpected finding and theorized that it was not the scrutiny itself that caused the increased productivity; rather, it occurred because the scrutiny made workers feel important and valued. In addition, the workers in the experimental group shared the study experience that strengthened the informal bonds between them. He concluded that the boost in productivity came from these feeling of value and the relationships formed between workers.

Although Mayo's ideas in their totality never became widely adopted within organizations, they have exercised a continuing influence on management theorists. The *theories of authority and incentives* of Chester Barnard provide a good example of the way that many successor theories included some of the principles from the human relations school, yet keeping many of the precepts from the scientific management perspective.[45]

Barnard was an executive and manager himself, serving as president of New Jersey Bell Telephone. On the one hand, he emphasized the need for managerial authority. But he also highlighted the importance of informal social networks and the need for managers to utilize them. Furthermore, he argued that authority is not just a matter of imposition from the top down – a manager's ability to manage rests upon the willingness of subordinates to accept that authority.

Barnard considered leadership to be the most important part of the manager's mission. And he tied values to that leadership, so that the manager motivated people to work together to achieve the goals of the organization, based on their shared values. One of the most interesting aspects of Barnard's theories was that communication was central to his thinking. He advocated:

- Explicit channels of communication
- Universal knowledge of the channels of communication within the organization
- Universal access to the formal channels of communication within the organization
- Short, direct lines of communication
- Competent handlers of communication
- Authentication of every communication

Theory Z

It's probably no surprise, but William Ouchi builds Theory Z by incorporating some elements from both Theory X and Theory Y.[46] However, by comparing American Type A companies to Japanese Type J companies, he shifts the focus from individualistic manager–worker relationships to a more collectivist perspective of the organization as a whole. Ouchi considers the overall philosophy of management and unique organizational culture that reflects a common consensus about the organization and how it is managed.

He notes that Type A companies would benefit from some management practices used in successful Japanese businesses, creating a culture that includes:

- Long-term employment
- Consensual decision making
- Individual responsibility
- Slow evaluation and promotion of managers
- Informal control, formal evaluation
- Holistic concerns for the organization as a whole

Modern Theories of Management

Yesterday's overarching grand theories of management have evolved into a complex array of theories that address a multitude of aspects of today's organizations: managing human resources, finance, organizational culture, decision making, quality control, communication, organizational knowledge, innovation and change, technology, administration, organizational structures, the business environment, or globalization. For every area, there is a body of theory, research, and how-to treatises that guides managers seeking to understand the tasks, and many books and articles detail these and even more topics.

In the media industries, communication technologies are the engines driving new ways of managing organizations in the creative industries to an even greater degree than in many business sectors.[47] They play a particularly key role in businesses that center on media, communication, information, and entertainment, because such enterprises depend on networked communication technologies to create, produce, package, distribute, and consume their products. In these efforts, there is virtually no role for manual labor. Indeed, many jobs require a high level of expertise that managers do not have and cannot acquire. The manager may have a view of how the skills need to be knitted together to achieve organizational goals and still rely on subordinates to guide specific parts of the overall effort.

In addition, the rapid rate of technological change at the heart of the creative industries means that companies must respond in alignment with environmental conditions external to the organization. In short, creating profitable intellectual property products cannot be accomplished with your grandfather's assembly line. In the same way, work in the creative industries cannot take place with the management styles that suited mechanistic industries.

A word often used to describe the way organizations must respond to constant innovation cycles is *agile*.[48] Agility means that the organization can change its strategies, processes, products, and revenue models quickly enough to respond to any large changes in their market environment. Conditions that make agility possible include close collaboration between units, departments, and partners, shared goals and values, openness to innovation, and a long-term perspective that serves as a context to short-term change.

So although communications technologies are the drivers of change, they can also help harness it. Digital networks with powerful computers on the desktop make possible rapid, inexpensive, high-bandwidth communication between large numbers of people. They reduce the cost of coordination, enabling widespread collaboration on complex projects. As a result, management processes must address larger, more open, and fluid structures and processes.

Many new organizational forms have emerged as the technological environment has evolved. *Matrix organization*, for example, is very important to the media industry, because it relies on creative projects as well as maintaining a hierarchical structure. Matrix management designs overlie the more horizontal, project-based structure on the familiar vertical hierarchy.[49] Project leaders have two or more reporting relationships: one to supervisors in the hierarchy and at least one other to people in other units to which they provide support or project elements. In a motion picture studio, this might mean that a special effects manager reports both to the head of production in the hierarchy as well as to the director and producer of the motion picture projects in production.

Another much discussed new organizational form is the virtual organization.[50] These businesses may not have a physical location, existing partially or wholly in people, computers, and networks to accomplish work. Many enterprises in the creative industries are at least partially virtual, such as universities, motion picture companies, music labels, and software developers. Research shows that virtuality brings both advantages (dynamic processes, permeable, edgeless boundaries, reconfigurable structure) and disadvantages (a high communication volume and greater difficulty understanding messages and forming a consensus).

Finally, a look at management theories through critical theory draws attention to some key aspects of management theories.[51] Critical theory is a stance that challenges conventional wisdom and accepted knowledge. It has a long tradition of literary criticism, so management is rarely a topic of discussion among critical theorists. These theorists observe that contemporary management approaches are dominated by rationality[52] and pragmatism.[53] They are characterized by an "implicit fiduciary relationship as agents of capital,"[54] as evidenced by the frequent references to the efficient use of resources.

As Theory Z theorist William Ouchi put it:

> In a "Type A" or typical American organization, the allocation of resources, the evaluation of performance, and other important matters are decided by and large on the basis of quantifiable, measurable criteria. Indeed, it would not be unfair to argue that the graduate school of business administration in the United States has specialized in teaching young people how to quantify and make explicit that which is ambiguous and subtle.[55]

LEADERSHIP AND MANAGEMENT IN THE CREATIVE INDUSTRIES

Some researchers[56] argue that leaders who have more concern for people than production are more successful, and in many types of businesses, this conclusion may be justified. However, research on creative workers suggests otherwise. Mumford et al. point to research that finds worker and team creativity are enhanced when leaders are task-oriented, provide task-related feedback, and establish structure.[57] However, one assumption of scientific management was that there is a single, best way to design tasks. Such a view may hold true for manual tasks, but it is unsuited to mental work. In modern organizations, particularly enterprises in the communication and information industries, nearly all work is mental. Executives supervise knowledge workers whose work involves the creation of intellectual property. In this work, there may be a single best way, but the skilled subordinate, rather than the executive trained in the principles of management, is more likely to know what it is.

MOVIE MOGUL: SHERRY LANSING

Sherry Lansing was the first woman to become president of a movie studio. She graduated from Northwestern University with a degree in Theater. She began her career as a teacher but quickly became a model and then an actress. Four years later, she decided to become a script editor and was rapidly promoted to fill positions with ever-increasing responsibility for creative development and management. She was a story editor at MGM and then VP of Creative Affairs. She was VP of Production at Columbia and then senior vice president there. Ten years after she went into the entertainment industry, Lansing was named president of Twentieth Century Fox. In 1992, she became chair and chief executive officer of Paramount Pictures Motion Picture Group and held that position for a remarkably long time in a revolving-door industry until 2005.

Lansing was known for her solid creative decisions, coupled with careful cost management. She brought Paramount a successful string of blockbusters, including *Fatal Attraction*, *China Syndrome*, *Kramer vs. Kramer*, *Forrest Gump*, *Braveheart*, and *Titanic*. She was responsible for six of ten of Paramount's all-time box office gross pictures, and 80 percent of the films that came out while she headed the studio were profitable – an extraordinary record of success.[58]

Example: Management in the Broadcast Industry

Consultant firm Noll & Associates has worked for many of the leading companies in the media industry.[59] The company describes today's successful manager in media companies as a "catalyst" or someone who creates conditions of excellence. Although this task sounds easy enough, it is quite common for the managers and employees to hold quite different perspectives along key dimensions of the working situation, as shown in Table 3-5. In essence, given the choice, an employee will choose a concrete payoff that is both immediate and benefits them while management utilizes praise as a means of payoff with a more long term view that benefits the company.

It's easy to see how the goals of employees and managers can collide. So how does the manager motivate employees to meet his or her goals while satisfying the employees? One key point is that events do not change behavior permanently. If a manager becomes angry and yells, it may change the behavior temporarily but not permanently. Systems of conditions change behavior, which in turn creates a culture of productivity.

In the Noll formulation, there are two philosophies of leadership: *Fish Giver* and *Fishing Teacher*. The Fish Giver creates solutions and constantly changes conditions. This allows the manager to remain strongly in control, but never allows the employees to develop their own solutions. On the other hand, the Fishing Teacher provides certain conditions and allows for follower-created solutions.

In order for a successful manager to effectively become a Fishing Teacher, they must create conditions of excellence that include:

- **Vision:** Defining where the organization is going and why it is worth going there
- **Purpose:** Stating why the organization exists and the core of how it provides value
- **Goals:** Establishing sequential actions and events that will lead to the organization's success in fulfilling its vision and purpose
- **Monitoring and feedback:** Paying attention to progress toward goals and objectives Providing employees with corrective guidance and direction
- **Support:** Putting resources into the hands of the employees and removing obstacles that block them from carrying out tasks and meeting goals

Table 3-5 Differing Perspectives of Managers and Employees

	Employee	Manager
Payoff	Concrete	Praise
Timetable	Immediate	Long-term
Benefits	Themselves	The company

- **Recognition:** Demonstrating appreciation when goals are achieved in the right way
- **Example:** Embodying the behaviors, attitudes, and work disciplines expected from employees

The "Manager-as-Catalyst" principle is expressed by the concept of the "governing power of example." Noll & Associates quotes a traditional Zen Buddhist story to illustrate how it works:

> The novice asks his master, "Master, what is the goal of all learning?"
> "Wisdom," replies the master.
> "What is wisdom?" asks the novice
> "Good judgment," replies the master.
> "How do you get good judgment?" the novice persists.
> "Experience."
> "How do you get experience?" asks the novice.
> "Bad judgment," the master replies.

Learning from failures is as important as learning from successes and adjusting conditions accordingly. Asking questions about the experience, beliefs, and behaviors that led to the success or failure to execute a plan allows for improved future projects. The other element of governing power is the transferring of complex skill sets from the manager to the employee. In a gradual transition of skills, a manager would follow these steps to develop an empowered work force that is able to perform necessary projects with little need for follow-up:

1. Manager performs task; employee observes and reports what he or she saw.
2. Employee performs task; manager observes and provides feedback on what was done well and what was not done well.
3. Employee performs task, calls manager in to inspect work, and manager makes corrections as needed.

TV AND MOVIE MOGUL: LEW WASSERMAN

Lew Wasserman was known informally as the "King of Hollywood." He began his career as a talent agent in Chicago, working at the Music Corporation of America. He eventually took over what became the MCA agency and grew to hold enormous power in the capital of U.S. entertainment. At one point in the late 1970s, MCA produced almost half of all prime-time television programming in the United States.[60]

Wasserman's programming innovations included the long-form TV series and the made-for-television movie. But more importantly, he laid the foundations for today's media conglomerates. He played a key role in moving the power center of entertainment from New York to Los Angeles.[61] His business innovations include giving performers percentages of box office in addition to salary and packaging programs – the practice of putting together stars, producers, directors, and script in a single package – all represented by his hugely successful talent agency, MCA. He pursued both vertical and horizontal corporate integration strategies, innovated extension of TV and movie properties across multiple media platforms, established blockbuster marketing and distribution, established TV content agreements, and used fundraising and political lobbying to allow the industry to support and then exploit tax loopholes.

4. Employee performs task, inspects own work, corrects own work, and turns it in to manager.

SUMMARY

This chapter looked at approaches to leadership, motivation, and management. It described how managers in creative enterprises, such as those in the media industry, need to interact with skilled subordinates, workers, and contractors. Finally, it presented biographical sketches of leaders and managers who have made a difference in the media companies they founded or worked for.

WHAT'S AHEAD

This chapter showed how important people are in leading and managing media enterprises. The next chapter discusses human resources, explaining how people are recruited and managed. It describes the different kinds of human resources that media companies require, from employees to contract freelancers, partners, and vendors – and how some companies even harness the efforts of their customers.

CASE STUDY 3.1 HOW WOULD YOU LEAD?

Joe is hired as general manager of a local television station. The television station has been slumping in news ratings and although the sales department has been selling out the inventory, they have not hit budget in more than two years. Joe has been handed the task of motivating the news division to garner higher ratings and work with the sales division to increase rates. The other divisions seem to be doing a good job.

Assignment

If you are Joe, what are your initial steps to solve the two major issues at hand? Keep in mind that the motivating factors used in a news division differ greatly from those used in sales. Develop a game plan for both news and sales that includes logic, standards of achievement, and creativity that will bring out the best in both departments.

CASE STUDY 3.2 LEADERSHIP OBSERVATIONS

Assignment

Watch a movie or DVD that portrays a corporate setting, such as *The Devil Wears Prada*. Complete a comprehensive analysis of the leadership, keeping the following items in mind:

- List and describe the main characters in the program.
- Observe and identify some of the leadership skills portrayed.

- Describe how these characteristics may have served to motivate employees or how they demotivated.
- Did the leader or manager of the firm use fear, comedy, or other technique?
- Watch closely for both verbal and nonverbal actions that support a specific style of management.
- What was your opinion of this style of management?
- Where would this style of leadership or management work best and in what situation would it not work?

REFERENCES

1. Bennis, W. (1988). Books & ideas: Review of leadership inside and out. *Fortune* 117:2, 173. Retrieved May 15, 2008, from ABI/INFORM Global database. (Document ID: 1493178.)

2. Accessed May 20, 2008, at http://www.carpenoctem.tv/military/caesar.html.

3. Kirkpatrick, S. A. & Locke, E. A. (1991). Leadership: Do traits matter? *Academy of Management Executive* 5, 48–60.

4. Zaccaro, S. J. (2007). Trait-based perspectives of leadership. *American Psychologist* 62(1), 6–16. doi: 10.1037/0003-066X.62.1.6.

5. Clegg, S., Kornberger, M. & Pitsis, T. (2008). *Managing & organizations.* Thousand Oaks, CA: Sage Publications.

6. Blake, R. R. & Mouton, J. S. (1985). *The managerial grid III.* Houston: Gulf.

7. Sheard, A. G. & Kakabadse, A. P. (2007). A role-based perspective on leadership as a network of relationships. *Journal of Management Development* 26(4), 331.

8. Sheard, A. G. & Kakabadse, A. P. (2002), Key roles of the leadership landscape. *Journal of Managerial Psychology* 17(2), 129–144.

9. Accessed October 7, 2009, at http://wapedia.mobi/en/Brandon_Tartikoff.

10. Finke, N. (June 23, 2006). The day I sucker-punched Aaron Spelling. *Deadline Hollywood.* Accessed online at http://www.deadline.com/hollywood/the-day-i-sucker-punched-aaron-spelling/.

11. Leavitt, H. J. (2005). Hierarchies, authority, and leadership. *Leader to Leader* 37, 55.

12. House, R. J. (1971). Path-goal theory of leadership: lessons, legacy, and a reformulated theory. *Leadership Quarterly* 7, 323–352.

13. Jermier, J. (1996). The path-goal theory of leadership: a subtextual analysis. *Leadership Quarterly* 7, 311–316.

14. O'Toole, J. (1996). *Leading change: The argument for values-based leadership.* New York: Ballantine Books.

15. Barker, R. A. (2001). The nature of leadership. *Human Relations* 54(4), 469. Retrieved May 26, 2008, from ABI/INFORM Global database. (Document ID: 90026830.)

16. Rost, J. C. (1993). Leadership development in the new millennium. *Journal of Leadership Studies* J(I), 92–110.

17. Scott, S. G. & Bruce, R. A. (1994). Determinants of innovative behavior: A path model of individual innovation in the workplace. *Academy of Management Journal* 37(3), 580. Retrieved June 2, 2008, from ABI/INFORM Global database. (Document ID: 2418.)

18. Scandura, T. A., Graen, G. B. & Novak, M. A. (1986). When managers decide not to decide autocratically: An investigation of leader-member exchange and decision influence. *Journal of Applied Psychology* 71(4), 579–584.

19. Tierney, P., Farmer, S. M. & Graen, G. B. (1999). An examination of leadership and employee creativity: The relevance of traits and relationships. *Personnel Psychology* 52(3), 591–620. Retrieved June 1, 2008, from ABI/INFORM Global database. (Document ID: 45165549.)

20. Hersey, P., Blanchard, K. H. & Johnson, D. (1996). *Management of organizational behavior: Utilizing human resources*, 7th ed. Upper Saddle River, NJ: Prentice Hall.

21. Jobs, S. (March 7, 2008). Steve Jobs speaks out. Accessed October 9, 2009, at http://money.cnn.com/galleries/2008/fortune/0803/gallery.jobsqna.fortune/9.html.

22. Bass, B. M. & Avolio, B. J. (2003). *Multifactor leadership questionnaire.* Redwood City, CA: Mind Garden, Garden, Inc.

23. Howell, J. & Avolio, B. (1993). Transformational leadership, transactional leadership, locus of control, and support for innovation: Key predictors of consolidated-business unit performance. *Journal of Applied Psychology* 78, 891–902.

24. Appelbaum, S. H., Berke, J., Taylor, J. & Vazquez, J. A. (2008). The role of leadership during large-scale organizational transitions: Lessons from six empirical studies. *Journal of American Academy of Business* 13(1), 16–24. Retrieved June 3, 2008, from ABI/INFORM Global database. (Document ID: 1413743721.)

25. Ibid.

26. Boje, D. M. & Dennehy, R. E. (1993). *Managing in the postmodern world: America's revolution against exploitation.* Dubuque, IA: Kendall/Hunt.

27. Dubrin, A. J. (2005). *Coaching and mentoring skills.* Englewood Cliffs, NJ: Pearson/Prentice Hall.

28. Kerr, S. & Jermier, J. M. (1978). Substitutes for leadership: Their meaning and measurement. *Organizational Behavior and Human Performance* 22(3), 375–403.

29. Politis, J. D. (2002). Transformational and transactional leadership enabling (disabling) knowledge acquisition of self-managed teams: The consequences for performance. *Leadership & Organization Development Journal* 23(3/4), 186–198. Retrieved October 23, 2009, from ABI/INFORM Global. (Document ID: 265997701.)

30. Luthans, F. & Avolio, B. (2003). Authentic leadership development. In K. S. Cameron, J. E. Dutton & R. E. Quinn (Eds.), *Positive organizational scholarship: Foundations of a new discipline,* 241–258. San Francisco, CA: Berrett-Koehler.

31. Dunphy, D. & Pitsis, T. S. (2003). Leadership wisdom. In C. Barker and R. Koye (Eds.), *The seven heavenly virtues of leadership.* Melbourne: McGraw-Hill.

32. Maslow, A. (1970). *Motivation and personality.* New York: Harper & Row.

33. Bing, J. (June, 2006). The new Hollywood. *WiReD.* Accessed October 4, 2009, at http://www.wired.com/wired/archive/14.06/hollywood.html.

34. McGregor, D. (1960). *The human side of enterprise.* New York: McGraw-Hill.

35. Taylor, F. W. (1895). *A piece rate system.* New York: McGraw-Hill.

36. Clegg et al., op. cit., 155.

37. Latham, G. P. (2007). *Work motivation: History, theory, research, and practice.* Thousand Oaks, CA: Sage Publications.

38. Adams, J. S. (1965). Inequity in social exchange. *Adv. Exp. Soc. Psychol.* 62, 335–343.

39. Fayol, H. (1916). *General and industrial management.* London: Pitman.

40. Hoskins, C., McFadyen, S. M. & Finn, A. (2004). *Media economics: Applying economics to new and traditional media.* Thousand Oaks, CA: Sage Publications.

41. Fayol, H., op. cit.

42. Clegg et al., op. cit.

43. Mayo, E. (1922). Industrial peace and psychological research, I–V. *Industrial Australian and Mining Standard* 67, 16–253.

44. Accessed October 7, 2009, at http://www.google.com/intl/en/jobs/lifeatgoogle/benefits.html.

45. Barnard, C. (1938). *The functions of the executive.* Cambridge, MA: Harvard University Press.

46. Ouchi, W. G. (Spring, 1981). Organizational paradigms: A commentary on Japanese management and theory Z organizations. *Organizational Dynamics* 9:4, 36–43.

47. Neff, G. (2005). The changing place of cultural production: The location of social networks in a digital media industry. *Annals of the American Academy of Political and Social Science* 597, 134.

48. Doz, Y. L. & Kosonen, M. (2007). The new deal at the top. *Harvard Business Review* 85(6), 98–104. Retrieved May 15, 2008, from ABI/INFORM Global database. (Document ID: 1276349631.)

49. Galbraith, J. R. (1971). Matrix organization designs. *Business Horizons* 14:1, 29–41.

50. DeSanctis, G. & Monge, P. (November/December, 1999). Introduction to the special issue: Communication processes for virtual organizations. *Organization Science* 10:6, 693–703.

51. Grice, S. & Humphries, M. (1997). Critical management studies in postmodernity: Oxymorons in outer space? *Journal of Organizational Change Management* 10:5, 412–425.

52. Barley, S. R. & Kunda, G. (September, 1992). Design and devotion: Surges of rational and normative ideologies of control in managerial discourse. *Administrative Science Quarterly* 37:3, 363–399.

53. Ball, S. J. (1990). Management as moral technology: A Luddite analysis. In S. J. Ball (Ed.), *Foucault and Education: Disciplines and Knowledge*, 153–166. London: Routledge.

54. Grice & Humphries, op. cit., 414.

55. Ouchi, W., op. cit., 39.

56. Likert, R. L. (October, 1979). Production- and employee-centeredness to systems. *Journal of Management* 5:2, 147–156.

57. Mumford, M. D., Scott, G. M., Gaddis, B. & Strange, J. M. (2002). Leading creative people: Orchestrating expertise and relationships. *Leadership Quarterly* 13(6), 705–750. Retrieved April 10, 2008, from ABI/INFORM Global database. (Document ID: 250033821.)

58. Accessed October 7, 2009, at http://www.filmreference.com/Writers-and-Production-Artists-Kr-Lo/Lansing-Sherry.html#ixzz0UU7DUXGZ.

59. See company web site at http://www.nollmedia.com/index.html. Some information presented here came from co-author Lisa Poe Howfield's attendance at Noll & Associates workshops for broadcast managers in 2007 and 2008. Noll & Associates media clients include Univision Television and Radio, NBC Owned & Operated Stations, Chum Radio and TV, Meredith Publishing, Sinclair Television, Cox Media and TV Group, Fox Sports Net Bay Area, National Cable Communications, Comcast Spotlight, Alliance Atlantis, Simmons Research, Scarborough Research, Nielsen Research, Entravision Television, Adlink, NAB, TvB U.S. and Canada.

60. Bernstein, M. (September, 2007). The Hollywood studio system: A history. *Modernism/Modernity* 14:3, 582–584.

61. _____ (October 13, 2003). Mr. and Mrs. Hollywood: Edie & Lew Wasserman and their entertainment empire. *Publishers Weekly* 250:41, 64.

CHAPTER 4

Managing Human Resources

Access to talented and creative people is to modern business what access to coal and iron ore was to steelmaking.

Richard Florida

CHAPTER OBJECTIVES

The objectives of this chapter are to provide you with information about:
- Human resources in the creative industries
- Vertical and horizontal staffing
- New organizational forms: distributed work groups and "follow the sun workflows"
- Ad hoc work groups and outsourcing
- Employees
- Guilds and unions
- Contract employees
- Partners and vendors
- Harnessing creativity: control or cajole?

INTRODUCTION: PEOPLE WHO NEED PEOPLE

Managers perform many functions that may differ from one organization to another. They may order or persuade; direct or educate; survey or monitor; control or guide. They may be responsible for scheduling, workflow, assignments, troubleshooting, putting out fires, and massaging egos. But one key task they must always take on is dealing with personnel matters.

Numerous organizational researchers have gathered evidence that the strategic management of people is a key factor in an organization's success.[1,2] A skilled, unified, nimble workforce conveys important competitive advantages to an enterprise because the relationship between an organization and its people

CONTENTS

91

DOI: 10.1016/B978-0-240-81020-1.00004-X

is subtle and complex and cannot be easily replicated by a rival.[3] Nowhere is this situation truer than it is for companies in the creative industries. Companies that create commercial content – motion pictures, television programming, news, video games, and Internet sites – face stiff competition on every side, from other creators of similar material, from user-generated content, from other types of content that also attract and hold the attention of consumers. And these consumers have a finite limit on the time, attention, and money they can spend on content.

The unceasing advance of consumer electronics technologies and services means that rapid change will be a continuing challenge. Being at the epicenter of innovation makes the media industries a dynamic and exciting marketplace, but it also makes a commercial environment that never stands still. Media companies that harness emerging technologies quickly to create profitable businesses know that a critical success factor is bringing in people who can keep up with the demanding pace and are willing to develop their skills constantly. Thus, salaries and wages are almost always the largest component of a media company's budget.

A recent survey of CEOs who head entertainment and media companies shows that executives are quite aware of the imperative to hire able individuals.[4] Seventy-one percent agree strongly that the people agenda is one of their top priorities, compared to a global average of 58 percent. The CEOs worry about their companies' ability to attract and keep talent and 21 percent said they agreed strongly that there is a need to change the way they recruit, motivate, and develop employees.

Media companies do hire recent college graduates. They need to hire people who know how to navigate the new digital, networked media markets and understand today's competitive, media-rich environment. For example, there is virtually an infinite variety of entertainment, yet consumer resources of time, money, and attention are finite. And although there may always be a few "must-experience" properties, in many instances, entertainment products substitute easily for one another. Each year, people probably want to see a handful of motion pictures. On any given evening, if the running times are not convenient or the lines are too long, most people will buy tickets for another choice. Or if someone wants to watch a live newscast and one of the news networks is airing a preproduced documentary, then it is very likely the individual will pick up the remote and try the other news channels.

Of course there are a few "must-experience" properties, the hits – *Titanic, Harry Potter*, Coldplay's *Viva la Vida*. They are hugely important, because so many sectors of the media industries are hit-driven. The problem for companies and artists in the Hit Economy[5] is that no one knows what will be a hit.

Nobody knows is a principle formulated by Richard Caves that has many implications for the creative industries.[6] One consequence for managers who must engage people to create unique content that has a chance to be a hit is that no one knows who the company should bring on board, what mix of skills are required, and how to know if the work produced by whomever is finally chosen will succeed in the market. Only companies that effectively manage creative people within and without the organizations are likely to perform well in this chaotic and competitive environment.[7] As a result, managers need to understand the work styles and motivations of creative workers.

The Creatives and the Suits

People who work in creative industry organizations are often divided into the creatives and suits. *Creatives* are people who write; design; develop; illustrate; photograph; compose, arrange, play, and sing music; touch up and manipulate photographs; produce, shoot, and direct video; and so forth. *Suits* are executives, managers, accountants who work on the business side of the house, putting deals together, hiring, budgeting, directing, controlling, and serving as liaison to clients and upper management.

Another way of describing the different kinds of work is by designating the type of collar they typically wear to work. People who work with their hands or in trades are sometimes called *blue-collar* workers. In the same parlance, managers and professionals are called *white-collar* workers. Jobs often held by women – such as teachers, beauticians, and nurses – are sometimes called *pink-collar* jobs.

Richard Florida calls creative workers *no-collar* workers. He describes the characteristics of no-collar workers as follows:

> Artists, musicians, professors and scientists have always set their own hours, dressed in relaxed and casual c'lothes, and worked in stimulating environments. They could never be forced to work, yet they were never truly not at work. With the rise of the Creative Class, this way of working has moved from the margins to the economic mainstream. (2002, 12–13)[8]

Florida goes on to say that creative people work more independently than other types of workers. They find it difficult to cope with managers who are incompetent or bullying. They may not have job security, preferring to trade some of the security they would have in other industries for greater personal autonomy. The meaning of autonomy is that it allows for lifelong learning and growth, influence over the nature of work, flexible work schedules, and the ability to express the self through work.

Florida's description points to important distinctions between the way creatives and suits approach work. Managers probably don't wear relaxed and casual clothes. Surprise: they wear suits! They do not work independently and they have less autonomy. They do not shape the content of their work or control their own schedules. Whether they learn and grow and express their identities through work depends more upon personal preference, rather than the imperatives of the job. Most managers work mainly for money and promotion, extrinsic rewards, although many executives also take pride in the products the organization produces.

Managers have resume careers. They build a resume showing a progression through increasingly responsible positions, supervising more people, bigger projects, and handling ever larger budgets. Naturally, their job titles and descriptions and salaries reflect their climb up the organizational ladder. Managers are also likely to hold positions in more than one organization over the span of their careers, but they often have a longer tenure than creatives. They are dependent upon the opinions of their supervisors; there is little concern for the opinions of their peer-competitors.

By contrast, though creatives work to make a living, they also work because they love what they do. The motivation of "art for art's sake" is a largely internal one, providing intrinsic rewards inherent in doing the work itself. Creatives have portfolio careers. They may perform work for a very long list of organizations, perhaps as an independent contractor rather than as an employee. When they look for new work, they keep or point to examples of their past work – their portfolio.

Creatives are at least as concerned about the opinions of their peers, other creatives, as they are about the opinions of managers, the suits. They usually participate in events that offer peer-to-peer recognition – awards, conferences, and similar creative get-togethers. Finally, creatives often possess deep knowledge and specialized skills that exceed those of both supervisors and co-workers.

It is important not to overstate these differences between creatives and managers. They often have warm personal relationships, and work together in an atmosphere of mutual respect. At the same time, it is important not to minimize the differences either, because they have implications for the interaction between the two types of workers. Because experienced creatives may know a great deal more than their managers, their cooperation in putting their knowledge and skills to work is essential for success.

In a marketing environment where *nobody knows* (what makes a hit, how much demand there will be for a content product, etc.), a well-known creative who has a history of success may well have greater clout than all but the highest level executives. Indeed, management careers have been built on the strength of relationships that an executive has with successful creatives. Clive Davis in the music business, Jamie Tarsus in television, and Julia Phillips are all examples of people who made it to the top of the entertainment business based largely on such relationships with hit-makers.

The characteristics of creative workers mean that managers who use persuasion fare better than those who use coercion or other bullying behaviors. Moreover, creatives may balk at producing work they feel will earn them the derision or contempt from their peers, even peers who work in rival organizations. All this means that managers face many challenges organizing and providing structure for the subordinates who carry out work to fulfill the organization's objectives.

HUMAN RESOURCES STRATEGIES

To align human resources (HR) with organizational goals requires a strategy to guide the search for and hiring of workers. HR units look to *vertical staffing* when an enterprise needs additional leadership and guidance. Vertical staffing means hiring people to fill positions in the hierarchy, building an authority structure to manage the organization's business. Sometimes vertical staffing is required when a boutique creative business decides to pursue major clients and needs to create more sophisticated account services and dependable work-flow processes.

Horizontal staffing means hiring people who will function at the same level as other employees and can strengthen a project or fill out the skills of an existing team. It might involve hiring an entire team. For example, a client may task the organization with a new project. Or the organization may acquire a new account.

Companies are increasingly adopting workflow processes that have an impact on HR activities and pose new challenges. HR professionals have to get background on people who live and work in geographies far from the organizational headquarters. They may need to learn about the legal and regulatory framework of other countries. And they are dependent on translations of resumes, letters, contracts, and other key employment documents.

The new working environment is made possible by connectivity over computer networks, using email, online meetings, and the telephone to complete their work. More and more, people are working in *distributed work teams and groups,* in which those who work together on the same projects or products do not live in the same place – perhaps not even on the same continent! One reason for the increase in this type of working arrangement is the rise in joint work undertaken by multiple organizations that are all parts in a web of partner and vendor relationships. Motion picture production offers one of the first examples of complex workforces assembled in this manner: When director Steven Spielberg was shooting *Schindler's List* in Poland in 1993, the postproduction editors for *Jurassic Park* needed his input and approval to proceed. The production staff set up a dedicated high-speed connection so that Spielberg could view the editor's work, make comments via voice, and approve the final editing.

A specialized method of distributed work that companies may adopt when they must finish a project quickly is a *follow-the-sun* strategy. Often used by software companies to ensure that work goes on 24 hours a day, the organization tasks people around the globe. As one group finishes working for the day, it passes the work to others just beginning work. In this way, a team may start work in San Jose, pass the day's output to Tokyo, who in turn passes the shift's output to New Delhi, and so forth, until the sun rises in San Jose, and work on the project has never stopped.

Project-Based Organizations

A very common configuration of staffing in the creative industries is the *ad hoc work group*, sometimes called a project-based group.[9] Companies in motion picture and advertising film production, music production, and *project-based organizations* (PBOs) may form groups as needed that disband when the project is completed or moves to a different stage. Often the people engaged in this type of team are independent contractors rather than full-time employees or there is a mix of staff members and freelancers.

Whitley has identified some important types of PBOs.[10] One dimension is the types of goals: Are they recurring or one-off? He calls this element the *singularity of goals and outputs*. The other dimension looks at work roles: Are they defined and stable or vague and changing? This is termed the *separation and stability of work roles*. Whitley shows how these two dimensions interact to produce four types of PBOs, as shown in Table 4-1.

Table 4-1 Comparison of Types of PBOs

Separation and Stability of Work Roles	Singularity of Goals and Outputs	
	Low	**High**
Low	Many and varied outputs, mixed and changing roles	One or just a few outputs, mixed and changing roles
	Examples: Consultancy and other service firms	*Example:* Internet start-ups
High	Many and varied outputs (although they may be related), distinct and stable work roles	One or just a few outputs, distinct and stable work roles
	Examples: Television series production, news shows, advertising and PR agencies	*Examples:* Motion picture production, recorded music (songs and albums)

Managing PBOs that fall in the high/high category (producing one or a few outputs, carried out by people performing in distinct roles) is challenging. People who move from project to project, who are hired based on their expertise, are likely to identify more with their professional association than with their current employer. In addition, unless careful attention is paid to documenting the project, the knowledge gained from the experience departs with the people who worked on it when the project disbands.

Companies that engage in similar projects (low on singularity of purpose) and retain a core group of workers over time have the best chance of achieving long-term success. Managers are helped by this type of PBO because it gives them the ability to create procedures for coordination, to identify and foster specific skills, and to learn from experience. Even when the work teams are challenged to produce unique and innovative content, managers can budget and organize with greater confidence than when they must handle one-off projects with ad hoc work groups.

Outsourcing

Outsourcing is a strategic choice for some creative industry companies. However, they tend to outsource humdrum tasks more often than work that involves the development of key intellectual property. However, software development and visual creation such as animation, illustration, photography, and skilled artistic tasks such as retouching are often outsourced globally.

Outsourcing isn't always an option. One motivation for keeping key creative work inside the organization is copyright considerations, ensuring that the company maintains ownership claims to the work. And some aspects of creative industry products, such as motion pictures, TV programming, and advertising messages, may need to be tuned to cultural and social dimensions. For these materials, outsourcing is likely to be to either domestic companies or offshore to companies in culturally similar environments.

DIFFERENT STROKES FOR DIFFERENT WORKERS

Companies in today's creative industries need to be flexible. Technologies and markets change, so it can come as no surprise that the way organizations interact with their workforce also changes. This section covers the human resources issues managers must address when dealing with employees, union workers, contract workers, partners and vendors whose workers carry out tasks, and customers, whose efforts may become part of the company's products or services.

EMPLOYEES

Employees are the glue of the organization. They embody the structure of the organization, transmit its collective knowledge and memories, and provide stability.

They carry out the day-to-day stability of operations. Management employees establish the company's formal and informal policies and procedures.

From the perspective of the organization, full-time employees are an expensive investment. However, they are the most easily monitored and controlled of any type of worker. Salaried employees in the creative industries, such as managers, typically work many more hours than the standard 40 per week, with no additional pay. The company can demand and, to some extent, enforce nondisclosure agreements. It can insist that the employee refrain from working for a rival company for some period of time, should they leave their position.

Many employees in the United States are hired under a legal umbrella known as *at will*, which means the employer can terminate an employee for any reason – or no reason. Workers who are guild and union members or who work under a contract are not at-will employees. Laws governing at-will employment are covered by state law, so they may vary depending on the jurisdiction. In the most protective environments, a state may establish an *implied contract*, even when there is no formal, signed document, protecting employees from termination without cause.

The tenure of an employee is called the *employee life cycle*, which indicates the stages of employment from the design of the job, recruitment, and hiring, through termination, as shown in Figure 4-1. There is no standard time line associated with the employee life cycle, as it depends on both the organization and individual factors. Some employees may be hired and stay until retirement, although such a career path is not common in the creative industries. Others may be hired and fired in a few months when there is a profound mismatch between the job requirements and the employee.

The employee life cycle falls into three broad categories: hiring, development, and termination, as shown in Table 4-2. Complex procedures and policies accompany every stage of the life cycle. In the past decade, the rise of the creative industries has highlighted how companies in these sectors handle human resources issues.

Phase 1: Hiring

Employee recruitment in the media industries is a much more open and flexible process than it is in many other industries and in previous eras. Work groups, entire divisions, or business units in multiple divisions may offer input about what duties the job entails, the qualifications and characteristics prospective employees ought to have, and at what level he or she should be brought in. In some sectors, desirable creative skills may be scarce and the market competitive, necessitating a recruitment strategy. The press of work and the need for a diversified campaign sometimes results in the hiring of a professional recruiter for difficult searches.

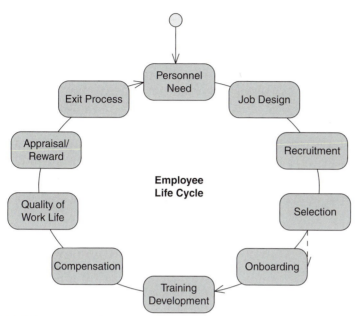

FIGURE 4-1 The employee life cycle

Table 4-2 Stages of the Employee Life Cycle

Hiring	Development	Termination
Personnel need	Training development	Exit process
Job design	Compensation	—
Recruitment	Quality of work life	—
Selection	Appraisal/reward	—
Onboarding	—	—

Recruitment efforts usually entail circulating announcements of openings within the organization. In addition, most companies place position announcements and ads in relevant trade papers, online employment sites, and in niche newsletters. They may visit campuses and attend conferences. Today, it may even include putting out information on social networks and other informal methods initiated by employees within the organization.

All these methods include requests that applicants send resumes to a person or department where they are collected. In some situations, all resumes may be forwarded to the manager who is hiring. More often, the resumes are prescreened to eliminate people who clearly do not have the requisite qualifications and a smaller number go to the manager. The HR department or the manager may conduct telephone interviews, often designed to narrow the field to the top three or four candidates.

The manager or HR department then invites these final candidates for an in-person interview. However, when the prospective employee lives in another region, increasingly first interviews may be conducted via videoconference. Second interviews occur in person, as it is important for managers and co-workers to get a feel for the applicant – and it is also an opportunity to present the company's goals, values, and expectations.

Some organizations may also take the opportunity of an in-person visit to require the applicant to take psychological tests or interview with a psychologist. And when the search is narrowed down to one or two individuals, HR or the hiring manager checks references usually by telephone. Many companies also conduct background checks at this point. Other organizations may require that the final applicants pass drug screening tests.

All procedures must take care to establish fairness in the hiring process. Managers cannot legally discriminate against a potential employee on account of race, age, gender, pregnancy, national origin, immigration status, language, marital and parental status, sexual orientation, or religion. Moreover, there are excellent business reasons for having a diverse workforce. For example, in the multicultural world of the media industries, where content products may have global distribution, companies need to have a *requisite variety*.[11] Requisite variety means that an organization that faces a diverse business environment must have a variety of employees in order to create products that appeal to the diversity of consumer interests, tastes, and habits. In short, it takes one to know one in the global business environment, and companies that recognize that need are more likely to produce content that appeals to specific cultural, social, and ethnic groups.

To avoid the suggestion of bias, even organizations that depend on the appearance of their employees, such as the news departments of television stations, cannot accept resumes that include photos. Only at the point when the hiring news director has determined that the qualifications provided in a resume are acceptable can they view or request a demo tape. If a candidate mails in a tape, the HR director will keep it until the news director requests to see it.

These processes ultimately result in the hiring of the person who appears to be the best match for the position: The organization makes an offer. Although the manager or HR extends the offer in a welcoming tone, it is actually a rather formal procedure. The offer includes a summary of the job requirements and duties, proposed salary and benefits, start date, and a deadline for the candidate to make a decision.

I've worked in media industries my entire career, for many different companies, both as an employee and as a freelancer. In my experience, the human resources department is just a formality – you know, the place where you sign the papers. Really, they've had little to do with the jobs I've gotten and the people I've hired. It's all informal. Maybe for entry level and assistant jobs, and some top corporate positions, HR is important. But for everything else, it's either who you know or the work you've done that comes to somebody's attention and you just get a call. Maybe somebody you know tells a friend or colleague about you. Or you run into someone at a convention or conference. Or there's an article in a trade mag about work you've done. Really, I've gotten my best jobs from interviews at someone's house by the pool. And that person just picks up the phone and says, "Hire her," and I'm in. (Anonymous producer)

However the hiring takes place, the next stage of employment is orientation. It may actually begin with the exchange of information that takes place in the first telephone and in-person interviews. But once the person accepts the organization's offer, the orientation starts in earnest. Even before the start date, the new employee receives an orientation package about the mechanics of enrollment in the benefits plans, typically including medical, dental, insurance, retirement plans and others. In addition, there are IRS forms and there may be nondisclosure and noncompetition agreements. At the same time, every contact includes a more subtle, personal process of acculturating the new employee to the organization that conveys how it does business, how it evaluates performance, how the informal structure and processes of the organization work, and the myths and legends that guide it.

Employee Development

Organizations have many reasons to develop the employees they have. It is likely to be the largest part of their budget. When people aren't in place, someone else has to do that work, taking away from their primary jobs. In addition, as we have seen, the process for hiring new people may be cumbersome and expensive. In a sense, employee development is protecting an organizational investment.

Development serves to reward employees, especially those who perform creative work and are likely to consider their professional growth and development an important benefit. It can improve the performance of employees and align their skills more closely with the needs of the organization. Finally, rapid technological change has an enormous impact in nearly all the creative industries, making continuous learning and development an essential part of responding to changes in the business landscape.

One study demonstrated the advantages of a leadership development program for managers within the British Broadcast Corporation. Employees "felt there was little collaborative work within the organisation, too much bureaucracy, silo thinking and internal competition. Moreover, leadership was regarded as a skill required only for those at the top of the organisation rather than something required whenever one person managed the work of another."[12] According to the BBC, most managers reported greater confidence in their leadership abilities and employees welcomed the formal and informal networks between managers that arose as a result of the program.

Termination

Employees leave an organization in one of three ways: (1) retirement; (2) employee chooses to leave the organization; (3) employer terminates the employee. The first case, retirement, is usually fairly straightforward. The second case, when the employee chooses to leave, is often without incident as well, although there have been disputes over recommendations and nondisclosure and noncompete contractual agreements.

Employee termination occurs when an organization ends an individual's employment against his or her will. Employer terminations have a potential for contention, including legal action, and so must be handled carefully. They can also negatively affect morale and productivity among the remaining employees.

There are two general situations that lead to such termination: *cause* and *reductions in force* due to downsizing or restructuring. Cause may involve an employee's inadequate job performance, a poor fit with the organization, the inability to carry out the responsibilities of the job, conflict with managers or co-workers, or employee misconduct. In these cases, the manager must initiate and maintain a detailed record of the problem and all actions taken to solve it or improve the situation.

Managers and employees have little control over the other cause of employee separation, mandated reductions in force. Reductions are often brought about by budgetary constraints or loss of business. Managers must review their needs and make difficult decisions about who will stay and who will not.

In all cases of termination, the organization needs clear, written policies, readily available to employees. The guidelines should define poor performance and misconduct, review procedures, and severance policies. The often uncomfortable termination meeting must be conducted in a professional and humane way that includes a discussion of the employee's positive contributions. It is important that the employee be able to leave with dignity. The terminated employee should receive a severance package that lays out termination procedures. It should include the amount of severance pay, benefits and assistance options, compensation for earned vacation, outplacement services, ongoing health insurance, and unemployment benefits.

Legal Considerations

Companies must take into account the many laws concerning employee termination. The most important laws deal with bias against protected groups – race, age, gender, pregnancy, national origin, and so forth. Large companies and corporations must also comply with laws that cover large-scale layoffs, such as the federal Worker Adjustment and Retraining Notification (WARN) Act of 1988. It requires organizations with 100 or more employees to provide 60 days' written prior notice before they undertake mass layoffs or reductions in work force. The act also mandates such services as benefits extensions and outplacement assistance.

Termination Procedures within the Organization

Before the employee is terminated, the organization needs to conduct an inventory that identifies the employee's access to systems, networks, applications, data, and physical facilities, equipment, and supplies. All these activities require coordination between the HR department, information technology (IT) units, and facilities security. Actions must be taken to shut down all accounts and privileges and to retrieve all physical access devices such as ID cards, badges, tokens, and keys. In some cases and organizations, the employee is escorted from the premises and IT installs enhanced intrusion detection software to make sure the employee is unable to gain access to organizational systems.

GUILDS AND UNIONS

Evolved from medieval organizations of individual artists, artisans, and craftsmen, guilds originally set standards and regulated the acquisition of skills through apprenticeships. By contrast, unions are organizations created to focus on conditions of employment. Unions do not set standards; rather, they negotiate with employers on behalf of groups of employees. Though medieval guilds did not negotiate with employers, over time trade unions have become increasingly similar to them.

Guild and union members who work for an organization are not the same as at-will employees. Members work for organizations under a collective bargaining agreement (CBA) or contract: The CBA governs hiring, compensation, discipline, and termination. Indeed, the CBA imposes drastic constraints on the ability of the organization to terminate an employee.

Further, CBAs establish grievance procedures that allow a member to challenge a disciplinary action or termination. If there is still a disagreement between the union and the company, the union usually has the right to take the issue to an impartial arbitrator who can impose a settlement on both parties.

Guilds and Unions in the Creative Industries

In the early years of the film industry, workers joined theater and electrical industry trade unions. However, as the industry matured, guilds and unions specific to the film, and later television, industry organized members. As a result, these worker organizations perform specialized functions. For example, the Writers Guild arbitrates screen credits for film script writers. And the Writers Guild, the Directors Guild, the Screen Actors Guild, and the American Federation of Musicians all help their members negotiate and collect royalty payments. They may also engage in political lobbying to advance the interests of the membership.

Guilds are often called *above-the-line guilds*; unions are called *below-the-line unions.* These terms are derived from the structure of entertainment budgets, which differentiate between creative workers (writers, directors, and actors) and craftspeople and technical and skilled laborers (camera operators, editors, etc.). The largest union is the International Association of Theatrical and Stage Employees (IATSE), which represents most of the below-the-line workers in the film and television industries: artists, story analysts, animators, set designers, graphic artists, teachers, set builders, editors, and so forth.

One key contribution unions made to the production environment is the definition of worker categories, with detailed descriptions of the duties associated with these categories. Although much humor has been made about the fact that no one but workers in the props department can touch a prop (except an actor), this strict categorization has allowed the industry to put together production teams that work together smoothly immediately, even when they have never worked together before; workers know exactly what they are required to do and the limits of what they are allowed to do.

Unions and Managers

In order to hire union workers, companies have to become *signatories* to the existing collective bargaining agreement. The ongoing relationship with union members is handled by representatives from the human resources department on the organization side and by the union rep for the members. Often, the union rep is the *union steward*, a union position held by an employee. The job of the steward is to represent workers by enforcing the terms of the agreement between the company and the union. However, stewards may not provide instructions about how to perform work – that is the job of management.

One study shows that in most industries, relationships between HR and union reps are relatively cordial, with some reservations on both sides.[13] In the entertainment industry, relationships can be quite strained, perhaps more so than in other industries. As a result, according to IATSE, fewer than one-third of motion pictures released in the United States were produced using union labor.

Table 4-3 Guilds and Unions in the Creative Industries

Guild or Union	Membership
Guilds	
Writers Guild (WGA)	Writers in the motion picture, broadcast, cable, interactive, and new media industries. About 9,000 members.
Directors Guild (DGA)	Directors, unit production managers, assistant directors, and technical coordinators. About 13,000 members.
Producers Guild (PGA)	Producers. (The Alliance of Motion Picture and Television Producers [AMPTP] is a trade organization that represents producers' power in the film and TV industries. It is the entity that negotiates with the WGA, DGA, and SAG to arrive at a collective bargaining agreement.)
Screen Actors Guild (SAG)	Actors, including extras. About 120,000 members.
American Federation of Television and Radio Artists (AFTRA)	More than 70,000 performers in radio, television, and sometimes, film, usually live and taped broadcast performances.
American Federation of Musicians (AFM)	Musicians in many industries, including radio, television, and film. About 90,000 members.
Unions	
International Association of Theatrical and Stage Employees (IATSE, pronounced "Yahtzee")	Behind-the-camera workers, including animation/computer-generated imagery, front of house, laboratory, makeup and hair, motion picture and television production, postproduction, projection and audiovisual, scenic artists, stagehands, television broadcast, trade show/exhibition, treasurers and ticket sellers, wardrobe.
Communications Workers of America (CWA)	Engineers.
International Brotherhood of Teamsters (Teamsters' Union)	Transport drivers, location scouts, and casting directors. About 1.4 million members, about 4,000 employed in film and television production.
National Association for Broadcast Employees and Technicians (NABET)	Now defunct – some locals and worker categories formed locals within the CWA and others within IATSE.

For managers, having union workers means that perhaps a significant part of the workforce that produces outcomes for which they are held accountable does not work under their control. In addition, the largest budget item may not be amenable to cost cutting. Such a situation is never comfortable or easy. However, managers typically make the hiring decisions with respect to creatives, so that high-level writers, directors, editors, and other key creative performers owe their jobs to management.[14]

Guild and Union Concerns

Long-standing concerns of Hollywood guilds and unions have been the growth of nonunion production; runaway production, which occurs when productions take place in other countries or in right-to-work states where producers can hire nonunion labor freely; and the trend toward conglomeration of entertainment corporations. Nonunion production is a common phenomenon, even in Hollywood. Producers and production companies that are not signatories to collective bargaining agreements can hire nonunion people. Guild and union members are not supposed to work on nonunion productions. But behind-the-scenes workers, even writers and directors, may work for such productions under different names. However, the producers will not be able to hire highly visible members of guilds and unions, particularly actors. The inability to hire known talent is an impediment to a production, from raising money through distribution, marketing, and sales.

The issue of runaway production to foreign locations, including Canada, Eastern Europe, and third world countries, and right-to-work states locations, because of lower labor costs, is of great concern for guilds and unions and their members. Runaway production is one of the major causes of the high unemployment among members. To make union production more attractive, guilds and unions now allow lower pay and more flexible working rules for low-budget productions.

A strike by the Writers Guild in 2008 demonstrated that workers are also concerned about their rights and royalties for new media uses under collective bargaining agreements. This issue had simmered for several years, as producers argued that new media channels of distribution were uncertain. However, by 2008, the DVD industry had virtually replaced videotape in the rental and over-the-counter sale markets, with the 2006 home video market exceeding $24 billion.[15] In addition, the popularity of videogames, which are produced using animators and moving images using methods similar to motion picture and television production, caught the attention of guilds and unions. Finally, it is clear that much distribution will occur over the Internet, supplanting and complementing traditional distribution channels.

The writers held out for a better agreement concerning new media and ultimately signed an agreement, over the bitter objections of some long-time members of the Writers Guild. A flavor of how high feelings ran is best provided by a statement from writer Harlan Ellison, characterizing the agreement in terms that cannot be entirely repeated here:

> My Guild did what it did in 1988. It trembled and sold us out. It gave away the EXACT co-terminus expiration date with SAG for some b – s – short-line substitute; it got us no more control of our words; it sneak-abandoned the animator and reality beanfield hands before anyone even forced it on them; it made nice so no one would think we were meanies; it let the Alliance play us like the village idiot. The WGAW folded like a Texaco Road Map from back in the day. And I am as ashamed of this Guild, as I was when … we wasted our efforts and lost out on technology that we had to strike for THIS time. 17 days

of streaming tv!!!????? Geezus, you bleating wimps, why not just turn over your old granny for gang-rape? You deserve all the opprobrium you get. While this nutty festschrift of demented pleasure at being allowed to go back to work in the rice paddy is filling your cowardly hearts with joy and relief that the grips and the staff at the Ivy and street sweepers won't be saying nasty sh– behind your back, remember this: You are their b–. They outslugged you, outthought you, outmaneuvered you.[16]

CONTRACT WORKERS

Throughout the creative industries, the highest paid, most well-known creative talent almost always works under a contract. In his seminal work on this topic, Richard Caves sets out the characteristics of such contracts in the motion picture and television industries.[17] Creatives have individual contracts with producers in the movie business, with the involvement and final approval of the movie studio that is financing the production. The terms of the contracts depend on whether the talent is *A-list* or *B-list*, which is based on a combination of ability, track record, and perceived contribution to the success of the project. Talent usually negotiates a *pay or play contract*, which means that they are paid even if the project does not go forward. Often key talent also negotiates contingent agreements, where they share in the profits of the project.

Many of the same conditions also apply to television industry contracts. In addition, because TV shows may involve years of production activity, producers often negotiate long-term contracts for as long as 5 years. If the show is a hit, there is usually intense negotiation when the contract comes up for renewal that forces producers to compensate star performers for their full value to the success of the program. As it is difficult to replace key actors, writers, and writer-producers, such talent can usually negotiate higher compensation.

In the television news industry, contracts are provided to on-air talent and quite often to key producers as well. The contracts typically cover a period between 1 and 5 years. They detail the annual pay amounts and any perquisites ("perks") that come along with the position, such as makeup, hair, wardrobe, dry cleaning, travel, cosmetic procedures, and even obscure inclusions like golf memberships. Usually, on-air anchors and reporters are represented by a talent agent who collects a percentage of their income to negotiate for them.

Enterprises in the creative industries have contractual relationships with many workers, not just stars and top talent, paying by project or by time periods such as yearly, daily, and hourly rates. Colorists, illustrators, photographers, retouchers, script doctors, editors, and hundreds of other specialty workers provide services via contract. They are typically boilerplate contracts, and those that involve high-value content often have nondisclosure provisions.

PARTNERS

Partnerships often presage mergers and acquisitions, as they indicate the existence of an ongoing dependency. Many companies oscillate between periods where they expand their activities to provide the work product for a greater extent of the finished product, as well as distributing and marketing it. At other times, they focus on their *core competencies*, leaving other activities to partners and vendors.

Overall, Caves characterizes creative industry contracts between partners in the following way: "Revenue-sharing joint ventures with up-front payments and real option contracts with successive transfers of decision rights make repeated appearances in the creative industries."[18] The *successive transfer of decision rights* means that complex creative properties are created in stages, with work finished by one group of participants, then handed over to the next group. For example, a production company may produce a program, which is then passed to a distribution company, all the while maintaining payment, revenue-sharing, and royalty agreements.

There are three types of partnerships, content–content, content–conduit, and conduit–conduit:

- *Content–content partnerships* occur when all the partners create content. One example is the co-production agreement between DQE and Method Films to produce the *Iron Man* animated 3D series in conjunction with Marvel Comics. Here, three companies that create content will partner on a series, each contributing to the finished product.[19] Another example is the deal between the Showtime network and Mark Ecko Entertainment to make a videogame based on the drama *Dexter*. A very common content–content partnership is one between content creation companies and marketing specialist companies that package, promote, and advertise the creative content. Other partnerships occur when a company reformats and repackages the content created for another medium.
- *Content–conduit partnerships* link content creation organizations with distribution channels. A good example is the 2004 deal between Sony Pictures Entertainment (SPE) and Comcast, one of the largest multiple system cable operators in the United States.[20] Previous to the arrangement, Sony had acquired Metro-Goldwyn-Mayer and its enormous library of motion pictures and television programs. The deal provided for SPE to create programming and for Comcast to manage the channels; thus the partners contributed to the effort in activities that draw on the core competencies of each.
- *Conduit–conduit partnerships* occur when the partners operate distribution channels. Satellite company DirecTV provides an enormous array of motion picture and television programming to its customers, but

its delivery does not allow efficient high-speed Internet service. The company partners with Verizon to provide its customers who live in Verizon coverage areas to receive Internet access through the telephone company, a conduit–conduit deal.

VENDORS

Creative enterprises almost always work with vendors. A complex production such as a motion picture may involve hundreds of vendors; a television show or videogame is likely to require support from dozens of vendors. Motion picture studios in the 1920s through the 1950s tried vertical integration, in which the studio carried out every type of work required to produce and distribute a film – scriptwriting, casting, camera operation, sound recording, editing, and so forth. However, in an industry where there may be periods when less production takes place, the overhead of paying enough workers to handle moderate- or high-volume production schedules is an impossible burden. Since the 1950s, studios have gradually divested themselves of all manner of activities, settling on the core competencies of developing content, financing it, and marketing it, with partners and vendors carrying out the other tasks.

Relationships with vendors are typically handled with contracts that may cover a single arrangement or a long-term relationship. Common vendor relationships include some production tasks, work at postproduction facilities of all kinds (video, audio, computer-generated imagery), marketing-related work, and content transcoding for digital distribution. As work increasingly takes place over digital networks, a need for network security has been incorporated both into the contracts and shared networks.

The problem of security with partners emerged clearly in 2003, when *The Hulk* appeared on the Internet 2 weeks before its theatrical release. Three weeks later, police arrested Kerry Gonzalez for felony copyright infringement. He had obtained the copy from a friend of a friend of an advertising agency firm tasked with creating the ad campaign for the film. One study used a sample of 312 popular films and found that more than half were circulated on file sharing networks.[21] Using forensic techniques to identify the origination of these movies, the researchers calculated that 77 percent of all unauthorized leaks of motion pictures came from insiders, as opposed to outsiders who *cammed* (used a video recorder) the movie from a theater seat.

Harnessing Creativity: Control or Cajole?

"You can't control creativity," says the research. The very nature of the work precludes managers from demanding highly creative work, whether it comes from designers, writers, artists, poets, researchers, fashion designers, musicians, or software developers. It can be nourished, fostered, supported, and guided, but it cannot be forced.[22]

The inability to command and control creativity, however, does not mean that creatives should operate in a vacuum. Creatives are more productive when respected managers provide structure, evaluation, and feedback.[23] One caveat for managers is that they need to have credibility with creatives, based on their own creative abilities, expertise, or superior knowledge of the market, the client, or the higher levels of authority within the organization.[24]

Human resources meets the theories of leadership and management in the workplace – the kinds of workers that organizations hire affect how leaders and managers can best get the results they want and the organization needs. When we consider the various theories of leadership and management covered in the previous chapter, it is clear that the classic theories like those of Taylor and Fayol are not likely to be effective. On the other hand, research shows that an unstructured workplace environment does not work well either. The more modern methods, such as Theory Z and matrix management, which invoke the norms and requirements of peers, in conjunction with management goal setting and structure and the respect for the individual suggested by the human relations school may prove to be the more effective combination.

SUMMARY

Media organizations need the services of many people who perform work under different rules and standards. From employees, to guild and union workers, to independent contractors, to partners, the demands of creative production and distribution require a greater combination of structure and flexibility than many industries of similar size. They also have adopted many innovative forms for working, including distributed work teams and project-based teams. The type of work, the kinds of workers, and the organizational structures all affect how leaders and managers motivate people and direct their work.

WHAT'S AHEAD

Is there anything more important than the bottom line? Top management and stockholders don't usually think so, so managers have to take seriously budgeting and understanding financial procedures, processes, and reporting. The next chapter looks at how managers deal with the financial aspects of their work.

CASE STUDY 4.1 MEETING WITH A HUMAN RESOURCE PROFESSIONAL

Contact the human resources manager for a local media or entertainment company and ask him or her to help you (in person, on the telephone, or via email) to understand the following:

- Guidelines and regulations specific to their industry
- Government requirements Equal Employment Opportunity (EEO)
- Legal stipulations

- Drug testing
- Questions that can (and cannot) be asked in an interview
- Required reports both internal and external
- Changes in human resources in the past year or longer

What did you find most interesting about the information you were able to gather? Did you see the value in some of the laws set forth or do you see them as overly regulating?

CASE STUDY 4.2 CONDUCTING THE INTERVIEW

You are the graphic artist director for a very successful online social network and need to hire a new web designer. How would you go about finding the best candidate for this position? Consider the following elements:

- How would you make your needs known: classified ad, newsletter, Twitter?
- Write up a job description.
- Research any legal or industry restrictions.

- Develop a list of questions for the interview.
- What qualities would you look for beyond experience and education?
- Create and write up a post-interview sheet for three candidates.
- What information needs to be conveyed to the human resources department?
- Who would you have hired and why?

REFERENCES

1. Becker, B. E., & Huselid, M. A. (1999). Overview: Strategic human resource management in five leading firms. *Human Resource Management* 38(4), 287–301.

2. Becker, B. E., Huselid, M. A., Pickus, P. S. & Spratt, M. F. (1997). HR as a source of shareholder value: Research and recommendations. *Human Resource Management* 36(1), 39–47.

3. Barney, J. B., & Wright, P. M. (1998). On becoming a strategic partner: the role of human resources in gaining competitive advantage. *Human Resource Management* 37(1), 31–46.

4. PricewaterhouseCoopers (2008). 11th Annual Global CEO Survey: Compete & Collaborate: What is success in a connected world? Technology, communications, and media & entertainment. New York, NY: PricewaterhouseCoopers. Accessed June 18, 2008, at http://www.pwc.com/extweb/pwcpublications.nsf/docid/9053F3FF30000F93852573D8000B7E83/$File/ceosurvey-tice.pdf.

5. Farrell, W. (2000). *How hits happen.* New York: HarperCollins.

6. Caves, R. E. (2005). *Switching channels.* Cambridge, MA: Harvard University Press.

7. Way, S. A. & Johnson, D. E. (2005). Theorizing about the impact of strategic human resource management. *Human Resource Management Review* 15, 1–19.

8. Florida, R. (2001). "The Experiential Life." In *Creative Industries*, edited by John Hartley, 133–146. Malden, MA: Blackwell Publishing.

9. Mintzberg, H. (1983). *Structure in fives: Designing effective organizations*. Englewood Cliffs, NJ: Prentice-Hall.

10. Whitley, R. (2006). Project-based firms: New organizational form or variations on a theme? *Industrial and Corporate Change* 15:1, 77–99.

11. Weick, K. E. (1995). *Sensemaking in organizations*. Thousand Oaks, CA: Sage Publications.

12. Kent, S. (2004). Leading the way. *Personnel Today* 31.

13. Willock, R. (January 7, 2007). HR and unions relationship: Cordial relations. *Personnel Today*. Accessed June 15, 2008, at http://www.personneltoday.com/articles/2007/01/30/39034/hr-and-unions-relationship-cordial-relations.html.

14. Wasko, Janet. (2004). *How Hollywood works*. Thousand Oaks, CA: Sage Publications.

15. Entertainment Marketing Association (2007). 2007 Annual Report. Accessed June 14, 2008, at http://www.entmerch.org/annual_reports.html.

16. Ellison, H. (February 18, 2008). Harlan Ellison reacts to the proposed WGA contract. *United Hollywood*. Accessed June 16, 2008, at http://unitedhollywood.blogspot.com/2008/02/harlan-ellison-reacts-to-proposed-wga.html.

17. Caves, R. E. (2003) Contracts between art and commerce. *Journal of Economic Perspectives* 17(2), 73–82.

18. Ibid., 82.

19. ——— (2006). DQ Entertainment Limited (DQEL) inks large co-production deals at MIPCOM. *Animation Express*. Accessed June 8, 2008, at http://www.animationxpress.com/index.php?file=story&id=1095.

20. ——— (October 1, 2004). MGM studio deal to spawn new cable channels. *Screen Digest*. Accessed June 12, 2008, at http://www.animationxpress.com/index.php?file=story&id=1095.

21. Byers, S., Cranor, L., Kormann, D., McDaniel, P. & Cronin, E. (2003). Analysis of security vulnerabilities in the movie production and distribution process. Accessed June 29, 2009 at http://www.dklevine.com/archive/movie_piracy.pdf.

22. Gil, R. & Spiller, P. T. (2007). The organizational dimensions of creativity: Motion picture production. *California Management Review* 50(1), 243–260.

23. Mumford, M. D., Scott, G. M., Gaddis, B. & Strange, J. M. (2002). Leading creative people: Orchestrating expertise and relationships. *Leadership Quarterly* 13(6), 705–750.

24. Powell, S. (2008). Management and consumption of organizational creativity. *Journal of Consumer Marketing* 25(3), 158–166.

CHAPTER 5

Financial Management

This film cost $31 million. With that kind of money, I could have invaded some country.

Clint Eastwood, Actor and Director

CHAPTER OBJECTIVES

After reading this chapter, students will understand:
- Structures for managing finances
- Fundamental financial concepts: revenue, expenses, capital assets
- Key financial documents, including Profit & Loss Statements, Balance Sheets, and Statements of Cash Flows
- Financial responsibilities in the age of Sarbanes-Oxley
- Financial management systems
- Managerial finance: strategic planning and budgeting
- Financial strategies

CONTENTS

INTRODUCTION

"We completed the project (program, initiative, or quarter) on time, on budget, and successfully reached our profit targets," may be the most powerful words in the world of business. The executive who can repeatedly make this claim is almost certainly slated for a fast-track promotion. However, success in such endeavors can be elusive, in many cases because the underlying market uncertainties are a profound barrier to accurate planning, sometimes reducing the proposed business models for the project to little more than an exercise in fantasy.

Today's market environment for the creative industries is vastly more unpredictable than it was two decades ago, because then digital technologies had not fully emerged to revolutionize the creation, distribution, and marketing of content, particularly the Internet. Estimating the potential for bringing in

DOI: 10.1016/B978-0-240-81020-1.00005-1

revenue from the sale and licensing of a creative work was difficult, even then, as there has always been considerable uncertainty about which products would become hits. Now, there are so many more markets and the number of outlets for creative products is growing so quickly that it is difficult to even conceptualize potential revenue, let alone the marketing efforts and expenditures that will be required to realize income.

The uncertainties plague many projects from start to finish. Investors are skittish about putting money with uncertainties about returns on their investments. When executives cannot estimate how well creative works (program, film, web site) will perform in the marketplace, they cannot make accurate decisions about how much to pay for production and distribution or how much to charge consumers for the final product.

Moreover, the profitability in the creative industries rests on the ability to enforce copyright and the control of distribution. Consider a motion picture, a CD album, a photograph, or a TV show released as recently as 1998. The company that owned the copyright could target a market, ship the product to a theater, music store, publisher, or TV station, and expect to be able to track (and charge for) its distribution to consumers with some accuracy.

Those days ended when powerful computers came into the hands of average consumers who are connected to broadband global digital networks. Today, once a creative work is released, high school students around the world can capture the property, copy it, convert it into the desired file size and type, upload it, and share it with several million friends over a peer-to-peer service. It is clear that artists, producers, and owners of copyrighted materials face considerable difficulty in reimposing the levels of control over their products that they took for granted a decade ago.

Although these developments make financial management difficult, particularly because of the uncertainties in estimating revenues, hit properties still bring in great profits; and companies still produce and distribute creative works to reap those profits. So financial management continues to be a key part of the creative industries – perhaps even more important than in earlier times, because the market moves so quickly that if companies do not impose and abide by efficient financial controls, they may miss substantial opportunities to make sales and bring in revenue.

Financial managers and even managers of business units who are responsible for budgets and financial projections need to be more knowledgeable than ever before. They need to understand the terminology, processes, and documents that provide the structure for financial management. This chapter will help students understand how they can participate in the financial planning and management process to strengthen the probabilities that the work they are involved in will be successful. It begins with general concepts and then moves to the key documents and budget items of *managerial accounting* that underlie the strategies that guide managers' decisions. Finally, it presents *financial statements* that companies prepare to represent their financial situation to people outside the company.

STRUCTURES FOR MANAGING FINANCES

In a corporation or large company, the highest ranking financial manager is the *chief financial officer* or *CFO*. In a smaller business, the title of the position might be VP or manager of finance and accounting. The other positions within the financial department might be:

- **Credit Manager and Department:** Reviews credit history and establishes credit line for buyers of advertising time.
- **Collections Manager and Department:** Makes sure company receives the money due to it for the purchase of products or services.
- **Accounts Receivable Department:** Prepares and sends out bills for money due to the company.
- **Purchasing Department:** Conducts research to find best value proposition for the company's purchases and issues purchase orders to obtain needed items.
- **Accounts Payable Department:** Writes the checks for purchases of products, programs, equipment, and services and posts invoices to the general ledger.
- **Payroll Department:** Collects, processes, and maintains all documents related to paying employees, as well as taxes and benefits. Content-producing organizations will also have a dedicated royalties department, where monies are sent to the copyright owners of content licensed by the company or to creative contributors to original products who have contracts that call for royalty payments.

The finance and accounting unit will interact with every other unit in the organization.

Without financial support, no dollar can be spent, no employee paid, no project undertaken. All incoming revenue and outgoing payments are posted to a document called the *general ledger*. It is the core financial document, which contains detailed records of a company's every transaction.

FUNDAMENTAL FINANCIAL CONCEPTS

A few basic ideas and documents underlie financial management and the activities associated with it. The definitions of four words are the foundational building blocks: economics, revenue, expenses, and profit. The edifice of financial management depends on a clear understanding of these ideas.

Economics is the context of all business, including its financial aspects. Economics is a social science that looks at the production, distribution, and consumption of goods and services. *Macroeconomics* is concerned with a whole economic system, whether it is international, national, regional, or local. It looks at indicators of performance and structure of the entire system. The data compiled by macroeconomists describes the overall, big picture of the business landscape.

By contrast, *microeconomics* is the study of individual actors and their behaviors, whether they are distributors, sellers, buyers, or consumers. (In microeconomic analysis, actors may be one person or an entire company.) As a result, microeconomics often focuses on the range of choices available, the choices actually made, and the market conditions that result from those choices.

Revenue is the money that a business takes in from the sale, rent, or licensing of products and services to consumers. Revenue is income. Each sector of the creative industries exists in a market that favors some kinds of methods for generating income over other methods. For example, the broadcast industries such as radio and television have an advertising-supported business model. Companies in these sectors offer programming free to consumers and receive income from advertisers, who pay for air time to reach consumers.

Cable and satellite companies have a dual revenue stream: advertising and subscriptions. Some channels, such as HBO, Showtime, and pay-per-view, which are available as premium offers requiring additional subscription fees or per-use payment, have no advertising. Other channels – basic and enhanced basic channels like CNN, ESPN, and USA – bring in a *dual revenue stream* that includes income from both consumers and advertisers.

Companies that provide packaged products, such as DVDs and CDs, may participate in rental as well as purchase schemes to bring in revenue. The rental revenue model has much in common with other products that are offered on a short-term fee-for-use basis, such as rug shampoo machines or vehicles. The purchase revenue model resembles over-the-counter retail sales, in which consumers buy the product for a fixed fee, take it home, and use it as they wish.

In the past two decades, the revenue models for many companies that distribute information and entertainment products have changed from pure purchase to licensing revenue models. This change means that consumers don't "own" the products they have purchased; rather, they own the rights to use the products under conditions established by the licensor. Such conditions typically include restrictions on copying, even casual copying, supported by law enforcement agencies or civil legal action against violators.

It costs money to bring in revenue. *Expenses* are costs – the money businesses spend to create or acquire products, to bring them to market, and to operate from day to day. The *cost of revenue* is the category of expenses that are spent specifically to garner income.

There are two broad categories of expenditures: business or *trade expenses* and *capital expenses.* Trade expenses are costs incurred in the day-to-day operation of a business. They include everything from payroll and maintenance to letterhead stationery and the taxi fares of traveling executives. According to the U.S. Internal Revenue Service:

> To be deductible, a business expense must be both ordinary and necessary. An ordinary expense is one that is common and accepted in your trade or business. A necessary expense is one that is helpful and appropriate for your trade or business. An expense does not have to be indispensable to be considered necessary.[1]

Companies in the creative industries account for business expenses on an *accrual basis*, as opposed to a cash basis, as this is the method required by U.S. tax law. Cash-basis accounting means that income is reported when the cash comes into the company, and expenses are reported when the cash flows out. By contrast, accrual-basis accounting means that income is reported in the fiscal period when it is earned, regardless of when it is actually received, and expenses are deducted in the fiscal period in which they are incurred, regardless of when they are actually paid.

Creative enterprises have many similar expenses, as shown in Table 5-1.

Capital expenses are those expenditures made to purchase items that have asset value – buildings, programming, technology, vehicles, and mailing lists. These expenses are usually *amortized* over the life of the asset. "Amortized" refers to the way capital expenditures are accounted for, particularly with respect to taxation. Capital expenditures are deductible, because they are improvements to the business. Instead of deducting the cost of the asset all at once, it is amortized and *depreciated*, so that its value is spread across the time the enterprise expects to use the asset.

Media companies in some industry segments have expenses not incurred by others. For example, cable companies install equipment in subscriber homes. Although subscribers pay fees for the installation, they do not always cover the entire cost of maintaining a skilled staff or contracting for this work. Satellite companies pay substantial fees for the spectrum they need to deliver signals. Broadcasters pay FCC licensing fees. Internet companies pay for network bandwidth and utilization.

Table 5-1 Typical Expenses for Creative Industry Enterprises

Area of Expense	Typical Expenses
Content creation and acquisition expenses	Development, preproduction, production, postproduction, and packaging for distribution to consumers. Such expenses might include personnel and talent costs, costs for creative work by independent contractors, location fees, costs for sets, wardrobe, props, license fees for music, graphics and other materials produced by others, special effects, and consulting fees
	Licensing fees to pay for use of acquired content, created by another entity
Sales expenses	Personnel costs, third-party marketing consultants and services, revenue monitoring service, audience research, sales commissions and bonuses, travel reimbursement, marketing materials
Marketing and promotional expenses	Personnel costs, advertising, event expenses, promotional materials, and premium merchandising items (T-shirts, banners, key chains, and other giveaways)
Distribution expenses	Personnel costs, transcoding of products into formats required for distribution over specific technologies, local transmission fees, Internet streaming costs, film prints and duplication, and satellite transmission fees
Technical and engineering expenses	Personnel costs, contract payments for third parties, power and utility expenses, repairs and maintenance, transmitter and other distribution technology rents, supplies, vehicle expenses, and travel reimbursement
Information/interactive technology expenses	Personnel costs, Internet connection and web-hosting fees, internal networking, computers and maintenance, software licensing
General and administrative expenses	Personnel costs, banking fees, business licensing fees (FCC), insurance, legal and professional fees, office equipment and supplies, postage and freight, printing, software licensing, office lease, telephone expenses, third-party provider fees, and miscellaneous expenses

Source: Table based on material from Understanding Broadcast and Cable Finance.[2]

Assets are items that have economic value for the organization. *Current assets* can be converted to cash easily or are consumed within a year from when they are acquired. *Long-term assets* are items that are not easily converted to cash or have a longer useful life than 1 year. Types of assets include *capital assets*, *deferred tax assets*, and *intangibles*. All these types of assets appear on the long-term asset section of the balance sheet.

Capital assets are tangible assets, sometimes called *fixed assets*, such as property, buildings, equipment, and so forth. Deferred tax assets are expenditures for assets that are carried on the books in one year and can be deducted from the pretax earnings the next year. Intangibles include brand reputation, trademarks, and other nonphysical assets.

Many media companies require capital assets, especially technology. Purchases of technology are difficult, particularly in the digital area, because products change rapidly, making the timing of the purchase a tricky issue. Anyone who

Table 5-2 Planning for the Purchase of Capital Assets	
Type of Analysis	**Analysis Method**
Breakeven analysis	Determines the breakeven point of the minimum revenue needed to cover the cost of the asset, if profits were zero – but not less than zero. If it is clear that the breakeven level cannot be reached, then the purchase may not be warranted.
Payback analysis	Establishes the length of time needed to pay for the asset. Unlike breakeven analysis, this analysis focuses on time rather than results. However, it encourages capital investments in assets that can be paid for quickly, rather than long-term investments.
Discounted cash flow analysis **1.** Net Present Value (NPV) **2.** Internal Rate of Return (IRR)	The two methods of discounted cash flow analysis both rely on the concept of the time value of money (TVM) and present value analysis. Money now is worth more than the same amount of money next year because money acquired now can be invested and earn interest. ■ NPV analysis looks at a long-term capital purchases in terms of how much it will cost and how much profit it will produce, with both elements calculated in terms of how much they are worth in today's dollars. In other words, future money (both expense and revenue) is discounted, because it is worth less than money received today. ■ The NPV indicates value or size of the purchase; the IRR indicates its efficiency by calculating how much the investment will yield. There are two ways companies can think about the IRR of a potential purchase: If the IRR is greater than the cost of the capital to make the buy (its hurdle rate), then it will add asset value to the company. A purchase is also considered to be a good investment if its IRR is higher than the rate of return that could be earned by alternative investments, such as another capital purchase or a savings account.

Source: Table based on material from Understanding Broadcast and Cable Finance.[3]

has bought a computer recognizes that if it is a very good price, there is likely a new model in the offing. Yet if the purchase is made too early in the product life cycle, there may be bugs or other defects that will be corrected in later versions. Such problems can occur with products that cost millions of dollars, as well as with MP3 players that cost $100. Table 5-2 shows some of the analyses that companies undertake to define the costs and benefits of the purchase and reach decisions about purchasing capital assets.

Liabilities go beyond expenses. They mean all the responsibilities a company has assumed, including everything the company owes – expenses, accounts payables, taxes, and loan replacements. They may also include any financial judgments or penalties incurred by the business as a result of legal proceedings. They are usually separated into short-term and long-term liabilities.

KEY FINANCIAL STATEMENTS

Managers use the main financial statements, shown in Table 5-3, to make both strategic (long-term) and operational (short-term) decisions. Investors

Table 5-3 Main Financial Statements	
Financial Statements	
Document	*Useful Analyses for Decision Making*
Profit and Loss Statement or Statement of Operations	What is the bottom line (how did the company perform in the most recent period covered, especially when compared to other years)?
	■ What was the profit margin?
	■ What were expenses in relation to revenues?
	■ How much should executives be compensated?
Balance Sheet or Statement of Financial Position	What is the company worth?
	■ What are the assets?
	■ What are the liabilities?
	■ What is the nature of liabilities (short-term or long-term)?
	■ What is the value of owners' holdings?
	Has there been an increase or decrease in the value of the owners' holdings?
	What is the level of the company's future borrowing capacity?
	What is the value of long-term assets?
	Over what period of time can the company pay down debt?
Statement of Cash Flows	Where does the money come from and where is it going?
	What is the ability of the company to reinvest in itself?
	What is the ability of the company to pay short-term debt?

analyze them to reach decisions about putting money into the company. And government departments use them to regulate and to estimate and monitor tax payments, and to carry out other agency-specific responsibilities.

Many of the terms that appear in financial statements were covered in the previous section, such as revenue, expenses, assets, and liabilities.

Statement of Operations (Statement of Profit and Loss)

The Statement of Operations is more widely known as the Profit and Loss Statement or just the *P&L*. The Walt Disney Company calls this document an Income Statement, as shown in Table 5-4. It reports the bottom line – how profitable is the business over some period of time? After all expenses are accounted for, it documents how much money the company made, its profits. Ideally, corporate boards of directors will decide how much to pay company executives based on profitability. (In light of the recent near-collapse of the financial markets, executive compensation is a controversial topic, as there are some instances where compensation was high, even though the company was brought to the brink of bankruptcy.)

Analyzing the Walt Disney Company's Income Statement, it is clear that the company is profitable. WDC brings in a great deal of revenue: more than

Table 5-4 The Walt Disney Company Income Statement

Walt Disney Company INCOME STATEMENT (PROFIT AND LOSS STATEMENT) (U.S.$, in thousands)				
PERIOD ENDING	12/27/08	9/27/08	6/28/08	3/29/08
Total Revenue	9,599,000	9,445,000	9,236,000	8,710,000
Cost of Revenue	—	—	—	(8,419,000)
Gross Profit	9,599,000	9,445,000	9,236,000	17,129,000
Operating Expenses				
Research and Development	—	—	—	—
Selling General and Administrative	8,382,000	7,993,000	7,215000	15,231,000
Nonrecurring	—	—	—	—
Others	—	91,000	—	—
Total Operating Expenses	—	—	—	—
Operating Income or Loss	1,217,000	1,361,000	2,021,000	1,898,000
Income from Continuing Operations				
Total Other Income/Expenses Net	261,000	188,000	32,000	—
Earnings Before Interest and Taxes	1,478,000	1,688,000	2,228,000	2,042,000
Interest Expense	139,000	301,000	141,000	147,000
Income Before Tax	1,339,000	1,387,000	2,087,000	1,895,000
Income Tax Expense	488,000	490,000	712,000	712,000
Minority Interest	(6,000)	(137,000)	(91,000)	(50,000)
Net Income from Continuing Ops	845,000	760,000	1,284,000	1,133,000
Nonrecurring Events				
Discontinued Operations	—	—	—	—
Extraordinary Items	—	—	—	—
Effect of Accounting Changes	—	—	—	—
Other Items	—	—	—	—
Net Income	845,000	760,000	1,284,000	1,133,000
Preferred Stock and Other Adjustments	—	—	—	—
Net Income Applicable to Common Shares	845,000	760,000	1,284,000	1,133,000

Source: Based on data from Yahoo finance, http://finance.yahoo.com.[4]

$17 billion in the first quarter (with some carryover from the previous year) and more than $9 billion per quarter thereafter. It also spends a lot to get it – more than $15.2 billion in the first quarter and around $8 billion in subsequent quarters. (Note that figures in parentheses mean a loss, reduction, or decline; in other words, it is a negative, the same as a minus sign.)

Statement of Financial Position (Balance Sheet)

The balance sheet provides a snapshot of a company's assets, liabilities, and shareholder equity, or value of their holdings. The formula for it is: Assets = Liabilities + Shareholders' Equity.[5] The statement assumes that if all the assets of the company were sold off, all the liabilities settled and paid, and the remaining cash distributed to the shareholders, the balance would be zero.

The assets include current and noncurrent assets and receivables. The liabilities include expenses, taxes, and other financial responsibilities. Shareholders' equity is the value of the company's stock plus any profits or losses incurred in the period covered.

News Corp.'s balance sheet describes a company with enormous assets – totaling more than $52 billion at the end of March 2008, and more than $62 billion by the end of June 2009, as shown in Table 5-5. The company acquired more than $10 billion in assets in a single year! Moreover, during the same period, it accomplished this increase in assets by increasing its current liabilities by only $1.5 billion and decreasing its long-term (noncurrent) liabilities by almost $6 billion. The decrease in long-term liabilities is reflected by the more than $6 billion increase in stockholders' equity.

Table 5-5 News Corp. Consolidated Balance Sheets

News Corp. CONSOLIDATED BALANCE SHEETS (U.S.$, in millions)		
Assets	March 31, 2009	June 30, 2008
Current assets:		
Cash and cash equivalents	6,054	4,662
Receivables, net	6,348	6,985
Inventories, net	2,581	2,255
Other	503	460
Total current assets	15,486	14,362
Noncurrent assets:		
Receivables	273	464
Investments	2,515	3,284
Inventories, net	3,280	3,064
Property, plant, and equipment, net	5,739	7,021
Intangible assets, net	8,848	14,460
Goodwill	14,521	18,620
Other noncurrent assets	1,383	1,033
Total noncurrent assets	36,559	47,946
Total assets	**52,045**	**62,308**

News Corp. CONSOLIDATED BALANCE SHEETS (U.S.$, in millions)		
Liabilities and stockholders' equity:		
Current liabilities:		
Borrowings	2,076	281
Accounts payable, accrued expenses, and other current liabilities	5,295	5,695
Participations, residuals, and royalties payable	1,309	1,288
Program rights payable	1,191	1,084
Deferred revenue	905	834
Total current liabilities	**10,776**	**9,182**
Noncurrent liabilities:		
Borrowings	12,186	13,230
Other liabilities	2,701	4,823
Deferred income taxes	3,251	5,456
Minority interest in subsidiaries	666	994
Commitments and contingencies		
Total noncurrent liabilities	**18,804**	**24,503**
Stockholders' equity:		
Class A common stock, $0.01 par value	18	18
Class B common stock, $0.01 par value	8	8
Additional paid-in capital	17,330	17,214
Retained earnings and accumulated other comprehensive income	5,109	11,383
Total stockholders' equity	**22,465**	**28,623**
Total liabilities and stockholders' equity	**52,045**	**62,308**

Source: Based on data from Yahoo finance, http://finance.yahoo.com.[6]

Statement of Cash Flows

Cash flow statements, as shown in Table 5-6, give information about cash coming in and going out of the company's coffers. This statement is a little tricky to analyze, because the numbers show whether cash went in or out: positive figures mean cash came in; figures in parentheses indicate that cash went out.

Viacom's Cash Flow Statement covers 3 years, from 2006–2008. It shows a company handling a volatile economic situation, reflecting economic conditions in the overall U.S. economy. Throughout, the company reported relatively stable income, although the decline in 2008 corresponds with the problems in the U.S. economy.

Viacom earns about one-third of its revenue from advertising.[7] The large negative figure listed under inventory (4,731,000) in late 2008 occurred because the company decided to wait to sell advertising time until market conditions were more favorable. The inventory is shown as a negative because, had it been sold, it would have brought in cash. Financial reports in 2009 indicate that the strategy was successful, as advertising sold later earned 10 percent more than it would have earlier.

Although income declined, operating costs were the same or higher. The company responded by decreasing its investments in other companies but buying back some of its own stock. In 2006 and 2007, Viacom borrowed money; in 2008, it started paying it back, a negative effect on the cash on hand. Note that in 2008, more cash went out than came in.

Table 5-6 Viacom Statement of Cash Flow

Viacom			
CASH FLOW (U.S.$, in thousands)			
PERIOD ENDING	12/31/08	12/31/07	12/31/06
Net Income	1,251,000	1,838,100	1,592,100
Operating Activities, Cash Flows Provided by or Used In			
Depreciation	5,213,000	392,600	3,090,300
Adjustments to Net Income	215,000	3,590,400	738,500
Changes in Accounts Receivables	279,000	(367,300)	(18,200)
Changes in Inventories	(4,731,000)	(3,809,000)	(3,249,200)
Changes in Other Operating Activities	2,036,000	1,776,200	2,269,900
Total Cash Flow from Operating Activities			
Investing Activities, Cash Flows Provided by or Used In			
Capital Expenditures	(288,000)	(237,100)	(209,700)
Investments	(71,000)	—	—
Other Cash Flows from Investing Activities	(212,000)	485,600	(723,200)
Total Cash Flows from Investing Activities	(571,000)	248,500	(932,900)
Financing Activities, Cash Flows Provided by or Used In			
Dividends Paid	—	(170,000)	(206,100)
Sale Purchase of Stock	(1,275,000)	(2,039,000)	(2,028,200)
Net Borrowings	(280,000)	377,600	1,221,500
Other Cash Flows from Financing Activities	—	—	—
Total Cash Flows from Financing Activities	(1,555,000)	(1,831,400)	(1,012,800)
Effect of Exchange Rate Changes	(38,000)	21,100	20,500
Change in Cash and Cash Equivalents	(128,000)	214,400	344,700

Source: Based on data from Yahoo finance, http://finance.yahoo.com.[8]

FINANCIAL RESPONSIBILITIES IN THE AGE OF SARBANES-OXLEY

The *Sarbanes-Oxley Act of 2002* was passed by the U.S. Congress in response to a series of business scandals, including Enron, WorldCom, and Adelphia (a large cable multisystem operator). It is named after its two sponsors, Senator Paul Sarbanes and Representative Michael Oxley, and it is commonly referred to as *SOX*. The purpose of the legislation was to protect investors and the public by increasing corporate responsibility, accountability, and transparency. The act has 11 sections (called titles) that provide accounting and reporting rules, defining the practices companies must adopt.

The act requires embedded controls to ensure that companies meet accounting standards, as set by a Public Company Accounting Oversight Board, established in the legislation. The management of publicly traded companies must take financial responsibility – *chief operating officers* (*COOs*) and CFOs have to personally attest to the accuracy and completeness of the organization's financial statements and disclosures. Sarbanes-Oxley stiffened criminal penalties for financial crimes such as insider trading, destroying or altering financial records, interfering with investigations, or manipulating financial disclosures. With few exceptions, it prohibits personal loans to corporate officers and directors. It also provides some protection for corporate whistleblowers.

Title 4, section 404, requires greater financial disclosure, including off-balance sheet transactions and stock transactions of corporate officers. The company's annual report must contain a statement of management's responsibility for establishing and maintaining an adequate internal control structure and procedures for financial reporting and an assessment of these internal controls for financial reporting by management.

The required internal controls are specified in a framework called COSO, an acronym for Committee of Sponsoring Organizations, a voluntary private organization set up to develop the framework. There are five components that set criteria for defining an appropriate control environment, risk assessment procedures, control activities, information and communication, and monitoring.[9] In media companies, these requirements apply to such routine activities as advertising sales, orders, subscriptions sales and authorizations, sales commissions, special offers, talent and program, and information technology. They also apply to more general business activities – accounts payable and receivable, capital assets and projects, cash management, and financial reporting. Section 404 and these controls and reporting requirements are controversial, because they add significant costs for compliance, despite the fact that the costs are declining.[10]

A DAY IN THE LIFE OF SAM BUSH

I am the Senior Vice President, Treasurer and Chief Financial Officer of Saga Communications, Inc. Saga is a broadcasting company whose business is devoted to acquiring, developing, and operating broadcast properties. The company owns or operates broadcast properties in 26 markets, including 61 FM and 30 AM radio stations, 3 state radio networks, 2 farm radio networks, 5 television stations, and 4 low-power television stations (http://www.sagacom.com).

I grew up in Indiana, receiving my Bachelor of Science with a major in Management from Indiana Central University (now the University of Indianapolis) in 1979. I continued my education at the Krannert School of Management (Purdue University), graduating with a Master's of Science with a major in Finance in 1980. My interest in finance began while I was still in high school. Between my junior and senior years I started working for Union Bank and Trust Company as a teller. I continued to work for the bank in various capacities on a work study program during my senior year, as well as working for them during the four years that I was in college. This was a tremendous experience, as I was able to strike a balance between "the books" and "real-world experience."

After graduating with my bachelor's degree, I looked at various opportunities in the banking field and determined to obtain the one I wanted I would have to obtain a graduate degree which I did at Krannert. After graduating with my master's degree, I began the pursuit of a banking career, working for a number of institutions over the years, until I ended up helping to found the Media Finance Group in 1988. Ultimately, the group became a part of AT&T Capital, the finance subsidiary of AT&T. The Media Finance Group specialized in providing financing alternatives to the media industry, including radio, television, cable, telecommunications, and programming companies, growing to almost $2 billion in loans outstanding. I ended up as the Senior Vice President/Manager of the group before leaving to become Chief Financial Officer of Saga in 1997.

As chief financial officer of Saga, I have numerous responsibilities including those to our public shareholders, as Saga is a NYSE-AMEX-traded public company. Our stock trades on the AMEX market with a ticker symbol of SGA. On any given day, I may interact with one or more of our shareholders, one or more of the nine banks that participate in our debt facility, one or more vendors with which we do business including our suppliers, accounting firms, our outside general counsel, our Securities and Exchange Commission (SEC)

FIGURE 5-1. Sam Bush

counsel, and our outside Federal Communications Commission (FCC) counsel. Additionally, I will interact daily with our CEO, senior vice president of operations, human resource manager, the accounting staff, internal audit staff, and the information technology staff that reports directly to me as well as the management teams at our stations/networks.

On a daily basis, the first thing I do each morning is scan my emails to read the daily reports, newsletters, bulletins, and messages that I receive (not to mention the spam that comes through, no matter what you do). While email is an extremely productive tool to use in business management, it can also be one of the biggest time consumers and even time wasters. With email, it is easy to copy anyone and everyone on even the smallest details of an item and it seems that it is in vogue to make sure that everyone that could even be remotely interested in the subject matter gets a copy. While this can be helpful at times, it also creates the need to manage your email time. I could spend almost every working minute of every day just with email if I let myself. I manage the process by sorting my email into a number of categories, including those that I will go back and read immediately, those that I will go back and read when time permits, or those that I send to my administrative assistant for her to accumulate and collate along with all other emails on the same subject (so that I don't end up with multiple readings of the same material) and those that I put in a file to be read when I am traveling or have down time at home. My basic rule is that if I put something in this file and don't get it read for three months and I have not heard anything more on the subject matter, I delete it, as I presume that the parties responsible for handling the subject matter directly have done so.

Following my reading of email, I then move on to my daily/weekly/monthly calendar for a quick review of what is coming up both for the day, which I should already have prepared myself for, but also for the week and the month, so that I can begin the preparation process if a future meeting will require some background research or the development of particular materials in advance. Always make sure that when you are attending a meeting, whether you are the person that called the meeting or not, that you are fully prepared as well as timely for the meeting. Meetings should be held to a tight schedule to be effective and not tedious.

In conjunction with this daily routine, my schedule on any given day will have seasonal and situational variations. The main variations will revolve around the following occasions or situations:

- Earning releases (quarterly and annual) including a public conference call to discuss the releases in more detail
- Annual budgets for each station/network
- Quarterly board meetings including preparation of the board book, attendance at the meetings and preparation of any requested follow-up material (these meetings can be more often than quarterly if specific subject matter requires)
- Acquisition opportunities including sourcing, due diligence and closing
- Debt facility including required reporting, periodic information disclosure, and requested alterations based on business changes
- Special situations that seem to always arise and can't be anticipated

I won't go into great detail as to how my day changes during these times, as it mostly revolves around who I am spending the most time interacting with. For instance, during the 3 weeks prior and for a few days after the four quarterly earnings release periods, I will be a lot more involved with Saga's board, accounting and internal audit staff, auditors, and SEC attorney although I will still spend time with all other parts of the organization for reasons associated with both the releases being prepared as well as to handle my ongoing day-to-day responsibilities that continue throughout the entire year. During acquisitions, I will spend more than my normal time with Saga's CEO as well as more time with our business and FCC attorneys, the selling parties including their business, financial, and legal resources. During budget season, more time will be spent with the station/network management, the director of operations, and our controller. It always varies, depending on the subject matter and time of year.

My days also change dramatically when I am traveling on business. My annual travels include trips to visit bankers, investors, financial advisors, and potential acquisition opportunities, as well as our existing portfolio of stations/networks. The one other variation to my "routine" schedule is that for the past 4 years I have been on the Executive Committee of the Media Financial Management Association (MFM). MFM's mission statement is to be the premier source of education, networking, information, and signature products to meet the diverse needs of financial and business professionals in the media industry. Over the past 4 years I have held the positions of treasurer, secretary, vice chairman, and chairman of the annual conference; this year I am chairman of the association.

Balancing these responsibilities as well as managing the process and people that I am directly in charge of in addition to playing a role in guiding the rest of the organization that I am not directly responsible for is my biggest challenge. Sometimes the hardest part of any person's job is to impact decisions that are being made that you do not have direct decision-making authority for. In this case, you must influence and convince but not decide.

Each day has its own highlights, from finalizing a project to closing on an acquisition, from hiring a new staff or management person to helping guide a current individual's career development. While I never like to lose a good person, I am always happy when the job opportunities and career development that Saga has provided for an individual results in their having the opportunity to move on to a more challenging career opportunity. While Saga has almost one thousand full-time employees, we don't have a lot of career advancement opportunities, as these employees are segmented in markets all over the country. We always look to provide career opportunities across the entire company operation, but have found in a lot of cases that individuals will choose to stay in a particular geographic location due to family and other preferences, seeking career advancement with another organization.

Finally, management of any organization or any part of the organization is like a living organism. It is a continuous process of evolution, growth, change, education, and development. One of my favorite quotes is from Tiffany Wilson. She said "Life is not about waiting for the storm to pass. It's about learning to *dance in the rain*." This could not be a truer statement in regards to management and in regards to your relationship with management. Always look to not only do what is right but to do the right things and your career will not be just a job but an enjoyable life experience.

Daily Planner

Date: 8/17/2009   Sam Bush

17 August, 2009
Monday

July 2009
Su	M	Tu	W	Th	F	Sa
			1	2	3	4
5	6	7	8	9	10	11
12	13	14	15	16	17	18
19	20	21	22	23	24	25
26	27	28	29	30	31	

August 2009
Su	M	Tu	W	Th	F	Sa
						1
2	3	4	5	6	7	8
9	10	11	12	13	14	15
16	17	18	19	20	21	22
23	24	25	26	27	28	29
30	31					

September 2009
Su	M	Tu	W	Th	F	Sa
		1	2	3	4	5
6	7	8	9	10	11	12
13	14	15	16	17	18	19
20	21	22	23	24	25	26
27	28	29	30			

Remember	Appointments	Notes

Appointments

7 :00
  :30
8 :00 Michael Martin, E5Y
  :15
  :30
  :45
9 :00 Call Office (Ed, Warren, Marcia)
  :15
  :30
  :45
10 :00 Lee Westerfield
  :15   3Times Square
  :30
  :45
11 :00
  :15
  :30
  :45
12 :00
  :15
  :30
  :45
1 :00
  :15
  :30
  :45
2 :00 Karim j McLean, Lloyds
  :15
  :30
  :45
3 :00
  :15
  :30
  :45
4 :00 MFM/INFE-
  :15 Inland Press Call
  :30 Steve Nettler - ING
  :45
5 :00
  :30
6 :00
  :30
7 :00 Kristen Allen = CSFB
  :30
8 :00
  :30
9 :00
  :30

☑ ABC **Prioritized Task List**
  Bill Lewis-Cohen Capitol AMEX
  Tickets u2 Lansing
  Melissa Evans-Kronnert
  Quentin-WTMT Tower site
  Schedule MFM Exec Comm. Call
  Jackie-OMT

Time   **People to Call**

$Amt   **Expenses**

FINANCIAL MANAGEMENT SYSTEMS

Financial management software has been in place for more than 20 years. In radio and television stations, the activities of the traffic department and the record-keeping behind customers order of advertising time, the receipt of the ads (first on tape, now on servers), the on-air scheduling of the ads, and billing the advertiser for them were also put on computers and increasingly computerized. In the 1990s, broadcasters and Internet content providers developed sophisticated content intake and playout systems.

Today, these systems have to be integrated so that contemporary businesses can operate efficiently and meet the requirements for financial controls and reporting. In addition, most of these stations are part of huge conglomerates that must track, monitor, and report their financial condition. Thus, both operations of business units and the demands on the parent companies have pushed the trend toward enterprise-wide integrated information systems.

Oracle PeopleSoft is a good example of an enterprise system that will integrate many functions. Jaguar System 7 is an interesting product, with many media company clients, including National Geographic, RHI Films, Major League Baseball and Basketball associations, and other unnamed clients. It provides for computerized contract administration, revenue accounting, royalties receivables and payables according to contractual participations, and modules for budgeting, workflow, materials billing, marketing communications, and broadcasting inventory. It is particularly attractive to media companies, because it allows them to identify and quantify royalty payments and to reduce the risk of noncompliance with contractual stipulations.

In addition, media companies are facing a host of challenges surrounding intellectual property rights, piracy, security, and digital rights management (DRM). Yet the pervasive digitization of content forces media companies to embrace digital distribution. To protect their valuable content, they need decision frameworks and operational processes to control it. Control includes security and usage and consumption tracking, the means for which must be deployed over networks and managed through automated server-side systems. All this requires sophisticated infrastructure that will also need to be integrated with financial systems, so that they report consumer purchases of protected content. For example, suppose that you want to send a protected song or video to a friend. Some digital rights management protections will allow your friend to pay for the content you've sent.

MANAGERIAL FINANCE: STRATEGIC PLANNING AND BUDGETING

Companies operate on a *fiscal year*, which is typically January through December or July through June. The strategic plan and budget are topics of conversation in businesses throughout the year, and executives prepare regular reports to describe progress toward implementing the plan objectives and meeting budget targets, usually every month. Part of the overall plan and budget are efforts to create more value, including creating or acquiring new content or providing new services and improving existing ones. Managers of these efforts will be guided by the objectives and constrained by the budget.

The strategic plan looks at the big picture: What is the overall economic outlook? What are the trends in markets where the company competes or plans to compete? What technologies are fading or on the horizon? How are competitors doing and what are they doing? How are existing and potential customers changing? Typically these questions are answered by a SWOT analysis (Strengths, Weaknesses, Opportunities, and Threats).[11]

The budget is based on the strategic plan – it puts the money where the planning is and makes it possible for the business units of the company to set goals and to fund their implementation. Estimates of revenues and expenses come from the market conditions identified in the plan and contracts in the pipeline. Developing the budget is a yearly exercise that involves every department of an enterprise.

The Capital Budget and Budgeting for Infrastructure

An earlier section discussed the analyses that managers make before buying capital assets, including such items as property, buildings, equipment, and, in the case of content-producing organizations, the costs to produce original content. They are accounted for differently from routine purchases. Capital expenditures, sometimes called *capex*, are usually *amortized*, which means spreading the cost of the asset across multiple budgets (usually years). The reason for this accounting is that putting the cost for a large capital asset in a single budget would cause the year to show a loss when, in fact, the company will use the item for years. Most often, the money for such purchases is borrowed from lenders and then repaid over several years as well.

Infrastructure is a category of capital expenditure often made by media companies that requires special consideration. For example, some media companies own and operate delivery infrastructure to transport content. Broadcasters must build and maintain towers and transmitters. Internet companies need servers and bandwidth. Cable companies construct systems that serve neighborhoods – even whole towns. The largest media conglomerates may own and operate several types of infrastructures to serve their broadcast, cable, motion picture, and Internet holdings.

Infrastructure is expensive – really expensive. Large infrastructure projects are so costly and there are so many trade-offs between performance, reliability, and durability that they usually involve years of engineering effort and planning before they can even start. Most of the money to pay for these infrastructure improvements is usually borrowed from lenders.

In the 1980s, the industry spent about $15 billion building hybrid fiber/coax (HFC) networks, one-way cable systems throughout the nation to deliver the signals of many television networks.[12] The cable industry learned that it often costs even more to upgrade infrastructure. Between 2000 and 2002, the industry spent more than $45 billion to make cable systems two-way, in order to provide interactive services. Then the industry spent $14.6 billion in 2007 and an estimated $16 billion in 2008 to upgrade those systems to offer television, interactive, and telephone services.[13]

The cost of a satellite system depends on how many "birds" must be launched. Each communication satellite costs $75 million.[14] The satellite itself accounts for about 40 percent of the cost, the launch is about 40 percent, ground control systems are about 5 percent, and insurance runs about 15 percent.[15]

Many of the same analyses used to reach decisions about purchasing capital assets are also used to make decisions about building or buying infrastructure. These analyses might include breakeven analysis, payback analysis, or some form of discounted cash flow analysis. As a matter of self-protection, lenders will require companies that must borrow the money for infrastructure to present detailed evidence that there will be a sufficient return on investment to justify the extraordinary cost.

Budgeting for Content Creation

In content-creating media companies, there are two types of content creation budgets: continuing projects and one-off projects. Similarly, marketing efforts mirror the kinds of products and services the company offers: Marketing may support ongoing products and services, they may start off in high gear and subside to low-level support, or they can start up and then stop altogether. Media companies and business units that produce content put together the budget for the cost of production just as companies in many other industries do, particularly when they are creating similar content over time. For example, the audience for a television series and the cost of production are reasonably predictable. Similarly, managers can make good estimates of the likely costs and opportunities in the creation of follow-up albums produced by an established, popular music performer or group.

Content creation budgets are often divided into above-the-line costs and below-the-line costs, as mentioned earlier. Above-the-line expenses refer to those incurred before the production starts. It includes such costs as story rights and salaries and other related costs for writers, producers, directors, and actors and other performers. Everything else falls under below-the-line expenses – labor, administration, equipment, services, location fees, wardrobe and props, sets, office rent, and expendables.

Generally, the production of filmed entertainment is labor-intensive, so the largest part of the budget is spent on labor. The cost of key talent (especially actors) is a significant part of the budget for a typical Hollywood film. Above-the-line talent can often represent 50 percent of a production budget, and has been identified as one of the key reasons why the costs of Hollywood films have skyrocketed.

Planning, Budgeting, and Managing the Finances of One-Off Projects

Many content products are created just once; they are often called *one-off projects.* Examples of one-off projects can include television specials, videos, recorded music, packaged entertainment, videogames, and motion pictures. If the content is a hit, there may be a sequel or a prequel, but even these are typically treated as additional one-off projects, and they do not have the stability of expectations of ongoing projects.

There are some established ways of managing budgets for one-off projects. When the material is produced in-house, expenses are often managed directly by the organization's accounting department. Sometimes an in-house production unit is created with its own bookkeeping and accounting unit.

When outside producers contract to create videos, films, and television programs, they usually receive money in thirds: one-third to start, one-third on completion of principal shooting, and the balance upon submission of the final version. Contract producers typically submit a proposal that includes a description of the project, a budget, and a schedule, including the due dates of *deliverables*, such as dailies, rough cut, digital intermediate, and finished content.

Budgeting for Union and Nonunion Projects

There are both union and nonunion productions, and each has its advantages. Union workers are well trained and knowledgeable, both about the industry and their area of specialization. They know the formal and informal work rules that prevail on the set and in postproduction. They often have an impressive list of credits and have worked with the top people in the industry. In an effort to make union hiring more attractive, many guilds and unions have a sliding scale of pay and differential rules, depending on the type of production – motion picture, basic cable, prime time network, multimedia, Internet – and the size of the budget, from $500,000 or less, $500,000 to $1,500,000, and more than $1,500,000.[16]

Nonunion workers usually earn significantly less money, although producers must pay for payroll fringe benefits for all hires. Payments for overtime are less (or nonexistent) and there are no union penalties. Producers have more flexibility with nonunion workers, as they can be moved from one position to another.

Monthly Financial Reports

Managing finances requires information that is provided in reports, usually monthly or quarterly and, of course, annually. Many organizations circulate a Monthly Budget Report or Review to managers, providing an ongoing record of revenue and expenditures, referring to the yearly budget to compare estimated and actual performance. These reports are often early indicators of how the company as a whole and individual business units are doing.

Some companies prepare and circulate monthly formal financial statements as well. Publicly traded companies are required to file the quarterly 10-Q report to the U.S. Securities and Exchange Commission. This report includes the key financial documents mentioned earlier in the chapter: Statement of Operations (Profit and Loss Statement), Statement of Financial Position (Balance Sheet), Statement of Cash Flows, and Statements of Equity. In addition, the 10-Q discusses financial controls and procedures and legal proceedings and other risk factors that might affect the value of the company.

The specific documents and their names may vary from one organization to another, but the information about the business overall and for each unit, present similar information to managers:

- Changes in income, receivables, payables, and inventory levels, overall and by unit
- Changes in annual budget – income, expenditures, remaining funds

In addition to monitoring the budget, managers are held to specific measures of performance to show the progress they are making toward reaching the objectives of the strategic plan. Such measures are usually called *performance metrics* or just *metrics*. There are measures of financial performance and operational performance. Financial performance metrics include cash flow margins, liquidity ratios, and return on assets:

- Cash flow margins
  - EBITDA
  - FCF
  - BCF
  - OCF and OFCF

- Liquidity ratios and DSO
  - Liquidity ratios
  - DSO
- Return on assets (ROA)

Operational performance metrics are often specific to a segment of the media industries, such as broadcasting, cable, subscriber-based businesses, or multiple-product businesses:

- TV, radio, cable systems: Power ratios
- Cable: Bundle discount percentage of monthly recurring revenue
- Subscriber-based businesses:
  - Churn rate
  - Net gain/loss
- CMPUL: Contribution margin per unit

FINANCIAL STRATEGIES

All enterprises need to have financial strategies in place. Even business units that produce content, such as the advertising or public relations departments within companies, will need to justify their budgets by showing how their efforts contribute to the overall bottom line. They may not need to bring in revenue, but they will have to demonstrate how they support the goals of the organization.

For revenue-producing media companies, there are four principal financial strategies:

- Make money
- Save money
- Raise money
- Manage taxes

Making money means selling products or services to bring in cash. Saving money means reducing expenses. Raising money involves bringing in more money through investments or loans to fund activities. And managing taxes means arranging investment, revenue, expenses, and losses in such a way as to pay the minimum amount of money in taxes to a governmental unit, local, state, or federal, regardless of the country of the organization's headquarters or operations.

Most for-profit companies use all of these strategies. All of them require commitment and guts. Each involves some level of risk, requiring business acumen to overcome. For example, innovation in content products or delivery is often rewarded, but the risks (costs) may be high and rewards slow in coming. Finally, managing taxation requires the counsel of highly qualified professionals.

Making Money

Selling or licensing products is the purpose of creative businesses, so bringing in revenue always occupies a central place in financial calculations and management. However, there is truth to the old adage, "It takes money to make money." Because creative businesses increasingly distribute content digitally, it may cost less money than it did in the past or than it does for companies that engage in physical delivery. But less money does not mean no money: There are still marketing, sales, distribution, customer service, and overhead costs. In addition, creative products often involve equity investors, employees with royalty rights, and other copyright holders who must be paid for the use of their materials in a final product.

Companies must implement other financial management strategies, especially cost controls and careful accounting, if they hope to turn revenue into profits. Otherwise, income can vanish into a spending extravaganza. Moreover, taxation issues loom large when there are substantial revenues, so expert accounting is essential.

Saving Money: Cost Controls

One way organizations keep expenditures down is by implementing cost controls. The process begins by examining each line of the budget or breaking out the budget by line items. Auditors and experienced executives can spot figures that appear to be too high, at least at first glance. Over the course of the fiscal year, accountants will analyze how costs of individual budget items vary, called *variance analysis.*

Another method companies with multiple business units use to lower costs is to consolidate buying items that are used across departments, systems, stations, and facilities. As any householder knows, buying in bulk often lowers the unit price of individual items. This principle holds true for office equipment, including computers, some software licenses, and some content packages, such as television programming and music license fees.

Automation is another way to lower operating costs, although the initial capital investment may be quite high. Many broadcast and cable groups have centralized and automated operations, including sales, traffic, broadcast control, cable headend, payroll, and accounting. Large companies may also automate management decision making with such enterprise-wide software as SAP and PeopleSoft and content development and creation, using content management systems. Over time, the initial capital cost is recouped by the savings in personnel costs, usually a substantial portion of any company's operating budget.

Outsourcing is another technique that may save money. Outsourcing can take the form of moving jobs from inside to outside the company, to another state, or another country.

Moving a job position from a staff job to an independent contractor eliminates the costs of benefits that may be as much as 50 percent of the cost of employing a full-time worker. Many creative industry companies hire freelancers to perform creative tasks. And they also outsource technical, information technology, engineering, accounting, billing, and customer service work. Sales commissions are a common target for cost cutting. It's something of a delicate task – commissions can only be lowered so much, as they must be high enough to keep outstanding salespeople. Every sector of the creative industries has some kind of sales force, brokers, or middlemen that must be incentivized by the commissions they receive if they are successful. The terms of the commission must be clear and unambiguous for receivers, payers, and accounting personnel.

Capital expenditures should be considered especially carefully, often because of their sheer size. Usually managers must provide written justification for large capital purchases and receive approval from higher levels of management. Companies need to make particular efforts to consolidate purchases to obtain additional discounts. They must contact multiple vendors to review features and price quotes.

Other forms of cost control are inventory security and management, especially when the product is in digital form. A company insider can distribute the product for profit; a disgruntled employee can release it on a peer-to-peer network, undermining its commercial potential. Finally, companies should carefully monitor, document, report, and analyze expenses on a regular basis, focusing managers on the importance of cost control to people at the highest levels of the enterprise.

Raising Money

Financial management also includes laying hands on the money to finance content creation – a movie, video, or song – and whatever funding the effort requires to keep going. Each sector of the creative industries has a set of accepted methods for raising money, although innovation is always welcome (if it is effective). For example, new media companies often follow the path of obtaining startup money from private investors and investor groups, then taking the company public as an initial public offering (IPO). The original private investors may have an *equity stake* in the startup and they also receive favorable positions in the IPO, picking up more equity in the new public company.

In the motion picture industry, *equity* means that investors will participate in the profits the producers of the film hope to make.[17] The expensive production and distribution of movies are usually supported by a unique and complex series of investments and loans, including a *completion bond*, a guarantor who gives investors assurances the film will be finished for distribution or, if the picture is abandoned, agrees to repay many of the costs incurred in its production.

In the music business, music labels pay for the production, marketing, promotion, and distribution of the CD and pay the artist royalties after the label recoups its costs, essentially giving the artist an equity stake while retaining the copyright. In the television industry, the producing organization usually provides internal working capital to get the project started; follow-up funding may come from many sources, such as distributors, advertisers, and a host of others.[18] Smaller companies in interactive entertainment, advertising, PR, design, and creative services often have a monthly fee structure to fund their activities or they may require advance payment of some percentage of the budget for the development and production of a large creative project.

When companies raise money to found a startup or to finance a project, they hire people and fund development. In short, they spend that money, often very quickly, and sometimes in large amounts. The speed at which they disperse the money they have raised is called the *burn rate*.

Managing Taxes

"Anyone in business has to deal with a variety of taxes. Sales and use taxes, real estate taxes, payroll taxes, income taxes, and the rest are the stuff that governments run on. Businesses must develop wise and adroit ways of paying just the right amount of taxes, no more and no less than what is required," write J. Michael Hines and Geoffrey Christian.[19] Few people are more valuable in a thriving business than a clever and wise accountant who can find that precisely right amount of taxes the company should pay, finding the balance between saving the company money and keeping the company free from expensive battles with the various tax authorities.

However, in addition to the standard menu of taxes that must be paid, creative industry companies can take advantage of methods of reducing their taxes used by all enterprises as well as some tax shelters that apply only to companies who create and distribute copyrighted products. The list is long of tax considerations specific to creative works in general and the film industry in particular, as shown in Table 5-7.

Table 5-7 Managing Taxation

Tax Issue	Description
Tangible/Intangible Property	Are creative works tangible or intangible? It's an even more difficult distinction when considering digital properties. There are problems converting laws and rules that apply to tangible property to intangible property.
Ownership	Ownership may be splintered so that many people and organizations could have equity in creative works. In this case, it is difficult to identify "the owner," also making it difficult to identify which entity is responsible for paying taxes.
Rents/Royalties	Income from the licensing of creative works may be classified alternative as a *rent* or a *royalty*. Each form has its own rules with respect to taxation, which may be difficult to disentangle, particularly when combined with uncertainty over whether the work is tangible or intangible property.
Inventory	Are the rights to a creative work inventory items or capital assets? It's an important distinction, because the sale of inventory items does not qualify for treatment of the income as capital gains, taxed at a lower rate than sale revenue.
Partnership	When partnerships are formed solely for tax purposes, the company may be liable for taxation in the countries of both partners.
Foreign Production and Distribution	Motion picture studios and producers seek to reduce the tax burden imposed by nations. They arrange international ownership and production agreements and facilities to subject their profits to the least amount of taxation in all relevant jurisdictions.
Depreciation/Amortization	Some costs of making motion pictures and other creative works are immediately deductible. The remaining costs are amortized (depreciated) over time; that is, they are spread across the life of the product. Most companies forecast the income by estimating gross revenues and then pay taxes based upon that amount. At the third and eleventh years of the life of the product, the actual income versus the forecast income is compared. If the amount owed is greater, the producer pays the difference (with interest and penalties). If the amount owed is less than forecast, then the producer applies it forward against future income or other productions.
Participations and Residuals	Producers pay other participants in a production participation fees and residuals. Producers may deduct them in advance against forecast income or deduct them as they are paid out.
Advances	Producers often receive funds in advance of production. Such monies may be taxed upon receipt (cash method) or accounted for as loans (accrual method). Many deals are put together that provide producers with a letter of credit, against which they may borrow.
Financing Production and Distribution: Domestic Tax Shelters	Domestic tax shelters used to play a greater role in financing motion pictures, before legislation made their use by individuals less attractive. Today, they are mainly used by corporate contributors.
Financing Production and Distribution: Co-Productions	Significant tax benefits may accrue when two independent entities make deals that allow them to take advantage of national quotas or subsidies of one or both partners.
Financing Production and Distribution: Foreign Tax Shelters	Some countries offer investors in film production significant tax shelters. The deals based on them are usually quite complex and subject to interpretation by the various national tax agencies.
Talent and Taxes: Wage Withholding	Typically, producers prefer to pay everyone as an employee because they operate under significant liability if a tax entity rules that they should have withheld tax payments. Many creatives prefer to be paid as independent contractors, responsible for their own tax payments.

Tax Issue	Description
Withholding: Payments to Foreign Persons	Producers must withhold 30 percent of the employee's salary for taxes in the United States. There are some exceptions established by contract or treaty (with some countries), but these are often difficult to uphold.
100 Percent Deduction of Cost of Certain Films	The entire cost of audiovisual works produced for less than $15 million may be deducted if it is shot in the United States and meets a host of other criteria. Television series fall under this rule, with each episode counting separately.
Partial Exclusion of Income for Films Produced in United States	Similarly, producers may deduct up to 50 percent of the income derived if at least 50 percent of the budget was spent in the United States and the film does not include sexually explicit conduct. (Clearly, Congress intended to exclude X-rated films.)

Source: Based on information in The Biz: The Basic Business, Legal and Financial Aspects of the Film Industry *by Schuyler M. Moore.*[20]

SUMMARY

A mere chapter barely scratches the surface of the topic of financial management. Although the work may not seem to be as exciting as producing or directing or performing, plenty of new Internet startups have found it to be a thrill-a-minute as they raise money to realize their dreams. It takes resources – money, time, and people – to accomplish projects, large and small alike.

The chapter described the titles and work of financial managers and departments. It provided definitions and some examples of the main concepts needed to consider financial management. Then it turned to the key financial statements, with documents reported by some media conglomerates. It also looked at some of the recent changes to financial management, including the requirements of Sarbanes-Oxley and the emergence of enterprise-wide financial management systems. Finally, the chapter looked at strategic planning, budgeting, and financial strategies.

WHAT'S AHEAD

The next chapter turns to audiences, whether they are audience members, viewers, listeners, readers, users, or players:

- Audiences: Viewers, listeners, readers, users, and players
- Media channels, including television, radio, cable and satellite networks, print, the Internet, and games
- Content types, such as visual, audio, print, and interactive media
- Content genres, such as entertainment, news, information, and user-generated content (UGC)
- Matching content products to audiences and audience segments by creating, acquiring, aggregating, and indexing content

CASE STUDY 5.1 PERFORMANCE REPORTS

Business managers for television and radio stations are required to complete quarterly performance reports on their syndicated programs. Your current contract requires your station to pay the program provider a set fee of $2,000 per week with a 5 percent yearly increase on a 3-year contract. Your station is provided with 5 minutes in local avails per day for a program that airs Monday–Friday. There are usually 13 weeks in a broadcast quarter.

Create a spreadsheet that determines an average rate per spot required to break even and another that generates at least $24,000 in the quarter. What average rate will the station need to sell the program for in years 2 and 3 to pull in an average of $8,000 per month in profit? These are just hypothetical performance reports but will demonstrate the need to keep a close eye on average costs per spot in order to generate a profit on syndicated programming.

CASE STUDY 5.2 SETTING THE BUDGET

As the CFO of ABC Video Games, you are assigned the task of providing a financial projection on a new action videogame the company would like to release for the upcoming holiday season. The president of ABC Video Games is looking for no less than a 30 percent profit margin.

You have been provided with the authority for setting the budgets for each division, estimating the number of units that will need to be sold, and setting a price point for each unit. Create a spreadsheet that provides the following elements:

PROJECTED REVENUES

Projected Units to Be Sold
Suggested Retail Price to Consumer
Price Per Unit to Distributor (50% of MSRP)

VARIABLE EXPENSES (Cost per Unit)

Manufacturing
Box Art
Shipping

FIXED EXPENSES

Research and Development
Advertising Campaign

PROFIT MARGIN

This exercise is designed to take you through the steps of how to project what would be required from sales to turn a profit as set by management. Feel free to research an existing game on the market to fill in this very condensed version of a budget. It is more important to walk away with a sense of taking a financial view of a product and recognize the pressure to reach sales goals and stay within budgets. Remember, many projects end up over budget, which requires additional sales or the willingness of management to be flexible on the profit margin, but that is not likely to happen.

REFERENCES

1. U.S. Internal Revenue Service. Accessed June 18, 2008, at http://www.irs.gov/businesses/small/article/0,,id=109807,00.html.

2. Bumstead, T., Lueders, J. & Quiralte, F. (2008). Expenses. In *Understanding broadcast and cable finance*, W. McDowell & A. Batten (Eds.) for the Broadcast Cable Financial Management Association, 39–48. Burlington, MA: Focal Press.

3. Rizzuto, R. & Hartmann, L. (2008) Capital assets. In *Understanding broadcast and cable finance*, op. cit.

4. _____ (2009). Accessed November 1, 2009, at http://finance.yahoo.com/q/is?s=DIS&annual.

5. U.S. Securities & Exchange Commission (2007). *Beginner's guide to financial statements.* Washington, DC: U.S. Government Printing Office. Accessed October 4, 2009, at http://www.sec.gov/investor/pubs/begfinstmtguide.htm.

6. _____ (2009). Accessed October 27, 2009, at http://finance.yahoo.com/q/bs?s=NWSA&annual.

7. Vanacore, A. (November 3, 2009). Viacom 3Q profit jumps 15 pct on strong box office. *Associated Press.* Accessed November 4, 2009, at http://www.wtop.com/?nid=111&sid=1801945.

8. _____ (2009). Accessed October 27, 2009, at http://finance.yahoo.com/q/cf?s=VIA&annual.

9. Collins, M. M. (2008). Sarbanes-Oxley and internal controls. In *Understanding broadcast and cable finance,* op. cit.

10. PR Newswire (April 30, 2007). FEI survey: Companies see only slight increase in 2008 audit fees. Accessed October 18, 2009, at http://www.reuters.com/article/pressRelease/idUS114229+03-Jun-2009+PRN20090603.

11. James, L. & Kober, A. (2008). Strategic planning and budgeting. In *Understanding broadcast and cable finance,* op. cit.

12. Corley, S., Taylor, M., Shaub, J., Selvakrishnan, B., & Patel, K. (2007). *Cable industry analysis.* Presented at Merrill Lynch 3rd Quarter Media and Entertainment Conference, September 17, 2007. Accessed September 4, 2009, at http://74.125.95.132/search?q=cache:Qv2Iv4380z8J:www.rdhawan.com/emba/Class08/Cable_Tv.pdf+cable+industry+spending+on+infrastructure+1970s&cd=4&hl=en&ct=clnk&gl=us.

13. Santo, B. (November 1, 2008). Hey Dad, may I have some spending money? *CED Magazine.* Accessed October 18, 2009, at http://www.cedmagazine.com/Article-Cable-capex-spending-money.aspx.

14. Whalen, D. Communications satellites: Making the global village possible. Accessed October 30, 2009, at http://history.nasa.gov/satcomhistory.html.

15. _____ (2006). *Satellite FAQs.* Accessed October 30, 2009, at http://www.telenorsbc.com/templates/Page.aspx?id=667.

16. Honthaner, E. L. (2001). *The complete film production handbook.* Woburn, MA: Focal Press.

17. Moore, S. M. (2007). *The biz: The basic business, legal and financial aspects of the film industry,* 3rd Ed. Beverly Hills, CA: Silman-James Press.

18. Blumenthal, H. & Goodenough, O. (2006). *The business of television.* New York: Billboard Books.

19. Hines, J. M. & Christian, G. J. (2008). Expenses. In *Understanding broadcast and cable finance,* op. cit.

20. Moore, S. M., op. cit., 215–227.

CHAPTER 6

Media Consumers: Measurement and Metrics

Then head of Programming for NBC Television Brandon Tartikoff … was commenting on the take-over of CBS by Lawrence Tisch. Tisch was a consummate businessman and was going to make CBS "mean and lean" (his actual words at a press conference). He owned and ran many very, very successful companies in tobacco, insurance, and hotels, none of which were remotely like TV or radio…. Brandon respectfully said something to the effect that Tisch, although a brilliant and successful businessman, had never had to bring in a hit television show. Nothing about that had to do with business. It was all about everything *but* business. And without hit shows you're out of business. I thought it was a brilliant line from a brilliant guy. Long story short, they dumped CBS nine years later to Westinghouse … still dead last and the company decimated. I'm sure the shareholders were thrilled with his stewardship.

Pat Holiday[1]

CONTENTS

CHAPTER OBJECTIVES

The objective of this chapter is to provide you with information about:

- Audiences: Consumers and customers, viewers, listeners, readers, users, players, friends, and followers
- Research and content
- Identifying market segments
- Media consumers: Demographic segmentation
- Media consumers: Psychographic (lifestyle) segmentation
- Media consumers: Behavioral segmentation
- Measuring audiences
- Measuring audiences: Television
- DMAs, sweeps, and Nielsen ratings

DOI: 10.1016/B978-0-240-81020-1.00006-3

- Local people meters replace people meters
- Measuring audiences: Radio
- Measuring audiences: Print media
- Measuring audiences: Internet
- Measuring audiences: Videogames and other emerging advertising channels
- Media consumers and media companies

AUDIENCES: CONSUMERS AND CUSTOMERS, VIEWERS, LISTENERS, READERS, USERS, PLAYERS, FRIENDS, AND FOLLOWERS

Media content can be fun, entertaining, moving, fascinating, compelling, informative – even life-changing. We are all very familiar with the media experience as consumers. But media professionals think about media consumers in ways that are different from how consumers see themselves, just as the doctors think about patients differently from the way patients think about themselves.

The first two chapters of this book talked about the nature of the media and the people and companies that create content. In this chapter, the focus changes from creators, marketers, and distributors of content to receivers of content – as seen by media professionals. It looks at the nature of the content people receive, and the methods producers and marketers use to match receivers with content products. Providing content to people who would like to receive it is as much art as science – but sustained success does require that the science be every bit as sophisticated as the art.

All commercial ventures involve transactions between buyers and sellers or, as is the case in the media industry, sources and receivers. Media creators, distributors, and sellers must begin with the same approach as companies in any industry do – with their customers. The kinds of questions they might ask are: Who are they and where are they? How much money and time can they spend? What do they like, dislike, care about, ignore? What are their characteristics and media preferences and habits?

Both questions and answers may change for different media industry segments. After all, even the names they have for the media consumers are different. Fans that go to see the latest Kate Winslet blockbuster are movie-goers or theater-goers (reflecting the fact that they go out of their homes to attend an event); however, they may also be termed *viewers* or *audiences*. Mass media consumers are TV viewers, radio listeners, print readers, cable subscribers, and, when they purchase DVDs, buyers. For interactive media, the Internet has users, videogames have players, and some online games have subscribers. Facebook connections are friends and Twitter receivers are followers.

They all have in common that they are media consumers. Creatives are thinking up ideas to attract and delight them. Marketers are making plans to reach them. And many consumers are eagerly awaiting the next big blockbuster.

RESEARCH AND CONTENT

Media companies have several purposes for collecting information about media consumers. Before they produce or acquire content, they need to make sure there is a market for it. They need to convince advertisers to pay to reach them. And, if they want to market content directly to consumers, such as motion pictures, DVDs, magazines, newspapers, and so forth, they need to understand what kind of appeals will induce people to pay to consume it.

This chapter begins with a consideration of what the research tells media marketers about the size and characteristics of potential and actual consumers for content of all types – movies, programs, publications, songs, software, and games. Estimating the demand for a product is the job of *market research*; gathering information about how to communicate about the product to motivate consumers to buy it is called *marketing research*. In some segments of the content industries, such as radio and television, these types of research are called *audience research*. In print media, they are referred to as *readership studies*.

The purpose of all these types of research is to inform marketers, guide them as to how they should proceed, and help them reduce *risk*. Risk means that there is uncertainty about an outcome – it could be good; it could be bad. The movie could be a blockbuster; the movie could be a flop. The TV show could be a hit; the show could get cancelled after two episodes. The Web site could have 8 million unique visitors; the Web site could have 54 unique visitors, half of them company employees. By learning as much as possible in advance about the potential demand for the product, the characteristics and preferences of the potential consumers, and their likely reactions to the content, managers reduce the risks inherent in producing and marketing content products.

In theory, there is a regular cycle of audience research and content development and marketing, as shown in Figure 6-1.

However, in practice, the picture is somewhat different. Marketing consumers to advertisers requires detailed information, because advertisers demand it. As a result, media companies draw upon sophisticated research procedures to capture such data. Yet compared to the rich array of consumer research to attract advertising dollars, as well as to support new product development within most industries, content-creating companies have historically been much less creative about their research, sometimes appearing even reluctant to gather information.

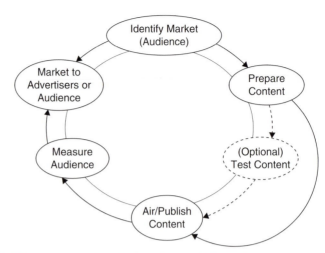

FIGURE 6-1 Audience research-content creation-marketing cycle

Some media sectors do use research. In particular, videogame companies conduct both formal and informal research before releasing games. Television executives and producers carry out some research before they put series on the air, although it is hardly extensive. For example, producers and networks conduct *concept testing* to see whether the idea of the show appeals to the potential audience. They also carry out *pilot testing* of a finished pilot, using the results to reshoot footage, change the ending, recast a role, or make other alterations. This type of research is sometimes called *formative evaluation*.

Companies that make radio programs, publish books, magazines, research reports and write papers, and design and publish Web sites conduct less research than television program creators. They certainly do considerably less research as companies in other industries, such as packaged goods companies. A review of consumer research in the project approval (green-lighting) stage of motion picture production by Eliashberg et al. (2005) notes that: "While maximizing the green-lighting success rate … is extremely challenging, it is staggering to discover how little 'science' usually goes into the process."[2]

To the extent that they collect data at all, there are two ways to get data. *Primary research* occurs when the organization gathers its own data. *Secondary research* is the use of data collected by others. In the media industries, market research typically begins with the analysis of data collected via secondary research – census, government-funded economic reports, and commercial data sources and market reports, such as credit card data or viewership data.

There are also two kinds of data and analytical methods: quantitative and qualitative. *Quantitative research* methods collect numerical data. It examines characteristics or behaviors that can be observed and counted – quantified.

For example, the number of people who play World of Warcraft online next Saturday afternoon between 3:30 p.m. and 5:30 p.m. (U.S. Eastern Standard Time) can be observed and counted by the game Web site's administrators. When there are large numbers of observations, it is not necessary to analyze all of them. Researchers can observe some of them: a *sample*. If the sample is representative of the whole, they can use statistical analysis to estimate the entire population or universe of potential observations.

Qualitative research collects information about a value or attribute that may not be observable by the researcher. An example is that a researcher can ask a group of people who watch *House* what they like about the show. She cannot observe their "liking." But she can ask them about it – what characteristics they like, how much they like them, when they like them, and so forth. She may even be able to tally the responses – quantify them – but that number will never be as important as the "qualities," the lead actors, the humor, Dr. House's snarky dialog, the medical animations, and so forth. Most likely, the research report will be a verbal summary of the session or interviews, with direct quotes highlighted to provide insight into the thoughts, beliefs, feelings, and attitudes of the respondents.

For most media content, if the information from secondary research suggests that there is a large enough market for a company to make the product and distribute it profitably, then the organization may go forward with that product. In the creative industries, there are established, known markets for content products. For example, in Chapter 1, the global market for entertainment markets, reported by PricewaterhouseCoopers as shown in Table 6-1, provides estimates that companies can use as a starting point to forecast the size of a potential market for a specific content product:

Table 6-1 Estimated Size of 2008 Global Entertainment Markets by Category

Industry Segment	Est. 2008 Market Size (billions)	2008–2011 CAGR (percent)
Filmed Entertainment	88.1	/4.9
Television Networks	181.4	/5.8
Television Distribution	172.3	/9.3
Recorded Music	36.4	/2.3
Radio	49.9	/4.5
Internet Advertising & Access Spending	242.2	/13.4
Videogames	41.5	/9.1

Source: Table based on report by PricewaterhouseCoopers.[3]

A DAY IN THE LIFE OF DEBBIE CARTER

**Debbie Carter, Vice President/Director of Sales,
Petry Media**

I am a VP, Director of Sales, and the thing I can always count on in advertising sales is constant change. Every day will be different from the previous. I have been in the business for 25 years. I started as a Sales Assistant and learned the ropes by taking messages on pink message pads and sending orders on a Twix machine that was similar to a typewriter but would produce a ticker tape of information; you would then dial up the station to send your order. There were no computers, no faxes, and no voicemail. Today, most transactions from ordering to invoicing are electronic.

The electronic advertising age is still evolving. We now have many more tools available with computers in the digital age. I work for a national television representative firm. My clients are television stations. Back in the 1980s, most TV stations were individually or family owned and operated. Now most TV stations are owned by a station group like Gannett or Sunbelt Communications, who own anywhere between 5 and 50 stations. Some groups will also own other media such as radio, newspaper, or digital.

My company is hired by TV stations to sell the commercial time they have available within their programming lineup. Some of the time is sold by the station's local sales team calling on smaller individually owned businesses within their market. My company sells to national advertisers, which include big names such as Wal-Mart, Wells Fargo bank, and McDonald's – large businesses that have multiple locations in many cities. These clients hire an advertising agency to plan, produce, and place their advertising dollars.

My day starts early, as I live on the West Coast and I have client stations in the Eastern and Central time zones, 2–3 hours ahead of Los Angeles. I begin by checking my email and reading the daily trades to make sure I am up on the latest information regarding the economy, updates on national advertisers and news to check what the competition is up to. As the director of sales, I am responsible for the national sales of our station clients. I am always planning the next quarter's sales and activity as well as monitoring current sales and revenue. My company has sales offices across the country that call on national advertising agencies in their region. I make sure all aspects of the business are covered from sales to planning to collections and troubleshooting. A typical day usually includes all of these duties.

Station sales managers will often schedule to come in and make calls to their most important agencies and buyers. A call sheet is made up with agency appointments prior to the stations arrival. Sometimes these calls are for a meal or event before or after hours. It is the sales rep's responsibility to accompany the client and make sure that they meet with key contacts and have a smooth and productive visit.

Organization and the ability to prioritize are key to success in advertising. I have approximately 25 TV stations across the country that can have several requests or needs. You think you have your day planned out until one phone call comes in with an urgent request that can change your entire day. You must have the ability to refocus and redirect yourself to the most pressing matter at hand. On a typical day, I will interact with TV stations' national sales managers, general managers, company sales reps, other directors of sales, as well as the president/CEO of my company. The most important tool I have is communication. It is critical to keep the flow of information moving to the stations, salespeople, agencies, and core management.

The most challenging issues I face often stem from lack of communication – a communication breakdown. People do their best work when they are working in partnership. Communication can help spark sharing of best practices, brainstorming creative ideas, or just keeping everyone focused on goal. When the lines of communication break down, people become frustrated and the doors open for misinformation and misunderstandings.

The best part about being in this industry is the opportunity to work and get along with many types of people. I have met people from all over the country and all walks of life. Getting to know and understand people and work together toward a common goal is very rewarding. There's a lot of hard work along the way, but it's well worth the payoff.

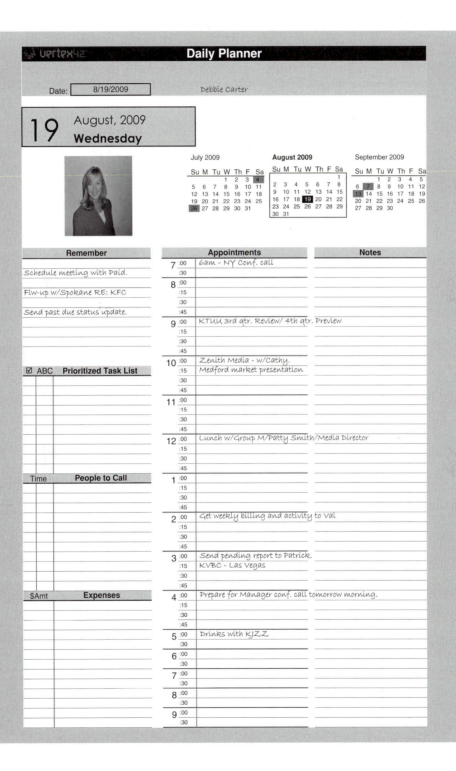

Daily Planner

Date: 8/19/2009   Debbie Carter

19 August, 2009
Wednesday

July 2009
Su	M	Tu	W	Th	F	Sa
			1	2	3	4
5	6	7	8	9	10	11
12	13	14	15	16	17	18
19	20	21	22	23	24	25
26	27	28	29	30	31	

August 2009
Su	M	Tu	W	Th	F	Sa
						1
2	3	4	5	6	7	8
9	10	11	12	13	14	15
16	17	18	19	20	21	22
23	24	25	26	27	28	29
30	31					

September 2009
Su	M	Tu	W	Th	F	Sa
		1	2	3	4	5
6	7	8	9	10	11	12
13	14	15	16	17	18	19
20	21	22	23	24	25	26
27	28	29	30			

Remember

Schedule meeting with Paid.

Flw-up w/Spokane RE: KFC

Send past due status update.

☑ ABC   **Prioritized Task List**

Time   **People to Call**

$Amt   **Expenses**

Appointments

7	:00	6am - NY Conf. call
	:30	
8	:00	
	:15	
	:30	
	:45	
9	:00	KTUU 3rd qtr. Review/ 4th qtr. Preview
	:15	
	:30	
	:45	
10	:00	Zenith Media - w/Cathy.
	:15	Medford market presentation
	:30	
	:45	
11	:00	
	:15	
	:30	
	:45	
12	:00	Lunch w/Group M/Patty Smith/Media Director
	:15	
	:30	
	:45	
1	:00	
	:15	
	:30	
	:45	
2	:00	Get weekly billing and activity to Val
	:15	
	:30	
	:45	
3	:00	Send pending report to Patrick.
	:15	KVBC - Las Vegas
	:30	
	:45	
4	:00	Prepare for Manager conf. call tomorrow morning.
	:15	
	:30	
	:45	
5	:00	Drinks with KJZZ
	:30	
6	:00	
	:30	
7	:00	
	:30	
8	:00	
	:30	
9	:00	
	:30	

Notes

IDENTIFYING MARKET SEGMENTS

Media companies use information they gather about the people who consume their products for many purposes: to forecast the appeal of a specific product to a particular consumer segment, launch new products, and refine and improve existing ones. For companies that own the means to exhibit, display, or present content to consumers (networks, stations, theaters, newspapers and magazines, popular Web sites and games, etc.), the most important reason to learn about consumers is to segment them into groups with specific characteristics to sell them to advertisers.

Consider this question: What is the product of television? Is it programs? Yes, television companies, particularly networks, do offer program products. They market collections of programs to other stations and overseas markets, a process called *syndication*. They repackage all the episodes of programs that aired in a season, put them on a DVD, and rent or sell the DVD through retail outlets and video rental stores like Blockbuster. They stream programs and parts of programs to enhance their web offerings, build traffic on a Web site, or sell them as downloads.

However, these revenue opportunities are not the media industry's only product: The other product is the audience. Specifically, it is people's attention that allows marketers to reach consumers with their messages, sometimes called the *eyeballs*. Consumers are a critical source of income to companies that bring media to audiences. Consumer segments are most often described with *demographic information*, such as geography, age, and sex. An example of a demographic segment is women 18–49 in the Dallas–Ft. Worth market or children 3–7 in the New York market.

Other consumer segment characteristics include psychographics and lifestyle (interests, opinions, attitudes, or values) and behaviors, such as voting, media preferences and habits, and so forth. Marketers rely on different combinations

Variable: Something that varies or changes. For example, a person can be male or female, live in an urban, suburban, or rural location, or earn between nothing and millions, even billions, of dollars per year.

Universe: A specified population of consumers. A universe could be all consumers, all women, all teenagers, all suburbanites – the universe depends on the group (or population) under consideration.

Sample: A subset of a population or universe.

Consumer segment: A group of present or potential customers with some common characteristic that is relevant in explaining (and predicting) their response to a supplier's marketing stimuli.

of variables, depending on what they are selling. They don't just sell products; some sell ideas or candidates. For these messages, the advertising effort may need to know other characteristics of the consumer. An effort to recruit for an anti–property tax campaign might seek registered voters, who vote or lean Republican, making more than $60,000, suburban, married with children, own their home, have strong religious beliefs, and support small government. In this example:

- **Demographic:** $60,000+, own home, suburban, married, have children
- **Psychographic (lifestyle):** Lean Republican, strong religious beliefs, support small government
- **Behavior:** Registered voter, vote Republican

Media companies try to attract consumer segments that have certain characteristics. Classic criteria for desirable segments are:

- **Identifiable:** It is possible to identify potential customers.
- **Accessible:** It is possible to communicate with people in the segment and to deliver content products to them.
- **Substantial:** The segment is large enough to justify a marketing effort that will result in a profit or other desirable outcome.
- **Unique wants and/or needs:** The marketer needs to be able to match a specific segment to their products or mix of products.
- **Durable:** The segment needs to exist for a sufficient time to communicate with them and to deliver products. This is a particularly important consideration for content companies, whose hit products may last for only a short time.

Media Consumers: Demographic Segmentation

Demographic variables of interest to most buyers of consumer segments include such characteristics as age, sex, ethnicity and nationality, marital status, location of residence, number of adults and children in the household, socioeconomic level, household income, employment status, occupation, education level, and so forth.[4] Virtually all marketers and communicators want to gather and analyze demographic information about actual and potential customers, because it is a crucial indicator of the kinds of products they need and want. Toy companies want to reach children. Food companies seek women. Beer makers target men. Many pharmaceutical concerns market to older consumers.

A key demographic variable that marketers usually want to know is geography: Where is the consumer? Traditionally, the answer to this question was a physical place – a city, a state, a region, a country, even a continent. Some industry sectors use the term *geographies* and others use *territories* to describe location-based markets; the two terms mean the same thing. Broadcasters use the term *designated market area (DMA)*, used by Nielsen to define a local television market. Some of the geographic considerations that can affect the kinds of content products consumers might buy are whether they live in a rural or metropolitan area, the climate of the region, and the availability of high-speed Internet access.

However, the question "Where are they?" takes on a different meaning in the Internet age. Today, the answer may be a virtual location: Which media platform does the consumer respond to and use to communicate? Which Web sites do they visit? Which social networks do they frequent? Which blogs do they read? How much information do they seek with their mobile phone?

In short, in some new media marketing efforts, physical geography takes second place to characteristics of media use. Brick-and-mortar retail establishments still want to reach customers who live in a particular place, even a particular neighborhood. But companies like Amazon don't really care where people live and work, and it makes little sense for them to try to reach consumers by geography; rather, they want to communicate with people who buy products online, no matter where they actually live.

Media Consumers: Psychographic (Lifestyle) Segmentation

Demographic data tells a marketer a great deal – but not everything. Two men may each live in Akron, Ohio; be 33 years old; be married with three children; earn $48,000 a year; drive Ford Explorers; and work in the computer industry. But these shared commonalities do not mean that they engage in the same activities, have the same interests, opinions, attitudes, or values. As a result, they probably consume very different content products.

Demographic variables describe external factors; psychographic variables describe internal factors. Psychographic information includes such items as interests, opinions, attitudes, values, and lifestyle – these are the criteria used to define consumer segments based on psychographic (or lifestyle) characteristics. A complete psychographic profile may also describe in detail the person or the segment's religious, political, and other personal preferences. A communicator is likely to choose a specific set of variables to narrow the universe of receivers down to the best potential prospect for the message. Demographic and psychographic variables work together to give a more complete picture of consumer segments.

Media Consumers: Behavioral Segmentation

If demographics describe what people are and psychographics describe what they believe, behavioral variables describe what they actually do. How do they vote? How often do they actually attend church? What organizations have they joined, and so forth? Most important to marketers are the answers to questions like how often they shop, where they shop, and how much they spend.

Media companies that market content want to know: What media do they use? What kind of content have they purchased in the past? What information do they need to know and where do the currently get it? How do they want to pay? As life circumstances change, such as a generation of college students graduating and entering the workforce, marrying, having children, raising children, and leaving the workforce in retirement, how do their information needs and wants change?

Most communicators want the target of their messages to do something, to take an action. Behavioral information offers a special value about a segment because the data offers insight into the likelihood that a message can convince receivers to act in the desired way. In short, it is directly linked to the goals of the communicator, whether encouraging a purchase, a vote, or some other action.

Measuring Audiences

Every content-based business needs to know how many people are listening, watching or reading their product and as much as possible about their characteristics. Each industry segment measures some specific aspects of behavior, yet they share some common methods as well. They all use technology to measure behavior – what do consumers actually do? They use surveys to ask individuals about themselves, their media habits, and their opinions about genres and specific content products. And they use focus groups and depth interviews to probe the deepest thoughts and feelings of a small number of consumers to understand more about why consumers act, think, and feel the way they do.[5]

At the same time, each industry segment has specific questions they want to ask that apply to their content products. They may also differ in the access they have to their customers. For example, Internet content providers can measure clicks and the amount of time they spend on a site precisely, down to the nanosecond. Using Portable People Meters™ (PPMs™) and personal diaries, as shown in Figure 6-2, radio broadcasters can measure listening behavior continuously. However, the Arbitron service that collects listening data reports listenership in 15-minute increments. Game companies, newspapers and magazines, and cable companies can measure subscriptions in addition to media use; free over-the-air TV companies and open Web sites can measure only usage.

When media students listen to the radio or watch a TV show, they should take special note of the advertisers they hear or see. They will notice distinct types of advertisers that appear on the media they consume, even the Web sites they frequent. They will quickly figure out who advertisers think is listening or watching. As a result, those who have become aware of such segmentation are unlikely to ever listen to a radio station, watch TV, watch movie trailers before a movie at the theater, or play a videogame without recognizing how advertisers are targeting *them*!

Your opinion counts

Use this space to make any comments you like about specific stations, announcers or programs.

Towards the end of this week my radio listening became somewhat ampical as the war w/irag began. I usually listen to classical stations, or XXXX my 10 yr old daughter prefers easy listening rock. This week I listened to NPR more than usual.

Your opinion counts

Use this space to make any comments you like about specific stations, announcers or programs.

Because of the on going talk of a possible war, I feel that I listened to talk shows more than usual this particular week of the survey.

FIGURE 6-2 Examples of Arbitron diaries. *Source: Arbitron.*

Measuring Audiences: Television

In the television industry, the results of measurements of the number of people watching a specific program on a specific channel, at a specific time, are provided by the *ratings*. They also provide basic demographic data about the audience that is watching the program, including geography, sex, and age. Thus, the overall rating might be 9.4, the rating for men 18–49 might be 14.2, and for women 18–49, 3.2 – this result could apply to a hockey game, for instance.

More detailed information about viewers, such as lifestyle, purchasing behavior, and media use, may be provided by the company that gathers ratings data for the television industry, the A. C. Nielsen Company. Data about viewers may also come from a third-party research firm, hired by the program producers, TV network, or advertisers who want to understand more about the programming environment where they are placing commercials for their products. For example, if a program has a violent or sexual content, the advertiser might want to make sure that it does not affect public perception of the brand in a negative way.

Knowing about potential and actual audiences is crucial to broadcasters. Thus, companies specializing in providing such information to radio and then television networks and stations emerged early in the history of the industries. These research firms are sometimes criticized for not being accurate. However, they have existed for nearly a century, constantly refining the methods by which media companies can determine the level of popularity of a product.

Each industry has its own most widely used research firms and *metrics*, just as Nielsen serves the television industry. For newspapers, ABC, the Audit Bureau of Circulation, has measured readership and circulation numbers for newspapers since 1914. Radio companies turn to Arbitron, founded in 1949, to identify listenership levels. Metrics are the specific measurements that are reported, such as viewership metrics (TV ratings), listenership metrics (radio ratings), readership metrics (number of subscribers and newsstand sales), and Internet metrics (unique site visitors, click stream patterns, conversion of click-throughs to sales), and so forth.

Both Nielsen and Arbitron are now in the process of developing new methods to measure demographic data for Web site traffic, mobile phone applications and out-of-home media habits. As technology advances, these long-standing companies are faced with the challenge of how to accurately identify these new behaviors and habits of consumers. An A. C. Nielsen subsidiary, Nielsen/ AdRelevance, is a leading data provider about advertising spending on new media. Another A. C. Nielsen company, Claritas, performs *market segmentation*, separating consumers into different groups based on demographic, psychographic, or behavioral characteristics. Claritas also uses these characteristics to predict how the people in a particular segment might behave in the future, a field of study called *data* or *predictive analytics*.

Sweeps, DMAs, and Nielsen ratings

Before examining the details of obtaining audience data for television, it is important to understand some of the basic terminology. It is difficult to over-estimate the importance of measuring viewers for the television industry. The industry business model, income, and ability to make a profit depend on confidence in the measurement of viewers. Now this measurement takes place daily, but in the early days of television when there were no people meters, it was only feasible to measure quarterly four times a year, in February, May, July, and November, the *sweeps*. The following sections describe some of the key terms used in the TV industry to describe the way the industry learns about its viewers.

Measurement Terms

- **Sweeps (sometimes called Ratings Months):** Four times a year, in February,* May, July, and November, Nielsen measures the television station audience in each DMA to determine the number of viewers by demographic categories. Sweeps begin on a Thursday and end on a Wednesday, a tradition begun many years ago by NBC. The ratings and share metrics reported by Nielsen are a report card of sorts, where television stations are graded on pure audience numbers.
- **DMA (Designated Market Area):** A geographic area, comprised of one or more counties, defined by Nielsen as a television market. Each year, Nielsen ranks each of the 210 DMAs by size. For example, New York City geographically reaches 7,433,820 TV households and is ranked as DMA #1, as it has the most in the United States. These rankings are reviewed yearly and based on changes in population can either move up, drop down, or simply stay the same.

---

* In 2009, Nielsen moved the February ratings to accommodate the original DTV conversion on February 17 that was then moved to June 12, 2009. This conversion was a government mandate that required TV stations across the country to switch from an analog to a digital signal.

For example, when New Orleans was devastated by Hurricane Katrina, the population dropped drastically and along with that change in population, so went the DMA ranking. For the 2008–2009 television season, New Orleans was ranked as DMA #53 with 602,740 households (HH). Before August 2005, there were over 672,000 TV HH and it was ranked #43. In fact, the devastation to that area resulted in Nielsen suspending ratings research for over a full year, until February 2007. This suspension of measurement had never taken place before in the history of the Nielsen Company.

- **Daypart:** The broadcast day is divided into dayparts to help programmers plan programs that people will want to watch at a particular time and to set prices for advertising. For example, few people want to watch *Desperate Housewives* at 7:30 a.m. or a morning talk show at 10:00 p.m. TV dayparts are:
  Early morning: 5:00a.m–9:00a.m
  Daytime: 9:00am–3:00pm
  Early fringe: 3:00pm–5:00pm
  Early news: 5:00pm–7:00pm
  Prime access: 7:00pm–8:00pm
  Prime: 8:00pm–11:00pm (M-Sat), 7:00pm–11:00pm (Sunday)
  Late news: 11:00pm–11:30pm
  Late fringe: 11:30pm–2:00am
  Overnight: 2:00am–5:00am
- **Panels:** Refers to the group of individuals who comprise those participating in the Nielsen ratings.
- **Diaries:** A paper booklet that is completed by those in the panel to represent the viewing habits by each person in the household.
- **Set Meters:** Devices that are connected to a participating Nielsen household and that capture the channel(s) being viewed.
- **People Meters:** A box that is hooked up to each TV set and is accompanied by a remote control unit. Each member of the family is assigned a personal viewing button, which is matched to that person's age and sex. Whenever the TV is turned on, a light flashes on the meter, reminding viewers to press their assigned button.
- **Local People Meters (LPM):** A new type of People Meter is in the process of being rolled out. The LPM offers several improvements over the older People Meter technology: (1) it measures continuously, not just during sweeps periods; (2) it captures data from individual viewers in the home by giving each person a code to punch in when watching TV.
- **Portable People Meter:** Carried by radio listeners, Arbitron gives these meters to people in their sample to measure their listenership when they are on the go because so much of radio listening occurs out of the home.

The Metrics (Results of the Measurement)

- **TV HH (Television Households):** The number of households with television sets within a given DMA. When calculating ratings, this number is often referred to as the *television viewing universe*.
- **HUT (Houses/Homes Using Television):** HUT levels can change throughout the day and typically reach their peak during prime time.
- **PUT (Persons Using Television):** Whereas HUT levels measure homes, PUT levels calculate the total number of persons viewing television with their sets turned on.
- **Rating Point:** The percent of the universe of households or persons viewing a program during the average minute. For example, *Days of Our Lives* earns a 5.0 HH rating point. That means that 5 percent of all television households in that DMA were watching to see if Sami Brady was up to her old tricks.
- **Share:** The percent of TV sets in use (or persons viewing) tuned to a program. This differs from rating as that number is calculated on a fixed number of TV households. As an example, *Deal or No Deal* earns a 20 share. That means that 20 percent of all TV households with their television set turned on were watching Howie Mandell open the next case.
- **Impression:** An instance of a consumer's attention to an advertiser's message.
- **Cost-per-thousand (CPM):** Advertisers pay an amount per one thousand television viewers or radio listeners. The *M* in CPM stands for the French word *mille*, which means thousand in that language.

The Pain of Precision as Local People Meters Replace People Meters

The traditional People Meter didn't so much measure people as it did sets. Placed on the back of the set, it measured the channel to which the set was tuned. For a number of years, it has been attached to a telephone line, so the meter could automatically dial up a remote computer and download its measurements. From that data, local stations who paid for the service received the *overnights* the next morning. In order to collect information about people, Nielsen relied on *diaries*, filled out by a member of the household appointed to track who watched what and when. Naturally, there was limited participation, flawed record-keeping, and heavy reliance on (perhaps) unreliable memory.

Local People Meters (*LPM*) make more precise measurements, because they really do measure people. The residents of a household are each given a code that they input when they watch TV. Nielsen has already gathered information about each person, so given the code, the ratings service can match the tuned in TV channel with demographic characteristics of the individual watching. In addition, without the imposition of writing diaries, using LPMs enables Nielsen to meter a larger number of households. This larger sample means that the statistics the company reports are more accurate and reliable.

Starting in 2004, Nielsen began rolling LPMs in the top TV markets, beginning with Boston, New York, Los Angeles, Chicago, and San Francisco. By the end of 2009, the top 25 TV markets had LPMs, accounting for nearly 50 percent of the U.S. television viewing audience. The original plan called for a continued rollout through 2011, putting LPMs in the top 56 TV markets.

However, in 2008, Nielsen announced that it would reconsider the rollout schedule after placing LPMs in the top 25 television markets:

> We all face a very challenging economic climate. Our clients have made it clear that we need to work closely with them to establish the right pacing of LPM rollouts, determine the right business model in light of current market conditions, and identify the most appropriate People Meter technology for these mid-size markets. As 2009 progresses and the economic condition becomes clearer, we will be better positioned, along with our clients, to adjust our moving forward plans.[6]

The introduction of LPMs has proved to be quite controversial. Although the more accurate measurements have generally increased size of the audience, it also redistributes a substantial amount of viewing away from broadcast channels and toward cable channels. The large change in ratings has negatively affected broadcasters, substantially reducing the amount they are able to charge advertisers. In Miami, the local Fox affiliate WSVN-TV is suing Nielsen, claiming that inaccurate data costs the station $12 million a year in lost revenue.[7] By contrast, cable companies are elated with the increased viewing of cable channels the new devices report.

From the Desk of Lisa Poe-Howfield, General Manager, KVBC-TV, Channel 3, Las Vegas

Leading up to the ratings months, the promotions and news departments are busy at work analyzing the competition, their previous ratings to search for success stories, and previous failed attempts to garner audience. Larger stations may have a full-time research analyst who specializes in reviewing and analyzing the measurement results to provide direction for the station to be more successful in attracting as many viewers as possible.

TV and radio stations live (and die) by the ratings. A good rating means receiving higher advertising rates to bring in more revenues to the company. They guide the development of content during sweeps and beyond. The news division will present ideas for *sweep pieces* that are targeted at raising viewership among favorable demographic audience segments – those likely to generate the most advertising revenues.

FIGURE 6-3 Lisa Poe-Howfield. *Source: Lisa Poe-Howfield*

Once stories are approved, producers write rough scripts, photographers shoot the footage, editors edit the pieces, and the on-air talent presents the story as you see it on television. The stories are strategically placed in newscasts that will have the potential to be the most successful. In the meantime, the pro- motions division will create teasers and promotional spots to air in specific programs that are most likely to drive eyeballs to a specific newscast. These promotional spots need to be creative and clever, but representative of the final product. (There is no worse backlash from the public if a TV station overhypes a story, but does not deliver.) It is a very fine line, as the goal is to create a *need* to watch a story.

Over the course of these four weeks, larger TV stations appoint a *ratings team*, composed of the top executives, such as the general manager, sales manager, news director, and research analyst, who will meet regularly to see how the game plan is working. Monitoring of ratings and shares can occur daily for those cities which are *metered markets*. In the larger cities, Nielsen connects People Meters to participating families, which are able to read every channel that is tuned in to a TV set.

The data from the meter is fed to Nielsen Media Research in Florida from 50 markets each night and transmitted back to the stations by the next morning. Considering that the broadcast day ends at 4:59 a.m. and starts at 5:00 a.m., it is very impressive that these numbers can be relayed so quickly. The metered numbers are broken out in 15-minute intervals, and, if needed, Nielsen can provide special reports that show minute-to-minute viewing habits.

Most People Meters only provide household data, although some meters allow individual household members to enter a code to indicate who is watching. For the most part, in order to determine the demographic characteristics of viewers, Nielsen collects diaries from a select number of households that provide data about all the programs people in the home have watched during one week. These diaries are mailed to a new panel of homes each week, and over the course of a year, the company analyzes about 2 million diaries.[8]

In smaller markets, viewers do not have set meters attached to their TV sets, so stations may have to wait as long as a month to determine whether they did well, until all the numbers have been received and calculated. In the larger markets with people meters, the diaries serve as part of an equation to determine the viewing habits of several demographic groups. Typically, age and sex define these groups, such as females 18–49 and males 18–49.

Usually within a month after the sweeps period, TV stations receive the much-anticipated ratings book. (Yes, they still send hard copies by snail mail.) Many stations also receive the electronic feed of the data and begin to decipher the numbers as soon as they are available.

If a station earns the #1 ratings in households for their evening newscast, the promotions department will quickly put a promotional spot on the air to let viewers know. When a station did not earn the #1 spot, the research analyst will look for a way to put the station on top. For example, maybe the newscast was first in the category of females aged 18–34. That qualifies for a promotion, right?

This practice explains why many people are not sure who is really number one in news, because every news station begins running spots about winning. Usually, the TV stations will provide the source of that message in the fine print of the spot, but in a 15-second or even a 30-second spot, most people are unable to read and comprehend the source data. It is also not unusual to see some TV stations run ads that they are #1 in a particular newscast without the source. When confronted on this matter, the promotions department can claim that they took a survey from their Web site that indicated they were first. That type of promotional strategy will drive many others in the business crazy, but it is difficult to stop.

After the ratings are completed, the fun is just beginning. The most recent ratings will now exercise a strong effect on the amount of money the station can charge advertisers to air a commercial on any program. The ratings are imported into a software system and the sales managers review them to see whether there is a need to raise or lower any advertising rates. The number of commercial spots, also called *avails*, available in a program will also influence the rate.

For example, if a program only has three avails (commercial spots), even though the rating is low, the station may be able to ask for a higher rate because there are so few spots. *Advertising clutter* is the reason – when there are many commercials in a row, viewers pay less attention to each one. So a commercial that runs in a program with fewer spots may actually perform better than one airing in a program accompanied by a large number of spots. Determining the correct rate that will make a program effective and attractive to advertisers is the job of the sales manager, and the task can be extremely difficult. In the end, the audience research is key to estimating how many households and persons are watching so that a television station can provide a proper rate and generate revenues needed.

It is clear that ratings are of paramount importance to the profitability of the station. However, programming managers, who determine the programs airing on the station, and the news staff more often look at shares. Shares tell them what percentage of the audience that was viewing at the time watched the show, as contrasted with ratings, which report the percentage of the audience that has a TV set in the home, on or off at the time. In other words, shares report how well a program did against the competition, and that measure means a lot to the people working day in and day out creating shows.

Advertising agencies and media buyers look at the same Nielsen data, but from a different perspective. They buy entire demographic groups that number in the thousands, even millions of individual consumers. They pay a dollar amount based on *cost per thousand* or CPM. They pay for consumers, but that's not what advertisers really want – they want consumers' attention to their messages. In order to ensure they capture that attention, they run ads over some period of time, sometimes called a *flight*. The term agencies use to describe an instance of attention to their messages is *impression*. An agency might say: "Our CPM is $(cost) and we will get 12 million impressions over the entire six-week flight."

Measuring Audiences: Radio According to Terry King[9]

There are more radio station frequencies, formats, and options for listeners than ever before in the history of the medium. Radio companies have conglomerated and streamlined resources as they determined, often cyclically, if they were swallowing up radio stations or divesting them, spending freely or cutting back. As listeners tune into different stations, they encounter formats and musical tastes that did not exist 20 years ago. With many radio groups providing first and second HD radio frequencies and web-only radiocasts as well as on-demand radio podcasts, advertisers are targeting their core customers like never before.

For example, suppose that an advertiser is trying to reach working moms because they are the most likely buyers of the company's products. It would make sense to advertise during radio *drive-time* – morning drive and afternoon drive when these women are most likely on their way to and home from work. The advertiser could be a grocery chain or a food company marketing quick and easy meals, for example. Restaurants featuring lunch specials or happy hours might target people listening at work – a primetime segment of the radio day. An air conditioning repair company might run commercials or *spots* during afternoon drive in the summer in the Las Vegas desert, the hottest time of year, when a poor air conditioner is bringing attention to its weak performance and the need for repair, before the commercials even air. Advertisers want to get in the heads of the right people at the right time.

Arbitron is a media and marketing research firm that measures network and local-market radio audiences throughout the United States, both nationally and in local markets. The company uses a PPM, diaries, and other research techniques to collect data. The PPM measures what people are listening to by tracking audio that is picked up by the radio through embedded identification codes in the audio portion of the transmission. One valuable application is measuring radio listening when people are in their cars or out-of-home radio usage.

The use of ratings information about radio usage – how many listeners are listening to which stations – is of value to radio stations and groups to help them sell time to advertisers and other communicators. They put messages on the air to reach consumers to persuade them to buy products or take other desired actions. Ratings information is also valuable to advertisers, who can use the data for media plans to buy time on behalf of their clients. As with TV, radio shares of the audience report how well a given program performs, compared to other programs at the same time in the same market.

Radio advertisers also want information about consumers that goes beyond mere numbers, radio advertisers increasingly seek data that tells them something more about listeners. Arbitron partners with the A. C. Nielsen Company in a venture called Scarborough Research that provides radio industry companies with qualitative data about listeners – psychographic and behavioral data. This information allows advertisers to go beyond mere demographics in targeting consumers for their messages.

Terry King, general sales manager for Clear Channel radio in San Diego, California, has worked in the radio industry since 1994. He created a list of terms for people who could not read through the legalese or "tech-ese" of the descriptions in an Arbitron book, some of which are available on their Web site at http://www.arbitron.com. He wrote simplified definitions because some of his clients had difficulty understanding the terms as explained in the book. And some terms such as cost per point (CPP) were not developed by Arbitron, but were nevertheless widely used in the industry. Terry's more user-friendly version of the terms, affectionately referred to as the *TK List,* is a must-have for radio professionals.

RADIO RATINGS ACCORDING TO TERRY KING: THE TK LIST

Cume: The total number of people that listen to a station, in a particular daypart and demo [demographic].

Net Reach: The total number of people that your client's SCHEDULE will reach in that particular demo during that week or flight.

AQH Rating: The # of people who listen to a station expressed as a PERCENTAGE of the population of that DEMO in the market. *(Example: A 1.4 AQH [Average Quarter Hour] rating means that 1.4% of the market in that demo listens sometime in that daypart that week.)*

AQH Persons: The AVERAGE # of persons that listen to a station for at least 5 minutes within that daypart during that week or flight. [Flight = a period of time during which an advertiser has purchased time to run messages; for example, a 6-week flight.]

AQH Share: The MARKET SHARE OF AUDIENCE within a daypart and demo that listens to THAT STATION during that time.

Exclusive Cume: The # of people who listen to only THAT station.

Cume Duplication: The percentage (or number) of people who listen to more than 1 station.

CPP: Buying term. A Cost Per Point represents the $ it costs to buy a GRP. Usually there is a goal for the market when an agency puts out an avail, rather than a goal for a particular station. Also, it's usually an arbitrary number determined by historical buying, the buying of a similar market size, or acquired from a "bible" of sorts that the agency used that gained ITS information from the same historical buying and the buying of similar market sizes.

GRP: (THIS ONE IS TRICKY. GRP is also not an Arbitron term – hence it's not in any Arbitron book – but rather is a "buying" term. Ad buyers pay a lot of attention to this, but many still don't know exactly what it is.) A Gross Rating Point is quantified from the AQH Rating info above. The problem is that the AQH Rating is a percentage of a population, and a GRP figures ALL listeners into a particular daypart and demo. THAT means that 4 people that listen for different 15-minute periods in an hour are looked at as the same as ONE person listening for an hour. So reach AND TSL are figured into this. *(Besides, if a GRP is a gross rating point, and rating points represent a percentage of the population, HOW COULD ANY AD AGENCY REQUEST 150 GRPs A WEEK? Can they reach 150% of the population?!)* Additionally, the term GRP does not take into account a duplication factor.

So, it TECHNICALLY may be easier to remember that a GRP represents about 1000 hours of listening per week in that demo and daypart, whether it is, say, 500 listeners or 50. But if a buyer thinks that it is a percentage of the population, versus a percentage of LISTENING, there's no point in correcting them. They just need to buy a certain number in the market, and mostly that's that they care about. Just work to get that buyer to buy as many points from YOU!

Terry King Explains Radio Research

The methodology of radio listening has always been inexact, since it was developed in the 1940s. At that time, radio programming largely consisted of 15-minute serials like *The Green Hornet* and *The Lone Ranger.* Arbitron, the media research product developed by the American Research Bureau (ARB), used diaries to determine who was listening to what and when. These diaries were filled out by household members to document their listening – the days, times, and radio station(s) to which they were tuned. This documentation of listening was the basis of an Arbitron-developed metric, the Average Quarter Hour, or AQH, used by the radio industry to this day.

Until only recently, this archaic methodology of *diary recall* was the sole origin of the data that ranked the listening level of individual radio stations. Pencil-scribbles and radio station *call letters* (e.g., KIIS-FM) and slogans (e.g., New Country) have determined which radio stations and programs are embraced by the public, capturing advertising budgets. Through Arbitron, the radio we listen to is placed in the hands of the small percentage of people who are sampled in each radio market.

Criticism of inexact measurement has abounded for decades, especially by radio stations that received poor ratings. Lower-rated stations have to overcome their ranking by either providing more value to advertisers by featuring lower rates or providing a desirable audience for specific advertisers that they could not easily reach anywhere else. (For example, a jazz station audience is a perfect target for someone wishing to market wine.) Of course, radio stations with great ratings often boast of their successes. Throughout many of our lifetimes, radio station formats have died or multiplied – and people have been hired and fired or become rich or poor – by the information provided in these diaries.

In 1992, Arbitron began investing in a new electronic metering technology to monitor radio listening that is used today, the People Meter, or PPM. It better documents listening habits

(Continued)

and, in 2009, started to replace the diary method in many markets and is continuing to expand. The technology itself looks like a small pager. Listeners wear it to allow it to capture and document radio station signals from radios as well as computer streaming sessions.

Arbitron's objective is to acquire more accurate listening information for advertisers and broadcasters alike, who need the most accurate measurement stick to determine value for the advertising rates on the stations they buy – or, more accurately, the audiences they buy. In 2008, the A. C. Nielsen Company, a competitor to Arbitron from the start, acquired the rights from Arbitron to do the radio audience sampling in 51 small and mid-sized markets for various radio companies, touting their own superiority to Arbitron's sampling methods. Competition is ripe even in sampling methodology and this will likely continue.

Measuring Audiences: Print Media

Print media, magazines and newspapers, measure how many people read their newspapers and magazines, or *circulation*. Total circulation includes subscriptions and newsstand sales, as well as copies sold in combination with events, educational programs, hotel delivery, and third-party sales. Market research firms measure and report back to publishers the result of their circulation research.

In addition, print media conduct readership studies to report the characteristics of their readers. Like broadcasters, they engage in demographic, psychographic, and behavioral research. However, as newspaper circulation has decreased over the past few years, they appear to be commissioning less of these kinds of research studies. For example, Dallas-based Belden Research, a 76-year-old company specializing in research for newspapers, closed its doors in early 2009 because fewer newspapers were willing to pay for such research.[10]

Circulation numbers have long been considered somewhat unreliable. As early as 1914, the Advertising Bureau of Circulation (ABC) was founded to provide independent *audits*, because the industry had earned a reputation for making exaggerated circulation claims. An audit means that the ABC examines a publication's circulation records, interviews circulation personnel, and examines internal circulation controls and practices.

Publishers issue a statement of circulation twice a year for 6 month periods that end on March 31 and September 30 for newspapers. Publishers of consumer magazines issue statements on June 30 and December 31. After the audit, the ABC publishes an audit report and verifies that the publisher's claims with respect to circulation are accurate. The report will also note any discrepancies between the publisher's statement and the findings of the audit.

Some publications will contract with ABC to conduct studies of readership and subscribers, as well as *passalong* information, which includes data about how much more actual readership there is due to one reader passing along the publication to others.

Measuring Audiences: Internet

So far the media we have considered are solely mass media whose messages flow in one direction from the content provider to many viewers, listeners, and readers. The Internet is an interactive medium, which means that messages flow both to users and from users. Sometimes the information doesn't even come from the users themselves – it might come from the user's device, a computer, mobile phone, or personal digital assistant (PDA), or from software loaded onto the device.

When users go to a Web site, they are called *visitors*. During the time a user is on the site, the *session*, the Web site server is constantly *pinging* the visitor's computer. In essence, a ping asks the question of another computer, "Are you still there?" and then waits for the user's machine to reply, "Yes, I am." The ping is the query–answer exchange between two machines. Throughout the session, the software on the Web site's server keeps a record, or a *log*, of the pings passed between the user's device and the Web site server. The log documents the length of the session, the identity of the device, the pages, downloads, web pages and services requested by the visitor, and downloads made by the visitor.

The Web site server is able to collect information about the device through the use of *cookies*. A cookie is a piece of software code that the server embeds in the memory of the user's local machine. Its purpose is to identify users or devices and to track user and device activities. Typically, when visitors request information or services, they must register, providing a user name, password, and email address. Often, they must enter more information, such as their first and last names, complete address, telephone number, sex, age, and even more personal data.

If the information is stored and kept in memory for more than a single session, it is called a *persistent cookie*, meaning that it lasts over time. Knowledgeable users can set preferences for how their personal information is stored: not at all, for a single session, permanently. (Some sites will not allow page views or downloads if the user does not allow the site to set a cookie.) If personal information is stored, the next time that machine accesses the site, it sends the personal data to the Web site server. The server can use it to:

- Authenticate previously registered visitors by comparing the new user name and password to the stored versions
- Display a personalized web page
- Track a user's activities across multiple Web sites

To avoid what they may believe is an invasion of their privacy, some users set the options in their browser to erase cookies when they leave the site. In these cases, only a *session cookie* is on the user's device, kept until the end of the session. However, the Web site's server log records all the information that is in the cookie during the registration process, so eliminating the cookie does not mean that the Web site, the content provider, or even an unknown third party, does not have the information provided by the user.

One of the questions a content provider, site operator, or advertiser might ask is: How many visitors have gone to this site during a specified time period? This metric is called *unique users* or *unique visitors*. If a site has a lot of visitors, then advertisers are willing to pay more than if the site has only a few visitors. However, cookies (and servers) cannot really identify visitors. They identify devices and authenticate user names and passwords. If someone else is using the computer and has access to the personal information, the site server will not be able to record that data. If a user has multiple accounts and devices, the same user may be counted as two users.

The Internet is the newest kid on the block: a recent media channel, compared to other mass media. The organization that hopes to standardize rules, policies, and metrics for Internet content providers and advertisers is the Internet Advertising Bureau (IAB). More than 375 media and technologies make up the membership of the IAB that, together, sell more than 86 percent of online advertising in the United States. Stakeholders in the standardization of measurement and reporting of usage are content creators and distributors, marketers, advertising agencies. The stated core objectives of the IAB are:

- Fend off adverse legislation and regulation
- Coalesce around market-making measurement guidelines and creative standards
- Create common ground with customers to reduce costly friction in the supply chain
- Share best practices that foster industry-wide growth
- Generate industry-wide research and thought leadership that solidifies the position of interactive platforms as mainstream media in the minds of advertisers and consumers.
- Create countervailing force to balance power of other media, marketing, and agency trade groups[11]

Being new means that the methods for gathering accurate measurements are still under development. The IAB conducts and sponsors research to develop the methods and metrics still needed to make advertisers comfortable in the online environment – and to increase their online ad spending. The IAB published guidelines for measuring the use of social media in June 2009, and metrics for audience reach in February 2010. The Internet and other interactive media are evolving rapidly, so measurement methods continue to evolve.[12]

The first order of business for the IAB is to standardized definitions and procedures to measure *audience reach*, or how many people does an advertiser reach with an ad placed on a web page? The IAB has proposed four ways to measure reach to a Web site "audience":

- Unique cookies
- Unique browsers
- Unique devices
- Unique users

Notice that these measurements are in order from easy-to-collect and least specific to hardest-to-collect and most specific. In other words, it is automatic for servers to identify and log a cookie. It is more difficult to know whether a single user visits a site using more than one browser. It is even harder to know if the same user is using multiple devices. Finally, it is almost impossible to know if there is one user who has multiple devices and browsers, or if multiple users surf the Net from the same machine. For example, a wife may know her husband's user name and password for commonly accessed sites. Indeed, there is some likelihood that roommates, friends, siblings, and significant others may know the registered user well enough to log on to some sites as that user.

In the online environment, the cost for reaching consumers is still evolving, and there are still many models and combinations of models for Web sites to charge advertisers:

- A reach-based fee, usually calculated by number of unique site visitors
- Click-throughs: Charge for click-throughs to the advertiser's page (*pay-per-click* or *PPC*)
- Part PPC, part information: Web site provides a link for the user to get more information, collects data from that requesting user, forwards data to the advertiser, and charges on a *pay-per-lead* or *PPL* basis – and keeps data
- Percentage of purchase
- Choice or combination: Fee structure is negotiated

Web sites seek to attract advertisers by providing them with precise information about users. For example, in addition to reach or the number of unique site visitors, they may offer behavioral data. For example, many sites tout *user engagement* as a key element in gauging the visitor's value to a communicator. User engagement is described by such behavioral measures as:

- Length of time spent on the site
- Number of pages visited
- Length of time spent on a specified page
- Number of times the visitor returns to the site
- Average length of time visitors spend on site or specified pages, over multiple visits

Why do consumers find some sites more engaging than others? There is some research that has explored some possible answers to that question. O'Brien and Toms[13] used earlier research to develop a scale to measure the factors that lead to user engagement. Their results found that the combination of the system and the task should be perceived as usable, aesthetically appealing, and enjoyable. The user is more likely to be engaged when there is an easy flow from one point to another, sufficient novelty to hold attention, and endurable.

Many Internet companies believe that video delivery is The Next Big Thing (TNBT). They believe that it will bring even greater success to the medium by increasing advertisers' online ad spending. So far, watching video has indeed proved popular, but it has not led to the bonanza Internet sites expected. One reason is the lack of standardized reporting of data about consumers that it is clear advertisers demand.

The IAB is working on standards for online video advertising. However, video content providers are not happy with the pace of development. In early 2009, Publicis, a worldwide advertising and public relations firm that has many clients active on the Internet, put together a high-level group of content providers called The Pool. Members include Microsoft, Yahoo, CBS, and Hulu (NBC) to work on developing standards and metrics for video search, social media, mobile advertising, and other new media channels and platforms.[14] More importantly, The Pool will develop additional video ad formats instead of simply moving the classic TV ad format, the 30-second commercial, to the Web.

The overarching purpose of the group is to attract more online video advertising, to *monetize* new media channels. A subsidiary of Publicis, VivaKi, has started the process by creating five new online video ad formats. The company will convene consumer focus groups to explore their responses to the new types of online ads and narrow that number to two formats. Then the group will conduct quantitative studies to determine one that it will promote as the new industry standard. The timeline for release of the new format is the fourth quarter of 2009.

Measuring Audiences: Videogames and Other Emerging Advertising Channels

As another new media channel, the videogame industry has not yet developed standard metrics that allow advertisers to quantify their media buys and to determine the value of placing their ads in games. In 2006, the A. C. Nielsen Company announced the launch of GamePlay Metrics to provide videogame companies the ability to measure game playing and to establish standards for buying and selling ads placed in videogames. As one Nielsen executive put it, "The value of an entertainment medium is directly proportional to how well it is measured. A reliable and accurate standard of measurement for video gaming will drive advertising investment in this medium."[15]

At first glance, measuring the reach of videogames seems like an easy task: Gather sales figures and online videogame subscriptions. From the perspective of videogame companies and game site operators, that simple procedure may be as much measurement as they need. NPD Group, a research firm, has tracked videogame sales for the past 25 years.[16] The company uses sales data directly from retailers in the United States and Canada and reports the sales of the top ten games monthly. Beginning in 2008, NPD started tracking online game subscriptions as well.

But advertisers want to know much more about how they can use this medium effectively – this kind of data is not quite as easy to acquire. To accomplish the task, GamePlay Metrics, a Nielsen company, puts measurement devices on consoles to monitor daily usage and playing habits. Interpret, a partner in the enterprise, looks at the activity on social networks and gaming Web sites to provide additional information.[17]

Advertisers that buy time on television and radio and ads in print publications and Web sites want to target their ads to customers who are likely to buy their products. Similarly, before they place ads in videogames, they require an accurate, reliable demographic profile of the people who play particular titles. As more games move online, it will be easier for game companies to provide usage and demographic information about players because they will be able to access information from their servers and from the credit card records required for ongoing payments for subscriptions.

One advantage offered by videogames is that they give advertisers a chance to put their messages before the eagerly sought young male demographic that advertisers cannot easily reach with other media. Nevertheless, media buyers want to make sure that they have the data they need to justify their decisions to their clients. For example, suppose 1,300,000 men aged 18–25 with incomes between $24,000 and $35,000 per year bought the latest version of *Grand Theft Auto*. Twenty percent of the group plays the game more than 500 hours; 20 percent plays between 250 and 500 hours; 20 percent plays between 100 and 250 hours; and so forth.[18] If you were an advertiser and could place your ad in 20 percent of the games, which group would you like to make sure had your ad in their *GTA* game?

Games figure in yet another new media channel – mobile devices, especially phones. NBC Universal Mobile recently made an agreement with Rentrak Mobile Essentials™ to analyze the consumption of NBCU's content that is distributed over mobile channels.[19] The company will track such materials as video clips, SMS messages, ringtones, videogames, wallpaper, and other content. The company's strategy is to collect data over time to shape promotional content that will lead users back to NBCU's television content.

In addition to video sites and online games, advertisers would also like to be able to reach consumers on social media sites – blogs and microblogs, social networks, and wikis. Social media (Web 2.0) cut across many different categories of Internet use, including retail sites, local listing sites like http://www.yelp.com, company Web sites, and even games. In a report about the role that social media play in the video gaming world, Networked Insights noted that in-game advertisers need to know about how the gaming audience is engaging, which elements it is engaging around in order to understand how to target players – in which games and what part of a specific game.[20]

Finally, publishing business reports and report excerpts, white papers, position papers, and press releases online is a new specialized form of reaching consumers about products and services. These activities combine marketing, PR, advertising, and promotion in an integrated package that endeavors to give consumers something to think about. Twenty years ago, a company offering expensive wares might have printed up a fancy four-color brochure, bought lists of executives and addresses, and mailed the brochure to them at the office.

Today, companies may still send such vehicles or give them away at meetings, conferences, and trade shows. But it costs far less to offer these materials for download. Moreover, people who download are taking an active role in securing the material, making it more likely that they will actually read it. Often the company will send out an email to existing and prospective customers, providing a link on their own Web site for download. Usually, the request to download requires registration, giving the marketer valuable information about potential customers – valuable because this is a prospect that actively seeks the information. The marketer then contacts the person. Success of the marketing effort is gauged by counting the number of downloads and, more importantly, the number of conversions from prospects to sales as the sales process unfolds.

SUMMARY

This chapter examined how media companies learn about their consumers through research. It covered both market research, which provides information about the potential demand for a product, and marketing research, which tells companies how to communicate with their customers to sell their content products. When it comes to creating new content, some media industry sectors do not do as much market research as companies in other industries.

Media companies almost always do detailed research to market consumers to advertisers, using sophisticated research techniques. They are likely to use a combination of primary and secondary sources of data and to use quantitative and qualitative methods to analyze the information. Each media segment has its own methods for gathering data about consumers and vocabulary for reporting results: television and radio meter media use and employ either meters or diaries to collect demographic information about their audience. Print media use readership studies and sales and subscription records. Internet media automate data collection by requiring personal data in registration procedures and monitoring activities. Learning about audiences that use emerging media platforms may be difficult until standards can be set.

WHAT'S AHEAD

The next chapter brings into focus one of the most exciting activities in which media companies engage: content creation and media production. It details the essential role managers play in fostering and leading creative projects, helping producers navigate the intricate development, budgeting, management, and completion of their works. And it looks at the new technologies that creators use to produce, market, and deliver content.

CASE STUDY 6.1 AUDIENCES AND PROGRAMMING

It is not uncommon for new hires as account executives (AEs) in radio or television to be handed the local Yellow Pages and guided by the sales manager with a simple task to "go get some business." Perhaps that is a bit exaggerated, but it is eventually your call to action. Most media organizations that take a chance on hiring someone without experience or even those who do have experience will typically put an AE through some formal training or perhaps a mentoring program with another AE, but at some point, it all comes down to making the "cold calls" to businesses in hopes of closing that first sell.

As the new AE at a medium-sized market, you have just completed your official training period and now you are ready to get out and meet with prospective clients. The company has a very strict policy that requires you to complete a "Customer Needs Analysis" for these prospects. These CNAs are brought back to the station where you then work with Marketing to develop a well-rounded advertising plan, which will require you to understand how to use ratings and demographic data to fulfill the client's needs. Choose a local TV or radio station that you would like to work for and complete the following assignment that will show you the value in conducting research completely that is designed to generate business and ultimately income. The successful AE will gain a full understanding of the audiences that his or her station is able to reach with its various programs and match it to the target demo or audience that advertisers are attempting to reach.

Assignment

1. Develop a full Customer Needs Analysis form. What questions would you need to ask a business owner that would allow you to develop a full marketing campaign? Keep in mind that your goal is to focus on determining that businesses target demographic group both from a quantitative perspective and also a qualitative description.

2. Team up with someone in your class who will play the part of a business owner and complete your own

Customer Needs Analysis. Now, switch roles, allowing the other person to ask you questions about your company. In order to do this effectively, you may want to either research a local business or simply talk to someone at a store where you enjoy shopping.

3. After you have conducted a full Customer Needs Analysis of the company that you are hoping to get on television, you can begin looking up the quantitative data that represents the media company you are representing. For example, you work at the local ABC station. What types of ratings or demographics do you have that would impress this business? If you are at a radio station, does the format lend itself to the company you have interviewed? If not, is there a specific program that airs on the TV or radio station that might be appealing? For example, every Sunday night, your radio station airs a Community Connection program or perhaps NASCAR in the second half of the year. What are the numbers?

4. Now, develop information on the qualitative aspect of the target customer for your client. Is it a high-price ticket that would require an upper household income? Are they more likely to be college graduates, parents with children, rent an apartment, own a home, concerned with the environment or strictly convenience driven as opposed to be price-conscious? These are examples of qualitative descriptions that will assist you in developing not only a strong advertising schedule, but also on how to develop a script.

5. Develop a : 30 television script that will be effective with the audience and sell the client's product.

6. Present your findings in the form of a presentation to include:

- Overview of client's business
- Quantitative data
- Qualitative descriptions
- Script
- Close the sell

REFERENCES

1. Simpson, G. (May 29, 2008). The FYI interview: Pat Holiday, Astral's gentle giant. Accessed December 18, 2008, at http://fyimusic.ca/industry-news/broadcasting/the-fyi-interview-with-pat-holiday-radios-gentle-giant.

2. Eliashberg, J., Elberse, A. & Leenders, M. (2005). The motion picture industry: Critical issues in practice, current research & new research directions. Accessed on October 8, 2009, at: http://www.hbs.edu/research/pdf/05-059.pdf.

3. PricewaterhouseCoopers (2008). *Media & entertainment markets, 2008–2013*. New York: PricewaterhouseCoopers.

4. Smith, P. R. & Taylor, J. (2004). *Marketing communications*, 4th Ed. London: Kogan-Page.

5. Kvale, S. & Brinkmann, S. (2008). *Interviews: Learning the craft of qualitative research interviewing*, 2nd Ed. Thousand Oaks, CA: Sage Publications.

6. _____ (2008). Ratings track: Update on Nielsen's Local People Meter rollout. Accessed October 30, 2009, at http://www.tvb.org/rcentral/viewertrack/weekly/lpm-schedule.asp.

7. Zurswik, D. (May 4, 2009). Will Nielsen People Meters rock TV news in Baltimore? Accessed October 19, 2009, at http://weblogs.baltimoresun.com/entertainment/zontv/2009/05/nielsen_people_meters_baltimor.html.

8. Figures taken from A. C. Nielsen Company web site. Accessed November 2, 2009, at http://en-us.nielsen.com/tab/measurement.

9. This section was compiled with the expert help of Terry King, general sales manager for Clear Channel, San Diego, California.

10. Mediapost (January 15, 2009). *Newspaper research firm Belden to close*. Accessed January 15, 2009, at http://www.mediapost.com/publications/?fa=Articles.showArticle&art_aid=98409&passFuseAction=PublicationsSearch.showSearchReslts&art_searched=belden&page_number=0.

11. Internet Advertising web site. Accessed January 10, 2009, at http://www.iab.net/about_the _iab.

12. Internet Advertising Bureau (December 8, 2008). *Interactive Advertising Bureau audience reach measurement guidelines version 1.0*. Accessed January 10, 2010, http://www.iab.net/media/file/ audience_reach_022009.pdf.

13. O'Brien, H. L. & Toms, E. G. What is user engagement? A conceptual framework for defining user engagement with technology. *Journal of the American Society for Information Science and Technology* 59:6, 938–955.

14. Mandese, J. (January 22, 2009). VivaKi takes plunge, pools resources with CBS, Hulu, Microsoft, others for new video ad format. *Mediapost*. Accessed January 2, 2009, at http:// www.mediapost.com/publications/?fa=Articles.showArticleHomePage&art_aid=98882.

15. Fox News (October 20, 2006). *Nielsen to actively measure video-game usage in households*. Accessed January 10, 2009, at http://www.foxnews.com/story/0,2933,222740,00.html.

16. *NPD Group*. Accessed January 11, 2009, at http://vgsales.wkia.com/wiki/NPD_Group.

17. Business Wire (March 21, 2007). *Interpret's new media reach and frequency study reveal measuring games by retail sales significantly under-values the advertising medium*. Accessed January 11, 2009, at http://findarticles.com/p/articles/mi_m0EIN/is_/ai_n27255577.

18. Sherry, J. & Lucas, K. (2003). *Videogame uses and gratifications as predictors of use and game prefer- ence*. Paper presented at the annual meeting of the International Communication Association, Marriott Hotel, San Diego, CA. Accessed January 10, 2009, at http://www.allacademic.com/ meta/p111471_i.

19. PR Newswire (January 6, 2009). *Rentrak inks audience measurement deal with NBC Univer- sal*. Accessed January 11, 2009, at http://news.prnewswire.com/DisplayReleaseContent .aspx?ACCT=ind_focus.story&STORY=/www/story/01-06-2009/0004949548&EDATE=.

20. _____ (2008). Networked Insights measuring the social report, part 3: Video games. Accessed October 18, 2009, at http://www.networkedinsights.com/blog/uploads/MeasureTheSocialRe- port_games.pdf.

CHAPTER 7

Managing the Production Process

We don't want the television script good. We want it Tuesday.

Dennis Norden (English TV Comedy Writer)

CHAPTER OBJECTIVES

The objective of this chapter is to provide you with information about:

- Managing content creation
- The process of content creation in the digital environment
- Creating content for multiple media platforms
- Pitching, budgeting, and scheduling
- Managing content creators
- Testing and evaluating content
- Acquisition and aggregation as content strategies
- Traditional media: Movie packages, TV syndication, cable program acquisition
- Internet: Portals, syndication and affiliation, search

INTRODUCTION

"Five, four, three, two, one" and "Lights, camera, action" convey the immediacy and excitement of media production. A romantic aura surrounds content creation. No matter how difficult it may be to break into the field, many people dream of doing creative work. The pleasure brought by a television or radio show, movie, album, or videogame may have been a person's first inkling that working in the media could be a satisfying career choice. For some, that choice becomes a lifelong ambition.

People who do not want to perform in front of the camera or the microphone, or even behind the scenes writing scripts, drawing animation cells,

CONTENTS

DOI: 10.1016/B978-0-240-81020-1.00007-5

or operating a camera, may still want to be involved in the media industry and the creative process. Entering management is one way to play an integral role in content-producing organizations. Executives bear the ultimate responsibility for approving and green-lighting projects and ensuring that the right resources for creating them are available in the right place, at the right time. They sign off on the administration of projects, including identifying partners and negotiating with them, hiring people, establishing budgets and monitoring expenditures, approving and monitoring schedules, and making regular progress reports to executives at higher levels of the organization. Most importantly, they share in reaping the rewards of hits, in terms of bonuses, career opportunity, and public acclaim.

This chapter covers the process of creating content – the content pipeline – from concept by creators to consumption by consumers. Managers need to understand a great deal about the process, because content is central to the media enterprise. At the many conventions, demonstrations, expositions, and shows that feature all forms of content, the phrase "content is king" is often heard. Less acknowledged is that the manager who controls the content creation process is the king-maker.

Today, there is more production taking place than in the past, because there are so many more content types and distribution channels, as discussed in the box below. The system of production was also different. Back in the day, producers created a program for television, radio, a magazine, or a book. Each distribution channel had a set of expectations about the program format, length, and genres. There was one set of technical standards for each type of content, such as the picture size, resolution, and signal quality in the television industry. Each area of content production had its own equipment, facilities, content producers, and skilled crafts and technical people.

Fifteen years ago, there were no DVD players, no mobile phones with video screens or web access – actually, the first graphics-capable browser had just launched, in 1993; the iPod debuted in 1994, along with the first .mp3 audio encoder. Interactive cable was still 2 years away. People who had high-speed access to the Internet were almost all using systems in the workplace; few people had broadband at home. There were no peer-to-peer networks and there was no Wi-Fi. In 1994, only 15 million people had cell phones; by 1999, 104 million people in the United States had them. There were no color screens, personalized downloadable ringtones and image backgrounds, photo sharing, or SMS services. There was no TiVo – no personal video recorders at all. No widescreen TV or high-definition TV, no home theater, or surround sound. Unbelievably, there were no commercially available DVD players or DVDs. Hotels didn't have pay-per-view. Hotel rooms didn't offer Internet access at any speed. Guests had to configure their modems to account for the need to dial "9" before calling the number of a local dialup service.

These changes complicate the content creation process. Creative ventures need more money, cost control, planning, and oversight than ever before. Thus, the greater complexity is also more likely to increase the importance of good management – and managers.

Today, executives and creatives think ahead to the ways the content can be extended to many different digital media platforms. TV producers consider DVD rentals and sales, online downloading, clip sales, and screen savers. Music labels now receive revenues from physical sales and streamed downloads. The global market for ringtones is estimated to bring in about $750 million in 2009,[1] and *ringbacks*, the sound the caller hears when the receiver's phone is ringing, should garner $235 million.[2] This development underlines the evolving content marketplace, a *slice-and-dice* future, where consumers can purchase the parts of content they want, with prices geared to usage.

The rise of user-generated content (UGC), made possible by more powerful computers and sophisticated software, has made video and photos as popular as text. Companies that own visual media can slice-and-dice, snippetizing their content to market the pieces or to promote content products. A clever scheme can even monetize user-generated content. For example, iStockphoto (http://www.istockphoto.com), which started with photographs submitted by creators, now posts them, as well as user-created illustrations, videos, and sounds. The company aggregates millions of these content items and licenses them to the public for less than $2 per photo, less than $20 for short Flash videos, and so forth. In the future, owners of movie and television show libraries may find similar opportunities to sell to users who want to put the footage in their UGC creations.

Managers can use existing content that has already been produced to increase revenues, without adding greatly to their production budgets. Today's commercial market encourages them to consider this strategy, because content intended for one media platform is routinely formatted, packaged, and marketed for one or more additional media platforms. The very nature of digital content lends itself to shape-shifting – reuse, repackaging, recreation – because it is easily copied, *transcoded* into other digital formats, and redesigned into completely different content types. This ease of refashioning content allows producers to package existing content into other profitable products without starting from scratch.

There are many examples of such repackaging. Whole seasons of popular TV shows appear on DVDs to be rented by Blockbuster and sent through the mail by Netflix. Movies are exhibited in local theaters, but like TV shows, they also stream over the Internet, play on television and cable networks, as well as on airplanes, mobile devices, and standalone DVD players. Music plays free over the radio and the Internet, and, for a fee, over satellite networks. Customers purchase it from retail outlets and Internet sites, and download it from millions of online "friends" over peer-to-peer networks.

THE MANY LANGUAGES OF DIGITAL CREATION

Many sectors of the media industry create content using digital equipment, but others continue to use traditional means. For example, some musicians play acoustic instruments, and filmed entertainment (motion pictures and high-end television programs) and large-format photographs are still acquired using analog cameras that expose the light to chemical-based film. However, printing is largely accomplished with digital printers (books, magazines, and newspapers), and most still photography, videogames, and local broadcast production of TV and radio programs now originate on digital equipment.

The motion picture, television, and radio industries began in the analog era and their vocabularies for producing media came out of analog processes. However, digital content industries typically have a somewhat different creation process, so creators have had to adopt new vocabularies to describe the new activities. Unfortunately, the digital creatives occasionally picked up analog terms and used them in different ways! The result is that people who move between analog and digital worlds have to watch their language very closely to avoid confusion and misunderstanding.

Here are a few examples. In the television industry, the images and audio presented to viewers are called programming, referring to programs and shows. But in the digital world, the term *programming* means creating a sequence of instructions that instruct a computer to do something, specifying the rules and variables that structure the operations of the computer; the people who do

Digital: Comes from fingers (digits), which leads to the idea of counting on your fingers. Fingers are *discrete* – something counted on them is one, two, three, four, and so forth. (You do not often hear of 3.765 fingers!) Thus, digital has come to mean a system of measuring in discrete units, no matter how large or small they are, and then numbering those units. Computers and other digital devices like iPods process 0s and 1s, a binary (two) digital system.

Analog: Analog means measurement along a continuous scale that is not broken down into discrete units. For example, human senses are analog. Take vision – people see a nuanced range of colors within the spectrum visible to humans, all the reds or blues or yellows. Digital devices translate binary streams into analog forms so that human beings can see and hear them, using a digital-to-analog processor. Some musicians report that they can hear the difference between sounds acquired by digital recording and those recorded on analog machines.

it are called *programmers*. In TV, programmers are executives who choose the programs that will be shown on a broadcast or cable network.

Digital creators call the material that appears on screens *content*. When material is not called content in the CD-ROM and DVD industry, the images, audio, and text that users get on their screens are sometimes called *software*. Writers, directors, producers, and programmers are collectively referred to as *content providers* (a much-disliked term among traditional creative practitioners). Content that is stored in quantity that can be accessed and repurposed for digital playback is sometimes called a *bucket* or *buckets of content*. In the analog, a movie was a movie, a book was a book, a TV program was a program – and there was no word to describe all these forms, except possibly "creative works."

In the entertainment business, the script is a blueprint composed of the scenes and dialog that will make up the finished product. In multimedia, a script is software programming in an authoring language that defines what is going to happen as the user progresses through the material. In television and film, the person who oversees a project is called a *producer*; in the multimedia and videogame fields, that individual is known as a *developer*. In show business, the finished product is a *program*, a *show*, or a *film*; in multimedia and videogames (and book publishing), it is called a *title*; for online projects, it is an *application*.

Beyond language, the computer-based creative companies (videogames, Internet dot-coms) have a different culture from the traditional creative companies (TV, film). The disparate cultures lead to profound disagreements over what content should look like, where it should come from, and how it relates to its audience. Even here, the defined reality is contentious: in the computer industry, audience members are *users*; in the entertainment industry, they are *viewers*; in the gaming industry, they are *players*. A clumsy compromise of sorts has been attempted by using such terms as *viewser* and *telewebber* to describe people who converge their usage of TV and the Internet.

TRADITIONAL PRODUCTION

The stages of content creation were formalized in the motion picture industry nearly a century ago, so they are familiar to creative people and managers alike. To a large extent, the well-understood stages still provide a useful way of describing the content creation process, in both analog and digital environments. From the beginning, managers played an important role in every stage, as shown in Table 7-1. Each of the stages of content creation takes place in an individual *silo* of activity, which means that each part is isolated from the other parts of the overall process. Some producers and directors (in motion picture

Table 7-1 Management Roles in Each Production Stage

Production Stage	Manager Activities
Development	Planning, budgeting, green-lighting, shaping through initial input and notes on scripts as they are written and rewritten
Preproduction	Budgeting, approving spending, and signing contracts
Production	Planning, budgeting, shaping through notes on dailies and approval process
Postproduction	Budgeting, shaping through audience/user research and approval process
Predistribution	Budgeting, planning, coordinating with marketing efforts

production) stay with the project from beginning to end. But in all cases, managers coordinate work throughout the life of creative projects.

The activities that take place in these stages of motion picture and television creation have not changed very much over the decades. Over time, the technologies advanced, but the fundamental techniques for analog production in 35 mm and 16 mm formats were well understood by the late 1940s; video production was standardized by 1953. Two stages became more complex over time and assumed greater importance in the latter half of the twentieth century: development at the beginning of the process and predistribution at the end. Development became a more prolonged, deliberate process as product development and marketing research rose to the forefront. Predistribution is now necessary because material has to be prepared to conform to the requirements of many different digital distribution channels and consumer viewing devices.

Development: Making Content Creation a Less Risky Business

Producing content is a labor-intensive and often a capital-intensive business. The high cost of production encourages television networks and stations, motion picture companies, and videogame companies to invest time and resources in development. As a result, development is increasingly important in all areas of visual content production, because careful consideration and planning at the beginning reduce overall risk. It is not unusual for creatives to express the glowing vision and for managers to consider the potential risks.

Development includes sorting through ideas for content products, choosing one or a few that need more consideration, and adding to each idea with increasingly detailed information about the potential market, the final shape of the final product, and the fit between it and the audience. It often involves close interaction between creatives and managers. The process ends when executives green-light the project.

Development begins with a concept or idea. It may come from a creative person, often a writer, producer, or developer. However, ideas sometimes come from market-savvy managers. Industry newcomers often worry about someone stealing their idea, and although such theft is not unknown, it does not happen often. On the whole, there is little incentive to steal ideas in a community where there are far more ideas than productions. Many writers can come up with several ideas a day, a treatment a month – so there is really no shortage of ideas. Moreover, some of the most prolific and creative people in the industry prefer to produce their own ideas; they are not dependent on others for them.

In practical terms, here is how creative people market their ideas. In the television and movie industries, well-known writers and producers (often writers themselves) with a track record make an appointment with development executives in studios and production companies to pitch their ideas. It is difficult for industry newbies to secure such a hearing. The movie *The Player* opens with a good example of a *pitch*. It is a five- to fifteen-minute verbal presentation of an idea for a movie or a show that describes the concept, the characters, the setting, the arc of the story, major plot points, the potential audience, and any special *hooks*. A hook may be a plot twist, an unusual combination of genres, a casting choice, a unique distribution scheme, a promotional idea: something that makes the idea stand out. When finished, the presenter gives the executive a *leave-behind* document that is usually only a few pages with much the same information that was in the pitch.

New writers almost always have to write a completed script and send it to agents for representation. The agent then submits the script to the studio or production company. Production entities rarely read scripts that come in "over the transom," or directly from the writer, because managers worry about potential lawsuits. Typically, they return such scripts unopened. When new writers do sell a script, it is common for it to be rewritten by another, more experienced writer. If the rewrite involves changing more than 60 percent of the dialog of the original script (and it almost always does), the rewriter gets screen credit as the writer. Such credits are automatically arbitrated by the Writers Guild of America if there is a dispute.

Ideas also come from producers and executives who may not actually write the script. For example, studio and production company executives may identify a potential market for a particular type of product. They then assign the idea to an experienced writer to develop and write a script.

At some point, management makes a final decision about what will be produced by sifting through the ideas that have been submitted to them and evaluating the potential attractiveness, value, and feasibility of the project. Most often, this work is done by a group of development executives. If the committee (or a powerful member of the committee) likes the idea, the creators of their idea will flesh out the idea, usually in a *treatment*. The treatment is a document prepared by the writer before the actual script is written, offering a detailed presentation of the story idea, including its elements of attraction to a specified audience, and its themes, characters, plot points, and story arc. Usually, many changes are made to the treatment before executives commission a script.

The process for other sectors of the media industries may be different – the venue of a pitch makes a difference. Videogame developers make a more detailed pitch than motion picture and television creatives, because they need to explain the technological aspects of the game, the gameplay, and the arc of the game, even when it is likely to involve user-initiated changes. In news-producing organizations and units, writers, reporters, correspondents, and freelancers contact an editor or news director. They make a quick pitch, either with a *query letter* or just verbally, over the phone or in person. In news, the pitch will address why the story is important or interesting and timely. It will cover how the proposer will go about gathering information or footage and their evaluation of the likely final form of the story. Both parties understand that the reporting process could change everything about the story – it could fizzle out, grow, or go pretty much as described.

Managers play an even more essential role in corporate and nonprofit organizations, where creative people are not pounding at the door to present new ideas. Several kinds of situations can motivate content creation in organizational settings. Some activities traditionally require content support, including marketing and promotional initiatives, where sales organizations and customers expect to receive DVDs, brochures, Web sites and pages, and other marketing communications materials. In large organizations, investor relations and employee relations units invest in content to make sure the company's message gets out. Finally, content may also address problems, such as damage control, a new organizational direction, an unexpected development in the environment that creates a change in the market.

Preproduction

In the digital environment, development activities are almost the same as they were 40 or 50 years ago – except that the work itself is done on computers and much of the communication online via email, chat, and IM. In addition, the digitization of content production has given executives much more management control over the process. One of the most important ways this occurs is through managers' ability to set the budget and to follow expenditures in real time.

Executives sign off on all major hires, including above-the-line creative people and work, including costs for rights to the script and salaries for the writer, producer, director, and actors. They negotiate and examine contracts, make suggestions, and insist on revisions. In television, executives set budgets for above-the-line expenses by week or episode for the run of a series. Below-the-line costs, which cover crew salaries, production stage and other location fees, equipment, travel, and catering, are usually fixed costs. For example, the amount paid to crew on large productions is governed by union contracts.

Throughout preproduction, managers monitor project spending to detect possible budget overruns. Computerized records of activities give them access to all aspects of planning and contracting that are brought together to produce the content, providing them with the information they need to control costs. They can find out all they need to know as the preproduction effort unfolds:

- Finalizing the script
- Creating *storyboards*, created using *previz* software
- *Breaking down* the script into actors' and performers' parts, crew needs, locations, lighting needs, wardrobe and hair and makeup, sets and backgrounds, props, equipment needs, etc.
- Setting final budget
- Beginning design of visual effects, special effects, and stunts
- Locating, negotiating, and arranging for all the required elements, as identified in script breakdown
- Casting
- Negotiating and executing contracts for required performers, talent, and crew
- Setting a production schedule
- Identifying and negotiating for downstream licensing partners and deals

Digitization has introduced a number of important efficiencies into the preproduction phase. For example, a few years ago, when artists wanted to be hired on a project, they submitted their work in bulky portfolios, sent by messenger or hand-delivered to producers' offices. The work sat in a conference room over a period of weeks to allow time for executives to walk down the hall and page through the submissions. Most artists lived in Hollywood or New York and could drop in for a subsequent interview.

Now this entire process occurs online. From their homes and studios anywhere in the world, artists make their work available to executives by emailing a file or sending a link to uploaded files on a Web site. Managers review them at their desks to choose the person or team they believe will do the best job on the project.

Similarly, preliminary location scouting may occur online, with scouts looking at photos for leads to locations before physically inspecting them. Even many of the casting calls for actors, the old *cattle calls* of the past, have gone online. Casting agents look at actors' photographs and *demo reels* online, making preliminary selections before calling them in for an interview.

Creatively, artists use *previsualization* or *previz* software to produce *storyboards*, artistic renderings and drawings that depict major scenes in the projected script, conveying the look and feel of the film. They used to be drawn by hand by one or more artists. Previz software provides more realistic, accurate, and detailed storyboards than were possible in the past, allowing managers and creatives to achieve a consensus about the final form of the content product.

Of course, business processes are highly computerized as well. Some companies simply digitally store contracts and other business documents. However, there are sophisticated entertainment and media contract management systems that automate contracts and agreements that deal with rights creation, segregation, and application as part of an industrial contract workflow process. In the entertainment and media industry, contracts and rights include such issues as licensing, clearance, audit, geographical and temporal exclusivity, finance, and royalties. Systems that provide for data analysis offer managers the opportunity to spot trends, anomalies, inefficiencies, and opportunities for cost cutting.

Production

The production phase of content creation is where it all happens, as shown in Figure 7-1 – the elements of the final product actually come into being. For the most part, studio-backed motion pictures, scripted television programs, and TV advertising spots are shot on 35 mm film and then digitized and stored on high-capacity drives to be edited on digital editing systems. However, many independent films are shot on videotape, with either high-definition or 24p standard-definition cameras. In addition, directors and directors of photography are considering the new high-resolution Red camera as a replacement for film. Production also includes the creation of graphics – illustrations, drawings, and animation cels.

Managers typically take a backseat during production, leaving the creatives to work their magic. However, they keep a close watch on the budget and

FIGURE 7-1 The language of digital entertainment production. *Source: http://www.wordle.net, licensed under Creative Commons.*

supervising executives in motion picture, television, and corporate production may be on the set. At the very least, they view the *dailies* – the material shot each day. If the production is on location, the dailies are sent over computer networks. If the footage departs from what is expected, particularly if there appear to be problems in the production, execs may decide to replace the director, the show business equivalent to replacing the pitcher in a tough game of baseball. Although such replacements are not common, they do happen.

Postproduction

In this phase, all the produced material is assembled in a final product through editing. In addition to being a highly creative process, postproduction is also procedurally and technically complex, as shown in Figure 7-2. In postproduction, managers again exercise considerable control through budget decisions and creative approval.

The first version of the product is called the *rough cut*. The rough cut may have blanks where elements are missing, or early versions of material that will later

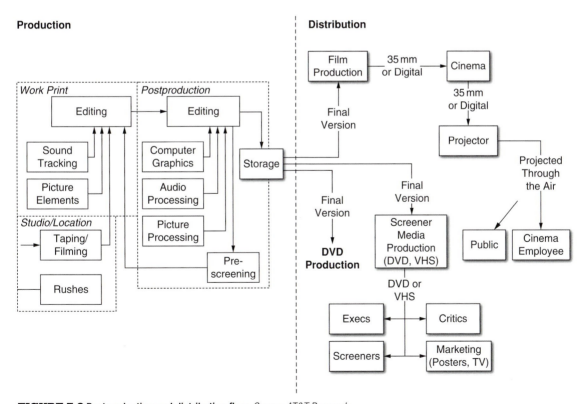

FIGURE 7-2 Postproduction and distribution flow. *Source: AT&T Research.*

be improved, in place of the yet-to-be-delivered final version. The elements have not been color corrected so that they match, a process known as *color grading*.

Digitally created footage (*computer-generated imagery* or *CGI*) plays a large role in many motion pictures. As of 1998, eight of the ten all-time highest grossing films were those that relied heavily on special and visual effects.[3] Subsequent research has shown that visual and sound effects have a strong positive effect on the box office success of motion pictures.[4] Most television programs use far fewer visual effects, although even shows such as *House* routinely employ a small number of them to show biological processes.

The workflow for computer-generated material runs parallel to the live action workflow until the two types of content are put together in postproduction. CGI and visual and special effects are usually contracted to artisans with special skills working in boutique digital facilities. The assignments may be carried out by people working anywhere in the world; it is a globally dispersed workforce. However, there may be limits to how much individual artists can do because the powerful, specialized computer workstations and software needed to do high-quality, cutting-edge work may be very expensive. Typically, images must be rendered in very high resolution. (High resolution is expressed as 2k × 2k or 4k × 4k. 2k × 2k means 2,000 vertical lines of resolution by 2,000 horizontal lines of resolution; similarly, 4k means 4,000 vertical and 4,000 horizontal lines of resolution.)

Managers set the budget for CGI and visual effects. For major motion pictures, the cost can take a big bite out of the production budget. Independent films and television shows do not usually have that kind of money to spend, so digital material for these projects is sometimes created on desktop computers (usually Macs, but sometimes Windows PCs) running relatively inexpensive software. In these cases, the output resolution is far lower than studio films, either at high-definition TV or standard-definition digital video quality.

Once the editor puts together a rough cut, including a rough audio track mix, it goes to the director, producers, and supervising executives. When all the players reach creative agreement on a final version, the editor generates an *Edit Decision List* (*EDL*). In the analog world, this begins a series of highly specialized activities to conform the camera original negative to the EDL and inserting the material from all visual effects and optical effects. The conformed negative is used to strike an answer print, which is screened by the director and a professional colorist. The colorist applies interpretative changes to the over color of the film and corrects any problems with color that may have originated in production. A series of prints are struck (produced) for final approval before prints and copies are made for distribution.

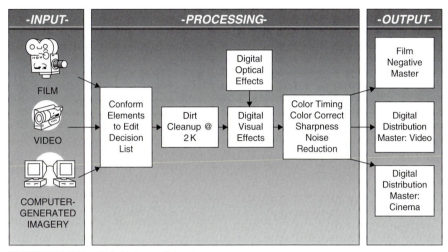

FIGURE 7-3 The digital intermediate process

However, all this is changing. Television shows and advertising spots may never go through the film process at all. Instead, the negative is converted to high-definition video and postproduction takes place in the digital environment. Even in motion picture creation, the *digital intermediate* (*DI*) process, as shown in Figure 7-3, is replacing the complex film postproduction process.

The change from analog to digital postproduction gives managers a larger voice in shaping the final content product. At any given point, the content can be displayed for examination. And changes are much easier (and cheaper) to make.

Predistribution

Predistribution is often treated as the last stages of the postproduction process. However, digitization requires specialized processes that cannot always be handled in the same facility. Consider all the channels used to distribute content: theatrical release, cable, network, and satellite TV, DVD, Internet, and mobile. Each channel requires preparing and structuring the content for its specific technology – and each of them involves several formats. These conversion activities are called *transcoding*. Many of the formats include some kind of compression to reduce the bandwidth to transport the content over networks and the amount of storage required on the *server*, a special computer that plays out the content on demand to a final consumer.

Any form of processing can always result in negative effects on the look and feel of the final product. With transcoding and compression, the effects can be drastic. The director and producers may still be connected with the project, but they may also have moved on to other work. In those instances, only the managers and executives may be around to step in to make the necessary decisions about the quality of the work. In all cases, executives will exercise final approval of the released content. (If there is a profound disagreement with the director, it offers another product opportunity – the Director's Cut.)

A DAY IN THE LIFE OF ANNE MARIE GILLEN

Anne Marie Gillen, CEO & Founder – Gillen Group LLC
Film Producer & Entertainment Industry Consultant

I wear two hats all day long: (1) as an indie film producer, and (2) as a film consultant to indie producers and film investors.

I am originally from Minneapolis, MN, and arrived in LA about 20–23 years ago. When I arrived I was coming here as a choreographer and actress with degrees and training in live theatre and dance. I had no background in film or media whatsoever. My first professional job was as the Executive Assistant to the President of a film distribution company. It taught me early on in my career that 50% is making a film and 50% is marketing and distributing that film. And a well-balanced film producer needs to know both sides of that coin equally. The company I worked for earned 12 Academy Awards the 3 years I was there. It was an incredible learning experience and prepared me for when I left and truly started my solo career as a film producer.

A typical day for me includes interacting with all the issues to move my film projects forward to completion, as well as consulting to my clients and assisting them in moving their projects forward to completion.

Examples:

My film in development: I will have a conference call with writer(s) to review my notes on the last draft of the screenplay they just completed. If there is a director attached, he/she will also be a part of this call. It is my job to be sure everyone's voice is heard, but at the end of the day I manage the conversation so we are all in agreement as to the next steps to take to get the screenplay ready for talent and financing submissions.

My completed film: I will have a meeting with the domestic distributor to discuss the marketing and advertising campaign; which theatres in which states we will be opening the film. How best to publicize the film and how best to utilize our lead actors to maximize exposure of the film just prior to the theatrical release date.

Client w/completed film: I will be submitting their film to potential buyers/distributors, so I will be on the phone pitching and doing follow-up calls.

Client w/film project seeking financing: I will write their business plan and research and do financial projections.

In any given day I will interact with a vast array of different people, and each one requires that I be a different person – boy does my acting training come in handy here. I will talk with bankers, talent agents, writers, directors, potential new clients, etc. It's what I love most about my job – I am constantly changing who I am for each person.

One of the most challenging aspects of my job is keeping positive and persistent. It takes 99 "No's" to get to the 1 "Yes" you need. There is a great Calvin Coolidge quote I like to review which inspires me through the rough times:

"Nothing in this world can take the place of persistence. Talent will not; nothing is more common than unsuccessful people with talent. Genius will not; unrewarded genius is almost a proverb. Education will not; the world is full of educated derelicts. Persistence and determination alone are omnipotent. The slogan 'press on' has solved and always will solve the problems of the human race."

So I press on!!

At the end of my day, I will do one of the following typically:

- View films and/or go to live theatre to rejuvenate the little creative soul inside me. Or
- I have dear friends over for a backyard BBQ. My husband is a great BBQ chef and plays a beautiful Kalimba. Great way to end a busy day and unwind. Or
- I will take a dance class or rehearse taiko drumming. I belong to a group and we perform throughout Southern California. So I still get the performance bug!!!

The most important thing for me is to have a "balanced life." I need family, friends, career, spirituality, community, health, exercise, and creativity. I try to be sure every week has each of those elements in it.

Daily Planner

vertex42

Date: 8/17/2009   Anne Marie Gillen

17 August, 2009
Monday

July 2009	August 2009	September 2009
Su M Tu W Th F Sa	Su M Tu W Th F Sa	Su M Tu W Th F Sa
1 2 3 4	1	1 2 3 4 5
5 6 7 8 9 10 11	2 3 4 5 6 7 8	6 7 8 9 10 11 12
12 13 14 15 16 17 18	9 10 11 12 13 14 15	13 14 15 16 17 18 19
19 20 21 22 23 24 25	16 17 18 19 20 21 22	20 21 22 23 24 25 26
26 27 28 29 30 31	23 24 25 26 27 28 29	27 28 29 30
	30 31	

Remember

Structure the day so all the
important stuff gets
handled first

☑ ABC   **Prioritized Task List**

Time   **People to Call**

$Amt   **Expenses**

Appointments

7	:00	Coffee in bed with the LA Times
	:30	Power walk with the dog
8	:00	Review all entertainment daily
	:15	news & box office reports
	:30	Answer overnight emails &
	:45	review daily calendar.
9	:00	Conference call with co-producers &
	:15	financers for next film project:
	:30	
	:45	
10	:00	Prep for the taping of my Seminars:
	:15	
	:30	
	:45	
11	:00	
	:15	
	:30	
	:45	
12	:00	TAPING: 2 back-to-back seminars on
	:15	the business of film producing for
	:30	upcoming DVD series.
	:45	
1	:00	
	:15	
	:30	
	:45	
2	:00	
	:15	
	:30	
	:45	
3	:00	
	:15	
	:30	
	:45	
4	:00	Download with production team
	:15	on taping and timeline for editing.
	:30	
	:45	
5	:00	
	:30	
6	:00	Dinner with girlfriend
	:30	
7	:00	
	:30	
8	:00	Go to Opening Night of the
	:30	Play my dear friend wrote and
9	:00	who I am now developing a film
	:30	with.

Notes

script changes; update on budget and tax
credit research options.

Review final approved guest list; approve
Power Point Presentation; get in make-up.

VIDEOGAME PRODUCTION

In 2003, the revenue brought in by videogames exceeded that of the theatrical box office revenue from motion pictures. Sophisticated videogames incorporate cinematic moving images, presented in an interactive content structure. Like the motion picture industry, videogame makers use big-name talent and spend big money to produce blockbuster hits. Spin-offs of successful motion pictures and comic books are common, as are prequels, sequels, and clones. Like the television industry, creatives plan for a smaller screen. However, interactivity brings an even more intimate relationship between user and content.

In recent years, the videogame industry has been going through a difficult readjustment period due to changing market conditions. The prices of games do not cover the cost of producing the games, because consumers will not spend more than $60 for a title. In 2004, it cost companies about $10 to produce a game. But now consumers are more demanding and consoles and computers are more powerful. Today's games cost $25 million on average, and some cost more.[5] With the sales of most games limited to about 150,000, companies cannot make a profit, unless they strike gold with a blockbuster hit.

Producing games involves three types of activities: creative, technical, and marketing. Interactive content depends on an intricate relationship between the material, the technological delivery platform, and the user. As a result, making games requires all the traditional phases and activities of production – creating story lines, writing dialog, casting, designing visuals, and directing and editing cinematic sequences – as well as several additional steps:

- **Longer, more complex development:** Establish functional requirements for interface, game engine, and technology; write story and script, technical documentation, and licensing of game engine and technology
- **Software programming:** Write code for game play, interaction, etc.
- **Asset integration:** Similar to postproduction
- **Testing, debugging, and quality assurance:** Make sure the game works!

The role of managers in videogame companies is larger than in other sectors of the media industries, such as motion pictures and television. The undertaking is so expensive and complex, the monitoring of costs, coordination, and communication between work teams falls to deeply involved managers. They also exercise the power of marketing planning and review and approval.

Game developers usually build a game around a licensed game engine that fits a popular game structure, such as a first person shooter or an MMORG (massively multiplayer online role-playing game) like World of Warcraft. Artists then create graphics around the engine that deliver a unique experience to gamers. The amount of advance money developers get varies from a nominal $30,000 to millions, depending on the track record of the developers. The creators usually get the advance plus 5 percent of the backend royalties.

The videogame development begins the launch of a new console. The old games – well, they are old hat. New games will take advantage of new console power and features. To make the pitch to videogame company executives, developers put together a one- or two-page description of the game and a list of the visual and sound assets that will be needed. Company decision makers sort through their product needs and submitted ideas. If the executives like the game, the developer builds virtual models and environments, programming a few of the pieces and linking them to the environments to demonstrate the elements of the gameplay.

If the project is green-lighted, work begins. Preproduction is spent writing a script, creating a budget and a schedule, contracting for skilled workers and performers, buying predeveloped elements such as the game engine and existing assets, and arranging for equipment and facilities. Programming and the production of visual and sound assets get under way, proceeding simultaneously. Critical gameplay decisions must be set out in software statements, such as how much user movement makes an effect, what happens when one piece bumps into another, and so forth. Even small companies have a library of code that allows them to cut and paste, and there are game developer sites on the Internet that post free software modules.

Once the programming is completed and the assets are produced, the game is created. Users are called in to test the game in *beta*, a prerelease stage that may still have features that do not work, objects that do not perform as expected, and databases that fail to store or retrieve data necessary to game play. Many game companies engage game players to participate in the beta tests, usually paying them to find the problems. Once the game is *user-tested* and *debugged*, it can be released online or as a standalone packaged product for sale. There are a few game specialty stores, but the majority of games are sold in *big-box retail outlets*, like Wal-Mart, Costco, Best Buy, Fry's, and CompUSA.

Although the popularity of online games lags behind console and PC-based games, they are nevertheless growing in influence. People like forming communities, so they flock to imaginative, well-designed multiplayer games. For companies, the Internet greatly reduces distribution costs, which are a major expense in the packaged game industry. This reduction in costs gives online game companies a lower risk factor. In addition, replacing physical distribution with online administration lets creatives tweak the product in fast cycles of innovation, responding to player feedback. In the online environment, developers can easily upgrade the game play, adding new features and characters to keep the game fresh and gamer interest high. Some observers believe that online games will soon be "programmed" in episode-like increments, encouraging players to log on often to make sure they do not miss important events.

Game developers must take into account the tribal culture that forms around a game, which can become remarkably elaborate. This characteristic emerged early in online gaming. For example, when players joined Ultima Online, a combined CD-ROM and online multiplayer game (http://www.ultima.com) that emerged in the late 1990s, they came into the Ultima world much as they do this one … naked, alone, owning nothing. Over time, they built identities and acquired possessions, including Ultima gold. Ultima IDs and gold have turned up for sale on eBay, worth real money there! Today's World of Warcraft MMORG also uses a CD or DVD to place graphics on users' local computers, reducing the amount of information that has to be transported over the Internet. Significant upgrades to graphically rich online games sometimes involve the physical distribution of a new disc.

MEDIA ASSET MANAGEMENT, DIGITAL ASSET MANAGEMENT, AND CONTENT MANAGEMENT

These systems are components of a *digital assembly line* or *pipeline* that enables workers to assemble a final product. Assets are the individual elements that make up a content product: live action footage, animation, computer-generated images and objects, music, and sound effects, and so forth. The artists and creative teams produce individual assets, which are then stored for access. As new assets come in, they too are stored. Over the course of a project, many people will touch the assets. Editors assemble the sequences. Colorists grade the material, standardizing the colors of the entire project. Audio editors add tracks and effects and normalize and sweeten the sound.

Media asset management, digital asset management, and content management systems are similar, but perform slightly different functions:

- **Media asset management systems** are optimized to handle a large number of media files, particularly video and audio files in a postproduction environment.
- **Digital asset management systems** are optimized to handle a large number of small and medium-sized files, such as text and graphics and sometimes audio.
- **Content management systems** are designed for any kind of media and are optimized for distribution to consumers. They are usually capable of transcoding material into multiple formats, slicing-and-dicing material, and joining elements together, depending on the demands of the specific distribution venue. They do this work on the fly, more or less in real time.

This section examines only media asset management systems (MAMs). (Chapter 11 looks at content management systems.) MAMs are essential in the production of animated feature films that are composed of millions of digitally created animation cels.

MAMs offer many benefits to managers. They provide regular reports, as a built-in function of the system. They let executives stay on top of costs by providing instant review of hours spent on projects and parts projects. Because the expense of skilled workers is the largest component of the budget, monitoring their time is a key part of controlling costs. Managers can also estimate time to completion and report project progress to their supervisors and internal and external clients. Of course, systems also let supervisors monitor the managers under them, so the computerized records may be a mixed blessing.

DreamWorks installed the first fully integrated digital studio for animation, and Disney and Warner Bros. implemented many of the same technologies. The music industry also benefits from digitization – one leading music company has attained nearly 100 percent business-to-business workflow in 2 years. In the television industry, one of the first MAMs was adopted by Paramount Television's *Entertainment Tonight* program, which draws on stored material for background and detail to create new packages based on current events.[6]

The functions of MAMs are to store assets, store information about the assets, provide security for them, and automate content-centric workflows. Companies can track who originates, reviews, approves, and revises every asset, saving an audit trail of the use of content within the organization. Thus, the three important kinds of information in a MAMs are:

- **Essence:** The assets themselves (text, graphics, footage and tracks)
- **Metadata:** The information about the content
- **Usage:** Information about who has permission to use, alter, name and rename, and approve essence and metadata

Metadata is the key to organizing content, as shown in Figure 7-4 – just try finding the can of soup in the cupboard without the metadata provided by the label on the can. Metadata means "data about data." In a digital environment, the

To create *Antz* with DreamWorks, Pacific Data Images built an enormous content management system that used an Oracle database to track and manage every drawing, frame, cel, voiceover, and sound effect. People working on the picture could log into the system using a Netscape browser and find the particular asset they needed by searching for it by shot number, description, artists, or department. They could check it out, examine it, continue working on it, and then check it back into the system – which also made sure that earlier versions were retained.

Carl Rosendahl, PDI[7]

FIGURE 7-4 Life is easier with metadata. *Source: J. Van Tassel.*

content (or essence) is itself data. Metadata is data that describes the essence. Metadata enables search engines. Metadata varies with respect to their quality, quantity, granularity, descriptiveness, searchability, and availability. Indeed, the overall value of the entire system rests on the quality of the metadata it uses.

At first, it is easy to think that metadata is just another weird digital concept that would be better to avoid. Think again, because anyone who uses the Internet depends daily on metadata. Consider Google: The user inputs a search term and the system brings up results, based on keywords the source of the material assigned to it. The "thing" a user is looking for is the "essence," a file, a photo, or a song. The key word, or search term, is the metadata. Without metadata, there would be no search engine; without search engines, how would anyone ever find anything on the Internet?

The importance of stored and matched metadata and essence can hardly be overemphasized. In 2004, Viacom surveyed departments and subdepartments on its Paramount Studios lot. The company's top managers were astonished to discover that employees had created more than 30 database projects on their own, just to track and retrieve information for the work they were tasked to carry out.

The need for MAMs does not just apply to motion picture studios. The scale of many digital projects, such as television commercials, programs and news shows, Web sites, even sophisticated brochures, makes content creation difficult to manage without automated systems in place. Members of a work team must locate particular pieces of stored content. The task would be daunting, perhaps even impossible, without metadata and the systems that match them to essence, retrieve it all, and track changes to them.

Most Internet companies, postproduction facilities, many production companies and studios, and television newsrooms have a media asset management system. A few of these integrate its MAMs with enterprise-wide business systems that allow automated accounting, billing, and other business processes. However, in many organizations, the MAMs is separate from the enterprise software.

ACQUISITION AND AGGREGATION AS CONTENT STRATEGIES

Identifying and negotiating for the rights to content may not seem as exciting as commissioning and supervising production. However, for managers it can be very interesting and profitable, involving considerably less risk, time, resources, and stress than the often-difficult content creation process. Once the material is acquired, managers will also make the key decisions about scheduling, marketing, and promoting it.

Acquisition is old-school; it has long been used in the broadcast industry. Acquisition involves buying programming that has already been produced. Money changes hands and a copyright license or the copyright itself is extended by the existing rights holder to the buyer. Traditional media channels do not typically engage in aggregation. One exception is on-demand TV channels, which are now popular on many cable systems. The menu for these offerings presents a wide variety of movies and programs that customers can see immediately. The choice of movies and TV shows is made easier by allowing viewers to search the listings by name, genre, year, stars, and other keywords. The cable operator or the on-demand movie service is the aggregator.

Aggregation is new-school. Anyone can provide a service by aggregating links to a specific type of information. Identify a need for existing information, aggregate links to it, and if it is valuable, find a way to derive revenue from the service. To be successful, managers spend considerable time exploring market needs, putting together a list of available material, and providing the resources so consumers can access it. Innovation can and does occur in any of these activities.

Internet: Portals, Syndication and Affiliation, Search

The push toward aggregation initially occurred because of Internet portals and search engines. The indexed material may or may not be owned by the Internet site that is listing the content. Internet search engines aggregate content by merely creating a list and links in response to a specific user keyword search: It is aggregation without creation or acquisition.

However, some Internet portals offer content to which the portal creator, subsidiaries, or partners own the rights. A good example of an Internet portal that offers aggregated content is Hulu (http://www.hulu.com), where consumers access a great deal of the most popular broadcast programming. Hulu is a joint venture of NBC and News Corp. (Fox) that was established in 2007, as the two broadcast networks sought to control consumer access to their valuable video content. In 2009, ABC joined the other two broadcasters in 2009, making the material of three of the four major broadcast networks accessible from a single Internet portal.[8]

An agreement of this magnitude requires months of planning by the executives in these organizations. Each company considered the advantages and disadvantages to an arrangement. Finance executives estimated costs and quantified the opportunities. Attorneys offered legal counsel and carefully examined the contracts. In the end, the decision-making managers of the companies negotiated with one another to reach a deal and then recommended approval to the board of directors. Investor relations reached out to inform and reassure big investors and the corporate communications departments of all the involved companies coordinated their release of the information to the public.

In the case of Hulu, the companies all produced and owned their own content. But not all content aggregators make their own content. For example, search engines are another way of aggregating content by listing the URLs where the material resides, in respond to user demand: aggregation without acquisition. Google and Yahoo! are the largest general search engine sites. There are also many specialized video, graphics, and audio search sites, like YouTube, Blinkx, Flickr, AltaVista, Truveo, and others. User-generated recommendations also aggregate by listing content for searchers on such sites as Digg, del.icio.us, and StumbleUpon. Finally, users can make their personal, customized "portals" on their own browser, aggregating content that fits specific criteria and keywords downloaded to the local computer automatically via RSS (Real Simple Syndication) feeds.

Syndication on the Internet differs substantially from television syndication. In television, it is a free, open market for distributing TV programs to any local television station. For producers, it is the second *window* exhibition for TV series episodes that were exclusive to a network for its first run. *Internet syndication* means the controlled, simultaneous distribution of content on the Web sites of multiple partners. RSS is the technological mechanism by which Internet syndication of content takes place.[9]

The content is made available on multiple sites, not by actually transporting the content to them. Rather, a descriptive snippet of the content and the metadata (the information about the material) appears on a site. Users click on a link to access the full version of the content, where it still resides on the server of the originating Web site. The content that appears on other Web sites, whether it is the complete content package or a summary, arrives in the form of a *syndication file*, written in the XML language, which is designed to deliver material to multiple Web sites, describing how the received content should be transported, stored and displayed. The file contains the name of the originating site, a headline, a description or the entire content package, and, if the material is a summary, a link to the site where the complete version resides. When it receives a request for the content, the syndication server provides the content.

The iGoogle customized page (http://www.igoogle.com) is a good example of Internet syndication. Users can place a few *widgets* on their page, out of the thousands that are available, to aggregate real-time data feeds of content and applications. The iGoogle page is refreshed by a feed of headlines from dozens of news services (Google, CNN, newspapers, magazines, and so forth). They can put widgets on their page for Google Maps, a weather service, a calendar, a to-do list, and continuous feeds from their Facebook, Twitter, Meebo, and other social network accounts. When users click on the headline or service, they go to the originating Web site. The elements that make content syndicated on the Internet of value to users include the quality, attractiveness, clarity, and timeliness of the information. Users choose applications that are useful to them.

Internet syndication began with Netscape in 1999, which allowed the early popular site to refresh its content without hiring a large group of editors to discover and move material to Netscape's home page. Instead, users chose their own *feeds* and the entire process was efficiently automated. Increasingly, content creators are dissatisfied with the current system of free circulation of material that costs a great deal to gather, edit, and produce. Rupert Murdoch plans to charge for newspaper content and believes consumers will pay for news material that has value to them.[10]

ORGANIZATIONALLY GENERATED CONTENT

The U.S. government produces hundreds of audiovisual titles every year, listed by the National Audiovisual Center at http://www.ntis.gov/products/nac.aspx. Several government agencies also archive still photographs and other graphic materials. Some of this content is available for free; other material must be purchased or copied for a fee. The total amount of money spent on government content creation is not known, either for individual countries or for global spending. However, a 2001 report to Congress noted that the U.S. Government Printing Office issued 18,000 new titles in 1999 – about 25 percent of the total of new book titles in the United States in that year.[11]

Both nonprofit and for-profit organizations produce content to further their aims. Such material includes films, videos, audio, brochures, emails, Web sites and pages, and still photographs and other graphics. As with spending on government-created content, there are no reports of corporate spending on media production, but it must be immense. A 2008 survey by Junta42 in conjunction with *B2B* magazine queried 150 business-to-business marketing decision makers.[12] They responded that, on average, their organizations allocated *29.42 percent* of their total marketing budget for 2008 on the creation and execution of custom content (the term used to describe media production in the report). The study noted that these findings were consistent with other industry studies. In 2005, the magazine estimated that B2B marketing spending at $15 billion, so 25 percent of that figure, even allowing for stalled marketing budgets, would amount to about $3.5 billion.

The survey looked at many types of "custom" content. The study found that:

- About 69 percent of companies elected to produce email newsletters.
- 50 percent created white papers.
- 47 percent produced case studies.
- Almost 31 percent produced webinars or webcasts.
- More than 20 percent of the surveyed companies created blogs, web portals and microsites, advertorials, and online videos.

USER-GENERATED CONTENT

Everyone with a computer is a potential content creator. Computers come with installed software to create text, graphics, even video and audio pieces. In many ways, the advance of technology has changed the nature of content creation. It used to be that the main barrier to expression was the cost and technical difficulty of production; today, the main barrier is one of discovery – when material is produced, how do others find it to consume and enjoy it?

Blogs, social networks, video sites such as YouTube, and personal and corporate Web sites are rich sources of material that increasingly compete with professionally produced content.

User-generated content (*UGC*) continues to grow – more than 82 million people in the United States engaged in content creation, just in 2008 (Figure 7-5), noted eMarketer.[13]

The market research company observed that more people spent more time creating such material than other users spent consuming it. Moreover, except for ad placement on popular social media Internet sites, it has proven difficult to make money from UGC. Advertisers worry about the uncertain environments of social media and still choose to market their wares in venues that feature professionally produced material.

One effort to *monetize* UGC was the development of *Podshow*. an Internet channel that focused on user-generated podcasts. However, facing competition from free sites like YouTube, the venture was not successful as a strategy to monetize

US User-Generated Content Creators, by Content Type, 2008–2013 (millions)

	2008	2009	2010	2011	2012	2013
User-generated video	15.4	18.1	20.6	22.7	24.9	27.2
Social networking	71.3	79.7	87.7	94.7	100.1	105.3
Blogs	21.2	23.9	26.7	28.5	30.2	32.1
Virtual worlds	11.6	13.9	15.4	16.9	18.4	19.9
User-generated content creators	**82.5**	**88.8**	**95.3**	**101.7**	**108.0**	**114.5**

Source: eMarketer, January 2009

100883   www.eMarketer.com

FIGURE 7-5 U.S. user-generated content creators, by content type, 2008–2013 (millions)

UGC, and the site has since morphed into two ad-supported efforts: http://www.vodpod.com, a community video-sharing site, and http://www.meveotv.com, a free Spanish-language entertainment site. So far, few sites have successfully monetized video on a large scale. One exception is ESPN's online video subscription service[14] – and some adult sites do pretty well too. (However, subscriptions to adult sites are on the decline, nudged out by social network–promoted, do-it-yourself, user-generated videos with nudity and sex that are pushing out the fee-based sites!)[15]

SUMMARY

This chapter looked at the how content in media-producing organizations is developed and produced. It described the processes and activities needed to create content in several sectors, pointing to their similarities and differences. It also gave information about the new, cutting-edge systems that enables complex digital production efforts. Finally, it looked at alternative content strategies: acquisition and aggregation.

WHAT'S AHEAD

Chapter 8 considers marketing strategies for content products. Marketing is a complex process that requires thorough research and careful packaging to be successful. The chapter describes how managers position material to consumers, bundle it, and price it to fit what they have learned about consumer needs and desires.

CASE STUDY 7.1 THE PRODUCER

Get ready to be the Producer of a breakout television show or blockbuster film. Visit your local video store and choose a title that you would have developed had someone else not thought of the idea before you. Map out the individual steps as outlined in this chapter, as if you had produced the show yourself and preparing to meet with the studio to pitch this incredible idea. You'll need to include compelling information on all of the following elements:

- Concept or Idea
- Characters
- Setting
- Arc of Story
- Major plot points
- Potential Audience
- Special Hooks (Casting choice, unique Promotional Idea)

Bonus: Present your information to the class without identifying the program and see if anyone can name the title. If they were the President of the studio, would they have said "Yes?"

CASE STUDY 7.2 THE GAME DEVELOPER

Using the movie or television show from Case Study 7.1, you will now develop a video game as a companion platform. Remember that there are 3 types of activities when developing video games: Creative, Technical and Marketing.

- Write a 1–2 page description of the game include list of art and sound assets.

- Discuss the technical features. What happens in the game?
- Identify your target demo.
- How would you market the game to the target demo?

KEY TERMS

- Beta
- Big-box retail outlets, big-box retailers
- Breakdown
- Buckets (of content)
- Cattle call
- Color grading, color timing
- Computer-generated imagery (CGI)
- Dailies
- Debugged
- Demo reel
- Development
- Digital assembly line
- Digital intermediate (DI)
- Essence
- Feeds
- Green-light
- Hook
- Internet syndication
- Metadata
- Monetize
- Pipeline
- Pitch
- Previsualization, previz
- Query letter
- Server
- Storyboards
- Syndication file
- Transcoding
- User-generated content (UGC)
- Widget
- XML

REFERENCES

1. ——— (September 22, 2009). More declines for music ringtones. Accessed October 9, 2009, at http://www.textually.org/ringtonia/archives/cat_random_stats.htm.

2. ——— (April 4, 2009). BMI Mobile music market projections: Ringback tones continue to lead and grow to tune of $235 million in 2009. *Wireless News*. Accessed July 18, 2009, at http://www.encyclopedia.com/doc/1P1-162667099.html.

3. ———. (February 12, 1998). Special effects. (Transcript of *PBS NewsHour*.) Accessed October 22, 2009, at http://www.pbs.org/newshour/bb/entertainment/jan-june98/movies_2-12.html.

4. Simonton, D. K. (2005). Cinematic creativity and production budgets: Does money make the movies? Accessed November 3, 2009, at http://escholarship.org/uc/item/9rv1c5q7.

5. Richtel, M. (March 29, 2009). Videogame makers challenged by the next wave of media. *New York Times*. Accessed March 29, 2009, at http://www.nytimes.com/2009/03/30/technology/30game.html.

6. Van Tassel, J. (2002). *Content management systems*. Washington, DC: NAB Press.

7. Rosendahl, C. (October 14, 1999). Personal interview.

8. Chmielewski, D. C. (May 1, 2009). Disney joins Fox and NBC as joint venture partner of Hulu. *Los Angeles Times*. Accessed August 20, 2009, at http://articles.latimes.com/2009/may/01/business/fi-wirehulu1.

9. Englehard, R. & van der Vliet, S. (2003). *Syndication: Sharing content across websites*. Accessed April 20, 2009, at http://evolt.org/node/60137.

10. Clark A. (May 7, 2009). News Corp. will charge for newspaper websites, says Rupert Murdoch. *Guardian*. Accessed May 10, 2009, at http://www.guardian.co.uk/media/2009/may/07/rupert-murdoch-charging-websites.

11. U.S. Government Printing Office. (2001). *Biennial report to Congress on the status of GPO access*, Appendix C; Accessed online June 8, 2009, at http://www.access.gpo.gov/su_docs/aces/biennial/index.html. For the number of book titles, see *Statistical Abstract*, Table 938.

12. Junta42 (2008). *Business-to-business custom publishing research*. Accessed April 18, 2009, at http://www.junta42.com/resources/Business_to_Business_Custom_Publishing_Research/.

13. eMarketer (February 5, 2009). *UGC phenomenon eclipses commercial possibilities*. Accessed March 18, 2009, at http://www.emarketer.com/Article.aspx?R=1006916.

14. Gubbins, E. (July 20, 2009). Move Networks' new CEO on monetizing Internet video. *Telephony Online*. Accessed October 2, 2009, at http://telephonyonline.com/residential_services/news/move-networks-roxanne-austin-qa-0720/index.html.

15. Blacker, C. (July 23, 2009). Porn: Still leading online advertising? *Search Engine Journal*. Accessed October 8, 2009, at http://www.searchenginejournal.com/online-adult-advertising/11977/.

Strategies for Marketing Content

I just believe that the cost of marketing is going to increase and the cost of delivery is going to decrease as the Net gets stronger and mass media gets weaker.

Joichi Ito

CHAPTER OBJECTIVES

The objective of this chapter is to provide you with information about:
- Marketing management and managing marketing
  - The marketing plan, marketing communications, and SOSTAC®
- Marketing strategies
  - Content as Product
  - Integrated Marketing Communications (IMC)
  - Branding, positioning, viral marketing, and other methods for marketers to build bridges between content and consumers
- Defining the content market
  - The global market for content
  - Audience/consumer segmentation
- Universal marketing appeals

INTRODUCTION

Content has two markets – the marketplace of ideas and the economic market. Whether it reaches a few million people or just a few depends on money, energy, strategy, and just plain luck. When an organization's success depends on the sale and distribution of content, the importance of marketing cannot be overstated – it is the very lifeblood of the organization – a smart, effective marketing effort is essential. As a result, almost every executive in a media company needs to understand something about it. Managers in the content areas

203

DOI: 10.1016/B978-0-240-81020-1.00008-7

need to know the market for material – what people want, what they buy, what will attract audiences that advertisers will buy. Facilities managers are involved in the planning, budget, and resource allocation of content product initiatives. Financial managers have to structure the deals.

In a sense, the process begins as part of deciding whether to create or acquire a content product. Will it sell? Who will buy it? How much will it cost, and how much will the consumer pay? The answers to these questions are at the heart of making decisions about content. Once the content is in hand – a video, a song, a newsletter – then the work to get it to consumers begins. An enterprise accomplishes this goal through marketing, defined by the American Marketing Association as: "The activity, set of institutions, and processes for creating, communicating, delivering, and exchanging offerings that have value for customers, clients, partners, and society at large."[1]

Marketing, like all communication activities, is undergoing enormous change, driven by rapid technological innovation. According to Smith and Taylor:

> Marketing and the marketing communications mix are changing. New insights, new tools, new opportunities and new challenges are emerging as the 21st century progresses. The world's 6 1/4 billion consumers and almost 400 million business customers are becoming increasingly accessible. And so too are your customers … ready targets for your competitors. New pressures also emerge as managers operated in delayered organizations, stripped of supporting services and yet free from the quagmire of tier upon tier of management. This means more managers need to understand marketing, which itself is changing.[2]

The emergence of the Internet as a platform that enables person-to-person communication between people who may never meet face-to-face is fundamentally changing communication. It empowers people to gather and exchange information on a scale that creates a qualitatively different environment for communicators. When the mass media was the primary source of consumer information, advertisers could control a great deal of what they could learn, although interpersonal social networks also exerted influence through conversations about people's experience with products and services.

However, now people can have online conversations with hundreds, thousands, and even millions of others. User feedback, comments, and ratings on many sites make it impossible for advertisers to control the conversation. At best, they can influence it. Figures 8-1 and 8-2 show how peer-to-peer connections alter the way information reaches consumers (and publics and audiences), compared to the process defined by traditional mass media communication.

Marketing has always been complex, requiring knowledge of the industry, the market, and the consumer. Yet mere knowledge is not always enough.

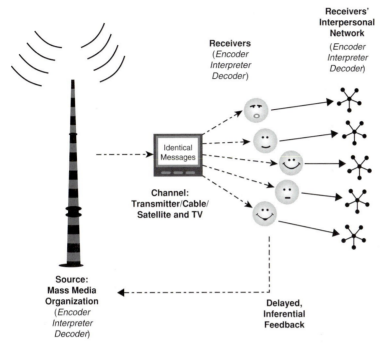

Schramm's Model of Broadcast Communication

FIGURE 8-1 Communication process of mass communication

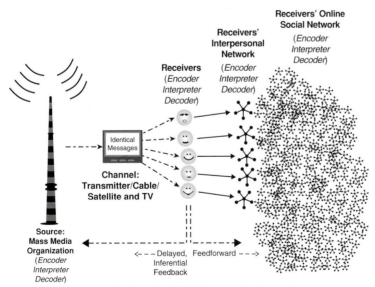

Feedforward Model of Viral Media Communication

FIGURE 8-2 Communication process of mass media and Internet media

Marketing is as much art as science, calling for innovation and creativity – and never so much as today, with new opportunities and challenges.

MARKETING MANAGEMENT AND MANAGING MARKETING

Marketing managers plan, implement, and oversee an organization's marketing activities, bringing to bear all of the available resources, time, money, and creativity, to the effort. In any industry, marketing is central to organizational success in fulfilling its business plan. In the content industries, there is a wide range of marketing needs and activities, making it difficult to generalize across the spectrum of organizations. It follows that marketing managers in different organizations exert varying levels of influence. Small content producers may hire freelance marketers; large companies can have managers who address narrow vertical marketing channels, such as healthcare titles, or broad horizontal channels, or all titles across multiple big-box retailers (stores like Wal-Mart, Best Buy, Costco, and so forth). Alternatively, a brand manager may be in charge of a line of products with the same brand, marketed via all available channels.

At the most basic level, marketing is matchmaking. It brings customers to the organization – buyers, consumers, viewers, audiences, advertisers. The job of marketing managers is to introduce the right prospects to the right products at the right time, or, as it is often expressed, to affect the level, timing, and composition of customer demand to meet organizational objectives.

In most content companies, marketing is not just the purview of the marketing department. According to McKenna, "Marketing today is not a function; it is a way of doing business. Marketing is not a new ad campaign or this month's promotion. Marketing has to be all-pervasive, part of everyone's job description, from the receptionists to the board of directors. Its job is neither to fool the customer nor to falsify the company's image. It is to integrate the customer into the design of the product and to design a systematic process for interaction that will create substance in the relationship."[3]

The marketing of content products is similar to those efforts in any industry. It follows well-known processes and uses familiar media platforms to buy radio ads, outdoor boards, public transportation posters and billboards, Internet banners, and television and radio ads. Specific segments of the media industries may market differently because of traditional practices, because they are too new to have traditions, or because the market of the sector, company, or product has changed. Some sectors, including motion pictures, television, and radio learn a lot about target audiences, but little about individual consumers. Others, such as newspapers, magazines, and especially Internet marketers, know a great deal about individuals. In many sectors, such as motion pictures, television, radio, newspapers, and Internet sites, the medium itself offers a way to market all the content the outlet owner distributes. For example, most television networks set aside a substantial portion of their commercial air time to in-house promotional efforts.

As indicated in the previous chapter, in media businesses, marketing is intertwined with the initial decision making about producing or acquiring content and continues to be a focus of discussion throughout the process. Even the finance department is involved in setting budgets for content acquisition, production, and marketing and product pricing. Virtually every manager in a media company understands something about marketing and its importance to the health of the organization.

The Marketing Plan, MarCom, and SOSTAC®

Marketing plans provide a roadmap for how an organization will fulfill its business plan and make its business model come alive. In decades past, marketing executives would develop or accept a product, set pricing, define marketing channels, and develop the marketing communications. (This array of decisions is immortalized as the four Ps of the marketing mix: product, price, place, promotion.) After making these decisions, managers would hire an advertising agency, develop a new ad campaign, design the product packaging and collateral materials, train the sales force, and engage a new public relations to reposition the company's image and enhance its reputation.

The focus of marketing is changing from one based on the product producer and the four Ps to one based on the customer or consumer and the four Cs:

Product	Consumer
Price	Cost
Place	Convenience
Promotion	Communication

This new focus and many other changes are making today's marketing plans infinitely more complex. The growth of media platforms, which bring more channels, more programs, and altogether more content, is causing rapid fragmentation of the mass audience. The rise of consumer-to-consumer communication through social networks and other interactive services, global markets, and the increasing multiplicity of product offerings and pricing tailored to specific consumer segments all combine to produce a more complex set of considerations and tasks for all marketers. Media companies also face new challenges such as the speed and scope of the market, professional content counterfeiting, and casual copying.

The new market for content changes how companies bring products to consumers, requiring flexible products, prices, delivery mode, and payment methods. Marketers are likely to have to market to ever narrower niches, even as the pressure for blockbusters continues. They must develop interactive conversations with customers, not just push communications one way to them. If marketers hope for their content to go viral on the Internet, with consumers forwarding recommendations to their online friends, content needs to be flexible, allowing consumers to forward material via email and posts. Marketers may also have to reexamine how they put products together so that they satisfy consumer wants and expectations. For example, music labels insisted on the sale of albums, refusing to allow the sale of individual songs. Their resistance to selling single songs was one of the driving factors behind consumers turning to peer-to-peer networks so they could get the music they wanted, without paying for music they didn't want.

A marketing plan describes how the organization will bring consumers to the company and its products. It will include a full SWOT analysis (Strengths, Weaknesses, Opportunities, and Threats) to help marketers understand the market. A strong marketing communications plan will be at the heart of the entire effort. Often shortened to MarCom, the plan to communicate with potential and actual customers is the operational blueprint for how the relationship with customers will be initiated, conducted, and maintained over time.

SOSTAC® is a framework for planning a marketing communication strategy, an acronym for these activities, as shown in Figure 8-3. SOSTAC stands for Situation

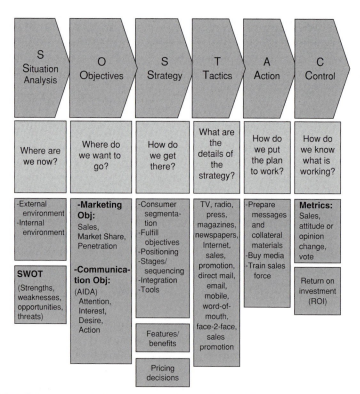

FIGURE 8-3 Planning marketing communications with SOSTAC. *Source: Joan Van Tassel based on (Smith & Taylor, 2004).*[5]

Analysis, Objectives, Strategy, Tactics, Action, and Control.[4] The situation analysis may constitute as much as 50 percent of a marketing communications plan. It describes the external environment – economic, political, and competitive landscapes – and the internal factors, especially resources such as the three Ms: men (human resources), money, and minutes (time).

A DAY IN THE LIFE OF DOROTHY HUI

Dorothy Hui, VP, Partnership Marketing & Sales, Wind-up Records

A typical Wednesday begins with a review of the "week in metrics." SoundScan sales reports from the week prior refresh on Wednesdays, so my data analysis starts by logging in to Nielsen SoundScan, the industry sales reporting tool which reports album and digital single sales: how many were sold this week and in which DMAs. Run reporting sets for each of our active albums and digital singles.

I print and review the weekly web trends report, including artist official Web site traffic, social networks traffic and streaming metrics; for example, for current artists with active singles, how many MySpace profile views did each artist profile receive this week, how many times was the single streamed on the MySpace profile this week; how many plays did the current music video on YouTube receive? The combination of web trends and sales metrics shows us how and where listeners are responding to exposure to our music.

In notable trends this week, Push Play's digital single sales for their new single "Midnight Romeo" more than doubled from last week as pop radio spins kicked in and the band's video recently premiered on Yahoo! Music. I note this and send out a highlighted DMA sales report to our promotion staff, so they can more closely analyze the correlation between digital single sales and airplay.

In the meantime, the Company of Thieves "Oscar Wilde" digital single and album sales spike in select markets where the band is getting alternative radio airplay and has recently passed through on tour. Our Alternative Radio promotions director and I discuss trends, as she is closely monitoring where we are finding new fans in airplay markets.

I write up a summary of notable traffic and sales trends to send to our marketing and radio promotion staff. This type of data analysis is useful information as we build out our marketing story and show our radio station supporters and interactive partners the listener response.

Time for a planning meeting to discuss the key release time lines associated with the release of the upcoming Creed album, Full Circle, coming out in October. The first single, "Overcome," ships to radio at the end of the month. With the radio plan in mind, our marketing team determines the release date for the digital single, which will follow one week after radio stations receive the single. The ringtones and ringbacks will be scheduled for delivery as soon as possible, to allow for ingestion time with the mobile carriers.

I meet with Sarah – our Manager, Digital and Mobile Distribution – to set the production process in motion for the release of the new Creed digital single and schedule the delivery date for the ringtone and ringback to mobile carriers. We discuss deadlines needed for album assets, such as audio and artwork, in order to set up a digital album preorder on iTunes.

Catch-up call with our Yahoo! Music label rep to go over our current singles and videos, highlighting notable radio growth and marketing news so that Yahoo's music team can consider our videos and singles for programming on their site accordingly. We confirm the date of our upcoming Emily Osment "All the Way Up" video premiere on Yahoo! Music.

I take a screenshot of Push Play's video "Midnight Romeo" rotating through YouTube's featured videos. I note the video is already garnering "YouTube Honors," showing up on Most Discussed and Most Favorite charts. I inform band management and marketing and radio promotion teams of this, as this provides a new insight into fan response. I add this feature to my marketing report spreadsheet, where my team tracks the promotional placements that have run for each artist.

Meet with Mark – Manager, Interactive Marketing – to discuss upcoming videos and identify potential online partners for future premieres. We evaluate metrics from Push Play's recent Facebook/U Stream live chat, which generated enough chatter for Push Play to register as a trending topic on Twitter.

I launch Tweet Deck and take a quick scan of new "tweets" to check on chatter on Wind-up bands. Looks like a lot of fans had a good time at last night's Company of Thieves show and that the band converted new fans from their performance.

Continued...

vertex42   **Daily Planner**

Date: | 8/19/2009 | *Dorothy Hui*

19   August, 2009
Wednesday

July 2009							**August 2009**							September 2009					
Su	M	Tu	W	Th	F	Sa	Su	M	Tu	W	Th	F	Sa	Su	M	Tu	W	Th	F	Sa
			1	2	3	4							1			1	2	3	4	5
5	6	7	8	9	10	11	2	3	4	5	6	7	8	6	7	8	9	10	11	12
12	13	14	15	16	17	18	9	10	11	12	13	14	15	13	14	15	16	17	18	19
19	20	21	22	23	24	25	16	17	18	19	20	21	22	20	21	22	23	24	25	26
26	27	28	29	30	31		23	24	25	26	27	28	29	27	28	29	30			
							30	31													

Remember
Tegan and Sara tickets on sale on Friday

☑ ABC   Prioritized Task List
	Reach out to LA partners re: setting up dates/times for music listening sessions on upcoming trip
	Book travel for LA trip
	Add new release information to digital platforms production queue
	Request proposals for October releases online ad plans
	Send invites to upcoming Civil Twilight performance

Time   People to Call
Return call from Jim

$Amt   Expenses

Appointments
7	:00	
	:30	
8	:00	
	:15	
	:30	
	:45	
9	:00	*Weekly Sales & Web Trends Report*
	:15	
	:30	
	:45	
10	:00	
	:15	
	:30	
	:45	
11	:00	
	:15	
	:30	
	:45	
12	:00	*New Release Planning Meeting*
	:15	
	:30	
	:45	
1	:00	
	:15	
	:30	
	:45	
2	:00	*Meeting with Sarah - Digital Distribution*
	:15	
	:30	
	:45	
3	:00	*Yahoo! Music Catch-up Call*
	:15	
	:30	
	:45	
4	:00	*Meeting with Mark - Interactive Marketing*
	:15	
	:30	
	:45	
5	:00	
	:30	
6	:00	
	:30	
7	:00	
	:30	
8	:00	
	:30	
9	:00	
	:30	

Notes

MARKETING STRATEGIES

Companies set sales goals, and it takes marketing to achieve them. They base their marketing efforts on certain assumptions they make about the nature of the markets in which their products compete, their consumers, and their resources. Then they develop the strategies that will guide them to achieve their objectives. Strategies are big ideas for how to approach a situation or problem; tactics are activities that, if undertaken, implement the strategies. If a strategy is the right approach, and the tactics implement the strategy, then the organization stands a good chance of achieving its goals.

Content as Product

There are three characteristics of digital content that make it different from many consumer products and affect content marketing strategies.

Table 8-1 Content Products and Market Strategies

Product Characteristic	Marketing Consequence
Digital content is completely digital from development through consumption. Unless it is replicated in the physical world (usually a CD or DVD), it may never assume digital form. This form makes it easy to copy and to pass around.	Implement copy protection and rights management systems and procedures.
Content is almost always a discretionary economic good, which means people buy and consume it based on choice. Unlike housing, food, and clothing, content is rarely essential to survival, requiring every person to acquire it in some way.	Direct appeals to psychological, emotional, and social needs.
Content is an experience good. Its use or consumption by one person does not prevent another person from using or consuming it. If someone has a car, a house, or a sweater, another person cannot have it at the same time. And in the case of a car or dwelling, there are legal provisions for ownership. Similarly, if one individual eats a salad, it is gone and cannot be eaten by someone else. By contrast, one person can consume a book, a music album, or a movie and nothing prevents another person (or another 2500 people) from also consuming it.	Sell the maximum number of products to first time-purchases as quickly as possible, before the product can be circulated.

INTEGRATED MARKETING COMMUNICATIONS (IMC): REACHING ACROSS THE WIRE AND THE ETHER

The basic concept of *integrated marketing communications* (IMC) is that all aspects of marketing communication, including advertising, sales promotion, public relations, and direct marketing work together across all available media platforms, as a unified force, rather than in isolation. It includes two key parts: the messages and the media platforms. The messages need to work together so that they reinforce one another. The multiple media platforms are all channels that are relevant to the marketer's budget and intent, including:

- Mass media advertising and public relations (television, radio, newspapers, magazines, Internet sites)
- Social media (blogs, wikis, social networks, content sharing sites, word of Net)
- Personal media (mobile phones, PDAs, palmtop computers)
- Direct media (email, postal media, point-of-purchase materials and displays)

Most media companies use IMC techniques in their marketing efforts. A new motion picture, TV show, videogame, song, or book that the marketer believes will be a blockbuster may well have IMC support across a wide array of media platforms. The campaign is likely to include some combination of TV and radio spots and newspaper, magazine, and Internet banner ads. There may be a dedicated Web site, fan pages in Facebook and other social networks, trailers on YouTube, and posts on blog sites. Mobile campaigns, while not yet common, are not unknown.

In 2008, Universal Pictures sent text messages to mobile users to support *Forgetting Sarah Marshall* and *Knocked Up*; a Paramount Pictures campaign used mobile phones to market *Eagle Eye*. In 2009, Universal Pictures developed a mobile campaign that included downloadable wallpapers and connection to a ticket-buying service for *Fast & Furious*. The use of mobile technology to vote for contestants on *American Idol* is well known – and provided a database of cell telephone numbers, allowing the show to send marketing messages to millions of mobile subscribers to promote the show.

Direct media such as email and postal mail are used infrequently by entertainment marketers, particularly after complaints about spam from email users against the Coca-Cola promotion of one of the Harry Potter movies. However, email campaigns to business executives frequently support company-sponsored free white papers that are designed to brand and position the company's products. Carried out most often in a business-to-business marketing environment, a company usually has a database of existing and potential customers that they can use to make the free offer via an email blast. If the white paper or other free document has been carefully written to provide new and valuable information, such campaigns can be quite successful in establishing *share-of-mind* in the targeted industry.

Product Placement within Content

Lehu defines product placement as "the location or, more accurately, the integration of a product or a brand into a film or televised series."[6] Product placement should not be confused with subliminal advertising, where the theoretical idea is to hide the message so that it works on the unconscious mind of the consumer. By contrast, placing a product in popular content seeks to maximize visibility.

For marketers, the technique offers a way to make a positive, credible association in the minds of potential consumers for the product. Marketers seek to clarify precisely how the product placement will be carried out. They come to the table with specific goals: They want a visible placement that will capture attention for as long as possible. And they try to minimize cost in an arena where costs differ greatly, depending on the show and the audience it reaches, and the availability of placement opportunities.

Many people may not realize how pervasive product placement in entertainment actually is. In the content industries, NBC and CBS have placed their brands in shows. Newspapers and magazines, software makers like Adobe and Microsoft, and even the videogame maker Activision have all placed products in entertainment vehicles. So have theaters, theme parks, and Internet sites. Consumer electronics makers frequently use product placement strategies.

There is some criticism of product placement. Though not subliminal, it is often subtle, and the consumer remains largely unaware that the material contains advertising. Criticism is particularly strong when the audience for the show or motion picture is children.

More Marketing Strategies

A brand is a name or symbol that identifies a product or company; over time, the association between the identity and product becomes rooted in the mind of consumers. According to Feldwick, "At its simplest, a brand is a recognizable and trustworthy badge of origin, and also a promise of performance."[7] In the media industries, *branding* is a marketing strategy that seeks to attract consumers to a content product because they have come to recognize it and attribute positive characteristics to it.

Sometimes the brand is the content itself. For example, Harry Potter is the brand of the motion pictures and other related content products. Or the brand might be an actor or performer, so people will go to see a movie starring Johnny Depp, regardless of the other characteristics of the content. In the early days of motion pictures, the ability of stars to attract an audience led studios to tie actors to long-term contracts, so that these popular figures became associated with the studio. The studio invested in building the actor's identity with the public because people would go to see a movie with Marilyn Monroe but were less likely to pay to see a movie merely identified as a Warner Bros. picture.

Now content brands are growing in importance because of the rapid increase in the number of choices consumers have. Thirty years ago, many viewers knew all the new programs on the network TV schedule. Today, no one can possibly track the programming of the 500 available channels available to them. Viewers will turn to a particular network simply because it is among the six or so channels they prefer. In this way, television networks' brands (ABC, NBC, Comedy Channel, Tennis Channel) provide a showcase for viewers to sample new offerings but will not, in themselves, sustain the content product. Success depends on qualities of the program itself, not just as part of a branded channel – or any other aspect of marketing.

In the case of business-created content that is given away free – such as research reports, white papers, and product brochures – the content itself is part of the branding effort, representing the company's approach to a particular topic. Often offered on the Internet, the marketer requires registration to download the document, thereby adding valuable information about potential customers to a database. That information can be used for other marketing communications aimed at turning the free content consumer into a paying customer.

Positioning is a specific form of branding, a strategy for competitive markets, where there are multiple products in the category. Marketers use it to create an identity in the consumers' minds that distinguishes their brand or product advantageously, as compared to its competitors. Branding creates a consistent strategic identity; positioning creates a specific, tactical identity that is not inconsistent with the brand, but places it within a particular market environment. Developing a position strategy begins with analyzing the marketing situation:

Microsoft Office dominates the market for bundled word processing, spreadsheet, and presentation desktop applications. How can another provider compete? Sun Microsystems was concerned about Microsoft's dominance in server markets as well, so Sun decided to provide competition in the desktop applications market. It developed a word processing software program called StarOffice that offers similar functionalities to MS Word and lets users create compatible documents that can be imported and exported between StarOffice and MS Office. Later, the mantle of StarOffice was picked up by open source software writers and was included in an application suite called OpenOffice.org (OO).

The targeted consumer segment was college students, who are sensitive to price. The most important difference between OO and MS Office is that OO is free. There are few other meaningful differences between the two products. The significant benefit the customer receives is that they do not have to pay the relatively high cost for the MS Office suite.

By 2007, OpenOffice could claim about a 20 percent market share.[8] It is difficult to estimate the precise market share, because OO is distributed freely on the Internet. The two reasons the product has not grabbed an even greater share is that the translation between documents is not always perfect and there is a cost to learning a new software program. Moreover, Microsoft moved to cut off competition by reducing the student price for MS Office to $59, well under the price point at which students would consider switching to OO, despite its flaws.

- Who is the consumer in this segment?
- What is the product?
- What is the most important benefit it offers to this consumer segment?
- What is the most important competitive product to this consumer segment?
- How is the marketer's product different from that of the most important competitor?
- What significant customer benefit does the marketer's product difference bring to the consumer?

Viral marketing is the marketing strategy relied upon by *The Blair Witch Project*. The three filmmakers posted messages on social networks and blog pages about missing film students. They gradually unfolded the pre-story of the film, continuing to post to blogs and social network pages and setting up their own Web site with video trailers from the film. By the time it was released, the audience had reached a fever pitch to see the movie, turning the $22,000 it cost to make the picture into $248 million.[9]

Viral marketers generate word of mouth (WOM) and buzz among consumers, turning potential customers into the marketing and sales force for the content product, influencing others in their social networks. They may also try to stimulate word of Net (WON), harnessing the activities of online users to use Internet platforms to transmit quickly and easily their preferences, thoughts, and intentions to a large group of friends and acquaintances. Dobele et al. (2005) conducted a study and found that a successful viral marketing effort, whether online or offline, must capture the imagination, promote visible, easy-to-use products, target the right audience or consumer, and come from credible sources.[10]

Spiral marketing strategies recognize that potential prospects use multiple media and that messages that reach them in one medium influence and are influenced by messages in another medium. A spiral campaign might begin on the Web, then be reinforced by broadcast advertising, with mentions of the Web site – effectively driving consumers back to the Web. The message on the Web should serve to reinforce the broadcast messages, so that the consumer is enveloped in a spiral of messaging that leads them to purchase.

Data mining strategies target specific groups of consumers and sends specific messages to them, based on what the marketer already knows. Increasingly, this type of strategy is called *micro-targeting*, because it tries to sell to small numbers of carefully selected consumers. For example, iTunes.com might use its database of music downloaded by a customer to suggest related music to that person. It is "micro"-targeting, because out of the millions of songs available, perhaps only 500 people bought one of the songs that the particular customer did, but iTunes might make a suggestion anyway.

It is easiest to carry out this strategy on the Internet, and many Web sites participate in micro-targeting efforts through such services as Google Analytics. The methods to gather and analyze data from Web site visits are still in their infancy. They are also controversial. Consumers worry about their privacy, and there has been enough expressed concern that the U.S. Congress is considering legislation to regulate the kind of data that is collected and distributed about users without their knowledge and permission.

To carry out data mining efforts, marketers gather the data by using cookies, a small file placed in the memory of the individual's computer that monitors all the Web sites they visit and perhaps what pages they access, how long they spend on those pages, and the merchandise they order. Of course, companies can always track visitors on their own sites and many require registration that asks for detailed personal information. Marketers can then buy data from credit card companies, the U.S. Census, and other Web site operators to put together a precise profile of individuals and niche consumer segments.

Once consumer segments are identified, marketers create messages that appeal to the specific needs and wants of each group. Such tailored messages almost always involve some form of social media (blogs, social network pages, etc.), personal media (mobile phone campaigns), or direct media (email and postal mail). The mass media are not generally suited to messages crafted for small consumer segments, although some cable systems allow targeted marketing to zip codes or even individual subscribers.

The best example of data mining strategies is Amazon.com. When an individual buys books from the site, the software keeps tracks of the purchases and makes recommendations for additional products, based on past buying behavior. Google and Wal-Mart also use the most sophisticated data mining and micro-targeting technologies available.

DEFINING THE MARKET

The market means consumers. Markets are people – individual and organizational buyers. Defining a market is a matter of identifying the number and characteristics of potential buyers. It is a process called market and consumer segmentation, which means dividing the market into groups that are likely to respond to different marketing appeals. Methods for segmenting consumers have changed dramatically over the past decade, with the appearance of ever more sophisticated means for data collection, analysis, and retrieval, including the micro-targeting mentioned earlier. Media companies sell content locally, regionally, nationally, and globally. Their chances of success are greatly increased the more they understand the market and the characteristics of their potential consumers.

The Global Market for Content

It's really big: In 2011, the global media and entertainment industries will account for nearly $2 trillion in revenue, including videogames but not including computer software. The global content economy is growing for the same reason it is growing everywhere – rising prosperity and the emergence of new platforms, more channels, more programs, and more user-created material. Another underappreciated reason is the increasing global interconnectedness of content producing and marketing organizations that makes it possible for companies to:

- Scout and identify local talent and promote that talent regionally, nationally, and then internationally
- Mount coordinated marketing campaigns across multiple territories
- Market content efficiently, using the range of marketing strategies, because local practitioners have deep knowledge of the marketing and promotional platforms in their geographies

Special issues must be considered when managers plan international marketing efforts for content. Keegan and Schlegelmilch identify the key decisions they should make before implementing the plan by examining the relationships between the market, products, and message requirements.[11] The *same product/ same communications* combination will work in markets where the market structure and consumers' needs and usage practices are the same or very similar. If usage practices are the same market but consumer needs are different, the marketer should adopt a strategy of the *same product/different communications.* A strategy of *different product/same communications* applies when the market structure requires specific product configurations but consumer needs and practices are similar. Finally, considering both *different product/different communications* makes sense when the market structure and consumer needs and usage practices are so different that the original product has little chance of succeeding.

Audience/Consumer Segmentation

Segmentation is such an important part of marketing that it often appears in several sections of the overall marketing plan – in the situation analysis, objectives, strategies, and tactics. Segments are groups of similar buyers. Targeted marketing consists of implementing a program of strategies, tactics, and communications to reach potential buyers to induce them to buy the product, change their opinion, donate to a cause, or vote for an issue or candidate. The data used to find appropriate segments most often begins with a company's existing customers. If the enterprise is new or the goal is to find new customers, the next source of data may be market intelligence, usually purchased from marketing research firms. Other sources of data include the U.S. Census, credit card companies, and, most importantly for content companies, reports about viewership and consumer electronic ownership by consumer characteristics.

It is often easy for marketers to identify the largest, most important segments. But other segments may not be so obvious. Smith and Taylor (2004) provide criteria for marketers to judge the viability of segments.[12] They argue that segments must be measurable (so they can be identified), substantial (so they are worth spending valuable dollars to reach), accessible (so they are reachable), and relevant (so they are likely buyers). Once identified, each segment should be analyzed in terms of size, income, lifestyle, likelihood of purchase, vulnerability to competition, and many other factors.

Traditionally, marketers segmented consumers by their demographic characteristics. In addition, marketers often want to know something about potential consumers' lifestyle, values, and psychological profile, especially those aspects that relate to the product category.

The most widely used methods to segment consumers are:

- **Demographics:** Variables like age, gender, marital status, occupation, location/geography, ethnicity, income, and educational level
- **Psychographics/lifestyle:** Activities, beliefs, attitudes, values, product preferences
- **Behavioral characteristics:** Brand loyalty, user category (first-time buyer, regular purchaser, etc.), product usage, and usage rate

Few content marketers carry out detailed consumer segmentation studies. Content products are usually one of a kind, much different from cans of soup or car wax or other packaged goods that may be on the market for several years, instead of several weeks. Rather, they may do rudimentary research (focus groups, audience testing with previews) to predict how an audience will receive a particular offering.

One area of rising interest to all marketers, including media companies, is media use.[13] The fragmentation of the mass audience makes it more difficult to promote content with their own content platform. To reach new consumers, they need to extend their messages to platforms where their potential consumers spend their time. Do they use Internet search engines, recommendation sites, or social networking sites to look for content? Do they receive content over mobile phones? Do they watch video or listen to the radio on their computers? If they spend time surfing the Internet, which sites do they visit?

The answers to these and other media use questions will determine how and where media companies need to promote their wares. Marketers must put their messages in front of potential consumers where they are already consuming media, and as consumer media habits change, they have to change along with it. It is worth noting that the 2008 Obama campaigns used their data about media use to conduct a sophisticated communication campaign.[14]

UNIVERSAL MARKETING APPEALS: THE NEW, THE FIRST, THE ONLY, AND THE NEW AND IMPROVED

The appeal is part of the marketer's tactical toolkit. Usually the appeal is based on the *unique selling proposition* (*USP*), an offer to a consumer segment that ties together product features and consumer benefits in such a way that only one product meets the criteria – it is unique. The feature/benefit pair for each segment is at the heart of most marketing messages.

There are four classic appeals that are effective in selling almost any product, including content, usually presented with great excitement, as depicted in Figures 8-4a and b and 8-5a and b. "New" is one of the most universal and effective words to get attention. "First" is like "new," and may also add an innovative dimension or competitive advantage that increases the value of the product. For example, a *first-run film* describes a motion picture that is being released for the first time. Because most movies attract the majority of their viewers in the first few weeks following release, theaters often pay more for them. *Second-run* films command a lower price and theater owners may be able

(a)   (b)

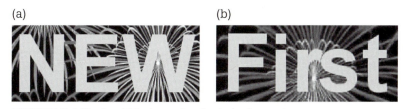

FIGURE 8-4 'New' and 'First' appeal to the desire for novelty

(a)   (b)

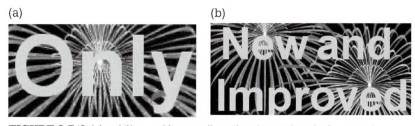

FIGURE 8-5 'Only' and 'New and Improved' are time-honored marketing appeals

to keep a higher percentage of the box office revenue. In television, "first run" refers to a program making its first on-air debut, whether on a TV network or in syndication (called *first-run syndication* like *Oprah*).

"Only" is a bid for *exclusivity*. This appeal is a traditional way that content marketers increase the value of an offering by driving consumers to a specific outlet to get the content – a particular theater, TV or radio station, print publication, or Web site. Because people can only view, listen, or use the material in a limited number of venues, the distributor and exhibitor alike can sometimes charge more for it. "New and improved" taps the appeal of a new product with the promise of something even better.

SUMMARY

Marketing is exciting and complex work that is essential to distributing content. Marketing professionals are key members of the management team who bring a detailed understanding of content products, marketing fundamentals and strategies, distribution technologies, and messaging to a successful effort. They are good students of human nature, tapping people's psychological, emotional, and social needs to craft their appeals to content audiences and consumers.

WHAT'S AHEAD

The next chapter will present a detailed look at all the imaginative ways that content marketers develop specific product offerings to sell to potential consumers. It looks at how they package new content and repackage existing content for new audiences. Chapter 9 explains the structure of markets at the wholesale, retail, and direct-to-consumer levels. Finally, it covers the pricing and tiered release of content products.

CASE STUDY 8.1 THE ROAD TO MARKETING A NEWSCAST

You have been recently hired as the new marketing manager for a local TV station. The station has a long history of holding the number 1 position in ratings for all of its newscasts, but over the years, the numbers have begun to slip, and research indicates that the station has failed to attract younger demographics. Management is looking for someone to reposition the station and utilize technology to garner new and younger viewers (adults 18–34).

Assignment

1. Utilizing SOSTAC, develop a plan and strategy that will meet the goals and objectives set forth for this TV station.

2. Spend the next week watching a local TV station's newscasts. What is the current slogan and brand of news? Identify the strengths, weaknesses,

opportunities, and threats. Are they making attempts to reach a younger demo? If so, what are they doing that you could possibly learn from? If not, what thoughts do you have on making that change?

3. Spell out where you want to take the station. What are your marketing and communication objectives? How do you get there?

4. Conduct a research study with eight to twelve of your fellow students. What are their current opinions about

the newscasts? Use this feedback to integrate into your overall marketing approach.

5. What are some new technologies you could utilize to get the word out about your new marketing strategy? How will the news department have to change to meet this new brand?

6. How will you measure the success of your campaign? Provide your projections on how you see this new marketing plan succeeding.

CASE STUDY 8.2 3, 2, 1 … LAUNCH OF A NEW WEB SITE

As the manager of business development with an up-and-coming interactive company, you have been tasked with launching a new Web site. Start with an idea that meets the needs of a specific market that is currently underserved. Provide logic that explains how this Web site would fully provide the needs and requirements for a niche market. Be prepared to explain how your Web site would differ from similar Web sites, if you chose a type of Web site that already serves this market. In fact, it's better to list those Web sites as your competition and understand their strengths and weaknesses. Keep all details in mind, including the overall look of the Web site, which includes specifics such as color schemes, animation, and so on. Who will contribute to the content? Will this Web site require the hiring of new employees?

Assignment

Conduct a research study to determine whether there is indeed a need for a new Web site for the area you have chosen. Utilize that feedback to move forward with the development of this Web site.

Develop a full marketing campaign that will generate loyal visitors to your Web site. What venues will you utilize to introduce the Web site to your target market? What research will you utilize to gather this information?

Finally, be sure to provide a thorough list of potential advertisers that would make this a profitable venture. What can you do with this Web site to make it advertiser-friendly?

Present your information to the class as if they are the board of directors for the company that employs you. Take a vote. Do they agree to launch your Web site?

REFERENCES

1. American Marketing Association Web site. Accessed April 18, 2009, at http://www.marketingpower.com/AboutAMA/Pages/DefinitionofMarketing.aspx.
2. Smith, P. R. & Taylor, J. (2004). *Marketing communications*, 4th Ed. London: Kogan Page.
3. McKenna, R. (1991). Marketing is everything. *Harvard Business Review* 69:1, 65–79.
4. Smith and Taylor, J., op. cit., 36.
5. Smith and Taylor, J., op. cit., 32.
6. Lehu, J. (2007). *Branded entertainment: Product placement & brand strategy in the entertainment business*. London: Kogan Page.
7. Feldwick, Paul (1997). *Understanding brands: Ten experts who do.* London: Kogan Page.,
8. ——— (October 10, 2007). To pay or not to pay: The world of office suites opens up. Accessed April 20, 2009, at http://knowledge.wpcarey.asu.edu/article.cfm?articleid=1483.

9. ———— (n.d.). Online movie marketing. Accessed April 11, 2009, at http://e-strategy.com/internetmarketingarticle.asp?section=Reports&story=online-movie-marketing-blair-witch-project.

10. Dobele, A., Toleman, D. & Beverland, M. (2005). Controlled infection! Spreading the brand message through viral marketing. *Business Horizons* 48:2, 143–149.

11. Keegan, W. J. & Schlegelmilch, B. B. (2001). *Global marketing management: A European perspective.* Englewood Cliffs, NJ: Financial Times/Prentice-Hall.

12. Smith and Taylor, op. cit., 37.

13. Heo, J. & Chang-hoan, C. (September 1, 2009). A new approach to target segmentation: Media-usage segmentation in the multi-media environment. *Journal of Targeting, Measurement and Analysis for Marketing* 17:3, 145–155. Accessed November 23, 2009, at http://www.proquest.com.ezproxy.nu.edu.

14. Van Tassel, J. (March, 2009). Politics 2.0: The Obama 2008 new media campaign. *Winning Campaigns* 6:2, 5–15.

CHAPTER 9

Packaging, Repackaging, and Marketing Content

By the age of six the average child will have completed the basic American education. ... From television, the child will have learned how to pick a lock, commit a fairly elaborate bank holdup, prevent wetness all day long, get the laundry twice as white, and kill people with a variety of sophisticated armaments.

Russell Baker

CONTENTS

CHAPTER OBJECTIVES

The objectives of this chapter are to provide you with information about:
- Defining the content product
  - Packaging the product
  - Content's long tail
  - Real-time content
  - Bundles and packages
  - Brand extensions
  - Formats
  - Licensing
- Channel marketing
  - Screens
  - Wholesale mechanisms: Partners, distributors, and aggregators
  - Retail outlets
  - Direct-to-consumer and Customer Relationship Management (CRM)
- Pricing strategies: We do windows

INTRODUCTION

The previous chapter looked at the big ideas and issues that face marketers in the content industries. This chapter carries the discussion further: "into the weeds" of the marketing process, the channels, the sales venues, and pricing and payment.

223

DOI: 10.1016/B978-0-240-81020-1.00009-9

DEFINING THE CONTENT PRODUCT

A movie's revelations, a favorite TV show, a song you danced to when you fell in love … some of life's most important moments are tied forever in our memories to the media that captured our attention at the time. Calling them "content" or "products" hardly seems to do justice to these powerful triggers of significant remembrances! Yet just as a fine steak is a profitable menu item to a restaurant manager, so is a motion picture, television show, or song, no matter how emotionally moving or technically brilliant, a product or a property to content industry professionals. On a personal level, they may be affected just as a consumer would be. But on the professional level, they must evaluate the material and make solid plans about how to turn it into a successful, profitable business venture.

Almost everyone dreams of writing a book, a screenplay, a song, or an influential blog. And many of them follow their dream. Some labors of love, made out of a desire to see the work created, may achieve commercial success, but there are very few: The vast majority of profitable content efforts are created as commercial products that are intended to appeal to a defined audience and market. Thus, from the very beginning, the creation of professional content products takes place with marketing in mind.

Of course, other factors come into play as well, including genre, innovation, and creativity. Content industry segments tend to develop particular genres of content, as shown in Table 9-1.

Packaging the Product

The bare content (a song, a screenplay, a book, a video, a white paper) itself is just the beginning. It is a creative work – a property – but it is not yet a product. In order to turn a creative work into a commercially viable product, it must be *packaged*. Packaging is one of the first steps in marketing, a way of shaping the content to appeal to specific segments of the market. Such shaping is essential to insure profitability. In other words, the prospective audience in the aggregate must pay more than it cost to produce, market, and distribute the material, so that all those who participated in that process (or *value chain*) will share in the profits. Once the content is packaged for maximum appeal and formatted in an appropriate manner for distribution, then the marketing experts have an offering they can make available to a potential buyer, user, or consumer.

"Packaging" has different meanings in different contexts:

- In industries that sell hard goods (toothbrushes, tea, and tents), packaging means to enclose or protect products for distribution, storage, sale, and use – the familiar plastic wrap, boxes, and clam-shell wraps that pose such a challenge for consumers to open.

Table 9-1 Preferred Genres by Media Segment

Content Segment	Content Products by Segment
Motion picture	Films, DVDs
Television	Audiences, programs
Television networks	Audiences, programs, networks
Radio	Audiences, programs
Radio networks	Audiences, programs, networks
Recorded music	Songs, albums, collections
Print	Books, magazines, newspapers
Advertising	Television commercials; radio commercials; mobile ads; kiosk ads; web page banners, ads, and video; ads in videogames; outdoor boards; print and display ads; brochures; and point-of-purchase and other collateral materials
Business intelligence	Research reports; white papers; newsletters
Software	Programs; applications
Videogames	Console, computer-based, mobile, and online games
Web content	Web site templates; animations; videos; photographs; text; cursors
Web digital services	Search engines and returns; online Web site and page creation; online content and data storage; online exhibition; communication aggregators and services; branded channels; utilities (such as currency exchange, maps and trip planning, etc.)
Social media content	Social network pages, widgets and gadgets, badges, and interactive logos
User-generated content	Personal Web sites; blogs; wikis; social network pages; Twitter; SMS text; photos; videos; music; slide shows; email

- In the motion pictures industry, it means putting together a combination of the major stars and creative personnel who will to work on or appear in the film. This "package" is used before production to raise money from investors and to arrange for presales to distributors.
- In television and other media that produce shows, programs, and videos, packaging refers to all the graphic elements that surround the actual program: intros, outros, bumpers, mattes, lower thirds, and credits.
- In the cable and satellite industry, packages usually mean a group of networks or programs that are bundled together, often offered at a special price.

All these definitions have one element in common: They are a way of "wrapping" the product for sale, whether it is a material wrapper or a digital wrapper. It's not only package materials that differ; so do the means of affixing them to the product, the manner in which they are removed, and the role they play (protecting, explaining, decorating, and promoting).

Increasingly, developing the content and its packaging is not just a case of the content creators producing a product and then marketing it to some audience segment. Many companies think of it as co-creation, where creating content is a conversation between creators, marketers, and consumers. In practical terms, before making a decision about what to produce, marketers often solicit potential prospects for their ideas and suggestions about how to design the content. At minimum, producers ask likely consumers to view the versions of the product with alternative packaging wrapped around it, comparing their responses to each possible configuration. This research may take place by depth interview, focus group, or special showing or exhibition and, based on the results, marketers can have more confidence in the final packaged product they will place before consumers at large.

A new feature of contemporary content marketing is to make the delivery mode a feature offering. It's a philosophy that says to make it easy and convenient to access the content – giving consumers the content how they want it, where they want it, when they want it. For example, a viewer can watch a motion picture through an on-demand television service, rented or purchased DVD, streamed live over the Internet, or downloaded from the Internet.

Content's Long Tail

Hits, fads, and fashions move at warp speed around the world, spreading across the global Internet.[1] Back in the day, people said, "Here today, gone tomorrow." Now, as Chris Rock observed about the contemporary music business, people say, "Here today, gone today." It's true that as a hit, a song or a program may be gone. And yet, because of the long tail, content only appears to be gone; it may only be in hibernation, waiting to return in a new season. Figure 9-1 compares how traditional content marketers thought about the life of content over time: It's a hit, then it dies. However, things have changed, and that formulation no longer captures an important feature of the market for content, the *long tail* of content, identified by Chris Anderson.[2]

(a)   (b)

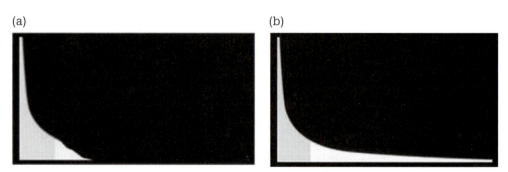

FIGURE 9-1 (a) Traditional consumer purchase behavior of content products and (b) new content long tail.
Source: Hay Kranen.

In the beginning was content with no tail, or only a short tail. Marketers who worked in traditional mass media did not commit many resources to marketing programs. Instead, they used their own media platform to promote their products to the mass audience already watching. Because that audience didn't have a lot of entertainment choices, it was not unusual for a hit show to attract 30 or 40 percent of the available audience. And marketers *were* aggressive in pitching their audience to advertisers. When a program stopped attracting, producers or networks packaged the shows for syndication and sold them as packages for additional runs on independent local stations. After a few years, the programs became so well known that they stopped attracting an audience and were retired altogether.

The technologies of television distribution make it cost-effective to send the same program at the same time to millions, even billions of people. Over-the-air broadcast television and satellite are one-to-many (or point-to-multipoint) transmission systems – it costs almost the same to send a program to five people as it does to send it to five million people. Originally, cable networks were designed the same way; instead of transmitting from the local TV station, the local headend pushed programs to TV households.

Now, content lives forever, or for so long that it approximates forever. The long tail of content became possible in the past two decades because of several advances. Cheaper digital storage made it possible to store a vast array of content products, both by individual sites and collectively, the totality of Internet Web sites. Cheaper transport over the Internet made it possible to send that content on demand to any individual consumer, at a reasonable price. And cheaper online on-demand payment processing reduced transaction costs to an acceptable level for both buyers and sellers.

When consumers can choose from a more or less unlimited catalog, they choose carefully and precisely, buying exactly what they want, without compromise. Anderson reported that in just about any huge catalog, 98 percent of the properties will be ordered.[3] It's true that a large proportion of sales accrue to hits – popular content that almost everyone sees. But, taken together, the total sales of properties extending out on the long tail will bring in as much or more revenue than the hits. Anderson argues that this trend will continue and that, over time, blockbusters will exercise a less powerful influence over the content market.

For example, Aris and Bughin[4] reported that Amazon makes almost half of its revenues from niche books that were previously unmarketable because the cost of maintaining such a huge inventory made it impossible to sell such books at a profit. However, they also make the arguments that managers must have a robust strategy for hit properties. One reason is that not only do current hits dominate the market of the moment, but past hits also account for a large percentage of

> It is becoming increasingly important to manage the existing stock of content and rights – the back catalog – aggressively to achieve maximum revenues over its lifetime. More than ever before, media companies will have to ensure that they have the rights and ability to exploit the full commercial potential of existing popular formats and brands. There are many opportunities to do this, depending on the media segment. For example, in the case of TV shows, reruns, relaunches, and spin-offs; in recorded music, the release of best-of albums and backlist compilations; and, in all sectors, vertical and horizontal brand extensions and leverage for nonadvertising revenues, such as content-branded merchandizing.[5]

sales of long-tail content. In other words, a hit today is a solid seller tomorrow, next year, and over the next decade. So though the influence of hits may lessen at any one point in time, marketers must still groom properties for large-scale sales.

Real-Time Content

Real-time content is a special genre that must be considered in a different light from other content genres. The category includes radio and television news shows, talk shows, sports, and live event coverage, traffic, weather, sports, and news and sports networks. Above all, one common characteristic of real-time content is that it must be timely to be successful.

Recent years have affected the markets for real-time content in very different ways. Some sectors are enjoying all-time high revenues; others are doing badly, facing severe budget and personnel cuts, and even bankruptcy. Generally, this content genre must be profitable in its first run because it does not sell as well along the long tail as other types of material.

Real-time content may be entertainment, such as sports and talk shows, or information-based, including news, traffic, and weather. The entertainment formats are maintaining their profitability and popularity – and even growing. Reality shows did well in 2008.[6] And for sports, 2008 was an extraordinary year on television, radio, and online.[7] There was a string of most-ever-watched sports events, including the 2008 Summer Olympics in Beijing with 4.7 billion viewers, the Super Bowl, cable broadcast, cable golf events, cable baseball games, NBA finals, NHL regular season games, and Wimbledon Finals. The Nielsen Company attributes these successes to:

- Compelling narratives
- High-definition-television picture quality
- More availability through more sports networks and Internet and mobile technologies
- Growing popularity of fantasy league sports
- Global market

By contrast, news presents a mixed picture that many people find worrisome because of the importance of journalism to democratic societies in informing the public. According to the Pew Project report, newspaper revenues fell 23 percent between 2007 and 2009 and the overall financial condition of the industry is dire.[8] Local television news revenues fell 7 percent in 2008 and ratings continue to fall. Network news audiences continued to fall, although more slowly than in the past. However, in some instances, the picture is beginning to improve. Cable news networks and some network news programs have shown audience gains, particularly those that display a "seriousness of purpose, a sense of responsibility and a confidence that the significant can be made interesting," notes the report.

It is not clear that the problems experienced by poorly performing real-time content can be solved through marketing – however necessary it may be. To some critics, news operations are adversely affected by the emphasis on the pursuit of market share and revenues, creating *tabloid* news coverage that emphasizes celebrity and other trivial stories.[9] Even the strongest supporters of today's news providers agree that companies must address changes in consumer habits and lifestyle, the overall economy, industry cost structures, and outdated business models before marketing efforts can succeed.

Bundles and Packages

Recall that, once produced, the additional (marginal) cost of providing content to one more consumer is negligible, essentially the cost of delivery. As a result, it is common for content companies to put several properties together in a package or bundle. They may aim to fulfill several marketing objectives through bundling, such as:

- Creating a viable product
- Reaching a larger audience by combining the appeal of the bundled products
- Creating price tiers
- Offering a price discount

There are many examples of bundles. The owners of popular television shows, such as HBO's *Sopranos* and ABC's *Grey's Anatomy*, package together a bundle of all the episodes shown during a television season for rental and sale from video stores and Web sites. Software companies often bundle products together. For example, users who buy Sony Vegas Pro® video editing software also receive NewBlue Cartoonr®. Cable and satellite operators bundle together many channels into *programming tiers,* such as the basic tier; the enhanced basic tier; and drama, sports, and premium tiers. They also offer special promotions of premium channels like HBO, Showtime, and Starz by adding a second channel for a lower price for a period of time if the subscriber orders one premium channel. This offering is particularly good for increasing the sampling of new channel offerings.

Brand Extensions

Content companies launch brand extensions to use existing successful content to reach new audiences. Extending the brand essentially means extending the market. There are two kinds of brand extensions: horizontal and vertical.[10] Horizontal brand extension means applying an existing brand name to a new product, which can be in a related category or entirely new to the company that is introducing the product. Vertical brand extension means introducing the product in the same category as the core brand, but the offering differs in some way, perhaps with different pricing, level of quality, focus, or features. Step-up vertical extensions mean the new product is an improvement or upgrade; a step-down vertical extension means the price or feature set of the new product is reduced.

Content industry horizontal extensions include turning a motion picture into a TV show or a Broadway musical, such as Disney's *Mary Poppins, The Lion King,* and *The Little Mermaid.* It could also mean the reverse, such as when Fox created a step-up vertical extension of the popular TV series *The X-Files* into a motion picture. Vertical extensions include movie sequels and prequels, TV program reruns and spin-offs, recorded music best-of and compilation albums, and software upgrades.

There may be risks to extending a successful brand.[11] Introducing a step-down vertical brand extension can hurt the core brand by taking away sales of the core brand, a process called *cannibalizing.* For example, pay-TV subscribers who might have otherwise gone to a theater and purchased an $8.00 ticket per person to see a motion picture may elect to wait for the movie to come to the on-demand service, paying from a few dollars to as much as $10 for at-home viewing. Essentially, the lower-cost option cannibalized the higher cost sale. Another risk is that the new product will be perceived as being of lower quality than the core brand. Public disappointment in sequels is common.

Step-up extensions can be problematic too. Consumers may become confused. Or the new product may make them uncertain about the quality of the core brand product. They can ask, "What was wrong with the original product?" or "Why wasn't the higher quality available in the original?" Such questions are particularly common in software upgrades, seen with such products as Microsoft Windows®.

Licensing

When content companies consider horizontal brand extensions – using the core brand to introduce products in an entirely different product category or industry – they often turn to licensing, rather than producing and marketing

Prior to *Star Wars*, merchandising was used only to help promote a movie and rarely lasted after the movie had finished its run. But *Star Wars* merchandising became a business unto itself and produced the most important licensing properties in history. The commercialization of *Star Wars* can be seen everywhere, from action figures to comic books to bank checks; there are even *Star Wars*–themed versions of Monopoly, Trivial Pursuit, and Battleship. Kenner toys once estimated that for most of the 1980s they sold in excess of $1 billion a year in *Star Wars*–related toys. In 1996, *Star Wars* action figures were the bestselling toy for boys and the second overall bestseller, after Barbie; in 1999 Legos introduced new models based on spaceships from the early movies. Even in the late 1990s, *Star Wars* toys based on the original trilogy before the prequel remained incredibly popular.[12]

the new product. Licensing is ample proof of the power of intellectual property, and the all-time champion of licensing is the *Star Wars* franchise.

The first three *Star Wars* motion pictures brought in about $2 billion in box office sales and more than $4 billion in merchandising. The prequel, *Star Wars I: The Phantom Menace* was an even more astonishing earner. Pepsi paid $2 billion to license the brand and Mattel paid $1 billion for a 10-year toy license. The soundtrack alone sold 1 million copies in its first pressing. A year after the film was released, students from a UCLA class counted 31 *Star Wars*–branded products in a local supermarket.[13]

CHANNEL MARKETING

A channel is navigable passage – the bed of a river or stream, a path for electrical signals, a route through which anything may pass. Marketing channels are ways of promoting and selling content products – the deals – that precede the distribution of content from license holders to consumers. The commercial pathways of content markets include existing wholesale, retail, and direct channels between marketers and consumers in some sectors of the content industry, while other channels are still being forged.

In the traditional motion picture and television segments, which have been around for decades, the wholesale mechanisms for marketing and delivering content are well developed. Internet and mobile marketing channels are still under construction. Direct channels, though well understood within some industries, are generally unfamiliar to most film and television practitioners. A content marketer might adopt a wholesale marketing channel strategy by licensing it to a syndicator, who in turn will mark up the price and relicense it to another syndicator or distributor or directly to an exhibitor. The exhibitor then delivers the content to the consumer, or they may choose a direct-to-consumer channel or some combination of both.

A DAY IN THE LIFE OF ELLIOT GROVE

Elliot Grove, Director and Founder of the Raindance Film Festival and the British Independent Film Awards
http://www.raindance.org; http://www.bifa.org.uk

I grew up in an Amish Mennonite community outside Toronto and was taught that the devil lived in the cinema. One day, when I was 16, I was sent into town to collect some welding from the blacksmith and had 3 hours to kill. So I walked up and down, and decided to see what the devil looked like. I paid 99 cents, went in, and sat down – it was a bit like church, except the fabric on the seats was red: the colour of the devil. Then they turned the lights off. The first movie I saw was *Lassie Comes Home*, and I wept like a baby. At the end I went up to touch the screen to see if I could feel the rocks or the fur – but it was gone, magic. And I was hooked on cinema forever.

I started Raindance in 1992 during a personal low. I had just gone bust in the previous global recession and I spent a long time feeling sorry for myself. I decided to retool in film – I had lost all my previous film contacts made while I was a scenic artist, and started a film training programme here in London. A year later I started the Raindance Film Festival, and in 1998, when the British film industry was wallowing in self-pity, I started the British Independent Film Awards.

My typical day starts by unlocking the office. More often than not I am the first one in. I love switching the lights on; it reminds me of that first frame of *Lassie Comes Home* that hit the screen. I open up my email to see if there is anything urgent or exciting. A colleague or two usually show up a few minutes later, and while they are settling we have an informal chat which covers these three really important things: what happened yesterday that could be better, what's happening at home (a couple of Raindance workers have small children; a couple others are single, so there is always plenty to discuss), and lastly, what's on the agenda today. These are really special moments, and if someone is late, or away, you really miss them.

The interns start arriving – we usually have four. I try and give each person a special project that plays to their strengths. Some interns excel in physical/practical things, others are really good on the telephone, and others have good web skills. I then have my second meeting of the day – with the interns – and again we discuss yesterday/last night at home/today.

I then check the metrics on the Web site: the number of new Twitter followers, unique visitors to our Web site, and how many people have opened our emails from the day before. It gives me a perverse pleasure to check these statistics – I'm never sure what they mean, but it is fun.

I have three problems each day. In fact, I don't like to call them "problems" – I prefer to say that in general I face three challenging creative opportunities:

1. As an art-based charity, we need to be very focused on money.
2. Administering our hectic training programme and the oldest, largest independent film festival in Europe.
3. Political issues. This area has started to demand a lot of my time, partly because we have grown in stature, partly because our competitors persist at taking cheap shots at us, and partly because of my own ego. I am terrible at politics – perhaps it is the pacifist teaching I got as a youngster, the "turn the other cheek" approach that Mennonites are known for. I try to assess the challenge and delegate our response to a colleague more adept and astute than me.

I know I have had a good day when everyone in the office has been totally immersed in their work. I love it when someone, intern or staff member, shouts, "Whoopee! Look what I found!"

Of course Raindance as a company has financial targets and goals like any other business, from dry cleaning to dentistry. But an important aspect of our goals, and my goals personally, is to help other filmmakers. Every once in a while we get a big slobbery thank you and that really makes it all worthwhile.

After the interns go home, I either have a speaking engagement somewhere in the city, or I go home to catch up on writing (like this) or I Twitter, or I watch yet another independent feature or short by someone, perhaps exactly like you, trying to break in. When I find something special, I feel like I have had the best day ever.

It doesn't get better than that.

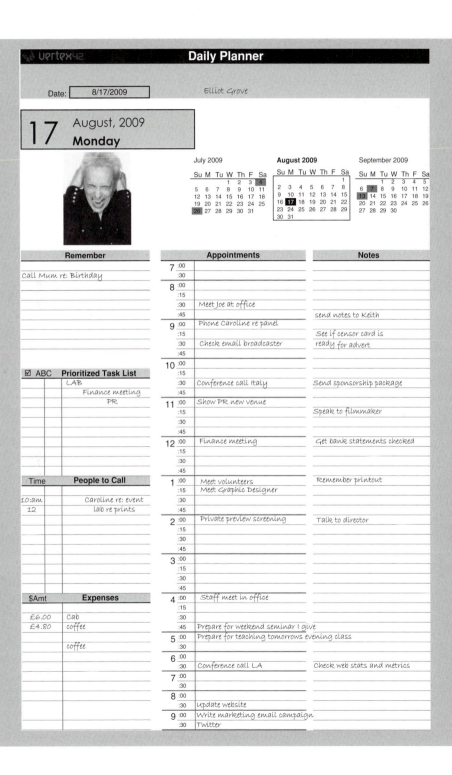

Daily Planner

Date: 8/17/2009   Elliot Grove

17 August, 2009
Monday

July 2009	August 2009	September 2009
Su M Tu W Th F Sa	Su M Tu W Th F Sa	Su M Tu W Th F Sa
1 2 3 4	1	1 2 3 4 5
5 6 7 8 9 10 11	2 3 4 5 6 7 8	6 7 8 9 10 11 12
12 13 14 15 16 17 18	9 10 11 12 13 14 15	13 14 15 16 17 18 19
19 20 21 22 23 24 25	16 17 18 19 20 21 22	20 21 22 23 24 25 26
26 27 28 29 30 31	23 24 25 26 27 28 29	27 28 29 30
	30 31	

Remember	Appointments	Notes

Remember

Call Mum re: Birthday

☑ ABC | **Prioritized Task List**
LAB
Finance meeting
PR

Time	**People to Call**
10:am	Caroline re: event
12	lab re prints

$Amt	**Expenses**
£6.00	cab
£4.80	coffee
	coffee

Appointments

7 :00
  :30
8 :00
  :15
  :30 Meet Joe at office
  :45
9 :00 Phone Caroline re panel
  :15
  :30 Check email broadcaster
  :45
10 :00
  :15
  :30 Conference call Italy
  :45
11 :00 Show PR new venue
  :15
  :30
  :45
12 :00 Finance meeting
  :15
  :30
  :45
1 :00 Meet volunteers
  :15 Meet Graphic Designer
  :30
  :45
2 :00 Private preview screening
  :15
  :30
  :45
3 :00
  :15
  :30
  :45
4 :00 Staff meet in office
  :15
  :30
  :45 Prepare for weekend seminar I give
5 :00 Prepare for teaching tomorrows evening class
  :30
6 :00
  :30 Conference call LA
7 :00
  :30
8 :00
  :30 Update website
9 :00 Write marketing email campaign
  :30 Twitter

Notes

send notes to Keith

See if censor card is
ready for advert

Send sponsorship package

Speak to filmmaker

Get bank statements checked

Remember printout

Talk to director

Check web stats and metrics

Vertical channels are all the available marketing paths within a single industry – the windows of opportunity that will be discussed in detail later in this chapter. Sometimes marketers will say, "I'm handling the syndicator vertical," to indicate their specialty. Most content industry marketing is done through vertical channels but horizontal channels add additional lucrative revenue streams as well. Horizontal channels are ways of marketing to other industries. For example, motion pictures and other programs might be available on aircraft through airlines or in hotel rooms through an aggregator for that industry, such as LodgeNet. The education market is another horizontal market, particularly for documentary and news content.

Screens

People seek content products through screens – even iPods have a screen. And increasingly, they consume media through them, too. Each screen has different format requirements and perhaps consumer usage patterns as well. Even books, magazines, and newspapers may soon be seen on screen devices such as the Amazon Kindle. The screens of interest to content marketers are:

- The big screen: Theaters, IMAX, and drive-ins
- The small screen: Television
- The smaller screen: Internet
- The smallest screen: Mobile telephones and devices

Wholesale Mechanisms

Market structures typically support four types of channels: wholesale (distributors, syndicators, and aggregators), retail, direct business-to-business, and direct business-to-consumer. Filmed entertainment content is more often licensed than it is bought and sold, although the purchase of entire libraries is not unknown. Typically studios and television production companies create content and license it to distributors or syndicators or directly to domestic and foreign exhibitors, such as local stations, broadcast groups, and cable, satellite, and telephone operators. In today's market, they may also make deals with Internet and mobile content distributors.

Each of the four content screens has its own set of marketing channels that have grown up around it. At the wholesale level, marketers in the motion picture and television industry participate in a structured series of conventions, trade shows, and private meetings with middlemen to put their content before consumers, as shown in Table 9-2. The television industry promotes programs to consumers and also markets audiences to advertisers. (Marketing to advertisers requires a separate set of trade events, meetings, and contractual relationships with independent media *rep firms*. Rep firms handle *spot sales*, unreserved commercial availabilities that are left after *up-front sales* that reserved time in advance for advertisers to place their commercials.)

Table 9-2 Trade Shows for the Four Screens

Screen	Industry	Marketing Events
Theaters	Motion pictures	National Association of Theater Owners (NATO)
		Film festivals: Cannes, Sundance, Monte Carlo market
Televisions	Television: Network and individual programs via local over-the-air stations and cable and satellite operators; audiences to advertisers	MIP-TV, MIP-Asia, National Association of Television Programming Executives (NATPE)
		Up-fronts; spot sales
Personal computers	Internet	COMDEX, CES, E3 (videogames), IPTV, Blog World Expo, ISPCon
Mobile phones, PDAs, and palmtop computers	Telecommunications	MIPCom, Mobile Entertainment Market, Wireless Association (CTIA), Mobile Business Expo

A great deal of business takes place at trade shows. Equally important is that marketers have the opportunity to meet potential customers face to face and to establish personal relationships. At international shows, they may be able to find partners who can provide marketing expertise in geographies where a content owner may wish to offer content to the public. Executives can walk around the show floor and spot trends and gather competitive intelligence that will prove important to their company.

In large markets for any kind of product, goods reach consumers through a *supply chain*. The supply chain stretches back to the raw materials that go into a product. The links forward include the product producer, one or more wholesalers or middlemen, and the retailer. The content supply chain works the same way as it does for other products.

Content companies may market their content through middlemen (partners, distributors, syndicators, and aggregators). For example, television production companies create a program and license it to a broadcaster for a certain number of showings, usually on an exclusive basis for a set period of time. After that license expires, the production company can again license the content to distributors or syndicators. Or it may bring the content to a program market and sell directly to an exhibitor, such as a local station, a broadcast group, cable and satellite operators and networks, and foreign television networks. In a wholesale transaction, the copyright holder to the content product might license it to a syndicator, who in turn will mark up the price and relicense it to another syndicator or distributor or directly to an exhibitor. The exhibitor, perhaps an independent station, then delivers the content to the consumer.

As discussed in Chapter 2, some large media and entertainment companies are vertically integrated. In addition to production studios, production services, and other production-related facilities, they own distribution units and many own media platforms where they can deliver content directly to the audience. As detailed in Chapter 2, they may own networks, stations, or cable companies.

In addition to the majors, there are thousands of distributors and exhibitors. Lacking the integration of the largest corporations, they take advantage of traditional marketing channels for buying and selling content. The attendees of such markets typically include sellers, suppliers of finished programs, packaged TV channels, and formats, and buyers, programming, acquisitions, and co-production executives representing TV stations, pay-TV operators, DVD and theatrical distributors, broadband and telephone company operators, web portals, closed-circuit networks servicing airlines, and retail points of sale, production companies, and territorial agents. Finally, when television programming is on offer, the attendees include advertisers, advertising and media-buying agencies, and direct marketers.

Everyone knows what finished programs are, but what are packaged TV channels and formats, which are also purchased at such markets? Packaged TV channels include a lineup of shows and programming buyers can schedule as a complete channel. It could be a channel dealing with cooking, golf, business, old TV shows – any theme. The key is that it is a channel that can be placed in a slot and airs a negotiated number of hours at a specified price.

Formats are not shows at all; rather, they are a design for shows – they are pure intellectual property and potential rather than actual content. A television program format is a license to produce, exhibit, and distribute a national version of a copyrighted program, using its name. They now make up a large part of the overall TV program market, accounting for about $3.5 billion in sales in 2007.[14]

The success of format sales has occurred for several reasons. Producers can avoid much of the risks and costs of creating original programming. Moreover, some program genres – comedy, reality-based programming, and game shows – do not travel well. But the pattern of such programs often do very well in many markets. Indeed, game shows make up 50 percent of global format airtime.[15] For example, successful shows created in the United Kingdom and recreated for the U.S. market include *Antiques Roadshow, The Office,* and *American Idol.* Shows created in the United States that did well in the United Kingdom are *Candid Camera, Jeopardy!,* and *The Apprentice.*

The get-togethers where the buying and selling of content take place are called *markets.* Some venues specialize in particular content genres. MIP-TV, a market for programming of all types, and MIPCOM, a market for entertainment programming, are held in October in Cannes, France. MIP-Junior, a showcase for children's and youth programming screenings, is a specialized part of MIPCOM. MIPdoc is also held in Cannes but in April; it is a showcase for documentary work. MIDEM, a market for recorded music, is held in Cannes, just before the various MIP events. MIP-Asia occurs in December in Singapore.

The National Association of Television Programming Executives holds a January convention where buyers and sellers discuss industry trends as well as make deals. In recent years, NATPE has been held in Las Vegas, but it is not tied to that city. NATPE also organizes specialized geographic programming markets, DISCOP East, occurring in June for television outlets in Central and Eastern Europe, and Eurasia, and DISCOP Africa in February, covering that continent. Other key markets are the London Programme Market, held in November in London and the Monte Carlo Television Market, taking place in February in Monte Carlo, Monaco.

The practice of buying multiple episodes of a television program in a bundle is called *syndication*. *Off-network syndication* means that the program originally ran on a broadcast network, where successful ratings increase the attractiveness and price of deals for subsequent plays. Because producers can typically recover only 80–85 percent of the cost of producing episodes, syndication is a key part of their financial estimates of future profitability.[16] Domestic syndication of TV series to local stations usually allows six airings over a 5-year period. *First-run syndication* refers to shows that have been produced for direct-to-market sale without having been aired first on a network. Talk shows often begin as first-run syndication offerings.

Motion pictures may be offered at television markets, but there are also specific venues for movie deal-making. The American Film Market (AFM) held in November in Santa Monica, California, is the world's largest market for films, where independent filmmakers make deals to bring their movies to consumers. Such films often start their journey to market via exhibition at the premier festivals, such as the Sundance Film Festival:

> Over 8,000 industry leaders converge in Santa Monica for eight days of deal-making, screenings, seminars, red carpet premieres, networking and parties. Participants come from over 70 countries and include acquisition and development executives, agents, attorneys, directors, distributors, festival directors, financiers, film commissioners, producers, writers, the world's press, all those who provide services to the motion picture industry.[17]

Retail Mechanisms

Motion picture and TV program DVDs, videogames, computer software, music CDs, and even books are for sale in video rental stores, supermarkets, drugstores, 99-cent stores – just about everywhere. But the most voracious appetite for content comes from the big-box retailers – Wal-Mart, Costco, Best Buy, and other large warehouse stores. In the case of videogames, a wholesale purchase by big-box retailers can make or break a title.

Big-box retailers are not easy for entertainment marketers.[18] The relatively low price of content means that it may be used as a *loss leader*, a product sold at a low price to attract customers to the store. They demand that every product be given a unique identifier, an SKU (Stock Keeping Unit), which adds additional steps to distribution. Increasingly, they want each product to be identifiable with a radio-transmitted ID, called *RFID* (Radio Frequency Identification), which would add to the price as well as the distribution task. There are disagreements about returned products and customer complaints, which the big-box retailers want content companies to handle. Other retailers do not sell on the scale that the big-box stores do, but they aren't as demanding, either.

Now there is the Internet, which is proving to be a formidable competitor to video stores, and many analysts believe the brick-and-mortar venues will not survive. Hybrid services like Netflix, a low-cost subscription service (that starts at $8.99 per month) that allows customers to order over the Internet but receives the content on a DVD through the mail. With the DVD comes a return envelope. Other Internet services allow the customer to download the content and watch it on their computer or to make their own one-time DVD.

Direct-to-Consumer and Customer Relationship Management (CRM)

Most content companies do not want to market directly to consumers. It involves a considerable organizational infrastructure at some cost to interact with customers and to handle rebates, credits, and product replacements. The relative low product cost of most content products makes it inefficient to set up such units, even on an outsourced basis. Even on the Internet, large content companies drift from their *core competency* of creating content by taking on direct-to-consumer marketing and sales.

By contrast, media platform providers who have regular subscribers do have customer service infrastructure in place. Cable and satellite operators, Internet service providers, and telephone companies receive monthly subscription payments that give them a regular cash flow and allow them to set up routine customer service. Most companies handle such service with a combination of in-house units and outsourced service providers.

Companies that deal with consumers recognize that beyond customer service, they must think of this activity as *customer relationship management (CRM)*.[19] CRM has an enormous impact on a company's bottom line. Although marketing may be able to attract customers and sales can get them to sign on the dotted line, CRM is essential for retaining customers and reducing *churn*, or the loss of customers. A well-trained personable *customer service representative (CSR)* will use the customer contact as an opportunity to sell more products (*cross-sell*) or more expensive products (*up-sell*), which, if done on a regular basis, can add considerably to the company's revenues.

PRICING STRATEGIES: WE DO WINDOWS

Windows is a shorthand way of saying *windows of opportunity.* It means releasing a motion picture over time in stages (or windows), protected from distribution in any other venue than the one contractually agreed upon by studios and distributors. The order of the windows is determined by the amount of revenue brought in per viewer in the shortest period of time. The strategy was first used by the motion picture industry to maximize its revenues over time. It is essentially a pricing strategy that moves the price down as the property gets older and exhausts its most enthusiastic audiences.

Motion picture windows are well-oiled paths for film distribution, and if that were all they were, it would be a relatively minor matter. However, increasingly, it is worth careful study because it provides a template for many forms of commercially distributed content in the future, particularly television programming. Given the long tail of content, pricing strategies by controlled window release may ultimately extend to other content types as well.

Movies are first released in theaters, sometimes called *fourwalling.* Between 4 and 6 months later, they are released on home video for both sale and rental. Four to 6 weeks later, they are distributed on pay-per-view and video-on-demand services. Four to 6 weeks after the pay-per-view window, pictures appear on premium networks like HBO or Showtime, called the pay TV window. Then begins a series of less lucrative TV windows, including distribution to network TV, foreign TV, independent stations, and basic cable networks. The revenue brought in to studios from licensing to television around the world was more than $16 billion in 2003 and nearly $18 billion in 2004, including licensing fees from world pay TV, U.S. broadcast and cable TV, and all foreign TV.[20]

By the time a property has been distributed in every possible window, the producers are making fractions of pennies per viewer.

The typical release windows for a film and the revenue each one brings in are:

- Domestic and some international theaters: Individual tickets cost $8–$10 each.
- Other international theatres: Individual tickets cost $2–$8 each.
- Home video sales (simultaneous with rental): $12–$25 each copy, viewing by unlimited number of people.
- Home video rental (simultaneous with sales): $4–$6 per rental, viewing by undetermined number of viewers, but between 1 and probably not more than 50 viewers.
- Pay-per-view/On-demand: $4–$6 dollars per order, viewing by undetermined number of viewers, but between 1 and probably not more than 50 viewers.

- Premium services (Pay TV): $10–$12 monthly subscription, viewing by undetermined number of viewers, but between 1 and probably not more than 50 viewers.
- Network TV: $10–$15 million for presentation to millions of viewers.
- Foreign TV: Networks pay millions for presentation to millions of viewers.
- Syndicated TV: Lowest cost movie packages that are shown to millions of viewers.

Creating Price Tiers

Individual products sell for a specified price and the transaction is over. However, marketing their services by price has proved to be an effective method for multichannel operators (cable and satellite). They have a monthly subscription business model, differentiated by price tiers for multiple channels as well as individual networks.

Every operator tiers products in their own way, but they share some general pricing characteristics. The basic tier usually includes local channels and other networks with broad appeal, produced at a relatively low cost. These networks are sometimes called *minipays* because the operator pays the channel from nothing to a few cents to a very few dollars per month, per subscriber, to add the channel to the lineup. (Some channels, mostly shopping channels, pay operators to get on the system and contract for a revenue split as well.)

Another tier that is included in the basic subscription is the on-demand tier. Most operators set aside numerous on-demand channels, providing pay-per-view (PPV) offerings. Typically, PPV revenues are split 50/50 with studios.

The enhanced basic tier adds widely popular channels such as CNN or MSNBC, TNT, TBS, and USA. Most systems have a *bouquet* of 30 or more networks that entice viewers to pay an additional monthly subscription fee. And the premium tier, featuring pay TV networks like HBO, Showtime, and Starz, adds another $10–$14 per month to the monthly cost.

Price Discounts

With many content items, especially blockbuster movies, consumers have a "first on the block" mentality. They will pay a premium and wait in line for hours to be among the first to see a new *Harry Potter* or *Lord of the Rings* release. In this environment, there is no incentive for marketers to lower prices.

However, once the gloss of newness has worn off, price discounts may be an effective marketing tool. A consumer who loved *Sleepless in Seattle* may buy the DVD on impulse if it is priced at a few dollars. Indeed, this situation is at the heart of long tail marketing, and marketers now have the technological means to maintain the title in a catalog, available from a server that fulfills just this type of content purchase.

SUMMARY

The chapter detailed how program purveyors define content products and how they can sell them. It described the structure of content markets and the venues where buyers and sellers come together to make deals. It looked at how consumers access the content via multiple screens and marketer's pricing strategies to maximize their profits.

WHAT'S AHEAD

The next chapter by coauthor Lisa Poe-Howfield provides a broadcast industry insider's view of the nuts and bolts. Selling advertising time, *avails*, to advertisers. Radio and television networks, local stations, and now Internet sites all seek to attract advertisers, selling marketers access to their viewers, listeners, and users. It has a rich 'how-to' focus, explaining how sales executives find, service, and retain advertisers.

CASE STUDY 9.1 DETAILS, DETAILS

The ability to package a product is a well-thought-out and carefully planned strategy that marketing experts utilize to attract their target market to the product or service being offered. If done correctly, it simply finalizes the efforts of developing a good product that is branded properly and serves as the final touch to being a huge success. On the other hand, if not done correctly, it can destroy the efforts and investments poured into even the very best of products.

For example, several years ago a company introduced a new healthier bread to the marketplace. The product was branded as home-style, fresh-from-the-oven bread. The advertising was directed at mothers looking for a healthier choice and was designed so that you could practically smell the bread baking in the oven.

So why wasn't the bread selling? Grocery stores had to remove the product from the shelves. What went wrong? The packaging was green. Why would *that* make a difference?

Turns out that people generally associate the color green with mold. Yikes. Not what you really want to envision when you're picking up a loaf of bread for the family. A small mistake that cost the company plenty of dough … no pun intended.

Another company set out to market a new brand of coffee. Hundreds of thousands of dollars were spent on research, establishing relationships with professional sports teams to get it placed into stadiums, not to mention the money behind the actual product of harvesting a special coffee bean in Brazil. When the owners of the company celebrated their first shipment by inviting investors and potential clients to their breaking out party, there was one glaring problem. The beautiful and perfectly placed cup of coffee on the front of the package did not have steam coming from it. It appeared to be a cold cup of coffee sitting on a table. That company ended up going bust because consumers have preset notions about products and even the smallest detail can spell disaster.

Could they have changed the packaging and continued? Yes, but the additional investments needed to recreate the packaging and the lost confidence from the retailers could not be restored.

Business is tough and when given the opportunity to get your product on the shelves, you only have one chance at bat. A product needs to generate a feeling or clear definition that consumers can depend on. It cannot simply be packaged in a pretty color; there has to be logic behind *each and every element.*

It is often easier to recognize the clever marketing strategies for tangible items such as cereal, soap, or perfumes. However, when marketing professionals set out to package an intangible item such as a movie, television show, or a syndicated radio show, the elements are far less glaring, but they are there – just as the toucan appears on your Froot Loops.

Continued...

Assignment

In this exercise, choose a tangible brand product, such as soap, deodorant, cereal, or laundry detergent, that you are loyal to and analyze the packaging:

- What colors were used?
- What words were used to grab your attention on the package (any "new and improved," "only," or "first" words used)?
- Did you find any elements to the product that might deter consumers from purchasing?
- Have you seen any advertisements for the product?
- How does that message match the packaging?

Now, for the fun part. Choose one of your favorite television shows, radio programs, or movie and identify the "packaging" for this product:

- What is the tone of this product?
- Are there color schemes used in the TV show or movie that you are able to identify?
- If you have chosen a movie that is now on DVD:
  - Describe the packaging and the description of the movie.

- Does it accurately portray the movie?
    - What stands out most on the packaging?
- If you have chosen a television show:
  - Does it have a theme song?
  - Describe the opening and closing of the show.
  - Any special elements about the program that makes it unique and appealing?
- If you have chosen a radio program:
  - Does it have a themed open and close?
  - What does the audience expect to get each time they listen to the program?
  - What does this radio program offer that others do not?
- In any of the previous choices:
  - Identify who they are attempting to attract to the program. Go beyond demographics. Write a brief description of the type of person you believe will be watching or listening to the program or movie.
- Determine whether you believe the marketing experts who "packaged" this show or movie were successful. Support your answer with research that indicates that they have attracted an audience that makes the product successful. If they have not, outline where they fell short.

CASE STUDY 9.2 YOU PACKAGE THE GOODS

After working your way up in the recording industry, you have reached a top marketing management position that puts you in charge of a well-known record label company's next top artist's musical release. Your portion of the project will be to successfully package a DVD for this new artist.

Assignment

Step out of your comfort zone on this project. Choose a musical genre that you do not normally listen to. Next, create a name for the band or artist. Begin developing your marketing plan that will make this a huge success and keep you employed in your dream job. Often, music releases will target multiple potential audiences. Do your research. If your artist is similar to another on the market, what audience do they attract? Do you want to go after the same audience or offer an alternative? If this is your plan, be sure to keep it in mind when moving forward with your future strategies.

Write out a brief description of the collection of songs that will be included on this release. When the consumer purchases your CD, what can they expect to get? Develop a theme for the release and begin making decisions on how you will work with the graphic artist department to design the jewel case for the CD. You don't have to be an artist for this portion of the exercise. Create a design that would best represent your artist's release. Do you want to include any special elements inside the packaging? Do you want any of the proceeds to benefit a charity?

At each step along the way, do not forget to keep in mind that the packaging is designed to support any marketing efforts and the product itself – don't forget the details.

Finally, decide which songs you will release to the market to be played on radio stations with an explanation of why you chose these songs. Create a one-sheet that outlines tour dates and a second sheet that includes a press schedule. What programs or shows would you want your artist to appear on to support this new release? Summarize all of your efforts and share this with your class. Did they catch any details that you overlooked? If not, you are on your way to being a big hit!

REFERENCES

1. Farrell, W. (2000). *How hits happen*: forecasting predictability in a chaotic marketplace. New York: HarperBusiness.

2. Anderson, Chris. (2006). *The long tail: Why the future of business is selling less of more.* New York: Hyperion.

3. Ibid., 12.

4. Aris, A. & Cughin, J. (2005). *Managing media companies: Harnessing creative value.* West Sussex, England: John Wiley & Sons Ltd.

5. Ibid., 68.

6. Blue, T. (2008). What TV shows earned more viewers. *The Insider.* Accessed March 9, 2009, at http://www.theinsider.com/news/1461605_What_TV_Shows_Earned_More_Viewers_in_2008_Plus_the_One_Tree_Hill_Anomaly.

7. Nielsen Company (2008). *2008: A banner year in sports.* Accessed March 16, 2009, at http://en-us.nielsen.com/main/insights/reports_registered.

8. Pew Project for Excellence in Journalism (2009). *The state of the news media: An annual report on American Journalism.* Accessed June 2, 2009, at http://www.stateofthemedia.org/2009/narrative_overview_intro.php?media=1.

9. Barkin, S. E. (2003). *American television news. The media marketplace and the public interest.* Armonk, NY: M. E. Sharpe.

10. Kim, C. K. & Lavack, A. M. (1996). *Journal of Product & Brand Management* 5:6, 24–37.

11. Ibid., 28.

12. Cobane, C. T. & Damask, N. A. (n.d.). Star Wars. *St. James Encyclopedia of Pop Culture.* Accessed on May 17, 2009, at http://findarticles.com/p/articles/mi_g1epc/is_tov/ai_2419101151/.

13. This count resulted from an assignment to attendees of a UCLA Extension School seminar in 2000, sending them to a nearby Ralph's supermarket to count *Star Wars*–branded products on the shelves.

14. Altmeppen, Klaus-Dieter, Lantzsch, Katja and Will, Andreas. (2007). Flowing Networks in the Entertainment Business: Organizing International TV Format Trade, International Journal on Media Management, 9:3, 94–104.

15. Buckley, S. (January 22, 2008). The Internet killed the video store. *Telecom Magazine.* Accessed April 18, 2009, at http://www.telecommagazine.com/article.asp?HH_ID=AR_3884.

16. Aris, A. & Cughin, J. (2005). Op. cit., 68.

17. ———. (n.d.). About the AFM. Accessed November 14, 2009 at http://www.ifta-online.org/afm/about.asp.

18. ———. (July 2006). Show review. *One on one.* Accessed April 9, 2009, at http://www.oto-online.com.

19. Hill, K. (June 8, 2007). CRM breaks into show business. *E-Commerce Times.* Accessed April 20, 2009, at http://www.ecommercetimes.com/story/57743.html?wlc=1244659308.

20. Epstein, Edward Jay. (n.d.). 2004 Worldwide TV Licensing Revenue For Studios. *2004 MPA Consolidated Television Sales Report.* Accessed November 14, 2009 at http://www.edwardjayepstein.com/TVnumbers.htm.

CHAPTER 10

Managing Sales: An Insider's View

Lisa Poe-Howfield

General Manager for KVBC TV 3—Las Vegas, Nevada

It is difficult to produce a television documentary that is both incisive and probing when every twelve minutes one is interrupted by twelve dancing rabbits singing about toilet paper.

Rod Serling

CHAPTER OBJECTIVES

The objective of this chapter is to provide students with an understanding of the following elements as they relate to Sales and Promotion:

Sales in Electronic Media
- Organizational Chart for Sales/Job descriptions

The New Approach to Selling Media (TV, Cable, Radio)
- Cold Calling/Prospecting
- 1st call and 1st impressions
- The need for Customer Needs Analysis
- Presentation Skills
- Closing the Business
- Servicing and Selling

Internet
- Revenues
- Standard Unit sizes
- Terminology

Promotions
- On-Air
- Public Relations
- Community Outreach
- Internet Campaigns
- Sales Promotions
- Production

INTRODUCTION

Although many viewers may not appreciate having their favorite sporting event, newscast, talk show or prime time show being interrupted by those annoying commercials, as indicated by Rod Serling in the above quote, they do serve a

245

DOI: 10.1016/B978-0-240-81020-1.00010-5

most important role in the media industry. And nobody likes those intrusive pop-ups on Internet sites, either. Primarily, those commercials are there to pay the bills and so you can still access your favorite content, DJs, and news anchors on the air.

In the broadcast world, commercials also support the public interest activities of stations. In 1946, the "public interest" standard was further delineated by the FCC in a document entitled *Public Service Responsibility of Broadcast Licensees*, commonly known as the "Blue Book." It states that devoting a reasonable percentage of broadcast time to sustaining programs is one criterion for operating in the public interest.* The FCC never ratified nor rejected the "Blue Book" guidelines which required four basic components: live local programs, public affairs programming, limits on excessive advertising, and "sustaining" programs. However, it did lead to new and stronger "voluntary" codes as set forth by the National Association of Broadcasters in 1948.† Although many rulings have occurred over the years that have both supported and challenged the federal government's authority, broadcasters are still required to serve the community by airing news stories and programs that serve the public interest. This FCC requirement translates to the broadcaster's ability to adequately cover issues and as one might conclude, requires money to cover the costs of employees, equipment, insurance, utilities, batteries, studio lights, microphones, computers, software – the list goes one. In order to cover these costs, it is imperative that broadcasters maintain a healthy state of financial well being. Although there have been expansions for broadcasters into new media platforms to generate revenues, the bulk of the income continues to be generated through "spot sales" – the selling of commercial advertising time. Now, we begin to understand the importance of managing a first-rate Sales and Promotion Department.

Many companies face what are called *two-sided* markets. This means that they market and promote to at least two distinct types of buyers. Content purveyors market their wares to consumers – series, programs, videos, Web sites, songs, games, and other individual content products. Some of them also sell time or space to advertisers – a completely different market.

In broadcast, the Sales and Promotion Department handles advertising sales. The Promotions/Creative Service department markets to consumers. Internet companies sometimes define the two markets as B-to-B (or B2B) and B-to-C (B2C). These terms mean *business-to-business* and *business-to-consumer*. Electronic media companies count on the strength of their B2C effort to attract consumers to increase audience share while concurrently depending on the B2C marketing to sell to advertisers, to sell commercial time based on those audience numbers. It is

---

* The Museum of Broadcast Communications
† The Benton Foundation

easy to see the delicate balance between these two efforts. The other glaring factor is the quality of the content. This obviously plays a role in the degree of difficulty to market or sell, but even material that is viewed as "bad" can generate revenues when priced properly – just not to the level of its successful counterparts. To fully understand the synergy between these two divisions, let's take a more in-depth view of each area beginning with sales. The chapter begins by focusing on broadcast advertising sales, because this industry segment has the most developed sales structures and processes. It then moves to considering promoting content to consumers. Many of the sales and promotion activities that take place in broadcast companies translate to the Internet and, later in the chapter, Internet selling is covered explicitly.

THE SALES DIVISION

Over-the-air reception simply requires the viewer to watch commercials in turn for receiving that signal at no charge. As technology advanced over the years, many viewers opted to begin receiving their broadcast stations via their local cable company which also enabled them to choose from hundreds of additional networks such as MTV, ESPN, CNN, and others that served the needs of niche markets. Later, satellite companies developed technology that no longer required running cable throughout the local neighborhoods and instead launched many of the same networks via a satellite signal, which required homeowners to install a satellite dish.

The telephone companies in many markets have now taken on the cable companies by offering their very own television/cable services utilizing their existing fiber optic lines. These services are referred to as TelCo. Television over the Internet (IPTV) will be following suit, in that it will utilize Wi-Fi and fiber optic lines currently utilized for Internet service to offer viewers yet another option by which to receive a collection of broadcast and alternative network signals. These alternative means for which viewers watch their favorite programs are referred to as *alternative delivery system* (ADS). There are obvious differences between traditional broadcast stations and the ADS networks, such as delivery system, but perhaps the most noticeable is the means from which each entity generates its source of revenue. Whereas traditional broadcast stations rely primarily upon selling advertising, ADS networks have the secondary source of revenues generated by subscribers for their service.

Over the years, electronic media companies have been forced to advance their methods of selling advertising due to the incredible growth in entertainment choices. There were only a handful of television and radio stations to choose from not so long ago. These stations enjoyed tremendous shares of audience in the early days. The method from which Account Executives sold advertisers air time during those golden years looked very different from those used in today's competitive environment. In fact, the sales representatives of that time were often referred to as "order takers." Those days are long gone. In the past 30 years, consumers have been introduced to cable systems, satellite, internet, ipods, mobile devices and game systems, all contributing to the erosion of audience for those traditional media outlets; television and radio. What this meant for those working in the media industry, besides a rude awakening, was the absolute necessity to change their methods of selling advertising. To assist in this area, several organizations formed in an effort to keep their respective industries both knowledgeable and competitive with new media platforms through education and training:

Television: Television Bureau of Advertising (TVB)
Cable: Cabletelevision Advertising Bureau (CAB)
Radio: The Radio Advertising Bureau (RAB)
Internet: Internet Advertising Bureau (IAB)

In this section, we will take a closer look at some of the new approaches and common practices used to generate revenues for electronic mediums to include television, cable, and radio. Many of these practices are applicable to the sales process for selling Internet, but the terminology varies and this area will be detailed separately.

The typical broadcast sales department does not include a traffic department, which operates software to ensure commercial and non-paid spots are placed properly on the log in relation to break structures. Many media companies have begun to move away from having this department report to sales as it has the potential to be a conflict of interest for a Sales Manager to have control over how the spots are placed. If the traffic manager reports to the Business Manager, it creates a "checks and balance" system. The chart shown below (Figure 10-1) is

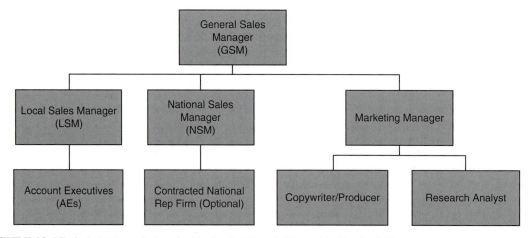

FIGURE 10-1 Typical structure of a broadcast sales department. *Source: Lisa Poe-Howfield.*

a general view of a sales department, recognizing that some media companies may combine some positions, while others may include more specific roles.

General Sales Manager (GSM): The general sales manager is responsible for the complete operations of the sales division. This position establishes budgets, projects revenues, sets incentives to motivate the Local Sales Manager and the National Sales Manager, handles personnel issues within the division, provides final approvals on rate cards and order processing, and reports directly to the general manager of the station. This person must also continually monitor inventory levels of available commercial spots and adjust rates accordingly to stimulate sales to open areas and raise rates on those that are selling out. It is a constant balancing act and if not done properly, can cost media companies hundreds of thousands of dollars. The GSM is considered a department head position and perhaps one of the more stressful positions. The numbers don't lie. If the station is not hitting budget, then the GSM is held accountable. It is not uncommon for a GSM to oversee the sales division of more than one radio or TV station in the instances where the parent company owns more than one station (i.e. duopoly) or has a Leasing Management Agreement (LMA) with another broadcast company. In most cases, this position can lead to the general manager position.

Local Sales Manager (LSM): The local sales manager is responsible for handling the day-to-day activities associated with the local account executives (AE). This means joining the AEs on sales calls, developing special projects to develop revenue streams, and approving spot orders. The LSM also works closely with the GSM to establish rates that are reflective of the market conditions. Often this position serves as an advocate for the AEs when the GSM is looking to make revisions or changes to the sales department.

National Sales Manager (NSM): This key position is responsible for generating revenues from national advertisers most often working closely with a National Rep firm such as Petry Media, HRP or Telerep to represent the station or stations in a group to larger, national advertisers. In this case, the NSM works alongside those media buyers at the rep firms to garner larger shares of business. If the station does not utilize a national rep firm, then they must personally develop business relationships with national advertising agencies to obtain that segment of the advertising business. Either way, this position is responsible for presenting rates, sales packages, and ratings information to either the rep firm or agencies.

Marketing Manager: The marketing manager oversees any and all functions that drive potential customers to the station. This entails gathering research from various sources and working alongside the research analyst to develop campaigns specific to either the market place or to the station's programming. For example, a radio station that is airing NASCAR would create a special package for advertisers to run spots in that broadcast.

The package may even include tickets for the business owner to attend a race. These types of packages and client incentives are put together to create "special packages" geared toward a niche marketing approach.

Copywriter/Producer: This position works alongside the AEs to write scripts, produce commercial spots and design web elements.

Research Analyst: The research analyst works with the Marketing Manager to research qualitative and quantitative data about the station or Web site to used by AEs presenting to prospective clients.

Account Executives (AEs): Account Executives are the "money makers" and responsible for generating the lion's share of revenues. The sales representatives are responsible for servicing and selling to existing clientele while also continuously generating new business. Later in this chapter, we will go through the many steps and training it takes to be a successful AE. This is typically where you will find some of the highest-paid employees. Most often, account executives are paid a percentage of the business they generate, creating a pay scale that has no ceiling. Some stations have moved to other methods of compensation to provide a more controlled system of staying within corporate budgets. One such approach includes paying a fixed salary plus an earned percentage of a pooled commission, based on accumulation of points set forth by management and bonuses for hitting budget as a group. Either way, the position requires those who are highly motivated by money and the willingness to handle rejection.

A NEW APPROACH TO SELLING MEDIA

One of the biggest changes to take place in the world or electronic media sales, has been the shift to incorporate a new approach to media sales by providing customized ad campaigns that are specific to the needs of the customer. Keep in mind that the success or failure of a media company lies in the hands of its sales department. That is why most media companies continuously invest in this division to keep each AE sufficiently trained, especially in light of the constant changing technology. Generally speaking, Account Executives, sometimes called Client Marketing Executives or Advertising Specialists, are responsible for developing new business and continuously selling and servicing existing clients.

Generating New Business

Creating new business is the lifeline to any AE and therefore is viewed as one of the top responsibilities. The process of generating new business can be accomplished through the following methods:

1. Cold Calls
2. Prospecting

Cold Calls

"Cold Calls" are one of those necessary evils of the position which requires the AE to pick up the phone or drive to a location without any prior introduction in hopes of setting an appointment to further present information on the station. New AEs are likely to describe this aspect of the position as their least favorite. However, more seasoned reps will tell you it is their favorite, because without them – one is likely to make very little money. Here is some good advice when making cold calls:

- Be prepared with a script designed to get their attention.
- Do your homework on the company or the industry you are calling.
- Keep the call short and to the point.
- Project an upbeat tone to your voice.
- Do not get discouraged.
- Get the appointment with the decision maker or influencer.

Prospecting

The verb definition of the word *prospect* is "to search or explore (a region), as for gold" (according to Dictionary.com). Here are some of the ways to … "search for gold":

- **Referrals:** Ask existing clients to provide names of businesses or other companies that could benefit from your type of marketing.
- **Monitoring:** Watch for businesses utilizing your competition, along with other advertising platforms in the market, including TV, radio, newspaper, billboards, Internet, and so on.
- **Yellow Pages:** Select a category and begin calling. Look up celebrated or honored months such as National Dental Month and begin calling that category.
- **Lead Groups:** Meet regularly with other AEs in the market to see if there are new businesses coming to town. This may require approval from the Sales Manager as some companies will not allow Account Executives to participate in lead groups.
- **Network:** Join a local business or community group that allows you to interact with people in the community.
- **Walk in:** Drive to an area of town where there are new businesses being built.
- **Business to Business:** A smart AE leaves business cards with companies they do business with – the dentist, dry cleaner, hair dresser, etc…
- **News:** Regardless of the type of news platform (TV, Radio Internet, Newspaper), it is a great source to discover stories about new businesses coming to town or grand openings.

The 1st Appointment

The ability to successfully prospect and make cold calls is all in an effort to set an appointment with a prospective client that should ultimately lead to a long term business relationship. Prior to going on the initial meeting, the AE will prepare with this simple "Pre-meeting" checklist:

- Dress professionally.
- Gather information about the company, its competitors and industry.
- Learn some of the industry terminology.
- Prepare information that fits into their marketing plans.
- Turn off the cell phone.
- Bring several business cards.
- Be equipped with a pen and paper to take notes.
- Practice your presentation.
- Bonus: Bring station goodies with logos as leave behinds.

Making a Good First Impression

There really is something to be said for first impressions. Account Executives recognize that this initial meeting is the foundation for which the client will formulate an opinion about them and gather enough information about the media company to determine if there will be a future business relationship together. Therefore, it is important for the AE to follow a game plan interjected with his or her personality. Following these simple steps can help in establishing a good foundation for a healthy business relationship:

1. Establish rapport.
2. Complete a Customer Needs Analysis (CNA).
3. Present company information clearly and concisely.
4. Set a follow up appointment.
5. Follow up.

Establishing Rapport

Establishing rapport requires an observant nature on the part of the AE and the ability to listen carefully to discover some common ground. Most of the time, it requires asking a few questions without getting too personal within the first few minutes of meeting. Are there photos on the wall of a favorite football team, college, kids, or awards? It's amazing how much one can learn about a person just by being observant and listening. After briefly exchanging introductions, the AE should waste no time in thanking them for taking the time to meet. This is the time to exchange business cards, saving both the AE and the prospective client from any embarrassment of forgetting names. The AE can then let them know what will be covered in the meeting; the completion of a Customer Needs Analysis, presenting important information about the media company and concluding with setting a second appointment to bring back a customized marketing campaign. This is a good time for the AE to assure them that the meeting will conclude on time.

Customer Needs Analysis

This should be the most time consuming portion of the meeting. The AE needs to dedicate most of his or her time to learning as much as possible about this business and industry. Completing a Customer Needs Analysis requires the AE to obtain great detail about the potential client that will play a vital role in preparing a marketing campaign designed to meet the goals set forth by the client. The ultimate goal is not to simply get a new client to advertise once; it is to create a long lasting business relationship which benefits the client. Many companies have existing Customer Needs Analysis (CNA) forms which an AE can bring along to the meeting. Some AEs may not feel comfortable using a form and will memorize a series of questions allowing them to take notes on the pertinent information. Here are just a few of the questions that one can ask:

- How long have you been in business?
- Describe your primary customer beyond age and gender.
- What challenges does your business face?
- What differentiates your business from the competition?
- What are you currently using to advertise your business?
- Is your business seasonal?
- What expectations would you have from this advertising investment?
- Can you show me around your facilities to better educate me about your business?
- Do you have a budget in mind?

Presenting Information on the Media Company

Once enough information has been gathered about the client, the AE will share pertinent information about the media company they represent. The presenting AE should never assume that the prospective client knows anything about the media company. The information should be enough to provide a basic understanding, but not overwhelming. Provide information on:

- The format of the radio station or affiliate of the TV station.
- Name the more popular on-air talents.
- Community events that the media company is involved in.
- Strengths of the station for advertisers.

The AE will end the presentation by opening up the conversation for questions.

Setting the Second Appointment

The AE will conclude this meeting by setting up a 2nd appointment within the next 2 weeks. The AE may meet with resistance if the prospective client does not yet feel comfortable with moving forward. It is the job of the AE to create an atmosphere of trust and clearly presenting the benefits of advertising on their medium. If this is not yet accomplished, it is likely that the AE will have a difficult time setting a 2nd meeting. Once this 2nd meeting is scheduled, the AE should thank them again for their time and present them with the media company goodies.

The Final Step

Not so quick…the 1st meeting may have concluded, but the process is never complete until the AE follows through with a most important step – sending a thank you note. Perhaps one of the more important steps, yet one that is often overlooked. This simple act reinforces the AE's commitment to service the client and also is a great way to confirm the date and time of the next appointment.

Preparing for the Closing Call

Over the next two weeks or so, the AE will have met with the marketing manager, research analyst and copywriter to develop a full scale marketing campaign. All of the information gathered and any additional items that the AE can include will be utilized to enhance the presentation for the closing call.

The presentation should include the following elements:

- Cover page – Includes the media company's logo, client's company logo, date of presentation, name of person being presented and AE's name and phone numbers.
- Introduction – This reiterates some of the facts gathered about the company including industry data that is pertinent to the overall marketing strategy.
- Research – Based on the identified target customer, provide detailed information about that individual specific to the market.
- Sample Script – The creative portion of the presentation allows the prospective client to visualize the look or sound of the commercial.
- Proposal – Provides a thorough explanation about the marketing schedule designed to specifically reach their target market and will include the investment required.
- Terms/Conditions – Information about the media company's business policies.

The Close

After the AE has presented information in the proposal, allowing for a two-way flow of information, the time arrives to close the sale. This is the most important part of the sales call; it requires the AE to ask for the business. Many articles, books and consultants have analyzed "The Close." The closing technique used by the AE is a matter of personal preference and style. Here is short list of some of the methods used to close a sale:[‡]

- **Assumptive Close** – acting as if they are ready to decide. Act *as if* the other person has made the decision already. Turn the focus of the conversation towards the next level of questions, such as when shall we start the schedule, how did they want to set up payment, let's set the production time now to get you on the air next week, and so on.

- **Bracket Close** – make three offers – with the target in the middle. Make the other person three offers. First offer them something sumptuous and expensive that is beyond their budget. Not so far beyond them that they would not consider it. Ideally, it is something they would look at wistfully, but just couldn't justify (if they do, it is your lucky day!). Secondly, offer them a solid good deal that is within their price bracket. It may not have all that they wanted, but it is clearly a good value for them. Finally, offer a severely cut-down deal in which very little of what they want is included. They should, of course, go for the middle option.

- **Handshake Close** – offer handshake to trigger automatic reciprocation. As you make a closing offer, extend your hand for a handshake. Smile and nod as if the deal is done. Look expectantly. If necessary, raise your eyebrows slightly.

- **Humor Close** – relax them with humor. Get them amused by telling a joke or otherwise making witty remarks. Then either go for a relaxed close with another closing technique or weave closure into the joke. This is particularly useful when they are tense. Beware of "http://changingminds.org/techniques/humor/pc_humor.htm" politically-incorrect humor unless you are sure it will be effective. Self-deprecating humor is often a safe bet and shows you to be confident and likable.

- **Summary Close** – tell them all the things they are going to receive. Summarize the list of benefits that the other person will receive, telling them the full extent of what they are getting for their money. Make it sound impressive, using full phrases and attractive words. Go into detail, separating out as many sub-items and features as you can. But also fit the description into a reasonable space of time. You goal is to impress them with what they are getting, not to bore them with excessive detail.

[‡] Changingminds.org

■ **Valuable Customer Close** – offer them a special 'valued customer' deal. Find a reason to show that they are of particular value, and then offer them a special, one time only discount. Tell them you need one more sale to complete your quota for the month/quarter and that you will offer an extra discount to get the sale.

A DAY IN THE LIFE OF WENDY Y. SHELTON

Wendy Y. Shelton, Sales Manager, KVBC TV-3 (NBC), Las Vegas

I am a native Las Vegan and started in the broadcast industry at KLAS TV-8 (CBS affiliate) in the summer of 1989, where I interned in the news department. In October 1989, I went to KVBC TV-3 (NBC affiliate). I began my career as a copy writer in Creative Services. I moved to the sales department in 1990, where I worked as a client marketing representative creating sales packages with the use of Leigh Stowell research. I was promoted to an account executive in 1991 where I sold television airtime for 16 years before being promoted to local sales manager in January 2007.

As the Sales Manager at Channel 3, I manage a team of ten outstanding, creative, and hard-working individuals. My primary responsibility is developing and implementing strategies to achieve local revenue goals. My personal goal is to motivate my salespeople to achieve their personal best despite the struggling economy and increased demands from our clients.

My day begins with greeting my staff and then processing advertising orders. I attend regular department head meetings. I lead a sales meeting every week. I participate in a Gatekeeper's meeting twice a month to review special projects that are being requested by potential media partners. Each week, I also take part in an inventory meeting to assure our commercial inventory is being sold at the appropriate rate based on supply and demand. I have a bi-monthly meeting with my general manager to discuss accomplished goals as well as future ones. I also attend sales calls with my salespeople on a regular basis.

I interact with various staff members and departments at the station, including the news, promotions, and traffic departments. Each department is essential to the success of our product, which is our news. The better our news viewership, the easier it is for my salespeople to increase revenues.

The biggest challenges I face as a television sales manager are the numerous competing advertising platforms that are now available to businesses, as well as the struggling economy. Most television stations generate most of their revenue from automobile dealerships, but with the economy being what it is, automobile advertising is considerably down, posing a big obstacle for media salespeople.

The highlight of my day is seeing my team excel and achieve. There's so much negativity regarding our economy, but I'm convinced that through stressful times, we can accomplish great things. Motivating a team to achieve amazing things during tough times is any manager's dream, so when I see my team thinking outside the box and going the extra mile to reach their goals, it's extremely rewarding to me. I'm convinced that my team is stronger, smarter, and more creative despite the current advertising environment. I believe that the obstacles we're facing force us to expand our horizons and at the same time make us appreciate the good things in life that we may sometimes take for granted.

I end each day recalling my many blessings. Outside of work, I have been married to my long-time love, Allen Shelton, for 14 years, and we share two magnificent boys, Allen and Christian Shelton. My entire family is here in Vegas, so my time outside of work consists of a host of family functions.

I regularly conduct workshops for various organizations addressing subjects such as Interviewing, Self-Esteem, Dressing for Success, and Selling Non-Traditional Revenue. I have been a member of Women in Communications as well as the Las Vegas Association of Black Journalists. I also worked with Make-a-Wish Foundation and the American Heart Association (Board of Directors, 2004–2006). I attend church and teach Sunday school.

My final words of wisdom: "Limitations live only in our minds. But if we use our imaginations, our possibilities become limitless." I challenge everyone to take advantage of these trying times and explore all your possibilities.

Daily Planner

vertex42

Date: 8/17/2009

Wendy Y. Shelton

17 August, 2009
Monday

July 2009							**August 2009**							September 2009						
Su	M	Tu	W	Th	F	Sa	Su	M	Tu	W	Th	F	Sa	Su	M	Tu	W	Th	F	Sa
			1	2	3	4							1			1	2	3	4	5
5	6	7	8	9	10	11	2	3	4	5	6	7	8	6	7	8	9	10	11	12
12	13	14	15	16	17	18	9	10	11	12	13	14	15	13	14	15	16	17	18	19
19	20	21	22	23	24	25	16	17	18	19	20	21	22	20	21	22	23	24	25	26
26	27	28	29	30	31		23	24	25	26	27	28	29	27	28	29	30			
							30	31												

Remember

Allen's Football Practice
Christian's Art Class

☑ ABC   Prioritized Task List

Revise Olympics Pkg.
Revise NFL Pkg.

Time   People to Call

ABC Agency
Internet Vendor

$Amt   Expenses

Appointments

7	:00	
	:30	
8	:00	Approve Time
	:15	AE Matrix Update
	:30	
	:45	
9	:00	
	:15	
	:30	Goals Meeting with GM
	:45	
10	:00	
	:15	
	:30	Client call with AE
	:45	
11	:00	
	:15	
	:30	
	:45	
12	:00	Marketing Luncheon
	:15	
	:30	
	:45	
1	:00	
	:15	
	:30	Conference Call with Agy
	:45	
2	:00	
	:15	
	:30	
	:45	
3	:00	Meeting w/ School District
	:15	
	:30	
	:45	
4	:00	AE Personnel Review
	:15	
	:30	
	:45	
5	:00	
	:30	
6	:00	Prepare Sales Mtg Agenda
	:30	
7	:00	
	:30	
8	:00	
	:15	
	:30	
9	:00	
	:30	

Notes

Upcoming sales promotions

Budget
Sales Contest
Sponsorhips

Terms and Conditions

Before allowing a client to sign off on the proposal, the AE will need to explain the terms and conditions. One can expect to answer the following questions about the client and payments:

- Will the client be cash in advance or pay on credit?
- When will future schedules need to be paid?
- Can the client pay with a credit card?

Production Appointment

Finally, set the appointment to shoot or record the commercial spot. It is important that the AE includes their new client on each step of the production. In fact, it's a good idea to have the new client sign off on a script. The AE does not want to complete a production only to have a client tell them that is not what they wanted. At the editing session, the client needs to be engaged in the process working with the editor of the spot. Ultimately, everyone involved needs to come together to produce a spot that generates results for the client.

Follow up

The AE should *always* follow up with a new client once the schedule begins running. Often, AEs are so concerned that they will hear back from the client that "it's not working" that they avoid checking in with the new client. It is the job of the AE to continually check in to see whether there are certain programs or dayparts where they are getting a higher response and others that are not delivering. The AE should be prepared to make changes to the schedule if needed, adjust the script, and do what it takes to service the client by making the campaign successful.

Selling and Servicing Existing Clientele

Now that the AE has built up a great list of clients from successful cold calling and outstanding presentations, just how does one maintain that business? For starters, be prepared for attrition. Many clients will not continue advertising on a particular station – that is simply a part of business. That is why a good AE constantly searches for new clients. The good news is that most AEs hired at a station are provided with an existing client list. In fact, many stations will lure AEs from other stations with a "Heavy/Strong List," meaning the list of accounts they will receive is known for generating large revenues and therefore high commissions. On the other hand, some AEs are hired to develop a new list of accounts and must start from scratch. There are two types of advertising business on these lists:

- **Agency:** Advertising agencies that usually handle a number of accounts and receive an agency discount (typically 15 percent) from the station.

AEs are also paid a commission on this business, but at a lower percentage than direct business (between one and five percent).

- **Direct:** Advertisers that deal directly with the TV station. Account executives are typically paid a higher commission than that which runs through an ad agency (between ten and fifteen percent).

Advertising agency business requires that the AE work directly with a media buyer. More easily translated, the AE is the seller and the media buyer is … well, the buyer. The negotiation begins with a media buyer requesting "avails" from the AE. "Avails" is a term that applies to the availability of spots on the station. The request can include information specific to the demographic group the advertiser is looking to reach, the flight date (date that the campaign will run), dayparts they are looking to run in, rating point goals, and total market budget for the campaign. Often, the request for avails will also include a list of programs that the advertiser has dictated as "blacklisted" where they will not run. Often, these decisions are made based on the subject matter of the program, cultural beliefs or political positions of company executives. When the AE is working with a direct account, they are dealing face to face with the owner or decision maker for the business looking to advertise. In both instances, the AE will provide the "buyer" with information about rates, ratings and programs or daypart areas where the commercial schedule should run based on the best efficiency to reach a specified target market. The term "dayparts" pertains to what time of day the advertiser is looking to run (i.e. Daytime, Overnight) which differs between Television/Cable and Radio.

TV/Cable Dayparts

Although television is often purchased program specific, advertisers may choose to purchase advertising by dayparts. It would be important for advertisers choosing this method to only buy those dayparts that would continue to reach their target market. These are the dayparts as established by the Television Bureau of Advertising, but are subject to vary by market:

- **Early Morning/Morning News:** 5:00 a.m.–9:00 a.m.
- **Morning:** 9:00 a.m.–12:00 noon
- **Daytime:** 12 noon–3:00 p.m.
- **Early Fringe:** 3:00 p.m.–5:00 p.m.
- **Early News:** 5:00 p.m.–7:00 p.m.
- **Prime Access:** 7:00 p.m.–8:00 p.m.
- **Prime:** 8:00 p.m.–11:00 p.m.
- **Late News:** 11:00 p.m.–11:30 p.m.
- **Late Fringe:** 11:30 p.m.–1:00 a.m.
- **Overnights:** 1:00 a.m.–5:00 a.m.

Not all television stations adhere strictly to these listed time periods. For example, in some markets, access may start at 6:30 p.m. These same dayparts are applicable to cable company advertising. However, the advertiser will need to work with their cable representative to determine which cable stations are ad-insertable. Some of the cable networks do not allow for local advertising. More importantly, the advertiser working with the cable AE should determine which networks are the best fit for their product. Cable companies sell advertising on a tiered structure. These tiers will be based on the accumulation of cable stations with higher ratings and/or higher demand which then warrant higher pricing. Advertisers also have the choice to run "scatter" ads which rotates the airing of the spot across various cable stations.

Radio Dayparts

Unlike TV, radio is primarily sold in dayparts – the commercial spots purchased run during the time periods as defined by RAB (Radio Advertising Bureau):

- **Morning Drive:** 6:00 a.m.–10:00 a.m.
- **Daytime:** 10:00 a.m.–3:00 p.m.
- **Afternoon Drive:** 3:00 p.m.–7:00 p.m.
- **Evenings:** 7:00 p.m.–12:00 midnight
- **Overnights:** 12:00 midnight–6:00 a.m.

The weekends for radio are much less structured allowing for advertisers to specify a time span that is more conducive to their business hours. These are called ROS/Run of Station spots. As an example, the spots can run 9 a.m.–5 p.m. or 6 p.m.–12 midnight.

Internet

Selling traditional media requires a great deal of knowledge about ratings, programming, cost per thousands, and psychographics, but when it comes to selling Internet, the selling situations may be very different. When television, cable and radio stations began to extend their brand to the internet, the question loomed about who would be responsible for selling it. The debate still stands. Many stations choose to have their existing group of account executives sell, while others dedicate a full-time person or staff to sell this entity.

Either choice seems to have created issues within the media companies. For media companies that opt to use existing account executives, it means teaching a brand new platform to individuals who are far more comfortable with selling the strengths of their existing medium. Companies going this route have found it slow going as most AEs spend their time explaining the details of television/radio advertising to clients and then outline the benefits of an extension of their company, yet an entirely different platform. On the other hand, hiring a full time staff or person to sell internet for the media company means that they are sure to be calling on existing clientele creating problems with the media AE already handling that account. It has been reported that some sales departments are sharing the commission on those accounts which would alleviate the tension that could develop between these two sales forces. Regardless of the path chosen, media companies recognize the strength of the world wide web and continue to develop methods from which to monetize it.

Internet Ad Revenues

In 2008, the internet generated $23.4 billion in advertising which was up 10% from 2007. Compare this figure to TV, Cable and Radio which all experienced substantial decreases in advertising during this same time period, and it's clear that there is a noticeable shift to this growing medium. After all, the internet has the capability to communicate more about an advertiser's business than the traditional 60 second radio spot or 30 second television commercial. It also allows the visitor to interact with the advertiser, automatically capable of establishing a relationship. Of course the advertiser will run the risk of losing a potential customer if not executed properly, but as time goes by, advertisers are learning more and more about the required means to reach their target market and the means from which to successfully engage them. To gain a better understanding about the growth of internet advertising, take a look at Figure 10-2, which shows the growth since 1999 when it generated $4.6 billion.

Further research by Pricewaterhouse Coopers, LLP on 2008 internet advertising revenue indicates that the format leader was "Search" at 45% ($10.5 billion), up 20% from 2007. Other formats garnering substantial ad revenues include "Display" at 33% ($7.6 billion) which includes Banner ads, Rich Media, Digital Video and Sponsorship. "Classifieds" revenues accounted for 14% ($3.2 billion) with "Lead Generation" coming in at 7% ($1.7 billion). In terms of advertiser category, Retail lead the way at 22% ($5.0 billion) of all dollars

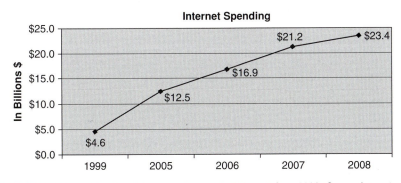

FIGURE 10-2 Growth in advertising spending on the Internet since 1999. *Source: Internet Advertising Bureau 2009.*

while Financial Services placed 2nd with 13% ($3.0 billion) and Automotive in 3rd with 12% ($2.8 billion). The numbers are big and by all indications, the internet appears to be a viable competitor with the traditional electronic mediums. Not bad for a platform that has revolutionized the way we communicate, shop, socialize and educate ourselves on any topic we choose. Quite impressive for an industry that celebrated its 40th birthday on October 29, 1969. This was the date when UCLA professor Leonard Kleinrock sent a message to the Stanford Research Institute from his school's host computer. He attempted to send the message "login," but the system crashed after 2 letters. Therefore making our first step into the World Wide Web with a simple "lo." There were other milestones over the years, but this was certainly the first step to a whole new world that includes e-mail, search, chat and social networks that forever changed our global society.

The Internet AE

A sales person for this media platform must be well versed in selling the value of his or her Web site to meet the needs of a potential client. In the world of TV, cable or radio, the AE sells the spot in lengths of 10, 15, 30 and 60 seconds. There are exceptions, but these are the generally accepted spot lengths. With the internet there are a host of sizes:

- **Banner & Buttons:** Full Banner, Half Banner, Micro Bar, Button 1, Button 2, Vertical Banner, Square Button, Leaderboard
- **Rectangles & Pop-Ups:** Medium Rectangle, Square Pop-up, Vertical Triangle, Large Rectangle, Rectangle, 3:1 Rectangle and Pop-Under
- **Skyscrapers:** Wide Skyscraper, Skyscraper, Half Page Ad

Each unit is available for animation as well.

These ad units are guidelines set forth by IAB, but will vary depending on the design of the web page.

As one can see, it starts with knowing what inventory is available to sell. Then, management must determine how to price these units. Similar to traditional electronic mediums, many ads are priced on a cost per thousand. Ultimately, the rate will be determined by what the market will bear.

Common Internet terminology that applies to advertising:

> **Banner:** A banner is an advertisement in the form of a graphic image that typically runs across a Web page or is positioned in a margin or other space reserved for ads. Banner ads are usually Graphics Interchange Format (GIF) images. In addition to adhering to size, many Web sites limit the size of the file to a certain number of bytes so that the file will display quickly. Most ads are animated GIFs since animation

has been shown to attract a larger percentage of user clicks. The most common larger banner ad is 468 pixels wide by 60 pixels high. Smaller sizes include 125 by 125 and 120 by 90 pixels. These and other banner sizes have been established as standard sizes by the Internet Advertising Bureau.

Caching: In Internet advertising, the cache server or the user's computer means that some ad views won't be known by the ad counting programs and is a source of concern. There are several techniques for telling the browser not to cache particular pages. On the other hand, specifying no caching for all pages may mean that users will find your site to be slower than you would like.

Click: According to ad industry recommended guidelines from FAST, a click is "when a visitor interacts with an advertisement." This does not apparently mean simply interacting with a rich media ad, but actually clicking on it so that the visitor is headed toward the advertiser's destination. (It also does not mean that the visitor actually waits to fully arrive at the destination, but just that the visitor started going there.)

Click stream: A click stream is a recorded path of the pages a user requested in going through one or more Web sites. Click stream information can help Web site owners understand how visitors are using their site and which pages are getting the most use. It can help advertisers understand how users get to the client's pages, what pages they look at, and how they go about ordering a product.

Clickthrough: A clickthrough is what is counted by the sponsoring site as a result of an ad click. In practice, *click* and *clickthrough* tend to be used interchangeably. A clickthrough, however, seems to imply that the user actually received the page. A few advertisers are willing to pay only for clickthroughs rather than for ad impressions.

Click rate: The click rate is the percentage of ad views that resulted in clickthroughs. Although there is visibility and branding value in ad views that do not result in a clickthrough, this value is difficult to measure. A clickthrough has several values: it's an indication of the ad's effectiveness and it results in the viewer getting to the advertiser's Web site where other messages can be provided. A new approach is for a click to result not in a link to another site, but to an immediate product order window. What a successful click rate is depends on a number of factors, such as: the campaign objectives, how enticing the banner message is, how explicit the message is (a message that is complete within the banner may be less apt to be clicked), audience/message matching, how new the banner is, how often it is displayed to the same user, and so forth. In general, click rates for high-repeat, branding banners vary from 0.15 to 1%. Ads with provocative, mysterious, or other compelling content can induce click rates ranging from 1 to 5% and sometimes higher. The click rate for a given ad tends to diminish with repeated exposure.

Cost-per-action: Cost-per-action is what an advertiser pays for each visitor that takes some specifically defined action in response to an ad beyond simply clicking on it. For example, a visitor might visit an advertiser's site and request to be subscribed to their newsletter.

Cost-per-lead: This is a more specific form of cost-per-action in which a visitor provides enough information at the advertiser's site (or in interaction with a rich media ad) to be used as a sales lead. Note that you can estimate cost-per-lead regardless of how you pay for the ad (in other words, buying on a pay-per-lead basis is not required to calculate the cost-per-lead).

Cost-per-sale: Sites that sell products directly from their Web site or can otherwise determine sales generated as the result of an advertising sales lead can calculate the cost-per-sale of Web advertising.

CPM: CPM is "cost per thousand ad impressions", an industry standard measure for selling ads on Web sites. This measure is taken from print advertising. The "M" has nothing to do with "mega" or million. It's taken from the Roman numeral for "thousand."

Fold: "Above the fold," a term borrowed from print media, refers to an ad that is viewable as soon as the Web page arrives. You don't have to scroll down (or sideways) to see it. Since screen resolution can affect what is immediately viewable, it is good to know whether the Web site's audience tends to set their resolution at 640 by 480 pixels or at 800 by 600 (or higher).

Hit: A hit is the sending of a single file, whether an HTML file, an image, an audio file, or other file type. Since a single Web page request can bring with it a number of individual files, the number of hits from a site is a not a good indication of its actual use (number of visitors). It does have meaning for the Web site space provider, however, as an indicator of traffic flow.

Impression: According to the "Basic Advertising Measures," from FAST, an ad industry group, an impression is "the count of a delivered basic advertising unit from an ad distribution point." Impressions are how most Web advertising is sold and the cost is quoted in terms of the cost per thousand impressions (CPM).

Unique visitor: A unique visitor is someone with a unique address who is entering a Web site for the first time that day (or some other specified period). Thus, a visitor that returns within the same day is not counted twice. A unique visitor count tells you how many different people there are in your audience during the time period, but not how much they used the site during the period.

User session: A user session is someone with a unique address that enters or reenters a Web site each day (or some other specified period).

A user session is sometimes determined by counting only those users that haven't reentered the site within the past 20 minutes or a similar period. User session figures are sometimes used, somewhat incorrectly, to indicate "visits" or "visitors" per day. User sessions are a better indicator of total site activity than "unique visitors" since they indicate frequency of use.

View: A view is, depending on what is meant, either an ad view or a page view. Usually an ad view is what's meant. There can be multiple ad views per page views. View counting should consider that a small percentage of users choose to turn the graphics off (not display the images) in their browser.

Visit: A visit is a Web user with a unique address entering a Web site at some page for the first time that day (or for the first time in a lesser time period). The number of visits is roughly equivalent to the number of different people that visit a site. This term is ambiguous unless the user defines it, since it could mean a user session or it could mean a unique visitor that day. With growing technologies, the world of sales and promotion on the internet is the most evolving and has the potential to move into the number source for advertising revenues. It is currently in third place.

Promotions

As mentioned earlier, the success of a sales staff depends heavily on the success of the programming they are sent out to sell. Meaning that the sales division is counting on high ratings to garner increased rates which in turn calculates to higher commissions paid out on their paychecks. The role of the Promotions department, sometimes called Creative Services, is specifically in place to increase ratings (viewers/listeners) through the use of various methods directed at a target market specific to the programs airing on their particular station.

> **On-air Promotions:** These spots will run on their own station promoting upcoming programs or specials. If the station has a slogan or brand that distinguishes them from the competition, the Promotions department will utilize these identifiable elements to further familiarize the audience with their unique characteristics.
>
> **Public Relations:** The PR department is responsible for generating publicity about the station which may occur in the form of a Press Release to the local media companies, newspapers, magazines and trade publications.
>
> **Community Outreach:** As mentioned earlier in the chapter, broadcasters are primarily in business to serve the best interests of the public. Many would say that they are a "Public Servant." Therefore, the Promotions

department will include a specific employee that is dedicated to being involved in community programs. This involves attending events for non-profit groups and civic organizations. This involvement further enables the station to get their name into the community while serving its citizens.

Internet Campaigns: The media company will have its own Web site allowing the Promotions division to execute interactive campaigns that furthers their exposure to the public. Some examples might include News, Traffic or Weather alerts to those loyal viewers or listeners who have opted in for the service.

Sales Promotions: Working alongside the sales division, Promotions will develop campaigns that will occur most often during ratings. For example, "Get Away May" runs in the morning news program encouraging viewers to watch and win in the month of May for a free trip to paradise courtesy of ABC Travel. This type of promotion can include on-air spots and internet elements specifically designed to get viewers to tune in during a time period that will be rated by Nielsen or Arbitron. In addition, they work with the Sales Department to sell these promotional ideas to generate much needed revenues for a station.

It is a collaborative effort on the part of the Sales and Marketing teams to generate revenues while also increasing viewership. In the upcoming years, there will be new and exciting methods from which both areas will evolve. On the initial horizon is the use of mobile devices, Hi-Def radio, Two-way cable and the further expansion into Digital Video. Most advances involve the interaction between the electronic media company and the end user. As long as the distribution points of these mediums continue to expand, it can only prove to be more beneficial to advertisers looking to reach their target customer and a place for Account Executives to show them the way in this bold world of media sales.

SUMMARY

This chapter examined the structure of a typical broadcast sales department and the responsibilities of those positions. It covered the new approaches and common practices, used to generate revenues for electronic media, including television, cable, radio, and Internet. Prospecting and generating new business were explored in depth, including guidelines on how to set a first and second appointment, performing the pitch, and multiple types of closing methods. In addition, we reviewed the role that Promotions/Creative Services plays in contributing to the success of the Sales division and described the various positions within that department. The ability for media companies to compete will be counting on these important departments to attract advertiser friendly audiences and generate substantial revenues, especially with the expansion into new technologies. Finally, the chapter considered selling time and space on the Internet and the developing terminology of this new field.

WHAT'S AHEAD

The next chapter discusses the distribution revolution and the profound changes in the way content reaches consumers, content management, and digital rights management. The impact of digital distribution has had a tremendous impact on the way content industries manage their businesses. The chapter examines both traditional and continuously emerging distribution methods.

CASE STUDY 10.1 CNA (CUSTOMER NEEDS ANALYSIS)

As a very persistent account executive for a local television-station, you have been calling on a local attorney's office for the past six months attempting to get an appointment. This high-profile attorney has a long-standing reputation in your city and has traditionally spent his advertising dollars in the Yellow Pages.

Today is your lucky day – the attorney is angry with the local Yellow Pages because they somehow misspelled his name in the recent directory. He has granted you an appointment, but advises you that you must really impress him before he takes a leap into television advertising.

You explain to him that you will not walk in with a pre-packaged schedule because you want to spend the first meeting gathering the facts, as he does when he first meets with clients. He likes your style and sets you up with a meeting in seven days. He'll meet with you in the morning because he has cases that begin promptly at 9:30 a.m., giving you 30 minutes to get the job done.

Begin laying out your strategy to make this a success-ful call. Choose a local attorney, and do some preliminary research on the firm. How long have they been in business? Are they associated with any charities? Do they specialize in a particular area of the law? Develop a Customer Needs Analysis form. What questions can you ask that will assist you in developing a well rounded advertising campaign?

Follow these guidelines when making your first call:

- Arrive 5–15 minutes early to the appointment.
- Introduction: Share commonalities or points of interest to client.

- Exchange business cards.
- Outline your meeting to the client.
- Present quick information about the station you are representing.
- Conduct a thorough Customer Needs Analysis.
- Set a follow-up appointment, at which you will present a customized advertising campaign.
- Thank him for his time.
- Get out on time.

Assignment

From beginning to end, describe how you intend to hit each of these actions points. Now, put this plan into action. Conduct your first meeting in front of your class. If there are time constraints, make this a 15 minute meeting. Keep your paperwork, because you will need it for part two of this Case Study. Allow your classmates to evaluate your meeting. If they were the client, would they grant you the 2nd appointment? By the way, make sure you set that next appointment no later than 5 business days from the initial meeting.

The more time that passes, the more opportunity that the potential client will find reasons to fall back into his tradi-tional advertising patterns, not to mention that word will get out on the street, and your competitors will be chomping at the bit to get an appointment, too.

CASE STUDY 10.2 THE PITCH

How did your meeting go with your potential new attorney client? What did you find out about his or her business that will enable you to formulate an advertising campaign that will be deemed successful? Did you ask him or her what his or her definition of a successful campaign would be?

Sometimes clients are looking to get a branding message out that may not generate immediate phone calls, but will grow a clientele base over time. Other businesses want the phone to ring off the hook yesterday. How do you accomplish this?

It is extremely important that you establish the expectations of the campaign and determine how you will measure this success. Now that you are armed with the information, it's time to put that data to use. For starters, when you created your own business card, what company did you decide on? Great! You'll need to conduct some research on the strengths of the station you represent and how that applies to your client's goals. Work these strengths into your Introduction page, which feeds back to the client some of the goals and information he or she has provided. This page should really communicate to the client that you were listening.

Target market page: Did you both decide on who the target market is for his or her business? If not, you are really going to have a difficult time moving forward, so make sure you have that critical piece of information. What can you tell your client about this target market that he or she may not know? Does your TV station deliver this audience? Where – what programs? How does that compare to your competitor? (By the way, it is likely they will be outside waiting for their opportunity to prove they have the better station.) Also, don't forget where he or she has been spending his or her ad dollars in the past. You do not want to make the client feel like he or she has been making a huge mistake – that is offensive. Simply offer an improved and expanded approach to his or her marketing strategy.

What extra research can you bring to the table that perhaps other stations did not consider? Is there data that tells you that attorneys who are now shifting attention to another area are reaping higher returns? Share this information. You need to become well informed about this industry. What challenges is the attorney facing? Do you have solutions to these challenges?

Assignment

Put together a schedule that reaches the client's target market and stays within his or her budget. Make sure to choose programs that are suitable to the client's target. Determine your flight dates and how many months you would like to start with.

Next, write a script for a 30-second television script. Based on the information you have gathered, what message do you want your viewers to hear that will make them react?

Before asking for the business, you will want to ask the client his or her thoughts on the presentation. This is a great time to hear the objections to the campaign. In this case, you might hear the client reveal that he has worked it out with his Yellow Pages sales representative and it was made clear to him that if he is not in this directory, he will lose business. Is that true? What answer do you have for that statement? What can you offer that the Yellow Pages cannot? Is there a compromise you can offer? Reduce the size of your ad and use the savings to branch out into television. If the client has no questions, be careful. It may be that he has made up his mind not to advertise and did not pay attention. Keep your client involved with the presentation. Stop and ask questions along the way to maintain interactivity.

Close the deal. Ask for the business. Use a closing line that would work best for you and this particular client. Have the client sign the contract, schedule a date for production, and let the client know when the commercial spot will begin running and how the schedule will be invoiced.

Okay, you guessed it: Do this in front of the class as well. Create a Microsoft PowerPoint presentation and obtain feedback from your classmates at the end. Did you meet your objectives? How did you handle objections? If you were successful, you'll not only have a new client on the air. You also get to pick up the lunch tab at the next meeting. Congratulations!

REFERENCES

Sources and Further Reading About FCC "Public Interest"

The Museum of Broadcasting 676 North LaSalle St., Suite 424, Chicago, IL 60654 | p. 312-245-8200 f. 312-245-8207, www.museum.tv

The Benton Foundation, 1625 K Street, NW 11th Floor, Washington, DC 20006 Phone: 202-638-5770 / Fax: 202-638-5771, www.benton.org

Federal Communications Commission, www.fcc.gov

Banning, William P. *Commercial Broadcasting Pioneer: The WEAF Experiment, 1922-1926.* Cambridge, Massachusetts: Harvard University Press, 1946.

Barnouw, Erik. *The Golden Web: A History of Broadcasting in the United States, Volume II–1933-1953.* New York: Oxford University Press, 1968.

"Cartoon Characters Enlisted in Anti-drug War." *Broadcasting*, 23 April 1990.

Federal Communications Commission. *Public Service Responsibility of Broadcast Licensees.* Washington: GPO, 7 March 1946.

Lichty, Lawrence W., and Malachi C. Topping. *American Broadcasting.* New York: Hastings House 1975.

Sarnoff, David. *Looking Ahead: The Papers of David Sarnoff.* New York: McGraw-Hill, 1968.

United States Congress. *Communications Act of 1934.* 73rd Congress, 2nd Session, S. Res. 3285. Washington: GPO, 1934.

Sources and Further Reading About Sales Division

Television Bureau of Advertising, www.tvb.org

Radio Advertising Bureau, www.rab.com

Cabletelevision Advertising Bureau, www.thecab.tv

Internet Advertising Bureau, www.iab.net

Warner, Charles, and Buchman, Joseph. *Media Selling: Broadcast, Cable, Print and Interactive.* Ames, IA: Wiley-Blackwell, 2003.

Weyland, Paul. *Successful Local Broadcast Sales.* New York, NY: Amacom, 2007.

Broadcasting & Cable Magazine, ww.broadcastingandcable.com

Sources and Further Reading About Promotions

Promax BDA, Promax Broadcast Design Association, www.promaxbda.org

Eastman, Susan T., Ferguson, Douglas A., and Klein, Robert. *Media Promotion & Marketing for Broadcasting, Cable & the Internet, Fifth Edition.* Bur lington, MA: Focal Press, 2006.

CHAPTER 11

Distributing Content

The speed of communications is wondrous to behold. It is also true that speed can multiply the distribution of information that we know to be untrue.

Edward R. Murrow

CHAPTER OBJECTIVES

The objective of this chapter is to provide you with information about:
- Distribution revolution
- Bricks and clicks
  - Legacy distribution channels
    - Film: Theaters
    - Print: Books, magazines, and newspapers
    - Broadcast media
  - Traditional electronic distribution outlets
    - Over-the-air local broadcast television and radio stations
    - Cable television
- Wired bitpipes
  - Cable networks
  - Telephone company networks
  - Computer networks
- Wireless bitpipes
  - One-way wireless systems: Satellites (GEOs, MEOs, and LEOs)
  - Two-way wireless systems: LMDS, MMDS, cellular wireless broadband (3G) and mobile television
- Content management
  - Mass customization
  - Personalization
- Digital rights management

271

DOI: 10.1016/B978-0-240-81020-1.00011-7

INTRODUCTION

The big headaches brought on by digital technologies began with distribution – a previously little-known backwater of the media and entertainment businesses. Sure, that's where consumers meet content and hand over their crumpled dollars at the box office, the counter, and the Web site shopping cart. Yes, distribution is where the money is made. But it's sadly low on glamour and coolness. No one ever came through the door exclaiming, "I closed this fantastic distribution deal with Telepix today!" like they might have crowed, "I had lunch with Sean Penn today and he's starring in my next project!"

Nevertheless, nothing has contributed as much to the transformation of the content industries as the disruption of distribution channels and practices. Beginning with the Napster peer-to-peer file sharing that decimated the music industry, every segment has been forced to deal with how to make a profit when consumers can share content without paying for it. But digitization seemed like such a great development at first!

Consider that the content industries differ from many industries because the entire product supply chain, from conception through delivery and consumption, can be carried out electronically. (You can't do that with carrots, cars, or cold storage equipment!) Write content, produce it, prepare it, and deliver it without ever leaving the digital domain. No more paper and ink, celluloid, reels, printing – many of the high costs of getting content to consumers can be eliminated.

Specifically, distributing content digitally makes possible efficient, cost-saving methods of automating the preparation and delivery of content such as *transcoding* the content from one format to another – repackaging a TV series from broadcast programs to a single DVD. Beyond doing old activities better, digital processing also enables carrying out altogether new actions that were not even possible with analog technologies, such as customizing and personalizing the content on demand and (perhaps) protecting it from being copied without authorization.

The impact of digital distribution has forced today's media managers to know a great deal about the technologies of both production and distribution. Just as earlier chapters looked at content production, marketing, and sales, this chapter turns to the means of media distribution from studios and producers, through middlemen, syndicators, and aggregators, all the way to the homes and devices of consumers. (Another way of referring to distribution is the *output supply chain*.)

Even the activities that describe the distribution process are changing. Traditionally, distribution really meant marketing, and the work consisted of negotiating marketing deals that granted distribution rights to another organization. For example, some common types of distribution agreements in the film industry are:[1]

- **Production/Finance/Distribution (PDF) agreements**, whereby a studio contracts with a production company and finances the production, while maintaining their distribution rights.
- **Negative pick-up deal**, where a studio agrees to pay a fixed amount for a completed film. Depending on the details of the agreement, the studio may retain distribution rights or may share them with the production company.
- **Presale agreement**, usually made between a production company and a foreign distributor to allow the foreign company to distribute the film in a particular country or territory.

Distribution in these agreements really means the sale of rights to distribute – a form of a sale that allows some entity to distribute the film to consumers. Similarly, in the TV industry distribution often means selling a content property to a broadcast or cable network, local cable operator or TV station, or a syndicator. In the traditional model, the process stops here. And for a long time, it could stop here, because every industry was associated with its own channel for moving the content to the consumer. Films went to theaters, TV shows to networks and stations, radio programs to over-the-air stations, newspapers to home deliverers or newsstands, and magazines in the mail directly to subscribers or to newsstands.

But like so much else in the content industries, the traditional view of distribution stops too short, because the number of content distribution channels has multiplied dramatically, increasing the complexity of getting content to consumers. Legacy distribution channels may still be the most common and profitable in some sectors, but others have seen traditional methods become anemic shadows of their former glory. The music business has been eviscerated by peer-to-peer networks and online sales. The newspaper business is experiencing many troubles, because people can read the news on the Internet without paying. In contrast, the motion picture business has been made more profitable by the addition of release windows beyond theaters and network and syndicated television – now encompassing the Internet and mail delivery services such as Netflix.

DISTRIBUTION REVOLUTION

Over the past decade, the proliferation of multiple content distribution channels, brought about by the emergence of global fiber-optic digital networks and the Internet, has opened many paths to the consumer. A company, a content creator, a studio – even a college student – can distribute content around the world in an instant. As we will see, the two-edged sword of anywhere, anytime electronic networks has made distribution a chaotic, thrilling, and dangerous enterprise for today's media companies.

Given the upheaval, it is easy to think that in the past, little time needed to be spent on distribution beyond contracts and deals, as distribution channels were already established. However, this cozy view of a static past marked by established customs and practices does not address the realities of technological change that marked the media industries throughout the twentieth century as well. For example, in 1891, when Edison Labs demonstrated the Kinetoscope "projector" to show moving pictures, the inventors believed that films would be shown to one viewer at a time. However, the projector quickly became used to exhibit in public theaters to large audiences – the first commercial exhibition of film took place on April 14, 1894, at the Holland Brothers Kinetoscope Parlor at 1155 Broadway in New York. For 25 cents, patrons could watch films that were less than 2 minutes long. According to contemporary reports, the owners took in more than $16,000 in gross receipts, an enormous amount of money for the time.[2] Not surprisingly, "parlors" soon opened in London and Paris as well.

By 1911, multiple-reel film enabled long-form movies to be shown, and there were permanent movie exhibition facilities, called "nickelodeons" because they cost 5 cents to attend, in almost every U.S. town.[3] This change meant that the people making films had to produce different properties to be successful. Moreover, as facilities had only one projector, the projectionist put up a sign that read "One Moment Please" while the reels were changed. Within a short time, a town with multiple nickelodeons would receive only one set of reels. Each theater would start the evening's entertainment at spaced intervals, allowing time for young people on bicycles to speed the just-finished reel from one theater to the next for exhibition. This practice became known as *bicycling reels,* and the term was still used as late as the 1990s to describe a process where a theater forwards content to the theater next scheduled to display the material. Bicycling continued to be used for syndicated programs in the early days of television.

The examples from the early days of motion pictures underscore the idea that rapid change has been occurring for more than a century – and it will continue into the foreseeable future. Today, the distribution channels of all media are undergoing almost continuous evolution. And when the underlying communication technologies change, every aspect of the medium can change with it, opening up entirely new distribution channels, driving the development of new display devices and altering consumption patterns.

Content distribution reflects the state of technology at any given time. The radio industry first transmitted programs by telephone line and played in hotel lobbies. Broadcast came a little later. Initially, national television programs were transmitted across the United States via coaxial cable and microwave for such live events as the 1953 inauguration of President Eisenhower and the

1953 coronation of Queen Elizabeth; by 1974, many TV programs reached stations via satellite and the consumer by local broadcast signals. Today, television content comes every which way – coaxial cable, satellite, microwave, and digital telephone and computer networks. Newspapers and magazines were originally posted as broadsheets, then sold on street corners, then from newsstands, and then delivered by boys on bicycles. Now, they reach consumers through the mail, by home delivery, or over the Internet.

For managers of companies that provide content, distribution is more important than ever because the delivery mechanism has become part of the content's marketing. Content sellers that want a competitive edge will make the purchase, receipt, and display of their material easy for the consumer, delivering it when and how the customer wants it. On Amazon.com, customers can elect to have books physically delivered to them or download them to a Kindle. Music lovers can buy albums in a music store or download songs from the Internet. Newspaper subscribers can have the paper delivered, buy it from a newsstand, or access it over the Internet. Film buffs may go to a theater, download the movie from the Internet, have it sent to them via Netflix or other service, or rent or buy it from Blockbuster or another local retail outlet.

The necessity to deliver material over multiple channels and networks has raised the visibility of distribution processes in media organizations. In addition, multiple preparations of content products for each distribution channel and consumption device entail a much more complex final packaging process than companies have had to support in the past. As each new channel arises, they have added resources to deal with it on an ad hoc basis. Now media organizations are looking at this disorganized array of distribution formats and procedures to see if they can put more efficient, cost-effective procedures in place.

If an organization enters into a distribution contract, then the actual distribution to the consumer is pushed down to that distributor. Traditionally, there was usually a separation between the companies that engaged in content production, distribution, and delivery: Creatives created, studios and labels marketed and promoted, technical people disseminated, and retail people sold and delivered.

But the growth of distribution channels makes it possible for all participants to distribute directly to consumers. And consumers can redistribute content among themselves via peer-to-peer networks. Figure 11-1 illustrates how legacy channels and direct channels are now available to everyone.

When a company chooses to handle the distribution of content products itself, managers begin by understanding how their prospective consumers want to receive and consume the content – when and where they want to buy it, how and how much they want to pay for it, and how, where, and when they want

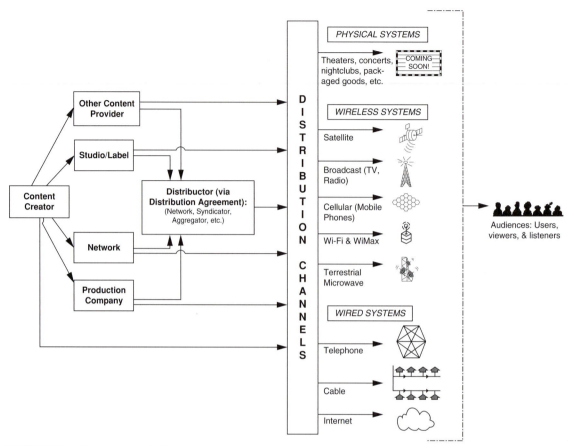

FIGURE 11-1 Contemporary distribution channels. *Source: Joan Van Tassel.*

to consume it. Based on that knowledge, one decision stands over all others – whether to deliver a content product to the consumer in a physical format, like a CD, DVD, book, or magazine, or in a digital, downloadable format – or both. This decision will direct the actions that managers will carry out to disseminate the content and deliver it to consumers:

- Contracting for distribution services that reach desired consumers
- Preparing content for distribution (formatting, customizing, and protecting)
- Scheduling and provisioning distribution services
- Distributing content through a delivery channel
- Delivering content (fulfillment)
- Displaying content
- Tracking content from dissemination through consumption
- Handling consumer relationships (customer care)

BRICKS AND CLICKS

Bricks and clicks is a light-hearted way of pointing to the division between physical and electronic delivery of goods, as shown in Table 11-1. The bricks, sometimes expanded to bricks-and-mortar, refer to buildings and the entire apparatus of retail physical supply lines – stores and warehouses, parking lots, trains and trucks, forklifts, inventory, shelf stockers, shelves and bins, counters, cash registers, checkers, and baggers. Most products necessarily come to consumers via physical means: pianos, peanuts, machined parts, and panel trucks.

Clicks won't take over everything in the physical supply chain, but they do replace many elements of it – retail buildings and associated costs, in-store personnel, checkout lines, and cash registers. Indeed, the entire payment mechanism is replaced by clicks. Warehousing of inventory can stay with the producer or go no further than a distributor warehouse operation, with products shipped directly to the consumer. Table 11-1 is a compendium of the difference between bricks and clicks.

For content distribution, each domain has its advantages and disadvantages. The retail world allows face-to-face contact between buyer and seller, engendering greater loyalty. In the long run, physical distribution is more costly. The costs of producing copies of motion picture prints, books, magazines, and newspapers are significant. Overproducing packaged content for retail sale leads to expensive returns of product. Underproducing it means lost opportunities to make a sale or establish a long-term relationship with a customer.

Many consumers prefer electronic purchase and download of content – it's instant gratification from a 24/7 store. Electronic distribution of content is also more efficient, but it may entail significant startup costs. It is also difficult to prevent consumers from redistributing the material to millions of their online peers, at a cost that can far exceed any possible savings from greater efficiency.

Table 11-1 Physical and Electronic Product Delivery Modes

Bricks	Clicks
Analog	Digital
Local retail store	Local device (computer, console, or mobile device with Internet access)
Physical or molecular	Electronic
Packaged goods	Electronic goods
Physical delivery	Download
Over the counter	Over the Internet
On the shelf	On the server

However, in the end, the physical and electronic worlds are inextricably tied together. For example, even now all of the information that surrounds physical products takes place in the electronic domain, and people in the physical goods industries need to master both domains. The product may be delivered in the physical world, but the design to create them and the promotional efforts to sell them take place in the electronic one. Similarly, all electronic content has its origination in the physical world, which includes computers, servers, cameras, drawing tablets, and so forth. Most persuasively, content may be digital, but human eyes and ears are analog, so all material must ultimately translate into the analog, physical domain if it is to be viewed by and listened to by media consumers.

The next sections look at traditional physical media distribution channels, then turn to analog and digital electronic channels. Finally, we'll explore new, as yet over-the-horizon wired and wireless media platforms that will support emerging channels.

Legacy Distribution Channels

The traditional distribution channels came into existence to support mass media as they emerged in the twentieth century. We all know them: They include motion pictures and theaters, broadcast media and local stations and cable systems, newspapers, via delivery and newsstands, and magazines, via mail and newsstands.

Film: Theaters

Studios usually distribute their own films through a specialized arm of the company. Independent producers may sign them with studios or with independent distribution firms. Distribution fees average between 32 and 40 percent of the gross box office revenues. Of course, if another arm of the studio is the distributor, then the studio pays this fee to itself. But independent producers can expect to make very real payments to distributors.

Once the deals are signed, the task of bringing the motion picture to consumers begins. The first decision the distribution organization makes is whether it will mount a wide release to reach a large audience from the start, or a *platform release*, a *niche-to-wide release* strategy that places the picture in a few theaters and building to a bigger audience through word of mouth, or a release that is somewhere between these two tried-and-true strategies. In the niche release, the distributor identifies audiences that are specifically interested in the genre or topic. The film is released in a small number of theaters, often only in urban areas, supported by local newspaper advertising. If the film generates interest and word-of-mouth "buzz," the studio expands the picture to additional screens, testing to see if it can attract a larger audience.[4]

This is a familiar story for garage band musical groups. Like the term suggests, the group begins by playing together in someone's home or garage. It then

> The country rock band the Cowboy Junkies was formed in 1985 in Toronto, Canada, by siblings Margo (vocals), Michael (guitar, songwriter), and Peter (drums) Timmins and friend Alan Anton (bass). The Junkies first performed publicly in local Toronto clubs. The group's first album was recorded in the Timmons family garage. Their second album, recorded in 1987, in one day with one microphone, at Toronto's Church of the Holy Trinity, attracted wider attention. In 1988, the album was named by the *Los Angeles Times* as one of the ten best albums of the year. Wide to niche: start with a big splash and reexpress for ever smaller audiences.[5]

moves to local venues and then catches on and attracts a large audience. A good example is the Cowboy Junkies, as described in the box.

Wide to niche is the blockbuster-or-hit strategy. It works well for multinational companies with big production, distribution, and marketing budgets. In the film business, the wide release is the most common, in which studios book the picture into several thousand theaters, sometimes in international venues as well as domestic theaters. The marketing effort can generate good sales for one or even two weeks, but then the product must have genuine appeal. If it disappoints early audiences, even an enormous marketing and promotion budget may not enable sustainable success. The same scenario holds true for new TV programs, CDs, and books – all those hit-driven content products.

Distributors reach a release strategy by looking at the performance of similar films released previously. They also consider the potential audience for the picture, including their demographic characteristics and where they live and work. Based on that information and analysis, the distributor sets out to match the marketing plan for the prospective audience with the availability of theaters and screens.

Once there is a decision about the number of screens, the organization will strike (make) enough prints of the film to execute the marketing plan, because the distribution of films still occurs in the physical domain. The distributor then messengers the prints to theaters. The physical distribution of motion pictures is a major budget item. There are more than 6,200 theaters that house more than 40,000 screens.[6] The average cost of a print is between $2,000 and $3,000,[7] and every theater showing the picture needs a print; multiplexes may require more than one print. As an example of the scale of costs, to distribute *The Negotiator*, starring Samuel L. Jackson and Kevin Spacey, Warner Bros. spent $12.32 million for "prints, trailers, dubbing, customs, and shipping."[8]

In addition, the theater owner gets a percentage of the box office revenue. Agreements between distributors and theater owners (exhibitors) have flexible terms that change over time, called *sliding-scale agreements*.[9] In the first week or two, the distributor may receive as much as 90 percent, with a guarantee of minimum revenues, *the floor*, after the exhibitor's expenses are met. As time goes on, the agreement may provide the exhibitor with a greater percentage, up to 30 or 40 percent.

(Exhibitors may make the greater part of their income from concession sales of popcorn, soft drinks, and candy. As one exhibitor executive said, "The profit margin on popcorn is enough to make a grown man cry with joy.")[10]

Slowly, the motion picture industry is moving to digital cinema. As of mid-2008, of the world's approximately 100,000 motion picture screens, about 6,300 of them were digital.[11] Digital distribution and display will eliminate celluloid reels, physically delivered to theaters and shown through mechanical projectors, and replace them with electronic data streams, delivered over networks to servers and played out to be displayed by digital projectors. Producing pictures on analog film may well extend for a number of years after the adoption of digital distribution. According to a postproduction facility executive, "It will be a long time till the hundreds of thousands of cinemas worldwide adopt the digital technology, which is expensive and whose equipment is short-lived. Furthermore, even if 35 mm print goes away eventually, filmmakers will want to originate projects on 8 mm, 16 mm, and 35 mm or 65 mm film for a variety of reasons from ease of use to look."[12]

Print: Books, Magazines, and Newspapers

With their centuries-long history, nothing is more "legacy" than books, magazines, and newspapers. Printed materials have been produced mechanically with expensive, precision equipment, using paper and ink – until now. Digital distribution of formerly printed products is proceeding at a rapid rate – Internet readership of newspapers reached an all-time high in 2009.[13] According to the Digital Future Project, Internet users spent 53 minutes per week reading newspapers online, compared to 41 minutes in 2008. Moreover, 22 percent of users reported that they dropped subscriptions to magazines or newspapers in favor of accessing the articles online.

One factor that has kept printed publication alive is the lack of portability of digital versions. People like to read them on public transportation, outside, and in restaurants and other public places. Advances in technologies to allow portable digital reading continue to emerge, including the Amazon Kindle, the Sony Reader, the Samsung SNE-50K, and a dozen other such readers that allow users to download material to read on the go. Current challenges facing the adoption of digital readers are extending battery life, improving readability, especially in outdoor and bright light, and cost. Farther out on the horizon is *digital paper*, which will use changing *digital ink* to reflect downloaded material and allow users to read in a manner similar to today's printed material.

Over-the-Air Local Broadcast Television and Radio Stations: Centralizing Broadcast Operations

The broadcast industry has already made the transition to digital distribution. In the process, the entire landscape of broadcast changed. For nearly a century, radio was largely local; television was also primarily local from its inception in the late 1940s. Today, both these media are largely national entities, offering programming to an ever-larger percentage of the total U.S. audience.

The consolidation in the media industry had many causes, but the result is that most radio and television stations are owned by broadcast groups – there are few family-owned stations left in the United States. The centralization of broadcast operations, including the distribution of programming to the consumer, occurred as part of the transition to digital television transmission.[14] Centralizing broadcast operations emerged as a way to reduce the cost of the transition – a case where one innovation brought about another. In the case of digital television (DTV), digital distribution actually brought about a change of much of television technology and many of the ways broadcast companies worked and organized themselves.

For example, as broadcast groups that owned multiple TV stations prepared to invest in the redesign of their physical plants to comply with the government-mandated transition, they became aware of the potential for reducing costs by building one master control room in one location rather than several of them, one in each station. Similarly, they realized they could carry out many tasks just once by putting the results of the job in a centralized, computerized traffic system. Such jobs include producing promos, inserting spots in a program stream, and preparing news and weather graphics for use by all stations, rather than performing these tasks at each station. They could also centralize billing, logs, and many other back-office functions, bringing considerable savings through reducing staff.

The process of centralizing broadcast operations has moved jobs from the local station into the broadcast group. In particular, many managers are likely to work at group headquarters rather than at the owned stations. However, the jobs that are moved depend on which tasks are centralized.

There is a spectrum of centralization that ranges from almost total centralization to very little. On the whole, radio broadcast operations are more centralized than television – on the ground in the local market, radio broadcast groups may only have a computer server and a transmitter, with everything else centralized at a headquarters facility. (The central facility is sometimes called the *NOC*, the *Network Operations Center*.)

Similarly, some television broadcast groups that own several stations in the same region have centralized almost everything, leaving only the local transmitter, news operations, and sales. Television groups that have high bandwidth and personnel costs may choose to centralize personnel to allow greater efficiency and reduce staff, while moving material over lower-bandwidth channels. Other television groups whose holdings may be scattered centralize programming coming from the satellite and forward it to the stations, leaving most other functions at the station level. In particular, most network-owned and -operated and affiliated stations continue to have a large news organization in major markets and at least a small news presence even in small markets.

Managers who want to succeed in broadcast companies need to understand the decisions their company makes about how to structure its operations and why they make them the way they do. They need to understand that as new technologies come on the market, it may affect the way the company operates, driving changes that affect jobs, processes, and profitability. There are several models of centralization, as shown in Table 11-2.

Table 11-2 Comparing Centralization Models

	Hub	Local Station	Connectivity
MODEL 1: Centralized monitoring	Transmission control and monitoring Remote automation air client Facility monitoring Traffic client	Transmission equipment Play to air equipment Automation system All media assets Media preparation and ingest Live production – news On-air promotional production	T-1 (1.5 Mbps) duplex
MODEL 2: Centralized operations	Transmission control and monitoring Play to air equipment Automation systems All media assets Media preparation and ingest Traffic system On-air promotional Production	Transmission equipment	Hub to stations: DS-3 or OC-3 Stations to hub: Lower bandwidth via Ethernet switch and network gateway
MODEL 3: Centralized resources	Transmission control and monitoring Facility monitoring Spot/program ingest – regional/national Syndicated program ingest On-air promotional production Media archivingTraffic	Transmission equipment Play to air equipment Automation system Media assets All local Regional/national, as required Local spot media preparation and ingest Live production – news	OC-3/DS-3 Duplex ATM WAN
MODEL 4: Hub and node	Transmission control and monitoring Play to air equipment Automation system Facility monitoring Spot/program ingest regional/national On-air promotional production All media except news Traffic	Transmission equipment Limited master control Local spot media preparation and ingest Live production – news Remote air client	OC-3/DS-3 Duplex ATM WAN

Source: Compiled by author, based on interviews and schematics from J. Adrick, Harris. Corp.

Cable Television

Like local over-the-air television stations, the owners of early local cable systems often lived in the same market, known as *mom-and-pop* systems. Today, nearly all local cable systems are part of larger companies known as *multi-system operators*, or *MSOs*. The local headend receives satellite signals, gathers them together (*multiplexes*), and pushes them out to subscriber homes. Handling analog signals is relatively simple and most cable headends automate the process. As signals come in, they are demodulated, scrambled, multiplexed, amplified, and demultiplexed for transportation to neighborhood nodes. If they are scrambled, the decoding will be done by the subscriber's set-top box.

Yesterday's cable networks were one-way, just shuttling cable networks to subscribers. Today's systems are much more complex, because they are two-way communication networks as well, providing Internet access, video on demand, and telephone service as well as cable TV. Content producers, networks, and middlemen do not have to concern themselves with the details of transporting their material over cable networks, because cable system engineers have worked out the mostly automated process. However, they may need to pay for all or part of the costs for the satellite feed to headends, particularly if they are distributing material they hope the cable system will run. Such content might include infomercials, video news releases, or *public service announcements* (*PSAs*).

Executives who work for cable companies and other content transport networks do need to understand how their company transports content in some

A DAY IN THE LIFE OF VALERIE GELLER

Valerie Geller, President, Geller Media International; Broadcast Consultant; Author: *Creating Powerful Radio*

Valerie Geller called her first talk radio show at age seven. The host of the program was complaining about kids who'd made too much noise at a restaurant. His idea: "Keep 'em quiet or leave 'em home until they're 18." Geller picked up the phone and told the host that the lives of most kids were so restricted, and that every aspect of a child's life is somehow controlled by his or her parents or other adults – the *one* thing a kid could do for freedom of expression (and to have fun), was to make noise, so could he please stop talking like that and leave the kids alone? Her message: "Let them make noise."

And so it began. Her experience in broadcasting prior to becoming a consultant: Geller was program director of WABC Radio in New York City, executive producer of KFI in Los Angeles, news director of K101 in San Francisco,

news reporter for KTAR in Phoenix and K-Earth-101-FM in Los Angeles, and a talk show host at KOA in Denver and at WPLP in St. Petersburg, Florida.

Over the past 20 years, Geller's worked with more than 500 stations in 30 countries, and is considered one of the top broadcast consultants in the world. In 1991, she formed Geller Media International, with a client list that includes NPR stations, CBS stations, the BBC in the United Kingdom, the ABC in Australia, Swedish Radio, and many more. *Radio Ink Magazine* named Geller one of the "50 Most Influential Women in Radio." An in-demand workshop and seminar leader, Geller is a popular keynote speaker at conferences for broadcasting, news, information, and new media and podcasting. She also lectures at NYU Film School and the Columbia University Graduate School of Journalism in New York.

A native of Los Angeles, Geller currently lives in New York City. But the work developing and training (and finding) on-air

Continued...

personalities, news reporters and anchors, producers, and programmers takes her around the world. Geller has trained and worked with some of the top people in the business, and has served on the board of directors of the Associated Press and NORCAL Radio & TV News Directors Association and is the author of three books about radio, including:

- *Creating Powerful Radio – A Communicator's Handbook for News, Talk Information & Personality* (M Street Publications, 1996)
- *The Powerful Radio Workbook – The Prep, Performance & Post Production Planning* (M Street Publications, 2000)
- *Creating Powerful Radio – Getting, Keeping & Growing Audiences for News, Talk, Information & Personality – Broadcast, HD, Satellite & Internet* (Focal Press, 2007)
- A new book, *Beyond Powerful Radio – A Communicator's Handbook for the Internet Age*, will be available from Focal Press in 2011.

For more information on these books, see http://www.creatingpowerfulradio.com. For more information on Geller Media International, see http://www.gellermedia.com.

Describe a "Typical" Day: If a Student Were Spending a Day with You on One of Your Busiest Days, What Could He or She Expect to See and Experience?

This is a tough question. I once had a film crew trail me – after shooting for three and a half days, they finally felt they'd captured an "average" day. While I live in New York City, I travel the world and over the past 20 years I've worked with more than 500 stations in 30 countries. Anywhere people want to learn the powerful radio techniques, and can bring me in, I'll go. It was easier to answer the question about "What is a typical day?" when I programmed a local radio station (WABC in New York) or was a news director at a major market station. A typical day was more structured, beginning with meetings with show hosts, news reporters and producers, marketing and sales and accounting, and other department heads, working to find and develop on-air talent, regular lunch meetings or breaks, basically all the tasks involved in running a station. But now I work as a consultant, and no two days are alike. I write books, lead training seminars and workshops, give speeches and coach individuals, lecture, and travel the world. That's part of the fun and why I love consulting: it's never routine or boring and you get to see the world, meet, talk with, and work with fantastic, creative, and talented people, experience other cultures. So a "typical day" may have me waking up in Moscow, Singapore, Sydney, Nairobi, Los Angeles, Toronto, Mexico City, Stockholm, or London,

working with radio and TV stations on-air, programming, news, and producing staffs.

How Does Your Typical Day Begin?

No matter where I am my day usually starts with a *strong* cup of coffee (in Europe I got hooked on Italian coffee, Turkish coffee, or just any great coffee – and now if I don't get a great cup of coffee in the morning, somehow my brain just doesn't get going the same way!). I wish I could be a great role model and tell you that I exercise (a long-term goal), but that wouldn't be honest. I have yet to start an exercise routine and stick to it in the morning.

When I open my email, even at 6:00 a.m., my message box is filled – usually from broadcasters in Europe, where the day has long been under way when we're just getting started in America or from clients in Australia where their day is wrapping up when it's morning here. These could be anything from requests from managers looking for talent for their stations or any one of a myriad of small "put-out-the-fire" problems, to larger issues involving format or management issues, research, or strategic planning.

What Is the First Thing on Your Agenda?

Each day is a bit different, though in looking over the past few months of days on my calendar – it looks like many days typically start either with an aircheck meeting, a programming or news meeting or a conference call with clients. I tend to do a lot of airchecking first thing, as that's when morning shows get off the air and have the time (and desire and inclination) to review their program.

Whom Do You Interact With?

I work globally and often in languages other than English, so many days, the most consistent person I interact with on a project would be the translator or interpreter, who helps me understand not only what went on air, but also helps put the content into context of the stories and helps me understand the customs and culture of each individual country. I also interact regularly with on-air personalities, those hoping to become on-air personalities, also producers, news directors, marketing and sales staffs, program directors, and general managers.

What Are Some of the Most Challenging Issues You Face? It Looks So Easy!

Because everyone can talk, most people falsely believe this work is easy! But just like a great actor, athlete, or dancer, the great ones just make it LOOK that way! This work takes craft, skill, training, experience, and talent. It's hard. *The curse of our business is that everyone can talk, so everyone thinks this work is easy!* But I believe there are NO boring stories, only boring storytellers, powerful storytelling can be taught, and everyone can improve, if people are willing to learn the techniques.

You Can't Make 'Em Do What You Want Them to Do

There's a joke: "How many psychiatrists does it take to change a lightbulb?" The answer: "Only one, but the lightbulb has got to want to change." As a consultant, you can make suggestions and offer ideas and solutions, and while you may have influence, you have no real power. You can never *make* clients do the things you know will help them. It's like being a stepmom or substitute teacher. These are not "your kids." So the hard part is when you watch the train heading off the rails and you *know* what to do to get it back on track, but the client chooses not to take the advice.

Broadcasting Is Changing

Our industry is in a technological shift and we're moving away from traditional delivery systems. Attention spans of audiences are shorter, people are busier, and there's much more information and entertainment out there and available to choose from.

But while our listeners and viewers are getting their information in a variety of ways, the basic principles to get, keep, and grow audiences are the same no matter what the medium and they work throughout the world. Tell the truth, make it matter and *never be boring*. Inform, Entertain, Inspire, Persuade, and Connect. No matter what the delivery system, if the content is relevant, listeners and viewers will be there. The work I do is to teach methods to help clients create relevant and powerful content that works across multiple and changing platforms

Cutbacks and Downsizing of Station Staffs

Even in times of economic downturn or cuts to staffs in the newsroom or at stations, the challenge is to keep the content relevant at all times and to train and teach powerful communication and storytelling – with the goal of broadcasters and podcasters creating powerful content. Creativity costs nothing. But it takes time and hard work. And getting, keeping, and growing audiences for stations is always hard work and a challenge.

Meeting Our Daily Goals

TV, radio, and Internet content producers have two goals: THE BIG DAY and THE REST OF THE TIME. Coverage of events on "the big news day," when what's happening is of such magnitude (weather emergencies, toxic waste spills in the local area, a tsunami, or earthquake, bomb blasts, etc. – where the lives, safety, and well-being of the public are in danger is different from other "regular days of programming"). The "big day" event coverage is special programming, and all broadcasters need to be prepared for those few days each year when the news events occur. On those days, our first responsibility, anywhere in the world, is to "keep our listeners and viewers safe from harm, broadcasting what they need to know immediately to stay safe, and verifying that the information we're giving is correct and credible."

Then there's the rest of the time, which is *most* of the time, our job as broadcasters is to inform entertainingly and entertain informatively and keep audiences even when not that much is happening. Our gig is to inspire, persuade, and connect listeners and viewers. My work involves teaching. The methods are in all of the "powerful radio" books and they are universal. Our job as communicators and broadcasters is to be powerful storytellers who chronicle the struggle to be a human being and reflect real life with a microphone. The work I do teaches powerful communication techniques, effective storytelling methods, and how to captivate an audience. The powerful radio principles are:

1. Tell the truth.
2. Make it matter.
3. NEVER BE BORING!

Jetlag

The only other challenge I face – other than the basics of working out of country and culture and language – includes the stress of constant "time shifting," getting off a plane in a different time zone, exhausted, and having to be "on, alert, awake, and creative" when you're completely jetlagged and wiped out.

Describe the Highlights of Your Work Day

When the work *works*! Breaking through to broadcasters who've been working one way for some time, then try new ideas to improve their work. The "highest" highlight for me is turning on the radio and hearing the personalities and newscasters creating compelling and powerful radio – as they "get it" and begin to work with and embrace these methods. Also of course looking at the ratings and seeing proof of audience growth! The "powerful radio" books and principles are universal and *work* everywhere. These books have been translated into several languages – and have made their way

Continued…

around the world, Each time the methods prove successful or a broadcaster contacts me saying one of my books has become his or her "bible," I'm thrilled. It doesn't get better than that.

How Do You End Your Day?

Well it sounds very boring, but at the end of the day when I'm on the road, consulting stations or working one-on-one with talent, I wrap up the day by writing client reports. (Or making notes, so I can remember details later. It's good to do while some of the key points of the work we've done together and the agreed-upon achievable goals are fresh in my mind.) At the office, at home in New York, you can work 24/7, as my work is international – and it's always business hours somewhere in the world where I have clients. So I have to put the stop to the day. Dinner or relaxing with the significant person in my life, or checking in with friends – when you do this kind of work, sometimes there's a fine line between work and the rest of your life. I don't worry too much about that these days.

Discuss Any After-Hours Responsibilities

When I'm on the road, there are those days of course when I'll have dinner with clients, and continue our day's work. Then there are other times when I'm so exhausted that I go back to the room and get quiet.

But one of the best pieces of wisdom I've ever gotten about this came from another consultant. The advice: "I'll still work with you this afternoon, but after 4:00 p.m., we have to leave the office. And you have to take me somewhere interesting. We can still talk about work, but we have to *go* somewhere and see something." That advice has been golden. I've seen the "Edge of the World" in southern Norway; the "Apostles" in Australia; watched a baby giraffe being born in Nairobi, Kenya; celebrated the Santa Lucia festival and parade in Finland; watched a magical sunset on a deserted beach in the Philippines; had a private tour of Red Square and the Armory Museum in Moscow, Russia; hiked the woods of southern Sweden; sipped tea in the home studio of a nation's poet laureate; taken a personalized tour of the Louvre with an architect involved in the redesign of the structure; shopped the Christmas Fair in Nuremburg, Germany; and much, much more.

What Is a Typical Day?

There's no such thing, for me; my work encompasses more like three or four separate work lives. If I'm in my New York office, that's one type of day, that might start with phone calls and email, but end up in a producer meeting, then being picked up in a limo town car heading to the Hudson Valley estate of a local celebrity who's starting a talk show in the fall, followed up by meeting with executives of a satellite radio company planning a new program.

If I'm attending a conference, speaking or holding training sessions, keynoting a conference, or leading a Creating Powerful Radio seminar, Powerful News, or Geller Media International Producer's workshop, that's a completely "other" kind of day! But when I'm on the road, as a consultant, working with a station either in the United States or overseas, it's one "typical day" (see following schedule). But if I have to pick a typical "day," here is what happens when I'm working onsite as a broadcast consultant at a station, on the road.

On the Road – Onsite – Consulting at a Station – Typical Day

5:30 a.m. Wakeup call.

5:45 a.m. Second wakeup call.

6:00 a.m.–10:00 a.m. Order room service breakfast, get dressed, monitor the station – by listening to the morning show – drink some coffee, make some notes. Look at the schedule for the day.

10:00 a.m. Grab my stuff and leave the hotel to head over to the station.

10:20: a.m. Arrive at the station. Grab a cup of coffee and get ready for our meeting.

10:30 a.m.–12:00 p.m. Begin the meeting. We're doing an aircheck session and one-on-one coaching with the morning show personalities and their team, listening to today's program, using the Powerful Radio Aircheck Criteria.

12:00 p.m.–1:00 p.m. Lunch meeting with general manager and producing teams.

1:00 p.m.–2:00 p.m. Take a bit of a break, check the email, return a couple of phone calls, write some notes about this morning's aircheck meeting.

2:00 p.m.–4:00 p.m. Station "Creating Powerful Radio News Seminar" for radio and TV news staff.

4:00 p.m.–5:30 p.m. Goals and follow-up meeting with management staff.

7:00 p.m. Dinner with station's general manager, program director, news director, and executive producer.

9:30 p.m. Go back to the hotel, then check email, take a hot shower, write up notes for the station consulting report, and call home.

11:00 p.m. Watch local TV news.

11:45 p.m. Try to get to sleep!

Daily Planner

vertex42

Date: | 8/17/2009 | Valerie Geller | On the Road

17 August, 2009
Monday

July 2009	**August 2009**	September 2009
Su M Tu W Th F Sa	Su M Tu W Th F Sa	Su M Tu W Th F Sa
1 2 3 **4**	1	1 2 3 4 5
5 6 7 8 9 10 11	2 3 4 5 6 7 8	6 **7** 8 9 10 11 12
12 13 14 15 16 17 18	9 10 11 12 13 14 15	**13** 14 15 16 17 18 19
19 20 21 22 23 24 25	16 **17** 18 19 20 21 22	20 21 22 23 24 25 26
26 27 28 29 30 31	23 24 25 26 27 28 29	27 28 29 30
	30 31	

Remember

Write up notes

☑ ABC	**Prioritized Task List**
	Radio Aircheck

Time	**People to Call**

$Amt	**Expenses**

Appointments

7	:00	Order Room Service
	:30	
8	:00	Review Schedule
	:15	
	:30	
	:45	
9	:00	Monitor Station
	:15	
	:30	
	:45	
10	:00	Leave for Meeting
	:15	
	:30	Start Meeting
	:45	1 on 1 with on-air personalities
11	:00	
	:15	
	:30	
	:45	
12	:00	Lunch with GM
	:15	
	:30	
	:45	
1	:00	Check e-mail
	:15	
	:30	
	:45	
2	:00	"Creating Power ful Radio
	:15	News" Seminar
	:30	
	:45	
3	:00	
	:15	
	:30	
	:45	
4	:00	Goals and follow up with
	:15	staff
	:30	
	:45	
5	:00	
	:30	
6	:00	
	:30	
7	:00	Dinner with GM, News
	:30	Director, Prog. Mgr., and
8	:00	Exec. Producer
	:15	
	:30	
9	:00	Back to Hotel
	:30	

Notes

detail, so we will discuss them further in the next section. As most content products are increasingly distributed in digital form, they are easily transported on both wired and wireless digital networks. Digital data streams are called *bit streams* and the channels over which they travel are often referred to as *pipes* or *bitpipes*. However, keep in mind that sometimes it is more difficult to move content to a home in a neighborhood on 30th Street in Athens, Georgia, than it is to get it to Athens, Greece. It's referred to as the *last mile problem*, and it has cost telephone companies and cable companies billions of dollars to bring high-speed bitpipes to consumers.

WIRED DIGITAL BITPIPES

Cable systems, telephone networks, and computer networks are all examples of wired bitpipes. And they all face a similar challenge: deliver all forms of content – video, audio, text, graphics – in two directions, to and from the consumer. Provide fast, always-on, reliable service at an affordable price. Each transport provider brings existing networks to the table, with its architecture based on the original purposes of the network. As requirements change, they must figure out how to use their networks to address the change or – in the worst case – reconfigure or rebuild their networks. In the past two decades, operators of all three types of networks have had to maintain a continuous schedule of design, redesign, construction, and reconstruction just to keep up with consumer demand.

Broadband Internet

Cable systems began life as broadband one-way systems in which signals ran over coaxial cable. Gradually, operators have introduced fiber optic cable into the backbone, extending it ever deeper into the network. A particularly sophisticated and elegant design is the hybrid fiber/coax (HFC) network, conceptualized by Dave Pangrac of Pangrac & Associates on the back of a napkin during an airplane flight.[15]

The HFC design was further refined and implemented by a team led by engineer James Chiddix of Time Warner Cable. By carefully thinking through the bandwidth usage, HFC allows every household in a 500-home neighborhood node to have an exclusive channel that carries a unique broadband stream. The term "500-channel universe" came from the HFC network that could allocate a complete channel per household.

Hybrid fiber/coax means that the main "pipe," the backbone, is fiber optic cable. Usually the wire into the home is *coaxial cable*, or coax. Almost all cable systems have upgraded to some version of an HFC design. Some cable systems are installing fiber to the neighborhood node to enable an interactive digital

TV tier, video on demand, and two-way high-speed Internet services that can grow as demand rises.

Managers who work for cable companies speak the language of broadband systems. For example, try reading this statement out loud: "This 750 MHz (megahertz) system passes 50,000 homes. To provide high-quality VOD (vee-oh-dee), assuming peak utilization of 25%, we'll need a server that can output 12,500 4-megabit per second MPEG2 (em-peg two) video streams simultaneously. Network capacity on the backbone will have to be about 50 gigabits per second."

That statement is fairly typical of the way a cable executive might describe a cable video-on-demand (VOD) system. It is easy to decode once people are familiar with the terms:

- The capacity of advanced cable television networks is measured in megahertz of bandwidth, i.e., 550 MHz, 750 MHz, or gigahertz for the largest systems, such as 1 GHz. When a system is described as a 750 MHz or 1 GHz system, the numbers refer to the capacity that can be delivered from the headend to each home or other receiver site, its end-to-end throughput along the downstream path.
- VOD stands for video on demand, a service provided by most large cable systems that lets consumers request video material and receive it right away.
- Peak utilization is the highest usage the system must be able to accommodate under normal circumstances. The capacity of the backbone must be the biggest part of the system, the sum of the bandwidth available for all the signals that are delivered to and from the neighborhood node, times the number of neighborhoods.

Broadband ADSL (Telephone Networks)

Cable systems began with a broadband system that was only one-way – their challenge was to develop a broadband two-way capability. It was an expensive proposition. Telephone companies began with the *PSTN* (*public switched telephone network*), a reliable two-way communication network, but it was narrowband, carrying only voice and data. Their challenge was to develop broadband networks – an even more expensive proposition.

The business decisions about transport networks that executives must make to provide content distribution services are complex. Mistakes are costly. Building a high-capacity network in which bandwidth goes unused can cost millions or even billions of dollars. Building a network that is too small, where consumer demand quickly outstrips availability, can cost millions or even billions of dollars as those consumers move to another source of content.

Some telephone companies just start over and adopt an HFC design when they build a network designed to deliver TV services. Often this choice involves *overbuilding,* or creating a separate network that follows the pathways of the existing telephone network, taking advantage of right-of-ways they have already negotiated. However, most telephone companies installed a version of a technology *digital subscriber line* (*DSL*), repurposing their existing networks.

The telephone company that provides service to most residences is called a local exchange carrier (LEC) or incumbent local exchange carrier (ILEC). If the LEC used to be part of old national AT&T telephone system, it might be called an RBOC, standing for regional Bell operating company. In many cities, large companies have the option of receiving telephone service from a competitive access provider (CAP), which are private companies that do not have a government-established geographical service area. There are a few private companies that do provide residential service; they are called CLECs, competitive local exchange carriers.

The basic telephone line is two wires between the telephone and the telephone company's central office (CO), sometimes called a *branch exchange.* Carrying signals and electricity in both directions between the home and the central office, this pair of wires is called a *drop,* a *loop,* a *pair, twisted pair, copper pair,* or a *circuit.* The local loop is the physical layer of the interface between customers and the PSTN, providing the familiar dial tone, touch tones, or DTMF (dual-tone multi-frequency), and busy signals.

The central office houses one or more switches that transmit each signal toward its final destination. The switch connects the two ends of the telephone call and holds open the path from origination to termination throughout the length of the communication (a dedicated circuit).

If the call is going to another neighborhood telephone, it might be switched directly to the terminated line; if it is within the local area, it will be forwarded to the switch in the central office where the terminated line is located. If it is a long distance call, outside the area of the telephone company's service area, then it goes to the switch of an interexchange carrier (IXC), a long-distance company. The location at the IXC is called a *point of presence* or *POP.*

Digitization has proceeded throughout the PSTN backbone and is now moving into the local loop. DSL technologies come in many flavors; xDSL refers to any or all of them. The various types are ADSL, ADSL Lite (G.lite), RDSL, HDSL, SDSL, and VDSL. *Asymmetric digital subscriber line* (*ADSL*) is the most common installation in homes.

Some telephone companies that want to deliver multichannel TV and high-speed Internet access built *VDSL* (*video digital subscriber line*) networks. For example, AT&T adopted VDSL for most of its localities, where it offers U-Verse television and Internet access services. Even though the maintenance is higher for VDSL than it is for HFC networks, many of AT&T's holdings are in low-density geographies, so it was cost-prohibitive for the company to construct new networks from the ground up. By contrast, Verizon has adopted a fiber network it calls *FiOS* (*Fiber Optic System*) because many of its systems cluster in the northeast of the United States, where population density is high.[16]

Computer Networks

When the Internet began, computer networks that delivered content across long distances used the PSTN, the telephone network, to transport content. Because in the early days content was all data, the tiny bitstreams were hardly noticeable in the ocean of voice calls. Now telephone networks and computer networks are interconnected in complex ways – telephone providers often use the Internet to carry voice calls.

Although as consumers, it would be easy to see content distribution over the Internet as free, it isn't. Yes, you can send emails, photos, even songs and videos without paying more than the monthly cost of Internet access. But private individuals aren't delivering video or audio content, day in and day out, 24/7. They don't have customers paying them for flawless, timely delivery who will dispute payment if they have to wait too long.

As a result, companies that deliver content to consumers pay to ensure that the process goes smoothly. Managers spend considerable time and conduct careful analysis to select vendors who supply transport services over the Internet. It's not easy to find reliable service at an affordable cost because the very structure of the Internet and other computer networks works against easy delivery of very large, time-based files.

Computer networks differ from telephone networks in that they are *packet-switched*, rather than *circuit-switched*. A telephone circuit stays open from the beginning to the end of the call. A computer network doesn't have a circuit at all. Messages are divided into packets – and they are very, very small. Each packet has a *header* that identifies the message destination and information about the length of the overall message and the position of the packet in the message. The message is held at the destination until all the packets arrive and can be assembled. Then it is delivered.

Each Internet subscriber has a unique address on a local network. Content arrives and goes out through a service provider's server, which sends and receives messages to and from other networks via a *gateway*. *Routers* take messages in, read the network destination with *packet sniffers*, and forward the packet to the next available destination that is closer to the final destination. Routing information is similarly dispersed. Each router makes a decision about how to forward a packet by referring to a lookup table that identifies the next node to which the packet should be forwarded to move it toward its destination. Lookup tables are loaded by the router itself, based on routing information supplied by other routers or on some kind of human input.

National traffic passes through four *network access points* (*NAPs*), located in Washington, D.C., New York, Chicago, and San Francisco. Traffic is carried on the Internet in three ways. *Peering* is an "I'll carry yours if you'll carry mine" type of agreement. Although all operators originally peered with one another, in the mid-1990s, small networks were dropped from the agreements and, since then, only the largest carriers peer with one another. The other agreements are called *peering payment* and *transit payment*, both of which involve some kind of fee by the larger operator for carrying the traffic of the smaller operator.

The actual architectures of the major carriers is proprietary information – no one knows how the Internet actually works in complete detail. In a router-based network, there is no dedicated connection open for the duration of the communication. This *connectionless* type of network is often represented in graphic depictions of networks as a *cloud*, a puffy curved entity that sits in the middle of diagrams of network architecture. It really misrepresents the complexity of network connectivity but it satisfies the descriptive needs of managers trying to explain how content will reach consumers.

The Internet does have a hierarchy and some geographically situated elements: NAPs, IXs, MAEs, POPs, ISPs, and users. The top of the hierarchy begins with:

- Level 1: Network access points (NAPs), large interconnection facilities where the largest Internet service providers (ISPs) and network service providers (NSPs) all mount racks of equipment in the same location.
- Level 2: Data emanates in and out of the NAPs along large lines that form the backbone of the network.
- Level 3: The information lands at the interconnection point (IX) of a regional network and then Metropolitan Area Exchanges (MAEs), located in most major U.S. markets.
- Level 4: Data is routed to the local Internet service provider (ISP), which maintains a point of presence (POP) on the network.
- Level 5: Customer premises: businesses and homes.

At almost every point on the Internet sits a server. A Web site is really a software construction that is stored in a server, so when a user "visits" a Web site, it really means that the graphics, text, video, and audio – the content – is transferred to the user's local machine by a server. Of course, in reality, the user isn't going anyplace; the bits that constitute the Web site move across the Internet to the user's machine.

Servers may be huge pieces of equipment, Big Iron, operated by ISPs or large private companies. Or they may be merely user PCs that are software-enabled to dish out data. Whether they are businesses or people in their homes, customers are at the fifth level of the Internet. If the subscriber is a business, then the organization often has a LAN that supports any number of employees, extending the Internet yet further. When a computer is connected to a network, data flows in and out. For many people, this is quite worrisome. Companies are in a position to act on their concerns, and security is manifested in hardware as *proxy servers* or *edge servers*. This specialized server maintains a *firewall* that protects unidentified data from entering the company's LAN or WAN. By providing instructions to the proxy server, companies can prevent employees from accessing some Web sites such as LimeWire or Facebook.

Companies providing video or even audio will use servers optimized for media. A media server is actually a special-purpose computer that enables commercial media delivery. A customer order comes into the media server; the server locates the desired information in storage, retrieves it, and sends it downstream to the viewer. It then sends a message to the billing software to charge the consumer. The ordered material might include video of movies, television programs, and direct-to-home programs. It may be entertainment-oriented or informational in nature. Other content could be music, games, catalogs, lists, and announcements.

One thorny challenge for media servers is simultaneous flows of a single on-demand video. For example, when a new movie comes out, everybody wants to see the new hit at once. Upward of 90 percent of the traffic could be generated by five or six current hit films. At the video store, all the copies of the popular film are gone and customers have to be placed on a waiting list – by contrast, an interactive system just crashes.

The technology of broadband wired bitpipes has continued to advance, enabling the Internet to grow and expand. From time to time, some Chicken Little will shout that "the Internet is falling, the Internet is falling!" but, so far, it has proven to be scalable and strong, just as its designers hoped. The next section examines wireless bitpipes.

WIRELESS BITPIPES

Wired bitpipes are expensive to build but, once constructed, can last for a long time. Moreover, if they are well designed, they are reliable, requiring little more than monitoring and routine maintenance. However, wireless bitpipes are not inexpensive to build. And they may be more sensitive to environmental conditions, because both the equipment and the signals are more exposed to the elements.

The barrier to the growth of wireless bitpipes is that the spectrum over which content must travel is expensive. The *electromagnetic (EM) spectrum* refers to the energy that travels and spreads out, a process called *radiation*. Radiation goes forth in waves of varying sizes – that range of sizes is the *spectrum*. Radiation includes light, radio (including TV and cellular mobile telephone signals), microwaves, infrared and ultraviolet light, X-rays, and gamma rays. The rate at which these waves travel is called their *frequency,* and each type of radiation actually includes a range of frequencies, as shown in Figure 11-2. When radio station 94.1 FM blares out its slogan – "94.1 is Number 1!" – it is encouraging consumers to set the *tuners* in their radio receiver to the 94.1 frequency, at which the station broadcasts its signals.

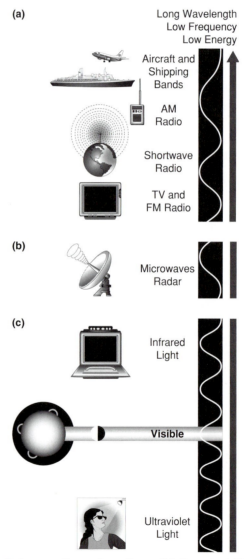

FIGURE 11-2 The electromagnetic spectrum. *Source: U.S. Government, NASA, http://imagine.gsfc .nasa.gov/docs/science/know_l1/emspectrum.html.*

The EM spectrum is regulated. Devices that emit radiation are measured and the waves must fall within the claimed range. For example, the U.S. Food and Drug Administration (FDA) measures and regulates the leakage of microwave ovens so that they do not cook a consumer's liver as it cooks their pizza. Certification of most appliances is performed by Underwriters Laboratories, an independent, not-for-profit product safety testing and certification organization.

The business issue confronting companies that want to distribute content on wireless networks is simply that it can cost a great deal. Radio waves have been regulated by the government since 1904. Early radio was competitive. Stations increased their signals and jammed the signals of other stations to win the commercial battle for listeners. As a result, the Radio Act passed by Congress in 1927 declared that radio waves are public property and the government would license the spectrum, essentially rationing the spectrum. In 1993, Congress authorized the Federal Communications Commission (FCC) to use competitive bid auctions to give out licenses of EM frequencies. It was a departure from a previous policy that allowed access to the public airwaves free of charge, as long as the broadcasts served a broadly defined *public interest*.

The auctioning of the spectrum brings in billions of dollars. For example, the 2005 auction brought in $13.7 billion to the government.[17] The auction – also known as Auction 66 – raised $13.7 billion dollars for the government. But such price tags also inhibit the growth of wireless services and makes them more expensive to consumers. This condition holds true whether it is the spectrum used by DirecTV or mobile telephones. Television and radio stations are an exception because their spectrum allocations occurred before 1993, and they continued to be honored. However, television broadcasters have been forced to move to digital transmission to reduce the size of their spectrum allocation, and the large swath of the spectrum they formerly occupied with analog signals will go to auction. (Some will go to local emergency use and other public uses.)

There are several advantages to wireless delivery systems:

- They are faster to build.
- They are cheaper to build.
- Maintenance, management, and operational costs are lower.
- They are easier to expand as demand increases.

One-Way Wireless Systems: Satellites

Satellite signals, though they can be bidirectional and allow traffic to be beamed up to the satellite as well as down from it, require a great deal of energy to push them far into space. There is also some latency, as anyone changing channels on a satellite TV system can verify. These aspects make it difficult for satellite operators to offer two-way services, such as Internet access and routine telephone service. News operations often give satellite phones (satphones) to correspondents who are reporting from remote locations. They use them to file audio and low-resolution video reports, as are sometimes seen from Afghanistan.

There are three types of satellites – the highest GEOs, geosynchronous earth orbit satellites, stationed permanently in one place at 22,300 miles above the earth; MEOs, middle earth orbit satellites, positioned between 6,000 and 20,000 miles above the earth; and LEOs, low earth orbit satellites, within 1,000 miles of the earth's surface. Satellite television programming services such as DirecTV send their signals over LEOs and low-orbiting MEOs.

Managers find satellite delivery of content over satellites very cost-effective if the content is going to many destinations. However, delivery to a single destination is much more cost-effective over a wired system, because satellite deliver costs the same no matter how many earth stations receive the signal. Sending content to a handful of destinations is a calculation exercise that requires precise knowledge of rates and delivery parameters.

LMDS (*Local Multipoint Distribution Service*) and *MMDS* (*Multichannel Multipoint Distribution Service*) are sometimes called *wireless cable*.[18] LMDS is a one-way network that delivers video content to consumers. Both LMDS and MMDS systems have fixed *base stations* and consumer equipment that transmit and receive signals. A *network interface unit* (*NIU*) connects the equipment to the network. LMDS is more powerful and complex than MMDS, but it is also far more expensive. LMDS may be useful for large companies or multiresidential complexes, particularly where wired cable services do not exist. One problem with LMDS transmission is *rain fade*, which occurs when raindrops adversely affect the ability of the system to transmit clear signals.

The lower cost and relative simplicity of MMDS make it more viable for distribution of content to and from consumers. It is also less vulnerable to rain fade. However, MMDS bandwidth is less than LMDS, so this type of system also has its downside. MMDS systems were deployed in many markets in Africa, the Middle East, Eastern Europe, the Caribbean, and Peru and Chile in South America because they were less expensive and faster to build than were cable systems in the early days of multi-channel delivery. MMDS is not used much in the United States or Europe, because these territories already have robust multichannel networks in place.

Another way to deliver content wirelessly, even video, is over mobile phones and other portable devices. Cellular carriers provide a service called *3G mobile broadband.* 3G came into existence in 2000 with the 3G designation from the International Telecommunication Union (ITU), which is authorized to set such standards. Cellular carriers have continuously added greater bandwidth to their networks. Before 3G, there was 0G in the 1980s, 1G later in the decade, and 2G (AMPS) in the mid-1990s.

There are several specific flavors of 3G technologies, but they all deliver the same bandwidth: peak data rates up to 2 megabits per second for stationary devices and between 144 and 384 kilobits per second for devices on the go.[19] As of mid-2009, there is no ITU designation of 4G. The iPhone, Sprint's broadband cards, and Verizon's mobile broadband service all meet 3G standards. Sprint is trialing a faster mobile service for what they market as a 4G service in Baltimore, although the ITU has not yet set the requirements for the 4G designation.

At the same time, the broadcasters are looking at another technology for mobile television as part of the Digital Television set of standards, to be set by the Advanced Television Standards Committee. The broadcasters will integrate the mobile signals into their over-the-air digital TV signal. Six stations will pilot test this new protocol in Washington, D.C., Boston, Dallas, Los Angeles, New York, and San Francisco.[20] Mobile DTV will assign 3.7 megabits per second to the transmission, which will display an excellent picture on mobile devices. The system uses MPEG-4 compression, which is the same algorithm used by QuickTime for sending video over the Internet.

CONTENT MANAGEMENT: TRANSCODING CONTENT INTO DIFFERENT FORMATS FOR DISTRIBUTION

Today, every content provider must deal with the issue of multiple distribution formats. For example, a previous chapter on marketing discussed "windowing," the practice of the sequential the release of motion pictures in different venues, in an order from the highest to the lowest return of revenue.[21] The release windows include pay-per-view and on-demand, home video (videocassette and DVD), premium cable, hospitality (airlines and hotels), network TV, and local TV syndicators (local TV stations and basic cable).

These multiple channels for bringing a property to consumers require multiple formats. On-demand, DVD, and hospitality versions all use digital formats, while many of the television versions are analog. The digital formats may have subtle but real differences in the way they are formatted as well. The process of re-formatting one digital format into another is called *transcoding*. The need for transcoding continues to increase. Even a decade ago, LucasFilm transcoded its motion pictures into 26 different formats,[22] even before the growing adoption of mobile video and high-bandwidth game consoles.

In order to accommodate the ever-growing list of distribution formats, business units responsible for disseminating content have adopted some form of content management. The earlier chapter on content discussed media asset management systems, which ingest, store, and retrieve the material that goes into the assembly of content. *Content management systems* (CMS) deal with the other end of the process – transcoding the finished content into a distribution that reaches the end customer.

CMS is a key to efficient delivery to media consumers. According to Fred Meyers, principal engineer at George Lucas's postproduction facility, Industrial Light & Magic:

> We see projects that are to be released at Digital Cinema and as 35 mm projected film. Right now, you transfer to the D-Cin master and cut the negative for the film master. We're looking to build a system that would master for both simultaneously so we would avoid having totally separate output systems, each with its own costs. Basically, we have to make masters for each release media – film, D-Cinema, video formats including standard definition broadcast and VHS, high definition broadcast, satellite, and DVD, and Web delivery. We're looking at moving this whole process to create a single mastering system for output for all release media.[23]

Mass Customization and Personalization

When a content provider uses a CMS, it opens up a new world of distribution. Suddenly, it is possible to put together the benefits of mass media distribution – reaching millions of people – with the advantages of tailoring material to satisfy audience segments and even individuals. Indeed, if the content is stored as modular elements, a sort of on-the-fly editing can take place. There are two methods of tailoring content to create different versions for different audiences: mass customization and personalization.[24]

Personalization is adapting or sequencing solutions to fit individual differences, expectations, and needs. In contrast, mass customization is adapting to fit common characteristics identified for *groups*. Thus, when content marketers identify audience segments, mass customization allows them to deliver a version that fits some desired characteristic of that segment. For example, a content item could be versioned for different age groups, so that young children get material that is shorter and simpler. Or suppose there is a database of snippets of material on a company's complex technological product. Individual consumers could check off the parts of the overall content they need and the CMS would create a table of contents and assemble the required pieces. Students might only want (and pay for) the required chapters from a text. Newspaper subscribers may only want stories on real estate and sports, or entertainment, food, and front page headlines.

Mass customization is actually the first step in building a relationship with individual consumers. It may not always be practical or cost-effective to support one customer at a time or to build in total personalization capabilities specific to one person. It may be preferable to start with a mass customized solution that identifies a few common critical success attributes that are key in satisfying the needs or wants of a particular group – well-defined objectives, analysis, and a personalization framework can guide these decisions.

Recognizing key aggregate characteristics organized by a personalization framework makes the individual personalization process easier to implement later with consistent, measurable results. A well-tested framework, based on sound scientific and design foundations, can help identify the capabilities, resources, and content issues that are relevant, useful, and attractive to the targeted group of consumers. Using measurement criteria implemented over iterative cycles of improvement, solutions can become increasingly personalized over time. A well-tested framework also helps designers tailor products and services to satisfy the wide variety of needs and gratifications for information and entertainment content.

The greatest benefit of mass customization done well is technology's ability to make complex messaging easier by alternatively presenting content for a particular media consumer – delivering what the customer wants in the appropriate manner and at the appropriate time. This kind of customization can apply to more than merely the content – it can also apply to the interface the customer uses. A good example of personalization is the iGoogle page (http://www.igoogle.com), which allows user to format their own Google search page, including graphic design background, widgets for services and applications, and widget placement on the page.

The very process of customization and personalization can work to the benefit to content marketers. As consumers choose the way they want information and entertainment, providers have the opportunity to gather valuable data about each consumer that they can use in the future. Moreover, they can engage their consumers in a joint effort to shape satisfying content.

DIGITAL RIGHTS MANAGEMENT

Media companies must search continually to generate revenue, particularly in an era where digital content circulates freely on the Internet. When content was in analog form, it could not be disseminated to millions of people at the push of a button, destroying much of the potential value of that material. To protect content the company has created or acquired, many are looking at technology to help them trace their assets and extract payment for them.

Consider the theater box office, as shown in Figure 11-3. It accomplishes many tasks at once:

- Sets an attractive "scene" for the coming experience
- Provides information about schedule
- Collects money
- Funnels customers to facility security: the ticket-taker

The theater box office has performed its job simply and effectively for nearly a century. It is the envy of digital content providers, whose content flies everywhere on the Internet, resides on millions of hard drives, forcing creators and distributors to choose between losing money or suing their customers. In an electronic environment, companies can only turn to technological means to protect their revenues, an array of technologies called *digital rights management* (*DRM*).[25]

Apple's pioneering online music store, the iTunes Store, provides an example of DRM in the marketplace. The iTunes Store launched in January 2001. The company had already negotiated deals with major music labels such as the Universal Music Group (UMG), EMI, Warner, Sony, and BMG. As part of the deal, Apple agrees to wrap the content in DRM, using the MPEG-4 AAC standard – Apple called it FairPlay, which is used by Apple in iTunes. The software essentially controlled access to the music by recording where it came from and how many times it had been copied.

(a)   (b)

FIGURE 11-3 The movie box office: Access management

The limitations of DRM, at least in the audio arena, soon emerged, evidenced by Apple's announcement in May 2007 that iTunes would sell DRM-free music. Apple was forced to abandon DRM by its customers because:

- Customers didn't think the restrictions on their use were fair.
- The DRM code caused some problems with legitimate use.
- Customers had alternative MP3 players that did not have DRM.
- Customers had alternative sources of music that were free (peer-to-peer networks).
- Hackers quickly figured out how to break the DRM code and strip it from files.

Someday, there may be the electronic equivalent of the theater box office – simple, elegant, attractive, effective. But that day is not yet here. Until it arrives, content providers struggle to develop business models that allow them to operate profitably, protect their content assets, and develop good relationships with media consumers.

SUMMARY

Delivering content over digital networks has become an integral part of the media enterprise. Although it is easy to get lost in the technicalities, the tradeoffs between reach, bandwidth, and cost are the practical foundation of business decisions. Consumers don't care about the details of how content reaches them – they just want to get it where, when, and how they want it.

WHAT'S AHEAD

The next chapter explains how technological innovation is changing the media industry business landscape. It explains how content generates economic value for media producers and companies. It charts the changing positions of media players and how managers consider new strategies to advance their business objectives.

CASE STUDY 11.1 CREATE YOUR OWN DIGITAL ASSEMBLY LINE

In order to fully understand the difference in how the value chain operates in today's business environment, one need look no further than how this same chain functioned only a few short years ago. In this case study, we will outline how an independent video company produced a product from beginning to end, utilizing platforms and methods of its time.

Video Industry

Create
- Development: Acquisition of film rights from independent filmmakers or in-house theatrical division; development of an original project involving scripts of various genres, including theatrical, self-help, musical,

Continued...

educational, etc. Companies that followed this method of development: Vestron, Media Home Entertainment, Rhino Home Video, AIP, Embassy.

- Preproduction: Develop concept for artwork, promotional campaign, advertising strategy, public relations, point of purchase. This can be completed in-house, but is often sent to art houses.
- Production: Ranging from high-cost produced films to lower-end video productions shot on VHS. New Line Cinema, Troma Films.
- Postproduction: Editing of film or video before being transferred to master tape for duplication to VHS and Beta. Tapes run through assembly line for packaging and shrink wrap. SI Video, Video Production House.

Distribution

- Marketing: Place advertisement in trade publications, radio/TV commercials, print ads, radio, develop co-op incentives for distributors (middleman). Sales reps travel and meet with distributor reps and take orders for release on specific date. Video distributors: Video Product Distributors, Baker & Taylor, Ingram, Comtron; Rack Job Companies: Handleman Company, Lieberman, Video Channel.
- Transport: Tapes are shipped to arrive at distributor locations just prior to consumer release date. Distributors deliver product to retailers in time for the official release date.
- Consumers: Consumers are able to purchase or rent video and watch on VCR.

Monetization

- Consumer payment: In this case, consumers pay the "retail" price of the VHS directly to the retailer. Blockbuster, Handleman Rack for K-Mart/Wal-Mart, "Mom & Pop" stores.

- Financial settlement: The retailer will pay the distributor the wholesale price. For example, a $39.95 videotape might cost the retailer $30.00 wholesale, allowing a $10 margin. The distributor has purchased this same tape from the manufacturer at $19.95, who is now making $10 per unit from the retailer.
- Royalties to copyright holders: Reports are generated and forwarded to the manufacturer's accounting department, where they calculate royalties due to the artists/actors in the video. Accounts payable will be provided all supporting documentation allowing them to distribute checks.
- Profit participants: Every tape that is sold has to cover the costs of the overhead, and box art, to turn a profit for the owners or stockholders in the company. The financial reports are reviewed on a daily basis to determine trends in genre success or geographical influences that will contribute to the decisions they make on the very next video release.

Assignment

Now, it's your turn to create your own value chain:

1. Research a media industry and begin by researching the history so you can create the value chain from its early beginnings.
2. Identify those platforms that remain the same for this business and identify those that have changed.
3. How has the business changed over the years?
4. Conclude your findings by sharing thoughts on how you see this industry changing in the future.
5. Do you think this business will survive at all?
6. Back up your findings with research that may indicate some very clear trends.
7. Provide a new value chain that shows the current way of conducting business in the industry you have chosen.

REFERENCES

1. Moore, S. M. (2007). The biz: The basic business, legal and financial aspects of the film industry, 3rd Ed. Beverly Hills, CA: Silman-James Press.
2. Dirks, T. Filmsite. Accessed June 2, 2009, at http://www.filmsite.org/milestonespre1900s_2.html
3. Kenney, K. A. (2003). Canton: A journey through time. Mt. Pleasant, SC: Arcadia Publishing.
4. Crabb, K. C. (2005). The movie business. New York: Simon & Schuster.

5. _____. (n.d.). Cowboy Junkies. Accessed April 22, 2009 at: http://www.soundunwound.com/sp/contributor/view/Cowboy+Junkies?contributorId=473.

6. Stein, B. (April 26, 1991). Holy bat-debt. *Entertainment Weekly* 63. Accessed May 15, 2009, at http://www.ew.com/ew/article/0,,314126,00.html.

7. Epstein, E. J. (August 8, 2005). Hollywood's profits demystified. Salon. Accessed May 2, 2009, at http://www.slate.com/id/2124078/.

8. Vogel, H. L. (2001). *Entertainment industry economics*, 5th Ed. New York: Cambridge University Press.

9. Ibid., 83.

10. Anonymous. (March 8, 2001). Comment overheard at the 2001 Sho-West convention of the National Association of Theater Owners, Las Vegas, NV.

11. _____ Taub, E. (June 18, 2009). More digital projectors, coming to a theater near you. *New York Times*. Comment on article posted by Robert Houllahan on July 2, 2009. Accessed July 7, 2009, at http://gadgetwise.blogs.nytimes.com/2009/06/18/its-a-4k-world-after-all/

12. _____ (July 31, 2008). There are now over 6,300 digital screens worldwide and major movies are now distributed digitally as well as with film. Press release. Accessed July 2, 2009, at http://www.researchandmarkets.com/research/5c9b68/digital_cinema_i.

13. Center for the Digital Future (2009). Digital Future Project 2009. Los Angeles: Annenberg School for Communication, University of Southern California. Press release. Accessed May 31, 2009, at http://www.digitalcenter.org/pdf/2009_Digital_Future_Project_Release_Highlights.pdf.

14. Van Tassel, J. (2002). Centralizing broadcast operations. Washington, DC: National Association of Broadcasters.

15. Van Tassel, J. (2001). Digital TV Over Broadband: Harvesting Bandwidth. Woburn, MA: Focal Press.

16. Morisy, M. (October 9, 2007). Can AT&T's VDSL compete in a fiber world? Telecom News. Accessed 7/2/09, at http://searchtelecom.techtarget.com/news/article/0,289142,sid103_gci1275983,00.html.

17. _____ (September 18, 2006). AWS spectrum auction ends. Accessed July 16, 2009, at http://www.phonescoop.com/news/item.php?n=1893.

18. _____ (n.d.) MMDS/LMDS Multipoint Distribution Services International. Accessed July 16, 2009, at http://www.mobilecomms-technology.com/projects/mmds/.

19. Smith, B. (February 1, 2009). The shift from 3G to 4G. Wireless Week. Accessed July 16, 2009, at www.wirelessweek.com/Article-Shift-3G-4G-020109.aspx.

20. Reiter, A. (July 12, 2009). Mobile DTV tests planned for seven Washington D.C. stations, other cities. Accessed July 14, 2009, at http://www.mobiletelevisionreport.com.

21. Vogel, H. L. (2002). Op. cit., p. 83.

22. Campos, T. & Rogozinski, B. (April 1999). Asset management across your facility: A case study of the Lucasfilm digital media management infrastructure. *Digital Mogul*. Accessed May 2009, at http://www.sugar-lab.com/digital_mogul/DM%202-5.pdf.

23. Van Tassel, J. (September 6, 2001). Personal interview.

24. Pine II, B. J. & Gilmore, J. H. (2000). *Markets of one: Creating customer-unique value through mass customization*. Boston, MA: Harvard Business Review Book.

25. Van Tassel, J. (2006). *Digital Rights Management: protecting and monetizing content* (NAB executive technology briefings). Burlington, MA: Focal Press.

The Changing Media Value Chain

This "telephone" has too many shortcomings to be seriously considered as a means of communication. The device is inherently of no value to us.

Western Union Internal Memo, 1876 (The Company Subsequently Declined to Purchase the New Invention for $100,000)

CHAPTER OBJECTIVES

The objective of this chapter is to provide you with information about:
- The digital content value chain
- The changing value chain
  - Power to the people: End-users control commercial content transactions
  - Content copyright protection and the value chain
  - Disintermediation: Cutting out the other guy (company)
- Disruptive innovation and the media industry
  - Responding to the challenge

INTRODUCTION: NEW MARKETS, NEW MODELS, NEW WWWORLD

The media industries bring together technology and creativity to produce content that touches the minds and hearts of nearly everyone in the world. These experiences are valuable to people for the information they learn and the emotions they feel. Experiential value for consumers is transformed into economic value for the media organizations that make and market content.

It takes a complex set of synchronized activities to bring content products into being and to deliver them to the customer. At each stage in the process, some value is added to the material. The writer brings concepts and a script; the producer offers vision and management ability; the director of photography and

DOI: 10.1016/B978-0-240-81020-1.00012-9

special effects producer bring images to life; marketers build demand for the work, and so forth.

When technology changes, the processes of bringing value to content products also adjust. In the last two decades, almost every aspect of the technology has become digital, including production equipment, computer-generated imagery (CGI), and the Internet and other networks. Thus, it is no surprise the processes to create and bring content to market have transformed as well.

Another key development is the increase in the speed and ease of communication. Improved communication makes it possible for media enterprises to participate efficiently in more markets. Beginning with the formation of the radio industry, early broadcasters marketed programs to listeners and on-the-air commercial time (or *avails*) to advertisers. This market structure is called a *two-sided market*, which brings together two different types of consumers, requiring a strategy for dealing with each market.[1] For example, television viewers are one market for broadcast, cable, and satellite networks and operators. They develop business plans for attracting, retaining, and bringing in revenue from the audience. Their second market is advertisers, who want access to those viewers. Content companies develop a second, different business model to address this market as well. Some companies sell products in multiple markets, facing what are called n-sided markets. Similarly, they develop products and strategies to satisfy the needs of all their customer groups.

THE DIGITAL VALUE CHAIN

Value means the relative importance, worth, or merit of something. In business, value generally refers to *economic value*, which describes how much someone will pay for a given property, product, or service. As beauty is in the eyes of the beholder, so economic value is in the pockets of the payer. Thus, the value of a company's product or service is determined by the willingness of consumers to pay for it.

Issues of how companies could increase the economic value of their offerings to consumers came to the forefront with Michael Porter's 1985 book, *Competitive Advantage: Creating and Sustaining Superior Performance*.[2] There are other methods used by managers to reach decisions about their business strategies. However, it is rare to attend a media industry conference or convention without hearing about the value or supply chain.

Porter coined the term *value chain* to describe a generic set of activities undertaken by an organization to create and add value. In the media industry, the content value chain includes these stages: development, preproduction, production, postproduction, marketing, and content delivery. Specific products call for a tailored value chain, so the chain for creating a Web site might

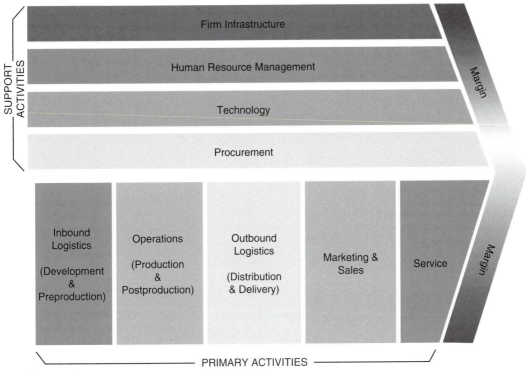

FIGURE 12-1 Generic digital content value chain. *Source: Based on graphic by Dinesh Pratap Singh, licensed under the Creative Commons Attribution ShareAlike 3.0.*

be: conception, planning and flowcharting; page wireframe modeling and mockup; user interface design; and content creation and image acquisition.

In Porter's general model, the four top rows shown in the figure are support activities – firm infrastructure, human resource management, technology, and procurement. They do not add value in and of themselves, but provide support to the activities that do:

- **Firm infrastructure:** Organizational processes, procedures, and culture; control systems
- **Human resource management:** Recruiting, hiring, development, and training
- **Technology:** Information technology and coordinating communications
- **Procurement:** Locating and contracting for the resources needed to create, market, and distribute the company's finished products

The five columns at the bottom of the figure – inbound logistics, operations, outbound logistics, marketing and sales, and service – are the activities that create and add value to the organization's offerings in the marketplace. The generic illustration of the value chain looks deceptively simple, but keep in mind that there may be hundreds of companies and thousands of individuals involved in the overall effort, and a large number of them in any one of the activity categories.

Furthermore, there also may be a multitude of consumers lurking behind each label. For example, the first customer for "inbound logistics" is the producer or the studio. Although the activities add value to the end consumer at a later point in time, it is a different level of value than occurs at the earlier point.

The idea behind the value chain is for managers to understand how each primary activity affects the overall value of the company in the marketplace. Based on that understanding, they can make informed strategies to increase that value. These activities, translated into the media industries, appear in Table 12-1.

Sometimes the term *value chain* is used interchangeably with *supply chain*. However, supply chain is an older formulation of business process management that emphasized such processes as Acquire, Build, Fulfill, and Support. (Support activities are those required to operate any business: administration, human resource management, and procurement.) Porter's conceptualization of the value chain extended the supply chain to add the processes of research and development, branding, marketing and sales, and services.

To understand the value chain, consider how much value a movie studio adds to blank DVDs. The final product will retail for at least $15, often more, and will ultimately go on sale for $5 or $10 – but the blank disc itself is worth less than $1. The studio develops and produces a motion picture, markets it, and replicates it on a DVD. Playing roles in this process, dozens of small and large businesses, as well as individual artists and skilled technicians, perform tasks that add value to the final product. All those activities increased the value of the disc as much as 30 times.

Table 12-1 Translating Porter's Value Chain Activities into Media Industry Activities

Generic Activity	Media Industry Activity
Inbound logistics	Development and preproduction: Creative blueprint Examples: Script, song, article, graphics, preproduction coordination, contracts
Operations	Production and postproduction Examples: recording equipment, printing, Web site construction, performers, locations
Outbound logistics	Distribution and delivery Examples: Transcoding, copyright protection. Trucks, trains, planes, and broadcast, cable, telephone, satellite, Wi-Fi, WiMAX, and cellular networks
Marketing and sales	Marketing and sales Examples: Two-sided marketing and sales efforts, where market programs to consumers and consumers to advertisers
Services	Services Examples: Consumers need few services beyond malfunctioning content products, like damaged DVDs. Advertisers need considerable additional services, such as make-goods and fast-track placement and spot-pulling

Chapter 2 introduced the idea of a digital assembly line that allows media companies to create content digitally, from beginning to end. Only live action production takes place in the physical world, and increasingly the action is captured on digital equipment. Even when it is filmed (an analog technology), the footage is rapidly, almost instantly, transferred into a digital format. Moreover, as the average blockbuster may contain a large number of digital effects, only a percentage of the film is shot on film at the outset. For example, the motion picture *Avatar* was 60 percent photo-realistic computer generated imagery (CGI) and only 40 percent live-action.[3]

Beyond the digital assembly line for much of digital content – books, magazines, newspapers, music, and much television programming – many segments in the content industry have the opportunity to create, market, distribute, deliver, and receive and disburse payments. In other words, they can operate online for most, and perhaps all, of their activities. Figure 12-2 shows the

ELEMENTS OF AN END-TO-END E-INDUSTRY

1. Creation: The Digital Assembly Line

	Development	*Preproduction*	*Production*	*Postproduction*
Platform:	Word processing software	Project management & pre-visualization software	Digital camera audio recorders	Editing software

2. Distribution

	Marketing	*Transport*	*Delivery*	*Consumption*
Platform:	Office/productivity software	Digital network	Digital network	Digital player

3. Monetization

	Consumer Payment	*Financial Settlement*	*Royalties to Copyright Holders*	*Profit Participants*
Platform:	Electronic banking via network	Accounting software	Royalty management system	Word processing software: contracts

$$\rightarrow \qquad \rightarrow \qquad \rightarrow \qquad \rightarrow$$

FIGURE 12-2 The end-to-end digital content industry. *Source: Joan Van Tassel.*

end-to-end digital platform that has evolved over the past decade to support media industry activities.

Now let us return to the idea of a two-sided market. One side of the market is made up of media consumers. In this value chain, media is created, marketed, and delivered physically and electronically to consumers, as shown in Figure 12-3. In this scenario, people pay for the media they buy to view or listen to on their consumer electronic devices.

However, when it comes to broadcast television and radio, consumers don't pay. So media companies turn to the second side of their market, advertisers. Figure 12-4 shows the value chain for selling access to media consumers to advertisers. In this model, the programming is part of what Porter termed *inbound logistics* – the raw material of this second value chain.

Value chain analysis begins at the end – with the market.[4] The manager looks at market research to determine the characteristics of the overall market and the specific demographic, psychographic, and lifestyle features of the company's customers (or prospective customers). Based on this understanding, the rest of the analysis can point to how the organization's activities can bring value to the market, as determined by the end consumers.

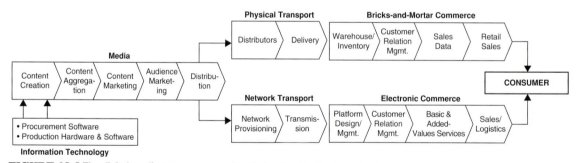

FIGURE 12-3 The digital media-to-consumer value chain. *Source: Joan Van Tassel.*

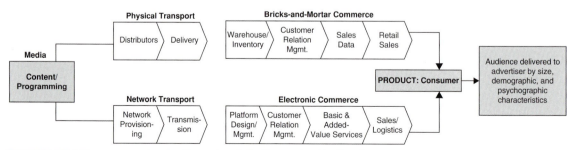

FIGURE 12-4 The consumer-to-advertiser value chain. *Source: Joan Van Tassel.*

The analysis continues with building the value chain: providing the unique detail of each of the five activities, described in the five columns at the bottom of Figure 12-1, that the organization undertakes. Each generic activity is replaced by the names of the business units that synchronize their efforts to prepare, market, and sell finished products, as well as vendor companies and individuals who provide products and services to the company. The list is likely to include hundreds of units, organizations, and individuals – sitting through the credits of a major motion picture shows just how many people are directly involved in its creation.

Once the manager understands all the elements in the value chain, it is possible to analyze how they work together. Porter identified structural factors and dynamic factors. The first structural factor, end markets, has already been examined. The analysis proceeds with a look at the other factors, as described in Table 12-2.

At this point in the analysis, the manager already knows a considerable amount about how the organization gets products to market. Porter also looked at how

Table 12-2 Value Chain Framework

Structural Factors	Description
End markets	Market size and characteristics, opportunities, competition, end consumer
Business enabling environment	Legal and regulatory system, taxation, customs, social and technological infrastructure
Vertical linkages	The coordination and connections between organizations that carry out different functions in different parts in the value chain
	Example: Production company and postproduction facility
Horizontal linkages	The coordination and connections between organizations in different parts of the value chain that draw on the same resources
	Example: Production (operations) needs performers to help create product; marketing needs them to help promote it.
Supporting markets	Markets that underlie the functioning of the organizations in the value chain
	Examples: Advances in information, production, and consumer device technologies affect the costs and market opportunities of media companies. The book publishing industry is often the source for creative ideas in motion pictures and television. Nightclubs and concerts bring performers to the attention of music labels.
Dynamic Factors	
Value chain governance	The power relationships between actors in the value chain: who sets and enforces the rules that define the workings of the value chain
	Example: Through its control of the operating system, Microsoft affects the price of PCs and the way software companies can participate in the PC market.
Interfirm relationships	Nature of relationship of organizations and individuals in the value chain: cooperative/competitive, friendly/hostile, ongoing/sporadic
Upgrading	The way the value chain initiates and responds to innovations that can affect its functioning

value chain activities affect profitability, pointing to two key ways the analysis can lead to success: cost advantage and differentiation. A lower price makes a product more attractive to consumers; differentiation makes a product unique, able to attract customers who cannot get these specific features from otherwise similar products.

Organizations can examine the value chain carefully, seeking to reduce expenditures at every possible point. They may look at saving by aggregating procurement, using their facilities more efficiently, negotiating with vendors and suppliers for lower prices, and many other cost-reducing actions. For example, a studio can centralize all the DVD manufacturing in a single company, demanding a volume discount.

They can perform the same kind of analysis by looking at how they can introduce unique features at various points in the value chain. This strategy is particularly important in the content industries because of the phenomenon of hits and blockbusters. A motion picture starring Brad Pitt is more likely to rake in profits than one starring an unknown actor. A high-priced market forecast report by technology and new media guru Esther Dyson will appeal to decision-making executives more than a similar report written by an unknown marketing professor from a small college.

THE CHANGING VALUE CHAIN

The multiple impacts of technological innovation are the primary sources of transformation to the media value chain. The reach and speed of communication networks, including the Internet, wireless, and mobile; more powerful handheld devices, such as the iPhone and palmtop computers; and faster, more powerful processing in computers, video cameras, and audio recorders all combine to affect almost every aspect of how media industries operate. Figure 12-5 shows the way a variety of technological advances affect the content creation portion of the media value chain.

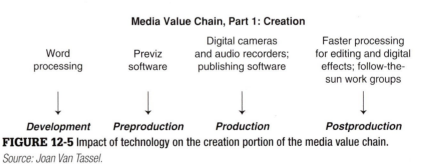

Media Value Chain, Part 1: Creation

Word processing	Previz software	Digital cameras and audio recorders; publishing software	Faster processing for editing and digital effects; follow-the-sun work groups
↓	↓	↓	↓
Development	*Preproduction*	*Production*	*Postproduction*

FIGURE 12-5 Impact of technology on the creation portion of the media value chain.
Source: Joan Van Tassel.

Word processing makes scriptwriting and revision a bit more efficient but does little to change the hard work creating original content in the development stage. Previsualization software, known as *previz*, replaces the script breakdown and storyboard processes that, in the past, were completed by hand. It increases efficiency to preproduction tasks and provides a solid foundation for the next stage of production.

But the real impact on the value chain is yet to come – cameras, audio records, desktop editing, and digital effects software change the economics of media companies by putting the means of production in the hands of consumers. Two decades ago, this equipment cost hundreds of thousands – even millions – of dollars. Skilled workers spent lifetimes acquiring the specialized skills to operate the various types of machinery that was needed for both audio and video production and postproduction. Today, hundreds of thousands of people have equipment that allows them to make sophisticated AV content. They may not be able to replicate the quality of Hollywood productions, but as the next section will show, the bar may not be set quite as high as it used to be.

The next portion of the media value chain is the one that has rocked the world of all the media industries – distribution. In the past, this stage was absorbed into marketing and the way content made its way to consumers was taken for granted. People who wanted to see movies went to the theater or rented tapes. People who wanted to watch television turned on the TV set. Listen to the radio? Turn it on. Read a book? Go to the bookstore. In other words, the distribution could be taken for granted, because each legacy medium had its own dedicated form of distribution. Today, consumers can see a movie on at least five different devices, read a book, listen to the radio, or complete computer tasks on at least three devices.

Distribution has gone from being an almost invisible commodity to a key way for companies to gain competitive advantage through increasing the value of their offerings to consumers. Content providers that give consumers what they want, when they want it, where they want it enjoy a competitive advantage in today's marketplace. An example of how it works was the Obama campaign's new media efforts in the 2008 presidential election. By sending messages via the Internet, social networks, Twitter, iPhone, texting, and email – as well as through traditional mass media – Obama was able to connect with the people who preferred those channels of communication and form a stronger bond with them than would have been possible through traditional channels alone.[5]

Figure 12-6 shows how technology affects the distribution activities of media companies. Here, it is not so much processing speed (except in consumer devices) as it is connectivity – the Internet and other content-carrying networks. Consumers can use peer-to-peer networks and viral email to send content around the world in nanoseconds, which forces media companies to

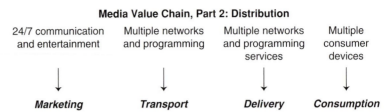

FIGURE 12-6 Effects of technology on the distribution portion of the media value chain.
Source: Joan Van Tassel.

distribute and monetize their products as fast as possible – a motion picture, a song, a digital book, an article – because they're almost as perishable as a head of lettuce or a bouquet of roses. Global distribution has stimulated alliances and partnerships between the largest media companies and regional and local entertainment managers and creatives to co-develop and co-produce material for such markets.

The need for speed pushes back into the marketing phase so that products are often released at the same time around the world, demanding global marketing support. Many media companies partner with local experts to execute some aspects of their marketing plans, in addition to co-creating content that will appeal to disparate geographies. These efforts are both driven by and made possible by communication networks underlying the constant contact and close coordination such work requires.

Technological changes in distribution both increase and reduce costs. Transport and delivery over digital networks reduce distribution costs in many cases, because it is so much cheaper to send bits electronically than it is to messenger motion picture reels, produce and ship DVDs, and print and warehouse books. In some cases, it may even be virtually free, as with reports and articles, which can be sent via email.

However, electronic distribution also increases some costs, including the transcoding of content into many different formats. However, the most staggering losses have been caused by three conditions that emerge as by-products of distribution over global networks:

- Consumer power over transactions
- Copyright holders' loss of control over content
- Disintermediation

Consumer power over transactions, sometimes called *power to the edge of the network*, occurs for two reasons. First, consumers have access to more content, virtually all the content in the world. They don't have the 500 channels predicted almost two decades ago – they have an infinite choice of material gleaned from their own searches and the searches of others, preserved in social sites such as Digg, Reddit, Last.fm, IMDB, Rotten Tomatoes, Metacritic, and other social recommender sites.[6] In addition, people can now compare product features and prices from many vendors and suppliers, allowing them to choose the lowest cost seller.

These difficulties are compounded by the problem of copyright protection – or, rather, the lack of it – in the digital world. Content must be generated as analog material for consumers to view or hear it. People cannot see streams of bits as other than 1s and 0s. In order to translate the bits into ships, pirates, and gangplanks, it must be visible to the oh-so-analog world of human hearing and sight. Once in analog form, content can be copied, one way or another. And this is a seemingly insurmountable difficulty, at least so far. Engineers are clever, so it is likely that there will be increasingly imaginative ways for media companies to protect their content, but so far, solutions have proved to be elusive.

The fact that there are many roads to the consumer means that media companies no longer have an exclusive path to deliver content to existing and potential customers. The Internet lets writers, artists, musicians, and other creatives reach consumers on their own. The process of eliminating steps between a buyer and seller is called *disintermediation*. It's a game that has many players. For example, creatives can disintermediate music labels, publishers, and studios. On the other hand, these large companies can buy their own over-the-air networks, theaters, Internet sites, and concert venues and disintermediate those existing companies. Conversely, large cable and telephone companies can buy their own production companies and disintermediate the studios.

Disintermediation has occurred in many places in the media value chain, even at the retail level. For example, managers of retail operations can communicate directly with sales personnel on the floor, access inventories and sales figures, and manipulate the data to give them a detailed picture of operations without waiting for written reports and summaries. Many people believe this capability has been responsible for the elimination of many middle management jobs, which traditionally involved gathering information from below and preparing it for perusal by higher management.

As we have seen, changes in the value chain have not always been positive for the media companies' activities in the creation and distribution portions of the media value chain. In contrast, technologies in the monetization part of the value chain have been largely beneficial for the largest media organizations. Figure 12-7 shows the development of large-scale systems that automate transactions at every level of payment, from the consumer to the seller, and back to copyright holders and profit participants.

Media Value Chain, Part 3: Monetization

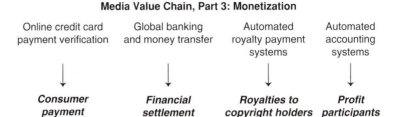

Online credit card payment verification	Global banking and money transfer	Automated royalty payment systems	Automated accounting systems
↓	↓	↓	↓
Consumer payment	*Financial settlement*	*Royalties to copyright holders*	*Profit participants*

FIGURE 12-7 Effects of technology on monetization portion of media value chain. *Source: Joan Van Tassel.*

A DAY IN THE LIFE OF RICHARD CONLON

Richard Conlon, Vice President, New Media & Strategic Development, Broadcast Music, Inc. (BMI)
Richard Conlon is Vice President of Marketing and Business Development for BMI. In his position, Conlon is responsible for the planning, development and implementation of licensing sales and marketing strategies to grow BMI's digital licensing business and increase BMI's, licensing penetration with existing media customers.

He supervises BMI's New Media Licensing team and marketing effort to radio, television, and cable. During his tenure, BMI has developed licensing agreements with industry leaders including MP3.com, Farmclub.com, Yahoo Broadcast, Live 365.com, and others. BMI also created the Digital Licensing Center, a digital end-to-end online music licensing utility.

After joining BMI in 1994, Conlon started BMI's New Media department in 1996. Prior to BMI, he consulted to

Showtime Pay Per View and held executive positions at Monitor Television and the Learning Channel. He holds a master's in Communications Management from the Annenberg School of Communications at the University of Southern California and a bachelor's in English from Boston College.

Typical Day
In the volatile world of copyright and digital media, there is no typical day – although most days not spent out of town on business trips start around 6:00 a.m. with a review and response to the previous night's email on the train on the way into my New York City office. Once in the office around 7:30 a.m., it's time to review the morning's digital media news clips online and review briefings for that day's meetings, as well as a once weekly review of the year to date revenue and expense reports for the New Media Business Unit. Before I kick off the day, I turn to my spiral-bound notebook

(a)

(b)

FIGURE 12-8

Daily Planner

Date: 8/17/2009   Richard Conlon

17 August, 2009
Monday

July 2009

Su	M	Tu	W	Th	F	Sa
			1	2	3	4
5	6	7	8	9	10	11
12	13	14	15	16	17	18
19	20	21	22	23	24	25
26	27	28	29	30	31	

August 2009

Su	M	Tu	W	Th	F	Sa
						1
2	3	4	5	6	7	8
9	10	11	12	13	14	15
16	17	18	19	20	21	22
23	24	25	26	27	28	29
30	31					

September 2009

Su	M	Tu	W	Th	F	Sa
		1	2	3	4	5
6	7	8	9	10	11	12
13	14	15	16	17	18	19
20	21	22	23	24	25	26
27	28	29	30			

Remember

☑ ABC Prioritized Task List

Budget Revenue

Time People to Call

$Amt Expenses

Appointments

7	:00	
	:30	Arrive at Office
8	:00	
	:15	
	:30	Day Sheet Review
	:45	
9	:00	
	:15	
	:30	
	:45	
10	:00	Open Deals Meeting
	:15	
	:30	
	:45	
11	:00	Client Negotiation
	:15	
	:30	
	:45	
12	:00	
	:15	Lunch with Client Attorney
	:30	
	:45	
1	:00	
	:15	
	:30	
	:45	
2	:00	
	:15	Demo of New Digital Technology
	:30	
	:45	
3	:00	
	:15	
	:30	New Deal Bid Sheet Review
	:45	
4	:00	
	:15	
	:30	All Industry Call
	:45	
5	:00	
	:30	
6	:00	
	:30	
7	:00	Industry Award Show
	:30	
8	:00	
	:30	
9	:00	
	:30	

Notes

Continued…

and jot down the key items that I want to accomplish that day as well as items that have a deliverable date to outside clients or internal departments at BMI.

Around 8:30 a.m., I review my calendar for the day and evening with the associate director of administration and discuss any upcoming calendar changes, travel plans, and meetings that need to be set up as well as any departmental housekeeping issues that need to be addressed that day.

After that, it's time for outside meetings to begin – usually the first outside meeting of the day is scheduled for 10 a.m.: working licensees and their attorneys negotiating license for the use of BMI represented music on online services, over mobile platforms, on social networks, and other new media platforms. There are different engagement teams assigned to different pieces of business – usually our leaders of business affairs and financial analysis will join me on these meetings. Lunch may be with a journalist or new media analyst at an equity firm discussing developments in the digital media and forecasts for the future. A typical afternoon would consist of another client meeting and working on strategy plans to address the monetization of copyright in the digital media or on conference calls or meetings with other interested parties in the copyright world monitoring development of issues such as the evolving nature of the governance of the Internet.

The digital monetization chain works mainly to the advantage of media giants, at least those that keep control of their own sales. If so, at the start of the revenue stream, when a consumer buys content, he or she receives immediate payment. However, because the royalty payment and accounting systems reside in the large media companies as part of their infrastructure, they can delay royalty and profit participants for as long as it works to their advantage. Disputes between media multinationals and creatives (profit participants), such as actors, writers, performers, and musicians, do not happen every day – but neither are they infrequent. (Of course, if a media company sells through an intermediary, such as many music labels do through Apple iTunes, then the seller is paid immediately and the media company depends on that seller for payment.)

DISRUPTIVE INNOVATIONS

All of these changes to the media value chain brought about by technological advances, even when they are at least partly favorable, are disruptive to stable business processes. They make forecasting and planning difficult and, when they have an impact on so many activities, may even make the overall business environment turbulent. Clayton Christenson, a professor of business administration at Harvard Business School, studied innovation in enterprises and developed a theory of *disruptive technologies*.[7] (He later changed the term to *disruptive innovations*.)

Figure 12-9 shows how disruptive innovations get their start – at the bottom of the price/performance curve. Notice that the incumbents – the companies making the successful products – have a relatively high price, but they also offer high performance. The higher the performance, the higher the price – buyers get what they pay for. These are excellent companies. They ask their best customers what additional features they want, and they add them. The product develops *featuritis*, a condition under which it does everything but

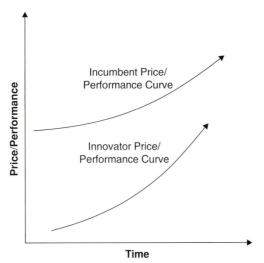

FIGURE 12-9 Incumbent and innovator price/performance curves over time.

Source: Joan Van Tassel.

tuck the customer into bed at night. And the price reflects the cost of all these features.

Now look at the innovator price/performance curve. It starts at a low price – but also a very low performance. Not many customers of the incumbent product are likely to buy the innovation. But people who can't afford the traditional product may be willing to spend a little just to get a fraction of performance they find useful.

Here's an example: the desktop computer. Developed in the period that was the height of "Big Iron," huge room-sized computers that wrote data to tapes, the first desktop computers seemed mere toys. They had little processing power and less storage. They were good for writing letters and keeping household accounts – and little else. The Big Iron companies barely took notice of these trifling machines that were hardly worthy of being called a computer. Why would they?

But techies, tinkerers, and household bookkeepers and letter writers found them interesting and even useful. These customers were never going to buy an enterprise computer –they constituted an entirely new market of computer buyers who wanted computers for personal use. Over time, as they gained experience with these new gadgets, Apple and IBM made computers that were better – and more powerful. Processors got faster. Memory increased. Apple made them aesthetically pleasing. IBM made them flexible and inexpensive. Pretty soon, desktop computers showed up on enterprise desktops. They didn't replace huge room-sized computers altogether, but today they are a much larger market than the multiprocessor monsters needed by NASA and the other alphabet government agencies and enormous multinational companies.

Now think about YouTube. A decade ago, it was just about impossible to put video on the Web. It could be done – but it wasn't easy or inexpensive. As late as 2004, it took an engineer several hours and several phone calls to the site host to configure a Web site and upload video to it. Today, a bright fifth grader can put video on YouTube in minutes.

Consider the price/performance curve of Internet video. The broadcast television networks weren't shaking in their boots when they saw the tiny 160-pixel × 160-pixel player, the pixilated video, the muddy audio, and the dumb stuff people uploaded. On the other hand, they weren't oblivious – they had seen what had happened to the music business, and the industry was abuzz with scenarios for the Death of Television.

So far, this scenario hasn't unfolded. Instead, as the performance of YouTube increased (the price is still zero), the television networks got on the bandwagon and contracted with YouTube or set up their own video site, such as NBC's Hulu (http://www.hulu.com). Flash video, compression advances, and higher speed networks are all rapidly improving the quality of the video viewing experience, and it is making a difference in viewership. According to a June 2009 study, "62% of adult Internet users have watched a video on these sites, up from just 33% who reported this in December 2006. Online video watching among young adults is near-universal; nine in ten (89%) Internet users ages 18–29 now say they watch content on video sharing sites, and 36% do so on a typical day."[8]

Figure 12-10 tells the whole story of disruptive innovations. They start small, well below the price/performance of existing products. Then they improve,

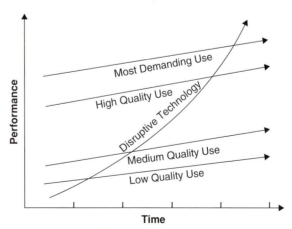

FIGURE 12-10 How little innovations disrupt more and more incumbent markets.
Source: Megapixie.

becoming capable of fulfilling ever more demanding uses. However, even as they improve performance, the innovative nature of the product allows them to keep the price below the incumbent products.

Disruptive innovations pose very real challenges to incumbent companies. They disrupt their value chain activities and, ultimately, their revenue streams. As the innovation improves and begins to encroach on more and more of their markets, the incumbents must respond. One reason the challenge is particularly intense in the media industries is that there are so many disruptive innovations affecting so many parts of the value chain. It has made it extremely difficult, even dangerous, for companies trying to navigate the tsunami of technology that has inundated them in the past two decades.

INDUSTRY RESPONDS TO THE TECHNOLOGICAL CHALLENGE: VALUE CHAIN SYSTEMS

The market is global, the competition is fierce, and the financial stakes are high. One solution available to media companies is to grow. Whether by merger and acquisition, alliance, or partnership, media companies try to put their arms around this new, complex environment by getting bigger. When organizations organize into a series of value chains that include suppliers and vendors, distribution channels, and customers, the resulting network of companies is a *value chain system*.[9] See Figure 12-11.

Camp-Building and Keiretsus

One way for organizations to cope with a tumultuously competitive environment is to merge or ally with others whose core business is complementary to their own. If it adds to horizontal or vertical control of a market, the deal is said to *leverage* the company's efforts or to provide *synergy*. In the 1990s, there was a virtual orgy of mergers. According to the *Wall Street Journal*, in the first half of 1995, there were 649 transactions in the information technology sector alone.[10]

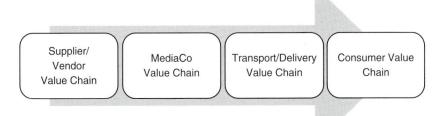

FIGURE 12-11 The value chain system. *Source: Joan Van Tassel.*

Some of these mergers were truly blockbuster alliances, including the acquisition of the ABC broadcast network by Disney, Viacom's acquisition of Paramount and Viacom, and the purchase of AOL by Time Warner. At the time, there was considerable discussion about the relationship of transport networks and content producers. It was a question of whether content producers should merge with other producers or with transport providers – called the *content/conduit* question. In retrospect, the content/content mergers worked out better than those between content and conduit providers.

This question is likely to come to the forefront again, because content providers need distribution and delivery and conduits need content to distribute and deliver. The organizational culture needed to create unique, one-of-a-kind products that reflect the uncertainty and richness of the human condition is far different from the culture required to deliver pushbutton consistency, reliability, and efficiency of the ideal transport and delivery network. Yet these two entities need each other, and on the floor of the digital assembly line, creatives and techies are forging ever closer ties.

When companies join together in a loose alliance to pursue a common set of standards around a product or system of products, it is called *camp-building*. (Standards are essential to the successful launch of products in which the format of the content must match the technology of the player or display.) Efforts to standardize the new generation of DVD players resulted in two rival camps: the Sony Blu-ray alliance and the Toshiba HD-DVD. Each proponent company had its motion picture studio backers, technology company adherents, engineers, and lobbyists that they organized in a camp-building process. Recently, the Sony camp emerged victorious and Toshiba has accepted the Blu-ray technology for its next generation of computers.[11]

The Japanese keiretsu and zaibatsu may provide a model for the operation of value chain systems. A keiretsu is a group of companies in an alliance that may have some cross-ownership at the top. Often, they are financed by a single bank. A zaibatsu has even tighter links through substantial cross-ownership and jointly executed strategies. This kind of organization may be necessary in a global media environment where many interconnected tasks must be undertaken quickly and nearly simultaneously, including such key activities as marketing and distribution.

SUMMARY

Chapter 12 presented the concept of value and the use of a value chain to show how companies transform the experiential value of content into economic value for the organization. It examined how and why the content value chain has changed in the past two decades. It looks at how media enterprises try to harness technological change to their advantage – and to reduce the risks it also brings.

WHAT'S AHEAD

The next chapter looks at how media companies think about their businesses. Managers make business plans and adopt business models that are the blueprints for their operations as they seek success and profitability. The chapter will cover the elements of media industry business models needed to describe fully how an organization will bring a content product to market.

CASE STUDY 12.1 A CASE OF "B AND C"

In today's competitive business environment, more and more companies are choosing to move away from the "brick" concepts as outlined in this chapter and move toward the "click" concept. Is this always the correct business path? Let's complete an analysis of a company that is attempting to do both and compare with your classmates.

Assignment

1. Identify a business that you do business with that has chosen to operate in both the world of "brick" and "click-through."
2. Name the company, the Web site, and detail the business.
3. How many "brick" locations do they have?

4. When did the "click-through" location launch?
5. Explain the advantages and disadvantages for each (i.e., costs, customer service).
6. Which portion of the business started first and approximately how long after the opening did they launch the other?
7. Name at least two of the company's competitors. Do they include a "click-through" location?
8. How does the company you chose stack up against the competition?
9. What advice would you provide this company for the future of its business?

REFERENCES

1. Eisenmann, T., Parker, G. & Van Alstyne, M. W. (October 2006). Strategies for two-sided markets. *Harvard Business Review* 84:10, 92–101.

2. Porter, Michael, E. (1985). *Competitive advantage.* New York: Free Press.

3. Campbell, R. & Downing, J. (2008). USAID briefing paper: The value chain framework. USAID: Washington, DC.

4. Van Tassel, J. (March 2009). Politics 2.0. *Winning campaigns* 4:2, 8–14.

5. Porter, J. (2006). Watch and learn: How recommendation systems are redefining the Web. *User Interface Engineering.* Accessed July 20, 2009, at http://www.uie.com/articles/recommendation_systems/.

6. Christensen, C. (1997). *The innovator's dilemma: When new technologies cause great firms to fail.* Cambridge, MA: Harvard Business School Press.

7. Meddin, M. (2009). The audience for online video-sharing sites shoots up. *Pew Research Center.* Accessed August 3, 2009, at http://www.pewinternet.org/Reports/2009/13--The-Audience-for-Online-VideoSharing-Sites-Shoots-Up.aspx?r=1.

8. Porter, 1985. Op. cit., 210.

9. _____. (July 25, 1995). North American information technology activity jumps 76 percent in first half of 1995. *Business Wire.* Accessed May 4, 2009 at http://www.allbusiness .com/technology/software-services-applications-information/7153791-1.html.

10. Calonga, J. (August 10, 2009). Toshiba exec: "The time for Blu-ray is coming now." Accessed August 12, 2009, at http://www.blu-ray.com/news/?id=3236.

CHAPTER 13

Media Industry Business Models

Deliver eyeballs? Sell ads. Deliver value? Sell subscriptions.
Industry aphorism (a concise statement of an accepted truth or insight)

CONTENTS

CHAPTER OBJECTIVES

The objective of this chapter is to provide you with information about:

- Business plans and business models
  - Content models
    - Content aggregation models
    - Audience aggregation models
    - Audience segmentation models
  - Distribution models
    - Windowing models
    - Cross-media/platform models
    - Walled garden models
  - Marketing models
    - Integrated marketing communications revisited: Spiral marketing
    - Viral marketing
    - Affinity models
    - Data aggregation and mining
    - Longitudinal cohort marketing
  - Revenue models
    - Transactional pay per
    - Licensing fees
    - Flat service fee
    - Subscription
    - Bundling and tiering
    - Access fees
    - Network utilization fees
    - Usage fees
    - Ad-supported
    - Data sales

INTRODUCTION: BUSINESS PLANS AND MODELS

For a company to be successful, it needs to raise money, either by borrowing it or attracting investors. Both of these funding mechanisms require the organization to prepare a forward-looking *business plan*, one of the most basic

325

documents for commercial enterprises. A typical business plan contains these elements:

- The specifics of the organization
- The management
- The products
- Analysis of the market and the competition
- Analysis of potential customers and consumers
- Analysis of marketing and sales opportunities
- Business model
- Financial plan and goals, including revenue and estimates of profitability

A generic business plan presents pretty much the same categories of information for any enterprise, whether it is making widgets, wagons, or wastebaskets. However, business models reflect the unique customs and practices that define a particular industry or sector. For example, during the difficult transition to digital broadcasting, an executive of a television network admitted that "Our business model right now is just staying in business through the digital transition."

A model is a smaller, less detailed version of an original, as a model car presents some features of the original automobile it models. Similarly, a *business model* is a small, less detailed version of the business that shows how the planned company's goals will be achieved if resources and processes are applied to the model. Ideally, if someone plugged in the numbers from the plan into the model, it would project the future financial position of the company. Business plans are confidential proprietary documents that managers cannot discuss, let alone reveal the actual numbers from the plan to anyone not authorized by the company to have that information. However, they can and do talk about their business models, usually referring to the operations and strategies that the company believes will lead to a profitable outcome.

This chapter examines the business models that have come to prominence as the marketplace of digital media and entertainment has unfolded in the past few years. Divided into content, distribution, marketing, and revenue models, as shown in Table 13-1, they can be combined with one another in any number of ways to generate unique overall models tailored to the particulars of content, audience, product, distribution, and transactions.

CONTENT MODELS

The content is the exciting part of the media, the reason people line up around the block for tickets to motion pictures; hold TV house parties to watch a game, a popular series, a much-publicized episode, or other media event; and rush

Table 13-1 Media Industry Business Models, by Submodel

Business Model Component	Description
Content model	The material that will be used to attract an audience, hold them, and influence them to act, usually purchase or view the content offered. Content models include the product genres and specific products the organization will offer and how the content will draw consumers and users.
Distribution model	Describes how the content will reach consumers. Distribution models lay out how the products will reach consumers and users and the conditions under which the audience members access the content.
Marketing model	Shows how a potential audience can be turned into an actual audience, how prospective consumers will learn about a content or service offering and be convinced to try it out.
Revenue model	Details how the company will make money. Revenue models show how the companies in the content value chain can make money, both directly from the content and indirectly by selling other products or services. (For example, television networks give away the content for free and make money by selling audiences to advertisers.)

out to buy the newest game console. The content model begins with creative people developing ideas for content that they believe will appeal to a particular audience. For example, the traditional broadcast network content model is called *least common denominator* programming. The audience is everyone, so the content is designed to appeal to the widest set of interests shared by the population as a whole and doesn't exclude anyone. Over time, the most universal interests turn out to be sex, violence, news, and music.

Broadcast and cable television networks, radio networks, and print publications may all appeal to a wide audience, like *Time* magazine, broadcast, and basic cable networks. Conversely, many target specialized more narrowly defined niche audiences, such as publications for quilters and Christian-oriented cable channels and radio stations. Television and radio create material for the consumer audience; the print medium is divided into consumer and industry trade segments, which always reach audiences.

Online content does it all. Sites may appeal to a broad audience, such as Google, or address a micro-niche audience, like www.thepontiactransam.com, The questions surrounding just how narrow a niche should be are important, as they relate to both creating content and products. Mark Cuban, Internet pioneer and current owner of the Houston Mavericks basketball team, calls it the *feature versus product* problem.

Suppose that someone is interested in Porsche automobiles and they want to turn a time- and money-consuming hobby into an online business. Specifically, this person collects the older 911S models. He is aware of the difficulty of getting some parts for the car: shock absorbers and carburetors. Should the site try to target Porsche enthusiasts; classic Porsche fans; 911S collectors; difficult-to-obtain parts for Porsches, classic Porsches, or the 911S; a parts exchange for classic Porsches or 911S cars; shock absorbers and carburetors for 911S cars – or incorporate all of these with different areas within a single Web site? Which choice will make a viable business, and how wide does the targeting have to be? Which choices are features of a larger overall product?

This problem permeates the development of products in many sectors of the new digital communications space. Take the set-top boxes (STBs) that are installed by cable companies. Should the STB have a hard drive in it? Should it provide input/output capabilities for web access? How much software should it offer? How many services? Should it be extensible to cable, satellite, phone, and DSL? Every selection has an implication for the final cost of the product, and media companies continue to wrestle with decisions about the scope of their businesses, product lines, and individual products and services.

Online efforts are particularly challenging in this regard because the costs to create Web sites are smaller than real-world markets – and there are fewer guidelines for decisions. However, like the print medium, plans for online content usually call for deciding whether it will be targeted to a consumer or trade audience. Specialized content, even an entire Web site, is created to appeal to the selected group. Large corporate Web sites can have a public area, supplemented by password-protected private areas devoted to vendors, suppliers, distributors and resellers, institutional buyers, and employees.

When a site serves the general public or consumer, it is engaged in business-to-consumer (B2C) activity. When the site serves businesses, then the content reflects a business-to-business (B2B) orientation. Depending on whether the activity is B2C or B2B, the content on the site is apt to be quite different.

Broadly, there are four kinds of online content types: information, entertainment, services, and applications. It is difficult to separate one from the other, and they are often combined or part of an overall mix of content provided on a site. Nearly all sites provide information, which includes news, facts, anecdotes, and opinions and associated text, graphic, and audiovisual (AV) elements. Entertainment is such material as fictional stories, games, and music. (Information about entertainment falls somewhere in the middle!) It is particularly difficult to differentiate services and applications. Services do something for people; applications let people do something.

B2C sites rely on information and entertainment, but increasingly they include applications and services – often in the form of *widgets*. Widgets are small pieces of software code added to a Web site. Even when there is no entertainment per se, developers try to present material in a pleasant and visually stimulating way.

B2B sites generally don't put much effort into entertainment. They may not invest the material with any overtly attractive elements at all, although there is typically a token effort to make content readable and actionable. B2B efforts are skewed toward product information and sales. They are increasingly likely to offer services and applications, selling them outright or offering them on a per-use or subscription basis.

Online services are products or free offerings such as file sharing (including documents, videos, music, presentations), document and file storage, 24/7 availability, price comparisons, online ordering, customer service, gift registries, live personal shopping assistant (voice or text), and legions of other helpful tasks. Applications are search engines, mapping, payment calculation, currency conversion, use of an online program to perform a task like photo or video editing, spreadsheet manipulation, and many other activities. Here again, there is some overlapping – search provides a service to the consumer but it invokes a program application in order to carry it out. On the other hand, a live personal shopping assistant calls upon a whole array of programs to provide the service.

Applications have led to a new class of online content providers called *ASPs*, or *application service providers*. These purveyors offer their customers the ability to use software to accomplish their objectives. An ASP can provide anything from quick lookup of stock market ticker symbols to extended sessions using sophisticated enterprise resource programs (ERP) or digital video editing. The ASP market is predicted to grow substantially to a multibillion-dollar market in the next few years, although estimates vary widely because the online business of providing applications is so new.

Whether they appeal to consumers or businesses, there are three broad categories of content models: content aggregation, audience aggregation, and audience segmentation models, as shown in Table 13-2.

Table 13-2 Content Models in Digital Media and Entertainment

Content Models	
Content aggregation models	Focus on the content and pull together enough attractive material to appeal to the targeted audience or audiences
Audience aggregation models	Focus on an audience and create or acquire content that appeals to a broadly defined audience or to more than one targeted audience
Audience segmentation models	Focus on an audience and create or acquire content that appeals to a specifically targeted audience, often quite narrow

Content Aggregation Models

Probably every digital content provider considers several of these models when they make their plans. They can combine them easily. A company that selects the consumer experience may also decide that the interface is the most important part of the process and that the landing page is the most important part of the interface, and they may also decide to syndicate their content or to add such material to their site. What content aggregation models have in common, as shown in Table 13-3, is that they call for a focus on the content first. The audience will select itself.

Consumer Experience Model

This model holds that the content – including how it is presented, purchased, navigated, and accessed – all taken together must provide the consumer a unique and pleasant experience, not just information, data, or service. The crux of this idea is that just as goods and services are products, so are entire experiences, and they are distinct from traditional product categories. In this view, the industrial economy was replaced by the service economy, which is now being moved over by the experience economy.[1] Joseph Pine II and James H. Gilmore say:

> Make no mistake: information isn't the foundation of the new economy. Information is not an economic offering. As John Perry Barlow likes to say, information wants to be free. Only when companies package it in a form customers will buy – informational goods, information services or informing experiences – do they create economic value.[2]

Shapers of media and entertainment utilizing this approach will want to ensure that the customer will not be confused, angered, frustrated, or otherwise

Table 13-3 Content Aggregation Models

Focus on the content itself and pull together enough material to appeal to the targeted audience or audiences.	
Consumer experience	Create best overall experience for the consumer, from beginning to end
Bundling and buckets	Put together a lot of content
Interface control	The key to the treasure is the treasure – controlling access is the key to maximizing content sales or use
Screen real estate	Try to control what can go on the screen and to place content in the best position
Enhanced TV	Add some combination of services to linear television: clickable hot spots, pause, fast forward/rewind, etc.
User-created	Make users the content creators
Syndication and licensing	Get content from others by contracting for it

affected negatively by the entire process of finding, retrieving, viewing or playing, sampling, ordering, buying, and ultimately using the product or site. It is easy to think that designing a positive experience can be taken for granted, but research shows that more than half of people who have started a sales transaction on the Internet do not complete it.[3] Because it takes many clicks to get through the process, such a result is not surprising. The high cost of usability and focus group research means that only the largest sites can afford detailed usability studies, but the content provider that hopes to offer an excellent user experience will absolutely require them.

In the nonprofit world, a site visitor who is highly satisfied is more willing to donate, volunteer, use the site, return to it, recommend it, recommend the organization, and leave with a favorable impression of the organization, as shown in Figure 13-1.

iGoogle provides a good example of how concern about the user's experience has been translated into site design, because the design has been given over to the consumer. The user has many choices of design, services and applications, position of widgets on the page, and widgets linking to other pages (GoogleTalk, GoogleMaps, Facebook, and many others).

Bundling and Buckets

Bundling means putting many different kinds of content together. The content can come from different sources and reflect many different types. In the cable, satellite, and PC software industries, consumers usually pay a single price for the bundled content. Online content is usually free. But large Web sites realize that in order to build traffic, they need to appeal to many people. One way they do it is by placing *buckets* on a page – an empty space where dynamically

	Highly Satisfied (Satisfaction 80+)	Dissatisfied (Satisfaction 69 and Below)	% Difference Between Highly Satisfied and Dissatisfied
Donate to Organization	76	51	49%
Volunteer with Organization	66	48	38%
Use the Site as Primary Resource	83	50	66%
Return to Site	93	60	55%
Recommend Site	89	54	65%
Recommend Organization	91	61	49%
Have a More Favorable Overall Impression of Organization	91	58	57%

FIGURE 13-1 Effects of visitor satisfaction with nonprofit Web sites. *Source: Foresee Results.*

provided material will appear. The bucket may be filled by a news feed, Twitter or Facebook feed, or some other third-party-developed content. It may be produced or commissioned by the site, licensed from copyright holders, or displayed through affiliate or affinity agreements with other Web site operators. Typically it is content that either has inherent usefulness or material people can sift through to meet their precise individual needs.

Interface Control Model

According to this model, what is really important is the consumer interface: control the interface, control the access to the content. If the content provider offers many products, users will have a difficult time finding what they want at all without a well-designed interface. This model recognizes that the interface is also content, a very specialized kind of content that engages the consumer throughout the session on a Web site, a television or music programming service, or even a list of published works, such as Amazon.com.

Control of the interface gives the ability to manipulate the customer's experience in a number of ways. The interface sets the context for the content; it establishes a thematic design, structures the choices a viewer can make, and provides mechanisms for navigation. It defines the numbers and types of choices customers can make and the procedures they must follow in order to execute them. The interface can add the element of consistency.

Powerful business incentives lead companies to provide the user interface. Beyond letting people find content, it also allows operators to present new sales opportunities. More profitable content can be featured over less profitable content. Moreover, the interface owner has the opportunity to own a piece of the revenue, as it is the vehicle through which the consumer orders products, or gets to the order taker. Finally, it may also give access to log files of consumer behavior, data that enables marketers to target consumers better, and consumer contact information.

"Navigation provided by the interface is everything," said Ken Papagan, SVP of the worldwide digital media solutions practice at iXL. "The name of the game is the race for the last interface. Every player, whether they are Google, TiVo, a cable or satellite company, a broadcast network, is looking to be that last interface so they can control the direct relationship with the consumer."[4]

The increasing complexity of communication devices poses problems for many consumers.[5] An interface that provides navigation is essential for customers on just about every device, from the television to the iPod or mobile phone. From the time they turn it on and get the "splash" or welcome screen, throughout the session, they will want to know where they are, where they are going next, and where else they could be. And it's even more important for TV viewers that have skill levels stretching from Nancy the Netsurfer to Grandma, the Regis Philbin fan.[6]

Mobile telephone operators provide good examples of this strategy. They now offer an enormous range of content and services including voice messages, email, business news, local living, mobile entertainment, shopping, games, financial information, and Internet access as a premium service. The operator controls every aspect of the interface – the look and feel, all the programs, content, application, products, and services that are available, and all the processes subscribers carry out when they are using the service.

From a business standpoint, this means that the operator stands to make money at every turn. They can charge content providers for reaching customers, and charge customers for accessing content and services. The company also commands a percentage of any transactions.

Screen Real Estate Model

This is a variation of the interface model. Many of the advantages conferred upon the company that controls the interface also applies to the control of screen real estate. This model assumes that of the entire interface, the two most valuable parts are:

- The welcome or landing screen (also called the *splash screen*), the first screen that users encounter when they turn on their devices. In some interfaces, the landing page may be called the *home page*; customers return to it over and over again throughout a viewing session.
- The *data glove*, the top (banner or marquee), bottom, and right-hand or left-hand side of the screen, as separate from the main part of the screen or the center of a web page, where the consumer-requested information is displayed.

The inventor of the concept of controlling consumer access to content and providers access to consumers was Bill Gates, whose masterful desktop real estate strategy was an important arrow in the Microsoft quiver until the advent of the Internet browser: first Netscape, now Internet Explorer and Firefox. Before the Internet, personal computers booted up into Windows and that was that. When the enormity of the threat to the Windows desktop hegemony posed by the Netscape Internet browser became clear, Microsoft moved decisively to package its own Internet Explorer browser with its Windows operating system. However, the browser does not allow for the execution of a screen real estate strategy, because it takes little expertise to set up a personalized home page.

An interesting contemporary execution of a screen real estate strategy on the Web is Google's iGoogle customized page, which gives control of almost all the page to the user, helping to ensure that the user will sign into Google and access their designed page. At the same time, Google still controls the all-important data glove that surrounds the user's elements.

Enhanced TV Model

The meaning of *enhanced TV* keeps changing. The basic idea of this model is to allow information from multiple screens to be co-presented on the large display in the home, usually the television screen. Originally, it allowed owners of linear programming, such as TV shows and movies, to make their content interactive. *Hot spots*, clickable areas on the video, allowed viewers to receive more content, usually text, on the screen, over the video. When clicked on, the hot spot might even open a Web site window and overlay it on the moving video.

More recently, Time Warner Cable in New York used it as a kind of built-in DVR, offering such capabilities as:[7]

Start Over: Restart program from the beginning

Quick Clips: Watch a video clip from a show

Look Back: Replay a missed show

PhotoshowTV: Subscribe to a service that puts a photo slideshow on the TV screen

User-Created Model

Think YouTube, Facebook, Twitter, Epinions, Blogger, Ning, del.icio.us, and Digg – all user-created content. Then there are the sites that rely heavily on it, like Yelp and every Internet *e-tail* site that solicits consumer and user ratings.

Early in the development of the graphically rich Internet, about 1998, it became obvious that populating a Web site with content is demanding and expensive. At the same time, many people want to express themselves and create material they can share with others. Sites that post material for the public often feature it as the majority of their content. Content providers following this model find that it does require some administration. The procedures for posting material must be clear. Similarly, rules must be prominently displayed and strongly enforced. Sites for the general public most often guard against pornography and other offensive graphics and language.

User-created material makes the most sense for the Internet. This type of content requires a great deal more tweaking in digital television venues such as over-the-air TV, cable TV, and even broadband TV. For example, home video compilation shows like *America's Funniest Videos* entail a staff to search out videos, gather them, order them into a rundown, and edit them. The producers then contract with (relatively) expensive talent to host the show, doing the on-camera pieces that introduce the show, each video, and the closing. The studio audience gives the program the added energy of live viewers.

Formats based on user-created content have not moved to radio or magazines, but music, podcasts, slideshows, and photos are everywhere – all on the gazillion-channel Internet.

Naturally, user-created content is the primary offering of personal Web sites, and many thrilled content creators – artists, musicians, writers, filmmakers – have enthusiastically pitched the Internet as the ultimate way for creative people to reach an audience. But there is some disagreement with this position. The counterargument is that there is such an avalanche of material on the Internet that no one person can be seen or heard. In fact, say these people, the ubiquitous Internet gives all the advantage to those with an existing brand name – stars and hit labels – because only a recognized and recognizable brand can break through the clutter.

Some observers believe that there may never be any real hits on the Net, in the way that other media, such as motion pictures, television, and music, all have blockbusters. In this view, the ability of people to match their wants and needs with precision undercuts the ability to aggregate large numbers of consumers for any length of time. The only way a site can build an audience is to aggregate enough content to attract a lot of individuals, a strategy that often involves including user-created content.

Syndication and Licensing

Syndication and licensing are simultaneously a content aggregation strategy, a way to build a bigger audience, and a revenue strategy to bring in money. Syndication and licensing are old hat in motion picture, television, radio, and newspapers. But they are still new and evolving on the Internet.

Web site operators and owners can populate a site with content that is geared toward their particular audience, without bearing the expense of an editorial staff. There are benefits for other Internet players as well, as shown in Figure 13-2.

There are two major types of syndicated distribution on the Internet, although the field is still evolving and could change. Full content syndication means that through some contractual arrangement, content is circulated to a Web site or a link is sent that allows the content to remain on the site where it is stored, but is shown in the window of the site where the link is accessed. Control of the content's distribution is generally retained by the original content creator or owner, although there may be some modification by the site displaying the content.

Party	Benefit
Content Creators	Increased revenue from:
	■ licensing fees from multiple publishers
	■ aggregation of larger audiences for advertising
Publishers	Affordable access to high-quality content
	More attractive site for users
	Increased user engagement, and:
	■ duration of user sessions
	■ page views
	■ advertising impressions
Advertisers	Aggregation of large, targeted online audience
	Controlled editorial environment
	Facilitation of online media-buying process
Users	More, higher-quality Internet content, easier to locate

FIGURE 13-2 Benefits of syndication on the Internet. *Source: Internet Syndication Council.*

RSS, or Really Simple Syndication, is a system whereby the content originator allows users to receive the content automatically. From the point of view of the content owner, RSS is a distribution model, but from the perspective of the user, it is a way of aggregating content. The user installs an *RSS reader* on the local computer, allowing the person to choose material and construct their own individually tailored "channel" of information. Control of content distribution passes to the receiver in this model.

Audience Aggregation Models

The content models we just looked at start with aggregating content and then look for audiences for it. Others models reverse that process and begin with strategies for aggregating a particular audience or set of audiences, then assembling content that will appeal to them. Broadcast television is the most successful industry ever to use an audience aggregation model, beside which all other media pale. Cable TV, radio, and print have a few broadly popular properties, but many more of their products serve niche audiences.

Horizontal Portals and Destinations

The early success of portals like America Online in capturing tremendous traffic on the Internet set off a race by media and entertainment giants to get their own branded portal. In rapid order, Disney, NBC, and Warner Bros. bought and built their way to mega-portal status. A portal is a way station; a destination is a place to spend time, a "sticky" site where people stick around for awhile. The

Audience Aggregation Models (Broad Audience)	
Focus on an audience and create or acquire content that appeals to a broadly defined audience or to more than one targeted audience	
Horizontal portals and destinations	Put together a wide range of material to attract a similarly wide range of people
Free content or service	Give away attractive, high-value content to draw an audience to it

most important feature of a portal is usually a search engine, which captures as many listings of Web site content and services as possible and displays the returns in an efficient and readable manner. A destination site requires many more services and bits of content than a site designed only to offer search engine services.

The distinction between portals and destinations is becoming more blurred as search engine–based sites expand to include many more services and applications. Of the following top 20 sites on the Web from the Alexa traffic ranking, eight of them are Internet search engine–based portals, six are communication-related portals (Facebook, Twitter, QQ.com, etc.), two are user-created destination blog sites (Blogger and WordPress), and the rest are informational sites of widespread interest (YouTube, Wikipedia, and Microsoft). One offers a service (RapidShare).

Google
Facebook
Yahoo!
YouTube
Windows Live
Wikipedia
Blogger.com
Microsoft Network (MSN)
Baidu.com (Chinese)
Yahoo! (Japan)
MySpace
Google (India)
Twitter
Google.de (Germany)
QQ.COM (Korea)
Microsoft Corporation
RapidShare
WordPress.com
Google.fr (France)
Google.uk (UK)

What does it take to be a portal? The best way to answer this question is to look at Google. The search site http://www.google.com is simple – use the search engine. However, on iGoogle, users can create their own portal, using thousands of themes and backgrounds, hundreds of individual applications called widgets or (on Google) *gadgets*, such as a to-do list, calendar, local map, local weather, a wide variety of news feeds, IM and Facebook sign-in and connection, and many others.

The difficulties of establishing a horizontal portal today should not be underestimated. The Walt Disney Company, no stranger to aggregating an audience, acquired search engine Infoseek and put it together with the company's other Internet entities to launch Go.com. In 1998, Go.com took in $323 million and lost $991 million for the year; in 1999, the site took in $348 million and went $1.06 billion into the red. Internet traffic measurement service Alexa ranks http://disney.go.com at number 96 in the United States and 303 in the world. Although this traffic is good, it is not sterling. The Alexa service describes the loading time of the site as "very slow," slower than 86 percent of rated Internet sites.[8]

Free Service Models

Building an audience by offering free service has a long history in broadcasting. That model has transferred to the Internet and become a popular strategy for many Web sites. Like radio and television, much "free" content is supported by advertising. Often called a "freemium" model, marketers offer some services for free, and pitch the consumer to upgrade to the premium tier for additional features or services.

- Internet access, web domains, and hosting
- Blog and social media page
- File space and file sharing
- Video, audio, and photo sharing
- Recommendations (Epinions, Digg, etc.)

Audience Segmentation Models

The Internet is the inverse of broadcast television – it has an unmatched ability to reach specialized audiences, and relatively low cash outlays for production and distribution make it cost-effective to do so. Interested in aviation history, aviary management, or .avi file conversion? There's bound to be a treasure of information on the Internet, just waiting for you to discover it. The following models all exploit this ability of the Internet to attract people who are united through some common experience or interest.

Audience Segmentation Models (Niche Audience)	
Focus on an audience and create or acquire content that appeals to a specifically targeted audience, often quite narrow.	
Vertical portal and destination model	Target consumers that have a specific interest and create content to appeal to them
Internet community models	Put together content that appeals to a group of people who already come together to interact with one another

Vertical Portal and Destination Model

A horizontal portal aggregates content to appeal to as many people as possible. A vertical portal defines a segment of the potential audience and then assembles content that relates to this segment. So how wide is a horizontal portal and when does it become a vertical portal? Or conversely, how narrow is a vertical portal and when does it become a horizontal portal?

The basic difference is that horizontal portals begin with assembling content, and a vertical portal begins with a segment or a content type. Verticals may be very wide. iVillage (http://www.ivillage.com) is designed for women; ThirdAge (http://www.thirdage.com) is a site for middle-aged boomers. Bolt.com (http://www.bolt.com) targets older adolescents and twenty-somethings, and Webkinz (http://www.webkinz.com) is for kids.

There are also portals that are very narrow, serving vertical interests like Bikersites.com (http://www.bikersites.com) and Adobe's file conversion info Web site (http://file-conversion.web-design-tools.com). Here's narrow for you: bird-lovers who want to know how to build an aviary for budgerigars can always turn to http://www.budgerigars.co.uk/manage/.

Internet Community Models

In some ways, making community a centerpiece of a Web site or digital service is often a particular case of user-generated content. However, all user-generated content is not based on a community, which involves creating Internet services that allow members of the group to participate in communication with one another. The means of communication may be an asynchronous message board or email discussion list, where participants post their comments, and then sign on later to read responses and post again. Or it might be real-time chat that lets participants conduct text-based or audio chats. Adopting the Internet community model doesn't mean there is no other content. Usually operators put additional material believed to be of interest to the members of the group on the site. Information, services and applications, and e-commerce interactives are quite commonly found on community sites.

Communities can form around any sort of interest or concern, and there are thousands – perhaps hundreds of thousands – of them on the Internet. Politics is a powerful community builder. On the Democratic side, http://www.dailykos.com has more than 215,000 registered users and receives 2.5 million unique visitors every month. The Republican equivalent, http://www.redstate.com, does not publish the number of the site's registered users, but says it has tens of thousands of readers. http://www.proteacher.net is a community for K–12 teachers.

Some entertainment sites, such as the online game World of Warcraft (http://www.worldofwarcraft.com), create a site-related community on their main Web site, like http://www.worldofwarcraft.com/community/.

The communication between people on the site, most of whom do not know each other in their "real life", may make up all or a large part of the content. However, bound by some commonality of interest, location, or circumstance, they may seek the same content. Content sellers may promote offerings they think will appeal to the community through membership or ads placed on the community site. Figure 13-3 shows how community-driven content brings people into an orbit of shared experience that can influence later behavior.

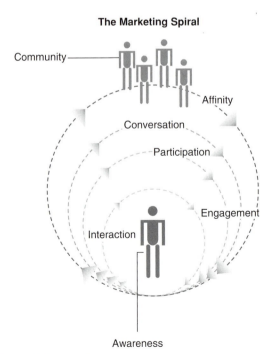

The Marketing Spiral

Community
Affinity
Conversation
Participation
Engagement
Interaction
Awareness

FIGURE 13-3 The marketing spiral. *Source: David Armano.*

A DAY IN THE LIFE OF BOB KAPLITZ

Bob Kaplitz, Principal and Senior Station Strategist for AR&D and Author of *Creating Execution Superstars with Budgets Cut to the Bone*

Bob Kaplitz is a principal and Senior Station Strategist for AR&D. He's a thought leader and influencer in an industry that requires unprecedented transformation and operational change to sustain long-term value. For close to 30 years, he's built winning strategies for clients, helping them become high-performance leaders in their local markets. Using market research from the company's analysts, he makes recommendations to clients for product development, marketing, and branding.

When he studied psychology as an undergraduate, he focused on learning and motivation. He assisted in experiments aimed at understanding how people learn and how to accelerate learning.

At Syracuse University's Newhouse School of Public Communications, he studied advertising and journalism for his master's degree. On a university-sponsored trip to Washington, DC, to visit news bureaus, he had the fortune to meet Dan Rather, who was CBS News's White House correspondent. Rather took time to show Bob around the cramped "press room." He didn't expect it to be glamorous, but it was no larger than a small cubicle.

After graduating, he became a reporter at a Greensboro, North Carolina, station where he also anchored the station's Sunday night news. He shot many of his own stories. Bob also taught broadcast journalism and TV production at the University of North Carolina several evenings a week.

When Dan Rather spoke at a university event, Bob reconnected. Rather said, "Send up a flare when you're in New York," and the two met for dinner in New York several months later. "Can I watch you put your show together?" Bob asked. He said sure.

Bob recalls that Rather, who was anchoring the weekend news for CBS, was driven to success. "He made anchoring a small part of his job. He was always in motion. Even though he had a producer and writers, he was actively involved in the program, calling correspondents about their story. And even after the show, he took the time to thank them for their reports, several of which were 'via satellite,' which was a big deal then."

After 5 years in Greensboro, everything changed. He revealed corruption in an area police department, and the police chief sued him for $8 million, pressuring his station to back off. The station supported Bob who continued his reports, the police chief resigned, and the Radio TV News Directors named Bob "Best TV Investigative Reporter in the United States and Canada."

A Miami TV station hired Bob as a reporter to cover the crime beat – from Miami vice to organized crime. Many of his stories ran on the *CBS Evening News* with Walter Cronkite and on CBS Radio.

After serving as an executive producer at a North Carolina TV station and as an investigative reporter in Dallas, Bob joined a relatively new TV news consulting firm, now known as AR&D, spending the first few months learning the ropes behind the scenes and then was allowed to conduct workshops at TV stations. His presentations were based on what viewers liked and disliked about TV news. The company would only trust him with smaller markets like Terre Haute, Indiana. Then he "graduated" to consult in major markets like Atlanta, Detroit, Cleveland, San Francisco, and Los Angeles. He created innovative workshops that engaged participants by involving them.

He also conducted several consulting "tours" to Australia and New Zealand, helping them to build their brands of journalism and ratings.

While with AR&D, he volunteered as Vice President for New Media for the Dallas–Ft. Worth chapter of the American Marketing Association, pioneering videos previewing the presentations of upcoming speakers. The videos posted on the organization's site drove up attendance. It was a valuable learning experience to interview many of the world's global marketing leaders.

Bob also occasionally taught international advertising, marketing, and digital marketing at the University of Dallas Graduate School of Management. It was an opportunity to teach and also learn from MBA students who came to Dallas from many parts of the world.

In 2009, Bob began playing a major role in the company's reengineering initiatives, which included training the new breed of multimedia journalists. This included reporters who need to learn how to shoot and photographers learning reporting. His blog, http://www.kaplitzblog.com, registered more than 100,000 hits over a periods of only a few months, with users from as far as China and India.

A Typical Day

When I'm in Dallas, I usually wake up about 6:30 a.m., checking email from my home office. I try to complete projects from the previous days because many clients have a "I want

Continued…

it now" approach, which I fully appreciate. Plus I don't want my to-do list to get too long.

I critique newscasts or newscast elements after viewing them on line. As brands of journalism are so crucial to ratings success, I focus on how successfully the shows deliver on their brand's promise. For example, if a station claims to be Watching Out for You or On Your Side, does it deliver? Because it's difficult for many journalists to understand the importance of a brand, I offer specific examples how they could have done better. The fun part is celebrating successes – whether big ones or small steps.

Anchors, reporters, photographers, producers, and news managers crave feedback, so I share a longer list in my What Worked section than in How to Raise the Bar? We all can only focus on a few new challenges to do them well.

Typical incoming emails and phone calls:

- News director needs help in explaining how an anchor can implement a franchise called "Fact Finder," which goes the extra step to reveal facts – like a crime trend in a neighborhood thought to be safe. In cases like this, it's often a matter of explaining the value of the concept to the anchor, reviewing actual examples and then discussing the steps necessary to implement successfully.
- Promotion director is disappointed with sweeps plans. Nothing strong to promote. I promised to set up a conference call with the news director to help. I usually review a Sweeps Planning Checklist, which includes questions like "Does the story interest the vast majority of viewers based on our research?" and "How will viewers appreciate the fact they can only get this new information on our station?"
- General manager asks for my help interviewing by phone a couple of news director candidates. As many candidates are practiced interviewers, knowing what to say, the goal is to learn how the applicant will handle actual challenges he or she would face at the station.
- A news director calls with a reporter in her office, asking me to walk her through the steps necessary to ask tough questions. The reporter doesn't want to upset the mayor, losing him as a source. But when I ask the reporter how many exclusives she turned thanks to using the mayor as a source, the answer is none. Even so, I suggest ways to state that the questions and complaints are from viewers, so the reporter is giving the mayor a chance to respond.

I'll also continue creating Learning Videos on my blog, http://www.kaplitzblog, which are primarily aimed at the new breed of multimedia journalists. As it's easier to learn by example, the blog shows examples often with my comments at the bottom of the screen.

I interact with a range of people including the heads of groups of TV stations, general managers, news directors, promotion directors, promotion producers, reporters, photographers, multimedia journalists.

Inside AR&D, I collaborate with a research analyst for project definition calls with clients – deciding what questions they want answered. We also work closely in crafting recommendations once we get the data back.

Because many news people believe viewers think like they do, the scientific surveys we do provide a reality check from our customers – viewers. For example, some reporters used to thrive on going live when nothing was going on. You probably have seen reporters standing in front of buildings, for example. Viewers find that a waste of time, seeing as "filler" when there's no "real news." Viewers find reporters reporting from the newsroom even worse. "Why don't they get out to the scene where the story is?" viewers ask.

As part of AR&D's transformation of TV stations, multimedia journalists will go directly from their homes to stories, posting stories to the station's Web site and feeding completed stories to the station for newscasts. No sitting around in the newsroom reporting away from the scene.

People issues are the most challenging – especially when they're failing but don't recognize it or don't want help. No matter how daunting the challenge, individuals who recognize they have something to learn can learn. We take it step by step, based on best practices applied to the specifics of their challenge. But those who resist can't improve because they choose not to.

Often they have good reason. For example, they got bad advice. Or they were set up to fail because their manager didn't believe in them. Whatever the reason, we try to show them they're not performing the way they should. Then we point out how the manager and I can take them step by step through solutions.

We all thrive on ratings improvements, but the deeper highlight and sense of accomplishment come from seeing the success of people. Sometimes it's a first-time news director who had difficulty at first gaining the respect of her staff – and finally does by following our plan. Other times it can be a promotion producer who admits he doesn't understand how to create an image campaign and then follows best practices and our strategy to develop one. Several clients who used to be at smaller markets have risen in the ranks to the

Daily Planner

vertex42

Date: [11/2/2009]   Bob Kaplitz

2   November, 2009
Monday

October 2009	November 2009	December 2009
Su M Tu W Th F Sa	Su M Tu W Th F Sa	Su M Tu W Th F Sa
1 2 3	1 2 3 4 5 6 7	1 2 3 4 5
4 5 6 7 8 9 10	8 9 10 11 12 13 14	6 7 8 9 10 11 12
11 12 13 14 15 16 17	15 16 17 18 19 20 21	13 14 15 16 17 18 19
18 19 20 21 22 23 24	22 23 24 25 26 27 28	20 21 22 23 24 25 26
25 26 27 28 29 30 31	29 30	27 28 29 30 31

Remember

Mediterranean Vac Planning

Final Cut software lesson

Prioritized Task List
☑ ABC

		Multimedia Training
		Re-engineering

People to Call
Time

	Florence
	Ellender

Expenses
$Amt

Appointments

7	:00	
	:30	
8	:00	
	:15	Blog: Create New Video
	:30	
	:45	
9	:00	Return Albany GM call
	:15	
	:30	Write GM's presentation
	:45	
10	:00	Critique Boise franchise
	:15	
	:30	Critique Vegas AM news
	:45	
11	:00	Write multimedia concept
	:15	
	:30	
	:45	
12	:00	Lunch: Reno ND candidate
	:15	
	:30	
	:45	
1	:00	Help Reno: Sweeps
	:15	
	:30	Interview by software company
	:45	
2	:00	Schedule Reno trip
	:15	Review Reno Scorecard
	:30	
	:45	
3	:00	Mentor MBA student
	:15	
	:30	Explore Webinar options
	:45	
4	:00	Re-engineering:
	:15	Develop updated model
	:30	
	:45	
5	:00	Discuss model with Rory
	:30	Return Fisher VP Call
6	:00	
	:30	
7	:00	
	:30	
8	:00	
	:30	
9	:00	
	:30	

Notes

Innovate re-engineering

Target 100,000 blog hits

Get global software company
to recognize value of
kaplitzblog.com

Continued…

networks, and it's always rewarding to see people achieve their potential.

After I complete the projects I'm working on and respond to calls and emails, I feel a great sense of accomplishment. Often that happens at 6:00 p.m., but sometimes 10:00 p.m., when I travel and need to respond after visiting with the client.

After normal work hours, I check email on my iPhone, responding to those questions that only take a few minutes. I like to put myself in the client's shoes, appreciating a quick response when possible. When issues require more thought or collaboration, at least I try to acknowledge the question, promising a time frame when I'll get back to them.

For those looking to enter the field of electronic media, I offer these three major points:

- **Learn as much as you can as fast as possible.** When you look at your career, it shouldn't be one year times five, for example, for five years of experience.

Rather, you grow in a big way every year. Every month.

- **Be flexible.** The "old ways" are disappearing fast. Simply put, "adapt or die" may seem threatening, but it's true.
- **Be bold.** Even the most successful people failed at their first attempts and then did better next time. Just make sure you're doing the right things rather than simply what you're used to doing, which may not benefit you or your TV station.

We have a unique point of view since we, as a company, are revolutionizing how local media produce and distribute content as they face their toughest business challenges ever. We create new innovative operating models, organizational and workflow strategies, and personnel alignment mapping for clients. The result is a stronger, more responsive organization with higher productivity levels and greater efficiencies from top to bottom and from beginning to end. To be part of that future I see, you need to get started now.

MARKETING MODELS

Marketing models (Table 13-4) explain how customers will find out about the content and the products and services and be convinced to view, access, rent, or buy them. They answer the questions: What appeals does this particular content hold for a given audience segment, and why should these people pay attention to it and consume it? How will they find out about it and how can the appeal be best communicated? The next section looks at marketing models to execute both brand strategies and media and entertainment product promotion and sales.

Revisiting Integrated Marketing Communications: Spiral Models

You've probably seen and heard all the broadcast advertisements that urge people to visit the Web site. Much of the new media advertising on traditional media is driven by the spiral model, which says that communicators can use multiple media to reach the consumers with messages about the same product but influence them in fundamentally different ways. The main idea is that each medium should be used for what it does best, as summarized in Table 13-5.

The original spiral model called for using traditional media first – TV, radio, print – because they reach the most people, and they are also best at raising interest and building an emotional connection between the brand and large

Table 13-4 Marketing Models

Traditional models	Branding
	Positioning
	Integrated Marketing Communications (IMC)
	Cross-media campaigns
	Product placement
	Viral marketing
	Audience/consumer segmentation
Spiral models	Drive people from one media platform to the next until they are persuaded to view, access, rent, or buy
Viral models	Create content that people will transmit to others in their personal and virtual networks, so that the others will view, access, buy, or rent the content
Affinity models	Partner with other content providers whose products are related or complementary to find people who are likely to want to view, access, buy, or rent the content
Data mining	Use information gathered about consumers in one context, venue, or transaction to market another content product to them
Longitudinal cohort models	Following the same demographic audience as it ages, marketing different content and other products to the group's changing tastes

Table 13-5 Use of Multiple Media in a Spiral Model

	TV/Radio/Print	Internet Web Sites	Social Media	Email
Medium offers	Content	Convenience	Communication	Notification
Content	:30 commercial, print ads	Searchable, informative web pages with purchase/access option	User-generated	Invitations, notices, and reminders
Communication structure	One to many	One to many (one at a time)	One to many or one to one	One to many or one to one
Content appeal to viewer/user	Richness	Information/Actionability	Immediacy/Trust	Need or interest
Medium's most effective marketing element	Selling	Service	Recommendations	Addressability
Element of influence (all provide information)	Emotion	Actionability	Personal relationship	Targeted information
Viewer/user reception behavior	Passive	Active	Interactive	Active/Interactive
Consumer cognitive response	Attention	Intention	Conversation	Attention/Response
Maximal consumer response	Interest	Access/Purchase	Engagement	Interaction

numbers of viewers.[9] The mass media message should direct consumers to a Web site for several reasons:

- It is an actionable medium – people can get more information and order conveniently if they want to purchase or access content.
- A Web site can incorporate multiple service components, like price comparison, customer support, gift registries, custom ordering, online price discounts, etc.
- A Web site offers an opportunity to collect information about individual consumers.

Once the marketer has the email address, he or she then circles to another medium: email, which establishes a one-to-one relationship with the consumer. Email closes the loop with a thank-you, followed up by notices and reminders, always sending the person around the spiral again by directing him or her to a TV or radio broadcast or print story.

The relationship can be maintained through the use of a fourth medium – social networks, particularly if the consumer is an *influencer* in the particular area of interest to the content marketer. For example, if the customer orders many movies or clicks on a lot of videos, then the content seller can ask this consumer to join a panel on a *wiki site*, where the consumer can be engaged further in the product presentation and choices. The marketer hopes such customers will buy more, but even more important, will involve their live and virtual friends, giving the campaign a viral boost.

It is important to repeat this spiral (mass medium, Internet, email, social media) as quickly and as many times as possible. It also calls for consistency in the marketing message so that consumers stay engaged with the brand and recognize it across media. Also, a consistent message allows customers to draw on their own experience to reexpress it to friends in their own authentic terms. An example of consistency is the NBC three-note audio signature and the peacock colors, no matter where their content appears, making the brand immediately apparent.

The power of spiral marketing comes from the fact that if it is repeated quickly and often enough, it builds a *virtuous circle*. This is a set of events where one propitious event leads to another, finally returning to the starting event to begin again. An example might be the development of an innovation, which leads to investment, effective marketing, increased productivity, higher economic growth, greater consumer buying power, which create profits that are used to underwrite efforts to develop more innovations. In this case, the virtuous circle leads to a seamless blending of brand management and customer relationship management (CRM).

The problem with spiral marketing is that it is very expensive. In some cases, the cost of acquiring customers is more than a content seller can hope to recoup in any reasonable amount of time. For this reason, some marketers start with a viral campaign, executed in social media venues and build toward a mass media exposure.

Viral Models

Viral marketing means to create a campaign where users act as your marketing agent, communicating your marketing message to their real-life and virtual friends. This is contagious communication, where "spreading the word" resembles how people pass colds and other viruses to each other. The genesis of the term probably came from Douglas Rushkoff's book *Media Virus*, which suggested that mass media programming contained hidden messages intended to spread counterculture attitudes and ideas.[10]

Viral messages can take place in face-to-face conversations, via email, and on social networks, and Twitter. Content sellers find viral marketing especially useful, as media is often the subject of such exchanges, and people pass on recommendations to their friends. Marketers can design materials with viral passalong in mind, encouraging customers to forward the message to their network of acquaintances.

There are many examples of successful viral campaigns. An early example was the *Blair Witch Project*. Since then, *Cloverfield* and the *Dark Knight* have launched notable viral efforts. Nine Inch Nails helped launch their album *Near Zero* by putting viral material on USB drives left for concert-goers to take home and upload to the Internet.

Affinity Models

There are two meanings for *affinity marketing*. The traditional model calls for marketing to existing groups of people, such as members of associations and clubs, employees of the same company or industries, students, other social groupings. Once identified, a marketing effort typically offers special arrangements, programs, or discounts for people who are in the affinity group.

On the Internet, *affinity model* refers to partnerships between Web sites that attract consumers who seek similar content. People may share an interest in the same content, but have quite different reasons for doing so. The common interest alone may propel them to look for compatible or complementary content, services, and products. To commercially exploit this relatedness, a partnership agreement between two or more Web sites that reach similar segments establishes URL links between them. Such partnerships are most widely used by sites that sell gambling, pornography content, and some retail products.

For example, a site that features real estate might partner with lenders, and a home improvement chain store. Similarly, a guitar manufacturer could execute agreements with a site that hosts a community of music creators, a songwriter's site, a musical instrument web store, a sheet music merchant, repair services, and so forth. It doesn't really matter that one guitar player wants to play funkadelic and another classic flamenco.

Data Mining

Viral and spiral marketing both focus on reaching new customers. Steve Milanovich of Merrill Lynch refers to monetizing customer relations as *hunting vs. gathering*. Looking for new customers using a viral or spiral marketing model is hunting. Pitching existing customers for an additional purchase is gathering.

Data mining is a gathering technique for using information about customers to create targeted value propositions to them. If a marketer knows a set of facts about a past buyer, analyzing that data in detail can provide guidance for such efforts. Sometimes additional information, such as zip code characteristics and census data can be added to the mix, giving powerful additional clues about how to approach a given customer. The more interactions a seller has had with an individual, the more targeted the approach can be.

Data mining is inherently cost-effective. Snagging a new customer for a retail site can be as much as $41, while some of the most well-known sites pay considerably less. For example, buy.com pays $22, Amazon.com pays $12, and eBay.com pays $8 for each new customer. Online stores can expect to pay 7–8 percent of their total revenues to acquire revenues.[11]

Over the past decade, data mining techniques have become very sophisticated. Supported by ever faster computers and better software, marketers can now simultaneously analyze multiple data sets, such as credit card data, census data, and consumer data. The result is that individual consumers can be targeted as narrowly as "Jane Murphy, 36, of Irish extraction, attended Boston College, earns $84,000 in a middle management job at an identified publishing company, owns a condo, a time-share in the Bahamas, and a Toyota Camry, views five on-demand movies per month, watches *House*, *Runway!*, and *CNN*, has a GlobalFit membership, donates to a political party and several nonprofit organizations, and uses an expressway E-Zpass for her daily commute to work."

Longitudinal Cohort Models

This revenue model goes particularly with audience segmentation content schemes, which offer material to a specific group of consumers. It tries to anticipate over time the array of wants and needs members of the group have in common, to provide content that interests and supports them, and to wrap around and embed appropriate ecommerce solutions. Mariana Danilovich, CEO and president of Digital Media Incubator, LLC, is an articulate advocate of this perspective. "This whole game is not about the creation of great programming. It is about serving a niche demographic. Now you can't serve a niche demographic with a single property. You can be very creative but it's the whole experience, designed with the entire lifestyle of the audience in mind, allowing you to fully serve the target demographic," she advises.[12]

A key element in this model is that it follows the same group over time, perhaps many years. A marketer using the model must continue to profile consumers at regular intervals so that the content and ecommerce opportunities evolve with the changing customer. The Web is still so young that this aspect of cohort marketing is only now surfacing as people in the Gen X cohort enters their thirties. E-tailers who focused on that group must now shift their strategies from urban, fashion-conscious, entertainment-driven singles to suburban marrieds with children buying their first home and entering the substantive years of their careers.

MTV is an example of a network that decided not to follow the longitudinal cohort model. Instead, it now programs to meet the needs of a core audience of adolescents, moving away from the Gen X group that made the network popular. By contrast, the CBS broadcast network appears to have adopted the model throughout the 1990s and the 2000s, putting on programs that appeal to an older audience, which in the 1960s, 1970s, and 1980s made the network the ratings leader.

DISTRIBUTION MODELS

Once content is developed, a distribution model lays out how the content will get to consumers, in terms of media platforms and technologies. In times past, the product itself defined its distribution: Movies were shown in theaters and later rented from video stores; songs were played on the radio and then purchased in stores that stocked vinyl record stores and later CDs; TV shows were shown on TV, and so forth.

In the digital environment, it is no longer clear how a given content vehicle will reach consumers. A song is played on the radio, on an audio pay service over cable and satellite, on the Internet, or over a mobile phone. Three distribution models that address this new reality are currently extant: windowing, cross-media/platform, and the walled garden shown in Table 13-6.

Before considering the models themselves, there is one further wrinkle in distribution – the relationship between providers and consumers in delivering material. The two-way Internet has fostered a new characterization of distribution media and formats as *push, pull,* and *opt-in,* or *pull-push.* Push means a distribution effort that sends out content to people whether they want it or not, such as broadcast TV and radio, spam email, and direct mail. Pull means a distribution that is requested by the receiver, such as going to a Web site and downloading a file: a request–receive format.

Table 13-6 Distribution Models

Windowing models	Distributing content in stages, using different time frames, media platforms, and prices
Cross-media/platform	Making content available on more than one media platform, such as letting consumers buy a book in a store (retail channel), download it in a .pdf file, and download it for an e-reader.
Walled garden	Making the consumers come to one place to get the content and not leave that venue for other choices. Before cable companies offered Internet, consumers couldn't ever leave the cable environment – a walled garden.

Opt-in might be characterized as pull-push. It reflects the need for companies to avoid irritating the consumer. The client makes a request which is then fulfilled at the sender's express choice. Examples of opt-in distribution are cable and satellite TV, requested email newsletters and other messages. In each of these cases, consumers ask to receive the content before they get it, and then keep on receiving the content until they *opt-out*, or request to end the service.

Windowing Models

This model is a marketing, revenue, and distribution model, depending on the context. When it is discussed as a way to reach ever less eager buyers, it is a marketing model; as a way to set ever lower prices, it is a revenue model; and as a way to plan sequential releases on different platforms, it is a distribution model. As covered in an earlier chapter, it is a marketing strategy and revenue model that originated with motion pictures and, to a limited extent, has now been adopted by some television series, networks, and programs as well.

Windowing means to release a property in stages for a specific length of time, the window. In the motion picture industry, it describes the wholesale level of film distribution. The order of the release windows is based on the revenue brought in per viewer. Domestic and international theatrical release comes first because each viewer pays for a ticket, $4.50 to $12.50. The pay-per-view window is next with a charge of $4.00 to $5.00 per household, followed by home video rental for $3.00 to $4.50 per night. After these windows follow premium cable, foreign TV, network TV, syndication packages for TV stations and basic cable channels, each window bringing in a smaller and smaller flat fee or package price.[13]

Revenue per viewer is not the only conceivable way to structure release windows. Strategies for reaching particular audiences or media platforms might define them. For example, one analyst proposes that film studios create an early release window via satellite HDTV channels, a *first-run HDTV channel*. It would feature pretheatrical releases of movies to households that have HDTV sets. Dale Cripps, who developed this idea, believes that there are about that many people who would pay $10–$20 to be the first ones to see new films.[14] The income would be substantial, and it could provide valuable word-of-mouth to support the theatrical release right afterward. (Maybe this wouldn't offer much good publicity for disappointing films!)

Digital windows include DVDs, video CDs, digital cable networks, and the Internet. Slicing and dicing of motion picture content permits the distribution of snippets, portions of text, individual scenes, and single photos. The distribution of music has been disrupted by sharing over peer-to-peer networks, but it is possible that windowing could apply to many other content types. For example, songs could launch at a concert, move to pay-per-song over the Internet (with expiring rights protection), then to CD-ROM, and finally to subscription audio channels over cable and satellite.

Cross-Media/Platform Models

The cross-media/platform model means distributing content across more than one medium or to more than one type of reception device. Like windowing models, it may be cited as a marketing and revenue model as well as a distribution model. Consumers differ in where they want to enjoy content, and many people use more than one device. The same person may watch a video on TV, on their mobile phone or portable DVD player, or over the Internet at different times and locations, with varied motivations. They may also combine media with the Internet, such as simultaneously watching the content while participating in interactive or social activities.

The changing content consumption habits of the public mean that content providers and distributors must now reach their customers wherever they happen to be, on whatever devices they choose to use. Creating material for different delivery platforms, network access speeds, formats, reception devices, and consumer characteristics is another way of saying that content must be customized, tailored to address many different environments, conditions, and consumers. In the digital world, more and more content companies think about distribution as *create once, publish everywhere*.

Sun called this strategy *chasing the consumer*, delivering content to consumers and tracking their responses across multiple media and platforms. The target audience may be broad or narrow, but the content is tailored to the needs and desires of that group. It is created once and automated procedures convert it to needed formats for distribution across multiple media. This means that content must be flexible. It must be an exciting print vehicle, a compelling television program, a sticky Internet attraction, and an e-commerce bonanza. The cost of the content is amortized from revenues derived from all sources, across the various media where it appears.

Martha Stewart Living Omnimedia, LLC, pioneered a cross-platform distribution strategy, with business ventures divided into four segments: publishing, television, merchandising, and Internet/direct commerce. At the height of the company's activities, the content creation empire included:

- A monthly magazine (*Martha Stewart Living*)
- A quarterly magazine (*Martha Stewart Weddings*)
- A syndicated one-hour television show (*Martha Stewart Living*)
- Weekly *CBS This Morning* appearances and periodic CBS prime-time specials, all in partnership with divisions of CBS Television
- Half-hour program twice a day, seven days a week on Food Network cable channel, that consists primarily of food-related segments from previous *Martha Stewart Living* television programs
- Books written by Martha Stewart and the editors of *Martha Stewart Living*
- A syndicated newspaper column (askMartha)
- A national radio show ("askMartha")
- A mail-order catalog and online merchandising business (Martha By Mail)
- An Internet Web site that features integration of television programs, radio shows, newspaper column, and magazines, as well as seven distinct channels on the site, each devoted to a core content area – Home, Cooking & Entertaining, etc. Each channel offered live discussion forums, 24-hour bulletin boards where visitors post advice, queries, and replies, and weekly live question and answer hours with in-house and guest experts
- Strategic merchandising relationships with Kmart, Sherwin-Williams, Sears, Zellers, and P/Kaufmann.

Walled Garden Models

Walled garden is a term often attributed to TeleCommunications, Inc. founder John Malone. It is a closed network that keeps subscribers within a restricted area. Inside the garden, the subscriber can choose from a bouquet of services that are carefully selected, controlled, and often created and operated by the network providing company. Walled garden services do not permit unfettered access to the Internet. Cable and satellite companies operate walled gardens on the television side of their operations, but when cable companies offer broadband network service, they market unlimited Internet access.

As media become ever more converged, walled gardens are likely to be more difficult to maintain. Mobile devices are a good example. These operators allowed users to choose only their own applications and services. Now that such phones access the Internet, consumers can find other sources. Most phones put limits in the device software, but hackers often defeat them. For example, telephones are often tied to a given service – in the United States, Sprint, Verizon, or T-Mobile. But on eBay, consumers can buy "open" phones (devices that have been modified to work with any service).

REVENUE MODELS

People will pay for content they want. Timeliness and time-to-market are always important, because information and entertainment products are highly perishable, like fresh flowers or lettuce. Freshness is especially critical for financial and business information, and companies and investors are sometimes willing to pay considerable sums to get it first. People like to be the first to receive entertainment but, more important, like it to be – well— entertaining.

Revenue models deal with product packaging, pricing, mechanisms for receiving money (or services in the case of barter), and revenue sharing schemes. Many of the models used by traditional media carry over into the digital marketplace. Not surprisingly, there are usually some unique twists when this analog to digital conversion takes place. Revenue models in new media markets may have the same name as those used in traditional venues, but they often mean quite different things. For example, pay-per models can cover smaller informational pieces than in the cable industry, which typically markets whole programs.

Of all the parts of business models, the list of revenue models is the longest. Perhaps this makes sense, in that business is primarily the pursuit of profit and nothing is more important to that effort than how the enterprise will make money. As the content business landscape continues to evolve, under the pressure of technologies, there is probably no way to capture all the possible revenue models. In addition, they can be combined into a nearly limitless set of combinations. Table 13-7 lists the more common revenue models.

Multiple Revenue Stream Models

It is hard to think of a content-based business that does not have multiple revenue streams and that does not spend considerable effort developing them. The over-the-air broadcast industry relied heavily on advertising budgets, but early in its development, began selling programs into the syndication market to add an additional stream of income. Today, successful programs become series DVDs as well.

The value of multiple sources of revenues in media and entertainment became clear to broadcasters with the rise of the cable industry as they competed with TV programming providers that could deliver multiple channels and brought in receipts from monthly subscriptions, advertising, premium channels, pay-per-view, and high-speed Internet access and telephony. Music labels have discovered the downstream market for ringtones based on popular songs. And some popular motion pictures make more money from ancillary merchandising deals than they do from the box office.

Table 13-7 Revenue models

Revenue Models	
Multiple revenue streams	Bring in money from more than one source.
Ad-supported models	Advertisers support content by paying to reach consumers.
Transactional pay-per	Content consumers pay directly for content.
Bundling and tiering	Place multiple content products together and charge for the package.
Big bite models	Monetize the content right away from its initial release.
Subscription models	Charge consumers a fee for a period of time – hour, day, month, year, etc.
Commerce-supported models	Content is a loss leader or free, supported by the sales of other products.
Usage fees	Charge consumers by how much they consume.
Piggyback models	One hit provides profits to content provider and may support other less profitable content.
Licensing fees	Charge content resellers or users a fee for using or consuming the content, while retaining ownership of the copyright.
Revenue sharing models	To make money by increasing demand by sharing customers and revenue with partners.
Affiliate revenue sharing	Setting up revenue-sharing partnerships with content providers to increase the total size of the audience.
Cybermediary models	Internet distributors aggregate links, replacing wholesale distributors in the physical world.
Consumer-generated content	Allow consumers to provide content and pay them some part of the revenue their work brings in.
Data sales models	Make money by selling data about consumers and users.

Ad-supported Models

Advertising is the stalwart of over-the-air television and a major source of revenue for basic cable and satellite channels, through 30-, 20-, 15-, and 10-second commercial spots. It is increasingly important to Internet Web sites as one of several sources of revenue. Marketers can buy a place on a Web page, usually the home or landing page. These availabilities include space for banner advertisements, pop-up windows, streaming video button boxes (V-boxes), and click-on animations, logos, banners, and buttons for audio clips. Sponsoring a Web site will give an advertiser access to all these forms of placement as well.

In traditional media, audiences are sold to advertisers on a CPM (cost per thousand) impressions. On the largest Internet sites that command millions of visitors, such as AOL and Yahoo!, this formulation works well. However, on the majority of Internet sites, advertising rates are less certain. Even though sites deliver customers with specific demographic and psychographic profiles, and their behaviors can be monitored and recorded, measurement issues still cloud the picture. Many new ways of accounting for customer behavior online now exist, as shown in Figure 13-4.

Guideline	Recommendation
Ad Counting	Client/Browser-initiated
Buffering and Caching	Measurement Standard = Opportunity to see
Measurable Activity	Includes, but is not limited to: • Delivery of a beacon, defined as any piece of content designated as a tracking asset • Delivery of a 302 Redirect or html/javascript • Delivery of digital video ad content
Reporting	Include disaggregated detail for placement or range of ad types
Filtration	Strongest possible combination of both specific identification and activity-based filtration
Auditing	• Counting methods • Processes/controls

FIGURE 13-4 Advertisers ask: How many consumers did my ad reach?

One controversy is that of impressions versus click-throughs. Internet Web site operators want to be paid for the number of targeted consumers they bring to the site. They have no control over the effectiveness of the ad itself, so they believe the number of site visitors should be the key metric. Advertisers prefer paying for click-throughs or sell-throughs.

The Internet Advertising Bureau issued guidelines for measuring a *digital video ad*, an ad that appears in streamed media, games, and other digital venues.[15] The group will continue as digital media evolve. They hope to standardize measurement and reporting procedures that will be necessary for the Internet to capture a substantial share of advertising budgets.

When high-speed broadband access becomes more widespread, advertising will play an important role in supporting content for it. Video and audio are much more expensive to produce than text and graphics, and broadband distribution will make content providers more dependent on commercial revenues to produce and distribute popular material – not that anything is likely to replace the Internet's current rich stew of irreverent, zany, flippant, obscene, snotty, thoughtful, and silly user-generated content.

Transactional Pay-per Models

Long before the term *pay per* came into being, people paid per ticket to attend movies, plays, and performances. Then telephone companies introduced pay-per-minute charges for long distance and local long distance. Cable systems launched pay-per-view service, which in the case of the NBC Olympic coverage was extended to mean pay-per-event or pay-per-package. And the advent of videocassettes and players brought about pay-per-night rentals.

Pay-per models are attractive to both buyers and sellers, and there are various Internet services that offer pay-per-download, pay-per-bit, per-article, per-photo, per-song, and per-video. The main problem with many of these schemes is that of *micropayments*, small transactions that are more expensive to meter and collect than the value of the payment. Until some form of *digital wallet* technology is standardized, it is likely to be difficult for content providers to make money on small units of information. However, the increasing automation of payments are coming close to providing this service, as evidenced by the growth of PayPal.

Bundling and Tiering

Bundling and tiering are pricing as well as marketing models. They are well-developed strategies by multichannel TV providers, but less used in other environments. Most bundling and tiering are implemented by product type – motion pictures, sports, or some other popular content genre. The more popular products cost the most, followed by ever-less-popular material. It is also possible to create bundles (or packages) and tiering based on timeliness so that the first buyers pay more than later buyers, when the material may be less timely.

The cable industry provides an excellent example. The first tier is basic cable. The second tier is composed of extended basic packages, each one costing an additional monthly fee. The third tier is made up of individual premium channels; the fourth is a digital tier of bundled channels; and next tier is pay-per-view, which charges for receiving individual programs, usually movies and sporting events; and the most expensive tier is individual on-demand viewings, usually motion pictures. High-speed Internet access and telephony are not considered a tier – they are added services. However, they are often bundled with cable services to provide an overall lower package price.

Big Bite Models

Big bite models are the opposite of windowing, which monetizes content by releasing it in stages to different distribution systems. "Forget windowing. It'll never work in the age of digital recreation and redistribution," cry the proponents of this model. Instead, they argue that content owners must monetize the first bytes out of the box and move on. The motto might be, "Eat the apple, then toss the core, because if the product can't make a decent profit when it first rolls out, it will probably incur a loss."

Content providers have to get the money while the getting is good – immediately. As soon as the product is widely available on the Net, its sales price will quickly drop to zero. Packaged video games are a good example: It takes 18 months to 2 years to create them and a couple of months to sell them out – or to bulldoze under the unsold product.

Subscription Models

Tiering is frequently an adjunct to subscriptions, but not always. A subscription is a revenue scheme where the subscriber pays an agreed upon amount for specified content for a fixed period of time. In the cable world, system operators charge a monthly fee for the basic tier but per-channel/per-month fees for premium channels. Many online games charge a monthly subscription. So do Internet service providers and many Web site hosting services.

Commerce-Supported Revenue Models

Content attracts people, so some marketers use it to draw customers for other products. When the material is sold at a price cheaper than the marketer paid for it or given away for free, it is called a *loss leader*. However, the content was probably sold at a profit to the copyright holder. Wal-Mart and Target used music CDs and video games as loss leaders. Apple uses iPhone applications to increase the value of its product, so that the thousands of applications give customers additional incentives to buy the phone.

One of the advantages that the Internet offers is that it is actionable, meaning that it can be acted upon immediately. On the Internet, a click and a credit card are all that are needed for a purchase. Contrast this ease of purchase with television and radio, where the viewer or listener has to drive to a store or place a phone call and execute a long series of actions to get a product. For this reason, e-commerce models are not suitable for one-way media; they apply only to interactive platforms such as the Internet and interactive TV.

One way designers conceptualize the development of Web sites is "wrapping e-commerce opportunities around content." So it is no surprise that there is some discussion that user-generated content may be the new loss leader to sell commercially produced content, evidenced by new Internet deals signed by some social media sites.[16] Efforts to push e-commerce using free content may be subtle sidebars or links, or they may be the obnoxiously intrusive pop-up windows, such as those employed by Netflix, consistently reported by users as the most disliked form of online advertising.

White papers and free reports are often underwritten by companies who want to establish themselves as opinion leaders in their market. They offer the information for free, using the registration process to gather information about possible customers. After the information has been downloaded, a salesperson uses the contact information to follow up.

Usage Fees

Usage fees are charged for time or a service. Typically they take the form of a flat service fee, network utilization fees, or access fees, as shown in Table 13-8. Often flat fees are designed to include costs incurred for network utilization or access. A good example is the mobile telephone industry. Users often pay a flat service for a *bucket* of minutes. However, that bucket includes the costs paid by the phone service provider for use of the wireless spectrum.

Table 13-8 Types of Usage Fees	
Flat service fee	Charge one price for a given level of service.
Network utilization fees	Charge for using the network.
Access fees	Charge for accessing the network.

When a customer pays for individual long-distance calls, they are typically *network utilization fees*, charges for using the long-distance network. Hidden in these charges is a *network access fee*, paid by the local phone operator. Another example is mobile broadband service Internet access offered by Sprint, Verizon, and AT&T in the United States. The operator charges the customer a *flat service fee*, although the operator pays a network utilization fee. At a hotel, customers often pay a daily fee for use of the Internet – this charge is a network access fee.

Piggyback Models

This model is a strategy of having one content product or service supporting the other content offerings. In the motion picture and television businesses, it is not unknown for a few successful hits to carry a studio, production company, or network for some length of time. A special case of piggybacking is the *tentpole* scheduling strategy, used by broadcast television networks. It means scheduling a popular show with high ratings between two new or lower-rated shows so that the tentpole show carries the two less popular shows – giving them a chance to build an audience.

Licensing Fees

A licensing fee revenue model works well for content types that have lasting value, such as well-produced motion pictures, television shows, and music. It means licensing the copyright to the property to a third party, allowing them to resell or redistribute the content for a fixed period of time. However, the copyright holder retains ownership rights over the content.

More time-sensitive materials, such as most sports events, newspaper articles, photographs, and user-generated content, have less value, unless they are part of a licensed package. It is possible that most content can be licensed. However, the long tail of content can be very long indeed, so that revenues are not necessarily high.

Revenue Sharing Models

There are many examples of revenue sharing models. Some of them are so entirely taken for granted that they receive little attention, such as royalties to book authors and percentage of the gross revenue deals received by some performers in the motion picture and concert music industries. Middlemen and distributors have always worked on a commission or percentage of their sales. In addition, the Internet has spawned some new versions of the traditional revenue-sharing models.

Affiliate Models

In radio and television, an affiliate station carries the programming of a broadcast network, and gives up commercial time that the network can package with stations all over the United States to sell to national advertisers. At the local level, stations make deals in which they air programming in return for giving some or all of the local *avails* (time available to run commercial advertisements), to the syndicator. The syndicator or programming supplier may find advertisers to buy the avails or turn them over to a spot sales rep firm to sell them on the open market.

On the Internet, an e-commerce site puts together an affiliate network of other sites, distributing clickable content, logos, banners, and links. When customers click, they are taken to the e-tailer's web storefront to make the purchase. In return, the seller shares the revenue with the referring site. The use of these kinds of agreements has grown as the cost of placing banner ads on portal sites has risen.

Essentially, it is a way of reaching out to potential customers instead of waiting for them to come to an e-tailer's site. If the affiliates have content compatible with the target audience, then visitors who are looking for similar products are reasonably likely to click on the link. Just as it is with cohort marketing, compatibility is crucial. Sites that offer information about entertainment are a natural for selling books, videos, music, and tickets. Sports sites can sell event tickets and sports equipment. Personal finance dot-coms might market research on individual stocks and mutual funds.

Here is how a site might analyze the business case for establishing an affiliate network:

- 250 affiliated Web sites, with 1,500 daily page views per site, to get 11,250,000 impressions per month
- A 3.5 percent click-through rate generates 393,750 targeted, self-selected sales prospects
- A 1 percent conversion rate of prospects into buyers results in 3,937 products sold per month
- If average purchase is $25, total sales = $98,425 per month
- Less 10–50 percent commission to referring Web site ($9,842–$49,212) + cost of goods sold = profit

Establishing and managing an affiliate network presumes a certain scale and sophistication of infrastructure. The e-tailer must have a product database and the means to process transactions and fulfill orders. Affiliate referrals need to be integrated into the database and tracked so payments can be calculated and distributed.

Affiliate commission rates on sales vary greatly, from a few percentage points to as much as 50 percent. Some examples of affiliate networks are Amazon.com, with hundreds of thousands of affiliates and partnerships with many booksellers and Barnes & Noble's agreement with the *New York Times*. Visitors to the NYT Web site who are reading book reviews can click and buy it from Barnes & Noble.

Cybermediary Models

The cybermediary is the online version of wholesale distributors, performing the functions of traditional intermediaries between product manufacturers and consumers. These online intermediaries, entities that facilitate the exchange between buyers and sellers, may do nothing more than provide listings where consumers can find items they want to buy, such as http://www.shopper.com or http://www.buy.com. Or they may provide customer service, such as handling returns.

There is a similar infrastructure in the physical world. In the United States and other highly commercialized business environments, wholesale distributors stand between the makers of products and the retailers who sell them in many product categories.. A study of the U.S. distribution and sales of high-quality shirts found that the wholesale-retail chain, the intermediaries that facilitate the exchange, account for about 62 percent of the final price to the buyer. At the same time, many analysts have advanced the notion that networking enables a direct communication between the parties to the transaction that could eliminate these middlemen altogether. They call this flattening of hierarchy *disintermediation*.[17]

In addition to wholesale entities, retailers are also intermediaries to the final sale, along with the more traditional definitions of wholesalers in the distribution process. And some intermediaries earn their money by performing valuable functions. They include packaging products into attractive, saleable merchandise categories, providing consumer-friendly product information, matching consumers to products, providing transactional economies of scale, and managing risks for both producers (verifying checks and credit cards) and consumers (handling returns).[18] Indeed, so valuable are some of these services, they have led to *reintermediation* by some cybermediaries.

Online fingers do the walking on Yahoo! and Google, instead of through the local Yellow Pages. Car buyers get the Blue Book value of their used car from Kelley's Blue Book online service (http://www.kbb.com) instead of calling their cousin Pete who works at the General Motors dealership. From http://kbb.com, the link goes to http://autotrader.com to shop for a car. Similarly, eBay.com acts as a cybermediary between millions of buyers and sellers, displacing the old intermediaries, newspapers. Business-to-business sites provide real-time spot market and barter networks. And shopping *bots* scour the Net, bringing back product and price comparisons.

A DAY IN THE LIFE OF VIVI ZIGLER

**Vivi Zigler President,
NBC Universal Digital Media Entertainment**

I like to say, "I am a TV girl in digital clothing." I've been very fortunate to work in many different areas in my career and believe that having a breadth of industry knowledge is more important than ever. I began my career in broadcast journalism while still a student at Cal Poly San Luis Obispo University. I fell in love with the excitement and spontaneity that surrounds news gathering and started working at the local NBC affiliate, KSBY-TV. I held many positions during my 12 years with the station, including Station Manager. From there, I moved to Seattle and was the Director of Marketing & Advertising at KING 5 (another NBC affiliate) where I oversaw all marketing, graphic design, press and publicity, public affairs, and community relations for the station.

In 1993, I joined the NBC Network as a Director in the Affiliate Advertising & Promotion Services group – dealing with our NBC stations around the country on a variety of marketing initiatives. I was later made Vice President of that group and took on added responsibilities for media planning and special projects.

As I continued my work in marketing at NBC, I took on a new challenge in 2003 as Senior Vice President, Advertising Services, the NBC Agency *and* as Senior Vice President of Marketing & Advertising for Bravo, our newly acquired cable network. While in the position, I was in charge of overall branding and marketing for Bravo, including the successful campaigns for *Queer Eye for the Straight Guy* and *Celebrity Poker*. It remains today one of the most rewarding periods of my career as Bravo saw amazing growth and attention.

In June 2005, I was given the opportunity to be Executive Vice President, Current Programs, NBC Entertainment, where I oversaw the production of NBC's slate of scripted series, working with many talented people on the show, studio and network sides.

Now, as President of Digital Entertainment, I am responsible for leading the NBC Universal Digital Entertainment team, which is comprised of the NBC Universal Digital Studio and NBC.com. Additionally, I work with all of the NBC Universal entertainment Web sites. I am fortunate to work with a number of digital business leaders who are fearless in this world that blends new media and entertainment.

There really is no typical day for me. No two days are the same – ever. And honestly I wouldn't have it any other way. Focusing on digital media inside an entertainment company is like trying to ride a wild horse inside a hurricane. Both areas are fast-paced, creative, and volatile, but digital media is also *new*. And new means there are no accepted practices, no long-held rules, templates, or obvious answers. We are creating the rules while on the horse in the hurricane.

Entertainment is undergoing the most significant challenges in its history, tech is changing at an incredible pace, consumers are adopting new behaviors at record speed, and our mission is to blend it all into a seamless and wonderful experience for our fans.

My day often starts with a meeting with NBC senior management to discuss strategy, programming, and a variety of business issues. After that I meet with various leaders in our business. Each day is different with a mix of talking to publicists, lawyers, creative executives, marketing folks, finance gurus, digital distribution, and of course members of my team.

Often the greatest challenge is moving from an analytic type of a meeting such as research or finance to a creative meeting to a tech meeting – quickly changing the "brain disk" can be tough! The biggest frustration in my work is a lack of non–meeting time to think or to connect with people. We are all moving so quickly it's very easy to forget how far we've come and what we've accomplished. I tell my staff to stop and look back at where we've been – it's a wonderful way to truly take stock of our successes.

An important part of my role is to serve as "translator" between television and digital. I currently live in the overlap of those two worlds. I constantly speak to groups internally and externally about digital entertainment. On a daily basis, I find myself explaining the uncharted waters of all things digital to the television side and the complex and evolving television industry to the digital side.

Continued...

vertex42   **Daily Planner**

Date: 8/17/2009   Vivi Zigler

17 August, 2009
        Monday

July 2009   **August 2009**   September 2009
Su M Tu W Th F Sa   Su M Tu W Th F Sa   Su M Tu W Th F Sa
          1 2 3 4   1   1 2 3 4 5
5 6 7 8 9 10 11   2 3 4 5 6 7 8   6 7 8 9 10 11 12
12 13 14 15 16 17 18   9 10 11 12 13 14 15   13 14 15 16 17 18 19
19 20 21 22 23 24 25   16 17 18 19 20 21 22   20 21 22 23 24 25 26
26 27 28 29 30 31   23 24 25 26 27 28 29   27 28 29 30
                         30 31

	Remember			Appointments		Notes

Remember
Steve's Birthday
Dry Cleaning

☑	ABC	**Prioritized Task List**
		email Lisa
		email Michael

Time	**People to Call**
	EP of Heroes
	Music Rights Lawyer
	CAA Agent

$Amt	**Expenses**

Appointments

7 :00
  :30
8 :00 Dentist
  :15
  :30
  :45
9 :00
  :15
  :30 Meet w/Sr. Staff
  :45
10 :00
  :15
  :30 site leader call-All NBCU
  :45 Entertainment Sites
11 :00
  :15
  :30
  :45
12 :00 Lunch with WB Marketing
  :15
  :30
  :45
1 :00 Publicity/Sales Call-NBC.com
  :15
  :30
  :45
2 :00 Show Rights- Call
  :15
  :30 Digital Studio/Financial
  :45 update
3 :00
  :15
  :30 iTunes deal-Call/Meet with Digital Distribution
  :45
4 :00 Sales Update-5 year projection
  :15
  :30
  :45
5 :00 Notes call-"The Office"
  :30 Webisodes
6 :00
  :30
7 :00
  :30 Speaking Engagement-
8 :00 Loyola Law School
  :30
9 :00
  :30

Notes

The highlight of my day is when I can get my emails under 100! An overflowing inbox seriously stresses me out.

I feel in order to maintain good relationships with people inside and outside of my company it's important to occasionally take the conversation outside of the office. About four times a month I meet someone for drinks or dinner. It allows for some serious conversations to become more casual and for some casual conversations to be taken more seriously. Sometimes we need a break from the confines of our offices and it's healthy to get some fresh air. I find the more comfortable someone is, the more he or she is willing to get to the bottom of an issue.

My best advice to students would be to "take care of the people parts first," as there is nothing more important. We spend a great deal of time teaching students about the financial, legal, and core business functions but we do not train them in the art of managing people. Nothing hurts productivity more than ignoring the problems of your staff. They are the front line and they are the difference between a successful and failed business.

Lastly, I would encourage anyone looking into a career in entertainment, digital or a combination of the two, to develop thinking skills. Fight against jumping to easy answers or solutions that come from throwing money at a problem. Learn to advance your own thoughts, to have the confidence to question your ideas, and to be open-minded to what you see around you. Never ever think you know it all – I guarantee you don't. Embrace learning and be curious!

User-Generated Content Revenue Sharing

iStockphoto (http://www.istockphoto.com) is a site where anyone can buy photographs, illustrations, video and audio clips, and Flash animations for a flat rate – about $1.30 for most photos and $15 for Flash animations. Users prepay with a credit card and download until their account is empty. However, not only can users buy – they can also sell. iStockphoto generates revenue from selling the content and distribute royalties from 20 to 40 percent back to the content creator.

Bloggers may also be able to *monetize* (make money from) their content. Some blogging sites offer bloggers revenue from advertising that is placed on their page. In addition, productive bloggers who write well for a site may be offered a stipend for their work by the site operator.

Data Sale Models

In addition to the dollar amount spent by customers, there is also the data the company owns about the consumers and their behaviors. Indeed, this information about actual purchasers may well be the most valuable asset the company will ever own. It can be used as a bargaining chip to partner with others or simply sold. Depending on the depth and breadth of the data, it can also be repackaged into segments for use or sale to multiple buyers.

SUMMARY

For 70 years, there were three media business models – sell retail, sell tickets, or sell ads. Today, managers mix and match the business models presented in this chapter to maximize their chances of success and profits. It is clear that the ways media enterprises now market, sell, and deliver content require much more complex business strategies than were needed in the past.

WHAT'S AHEAD

The next chapter looks at the web of legal and regulatory rights, obligations, and restrictions in which media organizations operate. Companies' products, marketing practices, and delivery technologies must all meet the requirements of the geographies where these companies are doing business. Laws and regulations are imposed at the local, state, federal, and international levels, each reflecting the cultural, social, and political environment of the area where they are enacted.

CASE STUDY 13.1 BACK TO THE FUTURE

As detailed in this chapter, the content or purpose of a Web site either appeals to a broad market or a niche market. Just how narrow that niche becomes will make the difference between the success or failure of an online business.

Assignment

For the purpose of this case study, you are going to become the creator of an existing online Web site that serves a niche market. Now, let's go "back to the future" as you draw up the business model for this particular Web site before it was actually launched. Get the idea? You get to explain how this Web site is going to become a success with your very detailed business plan without identifying the name of the Web site until the very end.

Content Model

- What type of online content will it produce? Remember that there are four types, and explain it in full detail.
- Is this a B2B or B2C operation?
- Create your content model, identifying "Content Aggregation," "Audience Aggregation," or "Audience Segmentation."

Distribution Model

- How will the content reach your consumers?
- What is your vision for the consumer experience? How will you accomplish your goals here?
- Describe your distribution model. Will it be push, pull, or opt-in technology?
- Will you include "bundling and buckets"? Explain how this will contribute to the success or why you would not include it.

- Provide information about the screen real estate. Are you including a "landing/splash screen"? Do you also have a "data glove"? If so, where is it located and how will it be used?

Marketing Model

- Who is your target market?
- What is your marketing strategy to turn potential audience into actual customer?
- What makes your business unique and different from the competition?
- Identify the brand and your plans to market the brand.
- What is your advertising slogan? How will you deliver this message? Will you be using traditional methods, a viral model or a combination?

Revenue Model

- How will your Web site make money?
- Will there be indirect sources of revenue in addition to direct?
- If you were to present this information to a group of investors, how do you think they would have responded?

Finally...

- Reveal the name of your online company and share information about its successes and/or failures, now that you're "back to the future."

REFERENCES

1. Pine, B. J., Gilmore, J. H. & Pine, B. J. (1999). *The experience economy: Work is theatre & every business a stage*. Cambridge, MA: Harvard Business School Press.

2. Pine, J. & Gilmore, J. H. (April 9, 2000). Are you experienced? *Industry standard*. Accessed June 18, 2001, at http://thestandard.net/article/article_print/0%2C1153%2C4167%2C00 .html.

3. D'Innocenzio, A. (August 21, 2009). More shoppers thinking twice in the checkout line. Accessed August 28, 2009, at http://www.huffingtonpost.com/huff-wires/20090821/ us-shopping-cart-abandonment/.

4. Papagan, K. (April 25, 2000). Telephone interview.

5. Christlieb, J. H. E. (2005). Reducing complexity of consumer electronics interfaces using commonsense reasoning. Accessed August 20, 2009, at http://dspace.mit.edu/bitstream/ handle/1721.1/33202/66528188.pdf?sequence=1.

6. Wolf, A. (2007). The future of content navigation. Accessed August 18, 2009, at http:// www.broadcastprojects.com/Janet_Greco_files/The%20Future%20of%20Content%20 Navigation.pdf.

7. This feature listing accessed December 18, 2009 at http://www.timewarnercable.com/nynj/ learn/cable/dvrhddvr/default.html.

8. See http://www.alexa.com.

9. Berst, J. (November 13, 1998). Secrets of spiral branding. ZDNet.com. Accessed November 6, 2005, at http://www.zdnet.com/anchordesk/story/story_2745.html. Also, see ibid., accessed September 8, 2009, at http://www.alexa.com/siteinfo/disney.go.com.

10. Rushkoff, D. (1996). *Media virus.* New York, NY: Random House Publishing.

11. _____. (June 3, 2009). Customer acquisition costs drop for online marketers. Accessed online on July 18, 2009, at http://www.internetretailer.com/internet/marketing-conference/03435- customer-acquisition-costs-drop-online-marketers.html.

12. Danilovich, M. (April 3, 2000). Personal interview.

13. Vogel, H. L. (1998). *Entertainment industry economics*, 4th Ed. Cambridge: Cambridge University Press, 75–77.

14. Cripps, D. (April 9, 2000). Personal interview.

15. Internet Advertising Bureau. (December, 2009). *Digital video ad impression measurement guidelines*. Accessed January 5, 2010 at http://www.iab.net/media/file/dig_vid_imp_meas_ guidelines_final.pdf.

16. Lacy, S. (February 2009). UGC: Just a loss leader in the end? Accessed August 21, 2009, at http://www.sarahlacy.com/sarahlacy/2009/02/ugc-just-a-loss-leader-in-the-end.html.

17. Sarkar, M. B., Butler, B. & Steinfield, C. (1995). Intermediaries and cybermediaries: A continuing role for mediating players in the electronic marketplace. *Journal of Computer-Mediated Communication* 1:3. Accessed November 9, 2009 at http://www.ascusc.org/jcmc/vol1/issue3/ sarkar.html.

18. Benjamin, R. & Wigand, R. Electronic markets and virtual value chains on the information highway. *Sloan management review* Winter 1995, 62–72.

CHAPTER 14

Legal and Regulatory Issues

August E. Grant, Ph.D.

Professor, University of South Carolina

The First Amendment is often inconvenient. But that is besides the point. Inconvenience does not absolve the government of its obligation to tolerate speech.

Justice Anthony Kennedy

No man's life, liberty, or property is safe while the legislature is in session.

Judge Gideon Tucker

CONTENTS

CHAPTER OBJECTIVES

The objectives of this chapter are:
- To introduce the role of the First Amendment to the U.S. Constitution in media regulation.
- To explore the range of Federal laws and regulations that impact media managers.
- To introduce regulatory facts at the state and local levels.
- To illustrate how a media manager copes with inevitable change in laws and regulations.

When you think of media regulation, the first things that may come to your mind are the Federal Communication Commission (FCC) and the First Amendment to the U.S. Constitution. But media managers must concern themselves with a much broader range of laws and regulations in order to do their day-to-day jobs. Consider the problem this author once faced in putting a new FM radio station on the air.

Without a doubt, the biggest barrier to putting any radio station on the air in the United States is getting the FCC license needed to broadcast on a specific channel in a specified community. That was, indeed, the biggest barrier, but other barriers from regulators proved to be challenging as well.

367

DOI: 10.1016/B978-0-240-81020-1.00014-2

As with most radio stations, our transmitter was located some distance from the studio. The transmitter site was a big expanse of nothing. It was a big field with a tall tower in the middle of it, the antenna on top of the tower, and a small building at the base of the tower to contain the transmitter and related equipment. Instead of using a portable building, we decided to do it right – a permanent concrete block building, with air conditioner, measuring about 10 by 12 feet.

To build a building in that area, you need to get a building permit from the county. I couldn't imagine anything simpler than a 10×12-foot concrete building. I took the plans to the county office to get approval for building permit, and after waiting only a few minutes, sat down with the inspector. "This should be easy," I thought.

The inspector perused the plans for much longer than I thought would be needed for such a small building. Finally, he looked up and asked me only one question: "Where is your bathroom?"

He's kidding, I thought. "Pardon me?" I said.

"Where is your bathroom?" he said again.

"Transmitters don't go to the bathroom," I responded slowly.

"Are there going to be any people there?" he asked.

"Once a week," I responded. "Only to inspect the equipment, once a week. And the tower is in the middle of a field, with lots of trees."

"You need a bathroom," he responded, rejecting our application for a building permit.

As it ended up, we did not need a bathroom, but we did need to allow an extra four days to appeal his decision and convince someone in that office that transmitters don't need a bathroom. We were cutting it close – our license required us to begin broadcasting within a fixed period of time, or we would have to file new paperwork with the FCC.

The lesson is that broadcasters, and for that matter all media organizations, have to be concerned about a wide range of regulatory issues. In media law in the United States, the primary governing principle is the First Amendment to the U.S. Constitution. But in media management, regulators, regulations, laws, and court decisions affect almost every area of media operation, from finance and sales to hiring and employee safety.

The first step in understanding the regulatory environment is knowing that laws and regulations affecting media organizations come from all areas of government, including state, federal, and local government. Most media law textbooks deal primarily with first-amendment and federal issues, because they are common to all media organizations in the United States. So it is important for media managers to become familiar with laws and regulations that are peculiar to their state, their county, and their city, because these will affect the day-to-day operation of your organization.

There are three broad sources of rules that must be followed. The first two are laws, which are passed by legislative bodies and range from Acts of Congress to city ordinances. The second are regulations, which are rules created by government agencies that have the force of law and are usually designed to implement the provisions of specific laws. The problem is that any law or regulation is subject to interpretation. In the U.S. legal system, the interpretations are provided by the courts when they resolve lawsuits and criminal cases brought before the legal system. This "case law" forms the third source of rules that must be followed, providing interpretations of laws and regulations that help to guide our day-to-day decisions.

You're probably asking yourself: How can I keep up with all of the laws, regulations, and court cases, especially as all three are found at the federal, state, and local levels? From a practical perspective, it is almost impossible to keep up with every single development that will affect the operation of your media organization. But you have help. There are law firms that specialize in each of the areas of regulation and law that you'll encounter. The key is knowing that no single law firm specializes in all of the areas mentioned so far. As a result, you should have the names and phone numbers of a couple of different sources of legal counsel available to you. The firm that can provide you the best guidance and representation on issues regarding employee contracts and sexual harassment issues is probably not the same as the firm that you'll turn to for questions or issues regarding FCC rules and regulations.

The solution is easy. When faced with a problem or issue or legal matter, pick up the phone and call your attorney. These legal experts are as well trained in their field as you are in yours, and having them at the ready will save you the trouble of having to be the expert on every area of law and regulation that you will encounter. At minimum, you need to have the numbers of four different types of attorneys on your speed dial: those specializing in employment (labor) law, contract law, tax law, and, of course, communication law.

Another resource that can help you keep track of changes in laws, regulations, and judicial interpretations is trade organizations. These organizations can be found for almost every industry, and they operate at different levels as well. For example, broadcasters are represented nationally by the National Association of Broadcasters (NAB), headquartered in Washington, D.C. The NAB serves broadcasters by lobbying for their interests in Congress and using a wide variety of communication media to keep member stations informed about developments or pending actions that could affect broadcast station operation.

Similarly, most states have their own state broadcast associations, such as the Texas Association of Broadcasters, which performs a similar role as the national organization, monitoring and representing broadcasters' interests in state laws and regulations. The motion picture industry has the Motion Picture Association of America, newspapers have state and local press organizations, and the cable television industry has the National Cable Television Association.

This chapter begins by exploring federal regulations, which are the most wide-ranging. Next is the state level, including a variety of taxes that concern media managers. The local level may also involve taxes, but also local zoning laws and other regulations governing where you can do business, what type of structures you can build, and even whether you are allowed to shoot video on public streets.

FEDERAL LAWS AND REGULATIONS

First Amendment

The cornerstone of U.S. communication law is the first amendment to the U.S. Constitution:

> Congress shall make no law respecting an establishment of religion, or prohibiting the free exercise thereof; or abridging the freedom of speech, or of the press; or the right of the people peaceably to assemble, and to petition the Government for a redress of grievances.

The "freedom of the press" protected by the First Amendment is not absolute. Courts have consistently found that certain types of speech, for example, political speech, are subject to less restriction that other types of speech – for example, commercial speech. The courts have also held that broadcasters do not have an absolute protection under the First Amendment because of a "doctrine of scarcity,"[1] the idea that because their waves are limited, the government must regulate the limited number of voices on those airwaves.

As a result, two distinct bodies of law have emerged governing media organizations: press law and broadcast law. But there is also a third body of law that must be considered: common carrier law. This is the body of law that applied to the telephone industry for its first century in the United States. It is interesting to note that common carrier law derived from railroad law. This evolution started when the first telegraph lines were strong alongside railroad tracks, so the same laws that applied to railroads, requiring them to publish their rates, or tariffs, charging the same rates to all comers on a first-come, first-served basis. When the telephone was invented and regulators were looking for laws to cover the telephone industry, the most logical set of laws were those governing the telegraph industry. As a result, the basic principles and many of the terms used in laws governing telephony were derived from the laws governing railroads. (You should know that many of the laws and regulations we deal with in the media industry are derived from similar historical accidents.)

Toward the end of the past century, legislators realized that the types of messages that could be communicated over the air, through wires, and through cables are more similar to each other than they are different. After decades of unsuccessfully attempting to unify these different bodies of law, Congress finally achieved success with the Telecommunications Act of 1996, which addressed a wide range of issues relating to broadcasting, cable television, telephony, and satellite communication.[2] It is not a coincidence that passage of the Telecommunications Act of 1996 corresponded with the rise of the Internet, the distribution medium that moved almost all media communication to digital formats, blurring the lines between traditional media and toward a converged media environment.

The basic provisions of the Telecommunications Act of 1996 include:

- Relaxation of ownership restrictions, allowing a company to own a larger combination of media outlets within a single medium
- Encouragement of additional competition in the media industries by allowing telephone companies to provide cable television service and cable television companies to provide telephone service
- Deregulation of cable television rates
- Other provisions designed to broadly encourage competition for advanced technologies in telecommunication[3]

As important as the Telecommunications Act of 1996 is, that act remains subordinate to the First Amendment, which remains the most important legal statement for American media. In recent years, the legal precedents derived from court cases testing the limits of the First Amendment have created a number of constraints that media managers must consider in the day-to-day operation of media organizations.

The greatest freedoms are afforded to journalists. Many journalists consider the most important freedom to be the limitations on prior restraint, the concept that the government cannot stop publication of information by the media. Although the First Amendment seems to prohibit prior restraint, Supreme Court decisions over the past 50 years indicate that information that threatens national security is subject to prior restraint by the government.[4]

Having the right to publish almost any other type of information does not mean that the media are not liable for any damage done by false or defamatory messages, but it means that such messages cannot be prohibited in advance except in the most dire of circumstances. Media organizations, including news organizations, are liable for damages if they are found to have libeled or slandered a person or company. Those in the media are responsible when they published false or embarrassing information about private individuals, although they have much greater protection when reporting information about public figures.[5]

If journalism receives more protection than other types of communication, the logical question is, "What is a journalist?" In an age where anyone can create a blog or call herself or himself a "citizen journalist," the legal definition of "journalist" has become an important consideration that will certainly be addressed in court cases over the next decade.

Another limitation on freedom of the press is related to "invasion of privacy." Although the word *privacy* is not explicitly found in the constitution, both federal and state courts have defined a "right of privacy" that protects individuals from intrusion into their private lives and appropriation of their name and likeness for commercial purposes.

The principle prohibiting intrusion is that a person has a reasonable expectation of privacy in most aspects of their daily life, including conduct within their home or other nonpublic place, private communication, and personal information. (But the right of privacy does not extend to actions in public.) Media organizations, along with everyone else, are prohibited from taking pictures, recording sound, or otherwise capturing information about a person when that person has a reasonable expectation of privacy.

The principle prohibiting appropriation is that a business may not use a person's name or likeness for commercial purposes without that person's consent. It must be noted that this limitation does not apply to news, underscoring the principle that journalistic content has more freedom and protections than commercial speech.

Copyright

Another body of regulation at the federal level concerns copyright laws. Ownership of media content is protected by copyright law. Copyright is one of the most complicated issues facing media managers because it governs the permissions that must be obtained before content is used. For example, U.S. copyright law provides a set of rules for content that is used or distributed in the United States, but other laws and regulations covering content distributed in other countries.

Although there have been numerous attempts to unify copyright law internationally, many countries, most noticeably the United States, maintain regulations and customs that are unique to those countries. For example, in most of the world, copyright law requires payment of music licenses for the broadcast of copyrighted music to the composers, artists, and producers of the music. But in the United States, broadcasters are required only to pay the composers (and lyricists) for using music on a radio or television program, with no payment to the artist. Another difference between countries is the term of copyright, which, in the United States, is the life of the author plus 70 years, or 95 years for work created for hire.

Internationally, most countries' copyright regulations comply with provisions of the Berne Convention and the Universal Copyright Convention, which have been negotiated to provide a set of common copyright rules worldwide. But each country has the right to adopt individual provisions of these copyright treaties, reject them, or create a new set of rules altogether.

On a practical level, the most common problem that media managers face related to copyright is knowing what rights they have to media content. Copyright law governs the payments that must be negotiated, but it does not specify the amount of those payments or other terms. Those provisions are usually part of the contracts that are negotiated when media content is licensed for distribution. For example, a television station can license a syndicated television program that may be broadcast on that station's assigned channel in that station's market. But, unless the contract specifically allows it, that program may not also be distributed by the station on its Web site. Similarly, a newspaper may license content from a news wire or a syndicated service, but that content may not also be published on the newspaper's Web site unless the contract specifically allows distribution in those additional media.

The challenge that media managers face in an era of converged media is that most media organizations no longer are limited to distributing their content to a small geographic area. Rather, content is distributed on Web sites, through email alerts, and even using "tweets," allowing users all over the world to enjoy the content.

Media organizations must therefore be aware of the reach of content distributed over the Web. A local newspaper that has offices in only one city does not need to worry about laws and other countries, but a multinational media organization must ensure that its web content follows all of the local rules for each country in which the content is distributed and consumed. One solution used by many organizations is the creation of separate Web sites for each country, not only using the local language, but also following the local laws and regulations, especially in regard to copyright and advertising.

The other major consideration with copyright law is that most media organizations also produce a plethora of media content, providing a resource that must be protected. In the United States, copyright protection is automatically granted to content when a new work is created, whether that "work" is a news story, photograph, video, or interactive presentation. This situation creates two opportunities for media managers. The first is that the managers have the opportunity to license use of work created by their organization to others, provided they have the appropriate rights in the employment agreements with their employees. The second is that the managers must conduct surveillance of media to ensure that their content is not being pirated and distributed by others. For example, anyone can record a piece of video off a television station and post it to YouTube, but YouTube is required to remove copyrighted content on request of the copyright holder. (In fact, in 2007, Viacom sued YouTube for $1 billion, claming that YouTube distributed more than 160,000 video clips of copyrighted content. Although that suit is still pending as this chapter goes to press in early 2010, YouTube quickly acted to remove Viacom's content from its servers. Viacom then posted this content, including clips from *The Daily Show with Jon Stewart*, on its own Web sites, where it could profit from distributing the content itself.)

Derivative Works

As discussed earlier in this chapter, laws and regulations are always subject to interpretation. One emerging area that has not been extensively addressed by the courts is the issue of derivative works. Derivative works are pieces of media content created by altering someone else's content. Consider a musical mash-up: the original pieces of music used in a mash-up are almost always copyrighted but the person creating the mash-up adds considerable creative input in selecting, editing, and arranging those works. The key question, then, is who owns the new work. Consider the iconic poster of President Barack Obama distributed during his election campaign with the word *hope*. The poster is an original work created by artist Shepard Fairey, but the work was based on a copyrighted photo from the Associated Press. The Associated Press claims to have an ownership interest in the poster. The suit is unresolved as this book goes to press in early 2010.[6]

From a legal perspective, there is no absolute percentage that content must be changed before it is considered a "new" work. With today's digital technology offering anyone the ability to edit, blend, and otherwise create new content from existing works, the right to create derivative works from copyrighted content will be the subject of a great deal of litigation for the foreseeable future. On a practical level, the solution is relatively simple: If someone in your organization is creating a derivative work from existing content it is best to get the permission from the copyright holder before the new work is distributed.

Other Areas of Federal Regulation

Almost any law or regulation that governs business in general effects media organizations. In this section, we will look at some of the most important federal regulations. But it should be noted that this list is not comprehensive.

It would be virtually impossible to discuss all laws, rules, and regulations pro-mulgated by the federal government in a single chapter. But this set will give you an example of the range of concerns for media managers:

Taxes: Among all powers of a government, the power to tax may be the most pervasive. At the federal level tax law is administered by the Internal Revenue Service. Any media organization, whether for profit or nonprofit, that receives revenue must file some type of return with the IRS.

Workplace safety: The Occupational Safety and Health Administration (OSHA) of the U.S. Department of Labor is charged with setting rules and regulations governing the safety of workers in the workplace. The goal of OSHA is to provide safe workplace and workplace conditions.

Labor relations: The National Labor Relations Board governs all aspects of unionization and collective bargaining in the workplace. If you work in a unionized operation, otherwise known as a *union shop*, you'll need to become familiar with the specific rules that govern your labor contracts and collective bargaining in general. But even if you work in an orga-nization that does not employ union labor, it is important to note that all workers have the right to organize and bargain collectively. The rules governing employer conduct are complex, so if the issue ever comes up, consult a labor relations attorney before doing anything else.

Financial reporting: If your company is a publicly held company – that is, its stock is offered for sale on a public stock exchange – you're subject to a variety of regulations regarding financial reporting that are promul-gated by the Securities and Exchange Commission. These rules govern when financial information must be released to the public, the nature of information that must be released, and the conduct of employees who have access to this information. For example, if you work for a company that is getting ready to report its earnings and you have inside infor-mation that the earnings are going to be much better than previously anticipated, so you expect the stock price to go up, it is illegal to act on that information by buying stock in your company before the public has access to the same information. Officers in publicly held companies are also subject to specific regulations regarding the accuracy of financial information that is reported to the public. Under the Sarbanes-Oxley Act, discussed in Chapter 5, a misleading earnings report can result in fines in or jail time for the corporate officer responsible.

Medical leave: If your organization employs more than 50 employees, those employees are entitled to request family and medical leave (without pay) for up to 3 months. While on family and medical leave, you're not allowed to permanently replace the employee, and the employee must return to his or her regular job or a like job at the original salary at the end of the leave.

Discrimination: The Department of Labor is in charge of enforcing antidiscrimination laws that are designed to prevent discrimination on the basis of age, sex, nationality, national origin, and sexual orientation. The same organization is also charged with promulgating rules preventing sexual or other forms of harassment in the workplace.

Advertising content: The Federal Trade Commission (FTC) promulgates regulations covering the content of advertising. These regulations are designed to prohibit false or misleading advertising.

Food and Drug Administration: The Food and Drug Administration (FDA) has responsibility similar to the FTC and governing advertising content, but its jurisdiction is limited to food and drugs.

Aviation: Many media organizations must also be concerned with regulations from the Federal Aviation Administration (FAA). The FAA governs the construction of the towers used by radio and television stations and cable television systems. Any structure that could be a hazard to aviation must be approved by the FAA and must use nighttime illumination to prevent towers from becoming a hazard to aviation.

Broadcast: Broadcasters are subject to more regulation than any other communications medium in the United States. Using the rationale that the amount of broadcast spectrum is limited, and therefore it is impossible for everyone who wants a broadcast license to have one, the courts have ruled that broadcasters do not enjoy all of the freedoms the First Amendment provides to other media, such as newspapers. For example, the courts have consistently held that the government may not exercise "prior restraint" with newspapers, prohibiting them in advance from publishing information unless that information threatens national security. But broadcasters have long been subject to a variety of rules that govern their content. For example, under the Children's Television Act of 1990, broadcasters are required to devote at least 3 hours a week to educational or informational children's television programming. Broadcasters are also required to sell time to any legally qualified candidate for federal office. Also the rates the broadcasters may charge for political advertising are controlled by the federal government. Within 45 days of a primary election and 60 days of the general election, broadcasters may not charge any politician a higher rate than the lowest rate paid by any other advertiser on the station.

In order to obtain an FCC license for a radio or television station in the United States, an individual or organization must first identify a vacant part of the spectrum in which a new station could broadcast without interfering with existing stations. In most parts of the country, especially the most populated, virtually all available spectrum was captured long ago. In the rare case that a new channel is identified, there are two steps to the process of starting a new station. First, the FCC has to agree that the channel is available in that area, and second, the FCC must select from all qualified applicants the one that will be allowed to operate a station on the channel. In the early days of broadcasting, the winner of the license was selected using a process known as a *comparative hearing* in which any person or organization that wanted the license could apply for it and make an argument that they would be the best steward of the public airwaves. Those rules were replaced in the 1980s by a lottery system in which the winner of the frequency was selected at random. Today, an auction procedure is held in which the company or person willing to pay the most for the right to broadcast receives the license.

If your company operates a broadcast facility, you're subject to a variety of reporting requirements by the FCC. In addition to reporting any changes in ownership or control of the organization, you must file periodic reports demonstrating your compliance with the Children's Television Act of 1990, demonstrating that you have ascertained and served the needs of your community and that you have followed the FCC's employment regulations. The FCC also charges regulatory fees that are related to the type of station and market served.

Broadcasters are also subject to a special set of regulations regarding the distribution of indecent content. First, it should be noted that there is a difference between "indecency" and "obscenity." Legally, *indecency* is defined as content that may be offensive, but is still protected by the First Amendment. *Obscenity*, on the other hand, has been defined as "(a) whether the average person, applying contemporary community standards' would find that the work, taken as a whole, appeals to the prurient interest, (b) whether the work depicts or describes, in a patently offensive way, sexual conduct specifically defined by the applicable state law, and (c) whether the work, taken as a whole, lacks serious literary, artistic, political, or scientific value."[7]

The courts have consistently held that it is illegal to distribute obscene content in any medium, but the courts have provided a broad range of protection for indecent content. At one point, Congress attempted to outlaw the broadcast of indecent content completely, but the courts held that such a broad prohibition on the distribution of legal speech was a violation of the First Amendment. What has emerged is a set of regulations identifying a "safe harbor," with indecent content prohibited on broadcast stations between 6:00 a.m. and 10:00 p.m., but allowed between 10:00 p.m. and 6:00 a.m.

Satellite television and satellite radio are also governed by the FCC, but not to the extent that broadcasters are. In the United States, satellite providers must be licensed to prevent interference between services, and content regulations for these subscription services are much less stringent than for over-the-air broadcasting, ostensibly because a person would not receive the subscription content unless they specifically request it.

Cable television is also regulated by the FCC, although not to the same extent the broadcast stations are. Cable regulations governing the right of broadcasters to control whether their signals are distributed on cable systems, ownership and reach of cable systems, nondiscriminatory provision of programming to all multichannel video service providers, and a limited set of technical standards.

Special Rules for Internet Organizations

As an emerging medium, the Internet has been the target of many regulatory attempts, but, at this writing, content distribution over the Internet is less regulated than almost any medium except newspapers. Advertising on the Internet is subject to the same rules and restrictions that apply to any other medium. In fact, in 2009, there was enough concern about misleading blog entries and other Internet content that the FTC proposed a set of rules governing the disclosure of payments or gifts to the operators of Internet sites and blogs.

The distribution in the United States of unsolicited commercial email, more commonly known as "spam," is governed by the CAN-SPAM (Controlling the Assault of Non-Solicited Pornography and Marketing) Act, implemented in 2004 by the FTC. These rules require identification of unsolicited advertising messages specific about information and disclosure of the sender's identity.[8]

Other attempts to regulate the Internet have not been as successful. The Communications Decency Act, passed in 1996, attempted to prohibit the distribution of obscene or indecent content to minors over the Internet, but the CDA was later thrown out by the courts for being overly broad.[9]

One of the biggest challenges in distributing content over the Internet is the global reach of the Web. Once posted on the Internet, content is available to any computer in the world with Internet access unless that region has specifically been blocked from receiving the content. With no international regulation of the Internet, scammers, pirates, and purveyors of questionable content are able to set up servers in jurisdictions with lax regulations, and then deliver content, games, or information services almost anywhere in the world.

The only consistent control over Web sites is related to the provision of web URLs. The Internet Corporation for the Assignment of Names and Numbers, ICANN, is the governing authority for the domain names system that allows companies and individuals to own specific web addresses.

STATE

Virtually any type of regulation that can be passed at the federal level could also be passed to the state level, but as a practical matter, most states do not choose to regulate as many aspects of business operation as the federal government does.

As with federal regulation, the most common state regulations involve taxes. These taxes take a variety of forms, from corporate income taxes and franchise taxes, to workers' compensation taxes. State taxes vary widely throughout the United States, and many corporations choose to incorporate in a state that has favorable tax rules rather than the state in which their primary operations are located. But, regardless of where the company is headquartered, if your company has offices and generates income in a state, you will need to comply with that state's requirements for income reporting and tax payment.

A special consideration is sales taxes. Most states charge sales tax on retail purchases, and those companies that charge for content that is distributed over the Internet are liable for paying state sales tax if the company has a physical presence in the state in which a purchase is made. As of early 2010, there is no requirement for collection of sales taxes from states in which a company does not have a physical presence, but that loophole could be closed at any time.

Every state has labor laws that govern the treatment of employees working in that state. Thes e laws vary widely from state to state. For example, many states are considered "right to work" states, in which employers are free to dismiss an employee for almost any reason, except for those prohibited by law, without notice. These states also allow employees the choice of joining a union or not when the workplace is unionized. On the other hand, in "closed shop" states an employee may be required to join the union in order to work in the unionized organization. You must thus make sure you familiarize yourself with the employment laws in every state in which your organization employs workers.

Within each state, there are counterparts to each of the three levels discussed for the federal government: the state legislature, state regulatory agencies, and state courts. Each of these has the power to create laws, rules, or interpretations that govern the way you conduct your day-to-day business.

LOCAL

Local laws and regulations rarely deal with media organizations in particular, but govern a number of concerns that media organizations must face the same as any business. These include taxes, property assessment, zoning, and employment.

As with federal and state government, the most important daily concern with local government is probably taxes. Most states require payment of property taxes on a company's real property, including real estate, vehicles, equipment, and inventories. The amount of property tax you pay is dependent upon the value assigned to your property by the local tax assessor. Fighting for a lower assessment of your real property can, for example, result in a savings of thousands of dollars per year or more.

The physical location of your offices can also be governed by local zoning laws, which control where residences, businesses, institutions, manufacturing, and other facilities may be placed, as well as a variety of other considerations relating to public access to your building.

A DAY IN THE LIFE OF BRAD WILLIAMS

FIGURE 14-1 Brad Williams

Brad Williams Vice President, Strategic Accounts – National Association of Broadcasters

Brad joined the NAB (National Association of Broadcasters) in 1997 as an Account Executive in Sponsorship and Advertising. This was followed by positions as Director of Sponsorship and Advertising, Director of Business Development, Vice President, Member Benefits and Business Development and his current position as Vice President, Strategic Accounts. Brad manages the NAB Show's strategic partners, which includes most of the show's largest exhibitors. He is also charged with business development for the Conventions and

Business Operations department, which manages the NAB Show and numerous other NAB events. Prior to NAB, Brad directed the marketing program and sponsorship sales for the Marine Corps Marathon, one of the highest rated and largest marathons in the world. Brad has a MS degree in Sports Management from Georgia Southern University and a BS degree in Communications from James Madison University. Brad serves on the Alumni Advisory Council for JMU's School of Media and Arts Design. Brad and his wife, Jennifer, have three children and live in Virginia. In addition to family time and work, Brad enjoys playing sports and is involved in a number of church activities.

What Does a Typical Day Look Like with Brad Williams?

Multitasking. I am responsible for a number of NAB Show projects and various business development initiatives. I could be working on researching, identifying and securing a new software vendor for the NAB Show, finalizing details for our foray into virtual events, on strategy calls with our leading exhibitors, or researching market trends in relation to the NAB Show.

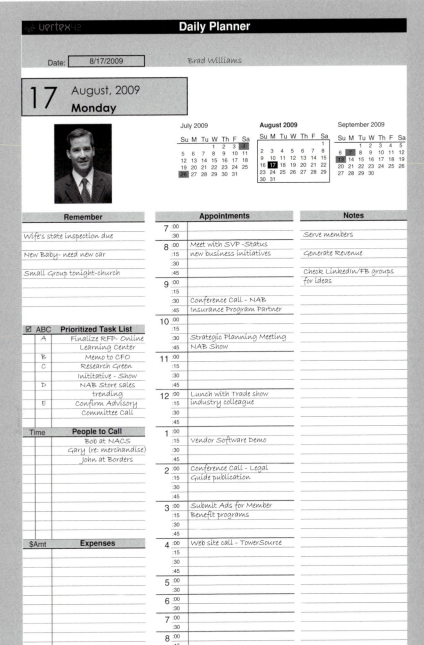

Daily Planner

Date: 8/17/2009   Brad Williams

17 August, 2009
Monday

July 2009	August 2009	September 2009
Su M Tu W Th F Sa	Su M Tu W Th F Sa	Su M Tu W Th F Sa
1 2 3 4	1	1 2 3 4 5
5 6 7 8 9 10 11	2 3 4 5 6 7 8	6 7 8 9 10 11 12
12 13 14 15 16 17 18	9 10 11 12 13 14 15	13 14 15 16 17 18 19
19 20 21 22 23 24 25	16 17 18 19 20 21 22	20 21 22 23 24 25 26
26 27 28 29 30 31	23 24 25 26 27 28 29	27 28 29 30
	30 31	

Remember

Wife's state inspection due

New Baby- need new car

Small Group tonight-church

Prioritized Task List

☑ ABC	
A	Finalize RFP- Online Learning Center
B	Memo to CFO
C	Research Green Inititative - Show
D	NAB Store sales trending
E	Confirm Advisory Committee Call

People to Call

Time	
	Bob at NACS
	Gary (re: merchandise)
	John at Borders

Expenses

$Amt	

Appointments

7	:00	
	:30	
8	:00	Meet with SVP -Status
	:15	new business initiatives
	:30	
	:45	
9	:00	
	:15	
	:30	Conference Call - NAB
	:45	Insurance Program Partner
10	:00	
	:15	
	:30	Strategic Planning Meeting
	:45	NAB Show
11	:00	
	:15	
	:30	
	:45	
12	:00	Lunch with Trade show
	:15	industry colleague
	:30	
	:45	
1	:00	
	:15	Vendor Software Demo
	:30	
	:45	
2	:00	Conference Call - Legal
	:15	Guide publication
	:30	
	:45	
3	:00	Submit Ads for Member
	:15	Benefit programs
	:30	
	:45	
4	:00	Web site call - TowerSource
	:15	
	:30	
	:45	
5	:00	
	:30	
6	:00	
	:30	
7	:00	
	:30	
8	:00	
	:15	
	:30	
9	:00	
	:30	

Notes

Serve members

Generate Revenue

Check LinkedIn/FB groups
for ideas

Continued...

How Does Your Typical Day Begin?
I arrive to work 2 hours before most of my colleagues, do some quick email work, then turn my focus to a project that requires my full attention such as a business plan, a proposal, a memo, or budgets. This may be the only time of the day when I have an extended period of time without disruption.

What Is the First Thing on Your Agenda?
Prioritize my day and send out necessary email requests in situations where I need input, data, or answers from colleagues. Put a deadline on every request in an effort to set expectations and keep projects moving.

Whom Do You Interact With?
I have an interesting position at NAB in that I interact with a broad range of people internally and externally. Internally, I work primarily with our Conventions and Business Operations group, but also with the various departments that support our events such as the Radio, TV, and Science & Technology departments. The only department I have little interaction with is our Government Relations group, which is wholly focused on broadcast lobbying efforts on Capitol Hill. I also work with these partners and the entire exhibitor base to create new opportunities to connect them with their customers. A good bit of my focus during the summer months is identifying the new players within the trade show technology space. With the NAB Show, we aim to provide cutting edge technology to our attendees and a show experience above all others. My focus is either on serving our show partners and advancing their business goals, or it is on a new revenue initiative. If a project is not related to generating revenue, then it is not on my plate. Externally, I work with our show partners such as Sony, Panasonic, Harris, Avid, etc., to ensure the NAB Show is serving their needs.

What Are Some of the Most Challenging Issues You Face?
Building the relationship with our top clients to a point where they view me as a valuable resource for their strategic planning. Funding new ventures is always a challenge. Keeping abreast of new technologies. Identifying the next big thing to showcase at your event when your show is still six to twelve months out. Getting the various internal and stakeholders to weigh in on new ideas and then buy in to new projects. You have to have your facts and projections ready and the ability to win over stakeholders.

Describe the Highlights of Your Workday.
When my kids call me to say "Hi Daddy!" On a daily basis, talking ideas with co-workers. I enjoy taking ideas from concept to the marketplace. Seeing a project develop, and others embracing it, is a highly rewarding experience. The feeling of camaraderie when you work toward common goals. I also get to do a lot of research in new media and social networking, which is an exciting and fast-paced industry.

How Do You End Your Day?
Before leaving the office, I set my priorities for the next day. Then, after putting the kids to bed, it's one last e-mail check.

Discuss Any After-Hours Responsibilities.
Outside of some emails and occasional paperwork when the workload is heavy, I try to keep my after-hour responsibilities to a minimum in an effort to dedicate that time and my undivided attention to my family. Most of my after-hours work comes at our events and trade shows. You can expect to work from sun up to sun down when on the show site, but the excitement of seeing months of hard work come together overrides the exhaustion. I think many trade show professionals are addicted to that feeling.

CYCLES OF REGULATION

Throughout the history of media organizations in the United States, there has been a continuing cycle of regulation and reregulation. For example, the twentieth century began with minimal regulations over electronic media, primarily because these media didn't exist prior to that time. The Federal Radio Act of 1927 and the Communications Act of 1934 heralded half a century of regulation in which increasingly complex rules were created for these new electronic media. That cycle ended in the 1980s with the advent of deregulation coinciding with the Reagan administration. One good example is the change in the rules that traditionally prohibited a company from owning more than seven

AM radio stations, seven FM radio stations, and seven television stations. In the 1980s, the rules were gradually relaxed, allowing the creation of increasingly large media conglomerates such as Clear Channel Radio and Citadel Broadcasting, each of which owned hundreds of radio stations.

If history is a guide, we should expect the return of a cycle of regulation sometime early in this century, followed later by another cycle of deregulation.

INTERNATIONAL MEDIA REGULATIONS

As of early 2010, there is no single organization charged with creating media regulations on a global basis. But there are a number of international agencies responsible for coordinating global regulatory efforts. These include:

- International copyright: Although there is no "international copyright law" per se, treaties between countries provide a limited protection for intellectual property. Each country has its own laws that govern copyright, and it is necessary to be aware of the local laws when creating or distributing media in any country. But there is limited protection to copyrighted works offered by the Berne convention for the Protection of Literary and Artistic Works (more commonly known as the "Berne Convention") and the Universal Copyright Convention (UCC). These treaties apply only to the countries that have signed them, and protection of work copyrighted in one country may be a function of providing notice of the copyright and awareness of when unauthorized copies are made.
- International telecommunications union: an agency of the United Nations responsible for coordinating the allocation of radio frequency spectrum used for radio, television, satellite, and telephony
- ICANN: As discussed earlier, the Internet Corporation for the Assignment of Names and Numbers coordinates the domain name system used for the World Wide Web, resolving disputes regarding ownership of domain names and related issues.

SUMMARY

Media organizations are subject to laws and regulations originating at all levels of government. Many of these regulations relate specifically to media organizations, but there are just as many, if not more, regulations that govern the conduct of business in general. Media managers are responsible for keeping up with all of these regulations, ranging from tax and labor law copyright law. Fortunately, we have the assistance of a broad range of trade organizations and legal experts that play an important role in helping us cope with the rapid pace of change in law and regulation.

CASE STUDY 14.1 NEWS FOR SALE

The United States has several federal agencies in place that are specifically created to protect the rights of its citizens. Within the communications industry, there exists one of the more well-known agencies, the Federal Communications Commission or the FCC. Most are familiar with the FCC's regulations placed upon the broadcasting industry that may include profanity or nudity resulting in substantial fines if proven. Perhaps more interesting are those cases where the violations are not as clear or fall into a gray area. In this case study, carefully walk through each of these steps and decide for yourself whether there appears to be a violation.

Kerry Johnson has been working for WNNN Television for the past 7 years. Over that time, she has worked her way up to handling some of the most lucrative agencies in the business. It has been a tough year and Kerry's managers have been pushing for her and the other account executives to develop creative campaigns to generate new or additional revenues. So far, their efforts have proven to be minimal, but indeed have been generating some new smaller accounts.

Kerry is one of the brightest AEs on the staff and prides herself in garnering the top shares of business from some of the top advertising agencies in her market. She is especially proud of her ability to work closely with the Ads Up agency, which handles a large group of fast-food restaurants in her market.

When Kerry receives an email from the media buyer, Jan Cummings, from the Ads Up agency, she is sure to handle the avail request immediately. Looking over the request from the advertising agency, Kerry discovers that Jan is requesting several "value-added" items in order to get on the advertising buy, such as bonus spots, a free promotion, and guaranteed news coverage of a grand opening at their newest location. Kerry knows that it is most important that she gets good rates to Jan and does not yet address the "value-added" request. After negotiating a few rounds, Kerry realizes that some of the rates are lower than she would normally go, but she has worked closely with the sales manager to get on this buy and now the manager is expecting another big share.

Jan then inquires as to how WNNN plans on handling the "value-added" items. Kerry advises Jan that she will work on providing some bonus spots, but they can not guarantee the news coverage. Jan is adamant that if she does not guarantee the grand opening event, there will be no advertising buy with her station. Kerry's competitive nature sets in and she agrees to speak with her manager about this stipulation. Kerry's manager takes a look at the request and recognizes that the TV station cannot "guarantee" news coverage of this event. However, the sales manager, Donald, realizes that the station needs to make money and makes a quick call down to the news director. Without disclosing information about the advertising buy, he provides details about the grand opening to see whether the news director finds the story newsworthy. When Dan, the news director, asks about the date of the sale and how it is newsworthy, WNNN's sales manager explains that this grand opening event will make a great story because it is the first restaurant to open in this area of town in the past 10 years, an area of town that the station has covered quite a bit recently and this would seem to make for a much needed positive story. Dan agrees and asks that they send down a press release to the Assignment Desk. Donald advises Kerry to tell Jan that they will cover the story.

Kerry is thrilled and advises the media buyer that WNNN is set to cover the grand opening. Jan moves forward with placing the advertising buy and provides a detailed press release to Kerry for their newsroom. The details of the requested news coverage include information about where to park the live truck and the name of the new restaurant's regional manager, who will be available for interviews and details about the positive impact this new location will have on this area of the city. This will make it all very easy for the news reporter who is assigned the story. On the date of the "Grand Opening," a news reporter is assigned the story by the news director. The reporter is provided with the press release, who then sets up a live shot and an interview with the regional manager and shows some of the featured food items. The following day, Kerry makes a copy of the newscast and sends it to Jan as proof of performance. Two weeks later, Jan contacts Kerry and lets her know how happy the client was with the last advertising buy and that they would like to place another schedule with WNNN, unlike one of the other stations in the market who refused to "guarantee" the news coverage. "Oh well, their loss," exclaims Kerry.

Assignment

1. In reading this scenario, were you able to identify any actions that could be deemed unethical or illegal? If so, which one, and is it considered illegal or unethical?
2. Go to http://www.fcc.org and research any topics that may pertain to this story.

3. If you were the TV station that did not get on the television buy, how would you handle this situation?

4. If a complaint was filed against WNNN, how could it be proven? Who would be held responsible?

5. If you are the GM of WNNN and a complaint is filed, how would you respond?

6. Summarize your thoughts on this case and determine whether the station was within its legal rights to air a news story.

7. How can managers prevent any questions or potential scenarios that the FCC may find in violation?

REFERENCES

1. *Red Lion Broadcasting Co. v. Federal Communications Commission*, 395 U.S. 367 (1969).

2. Telecommunications Act of 1996, Pub. L. No. 104-104, 110 Stat. 56 (1996). Retrieved October 10, 2009, from http://www.fcc.gov/Reports/tcom1996.pdf.

3. Berquist, L. (2008). Communication technology and policy. In A. E. Grant & J. H. Meadows (Eds.), *Communication technology update and fundamentals*, 11th Ed. Boston: Focal Press.

4. See *New York Times v. U.S.*; *U.S. v. Washington Post*, 713 U.S. 403 (1973), and *U.S. v. Progressive*, 467 F. Supp. 990 (1979).

5. See *New York Times Co. v. Sullivan*, 376 U.S. 254 (1964).

6. *Fairey v. The Associated Press*, 09-01123 (S.D.N.Y., Complaint filed Feb. 9, 2009).

7. *Miller v. California*, 413 U.S. 15, 93 S. Ct. 2607, 37 L. Ed. 2d 419.

8. The CAN-SPAM Act: A compliance guide for business. Accessed October 22, 2009, at http://www.ftc.gov/bcp/edu/pubs/business/ecommerce/bus61.shtm.

9. Napoli, P. M. (2001). *Foundations of communications policy: Principles and process in the regulation of electronic media*. Cresskill, NJ: Hampton Press.

CHAPTER 15

Ethical Issues

*Chris Roberts, Ph.D., **August E. Grant, Ph.D.

*Assistant Professor, University of Alabama, **Professor, University of South Carolina

Divorced from ethics, leadership is reduced to management and politics to mere technique.

James MacGregor Burns, presidential biographer and author of *Leadership* (HarperCollins, 1978)

Always do right – this will gratify some and astonish the rest.

Samuel "Mark Twain" Clemens, 1901

CHAPTER OBJECTIVES

The objective of this chapter is to provide you with information about:
- The nature of ethics
  - The difference between ethics and morality
  - The peculiar nature of media ethics and its competing demands
  - How what's legal is not necessarily what's right
  - Codes of ethics useful but not a panacea
- The Potter Box: A systematic approach to ethical decision making
  - Define facts
  - Identify values
  - Consider ethical principles
  - Balance loyalties
  - Limits to the Potter Box
- Specific considerations of ethics and the following:
  - Entertainment
  - News
  - Sales
  - Content ownership/distribution
  - User-generated content

387

You are general manager of FMRX, the second-ranked television station in the three-station market of Freedonia. Your station hopes to make a move on the top-rated station by introducing *Good Morning, Freedonia*, the area's first local news/entertainment show. It will be expensive to add the staff and equipment needed to produce a 90-minute weekday show, and in these difficult economic times, you expect that the program may not break even within its first 2 years. Your career may be riding on the decision: If the program is not profitable by then, the bean counters at your corporate headquarters might fire you.

Your advertising director says he has a way to make the show profitable within 9 months: Let the advertising department sell product placements in one or two "soft" segments in the program each day. Local car dealers and area restaurants are among potential clients who would be eager to pay for host-sponsored segments that highlight their products and services, your ad manager tells you.

Your station's news director hates the idea, saying that it violates the news directors' code of ethics. The news director is worried that an anchor who sings the praises of a restaurant client one day might have to report a story about a deadly salmonella outbreak there the next day, which would hurt the credibility of the news department.

What do you do?

Though Freedonia is the fictional country in the Marx Brothers' 1933 movie *Duck Soup*, the *Good Morning, Freedonia* case study is similar to real dilemmas that faced several general managers at stations across the United States. The word *dilemma* – derived from a Greek phrase that translates as "double proposition" – may not be the best word choice, because many decisions are not binary, yes-or-no decisions. This case study has no simple solution, but it is the type of bottom-line decision you might face one day as a media manager/ entrepreneur as you balance your beliefs and goals against economic realities.

Further complicating matters is the fact that most media managers believe that the messages their organizations produce include intrinsic societal values that are different from, but at least as important as, their dollars-and-cents value in the marketplace. That implies that it may be harder to manage a media operation than, say, a department store, because your product often is inexorably tied to your own sense of worth and values, as well as the worth and values of society. Yet those intrinsic values must be balanced against the reality that media organizations do not survive unless they (at a minimum) pay for themselves or turn a profit for their owners. Most media organizations are parts of conglomerates whose underlying ethic is based on Pareto Optimality, an economic theory that "assumes a social state is optimal when no one's utility can be raised without reducing the utility of someone else."[1] This assumes that a business's key contribution to society comes when it maximizes its profits. Hosmer states it more plainly: "Profit maximization, again according to management, is the only moral standard needed for management."[2] No wonder, then, that the varied and competing interests of today's media organizations make many managers feel like the guy at Venice Beach who juggles a roaring chainsaw, a 10-pound bowling ball, and a navel orange.

Although the *Good Morning, Freedonia* case study comes with concrete ramifications involving money and jobs, it is ultimately a choice about ethics. You must decide whether, or to what extent, you would trade the credibility of your news organization for money (and, maybe, to keep your job). The study of ethics is the study of character and the decision-making processes that influence our morality. Although it's easy to confuse "ethics" with "morality," the two are not the same. *Ethics* comes from the Greek word meaning "character," and it has ties to the word for *custom*. The word *morality* comes from the Latin word for "mores," or behavior.[3] Black and Bryant suggest you think that ethics is behavior above the neck, while morality is behavior below the neck.[4] Simply put, how we think about ethics – our values, our conscience, our sense of right and wrong – helps determine how we act.

When thinking about ethics or any other tough decision, it's useful to start with what we agree upon. Ethicist Cliff Christians has long argued for a global media ethic based on what he calls *protonorms* – concepts of good that are rooted in universal human understanding. Atop that list is the sacredness of human life, which he says necessarily leads to moral actions that require us to respect dignity, honesty, and nonviolence.[5] Yet even when we buy into these fundamental standards, the world remains closer to charcoal than black or white, because even these standards can compete with one another. (Is there ever a time when telling the truth should take a backseat to human dignity, for example? Is there ever a time to be violent? Are there individuals who are so evil that we should not hold their lives as sacred?) These top-line values provide a good place to start, but they may not be sufficient in helping us make day-to-day decisions.

Agreeing upon ethical standards can also be difficult, because of the influences of the prevailing cultural standards of our nation and region. Often times, the ethical standards of a culture have more to do with tradition or religion and nothing to do with universal protonorms and ethics. For example, men wear short pants in warm weather in the United States, and you see people wearing shorts in advertisements for shorts and for products that have nothing to do with shorts. In the West African nation of Senegal, however, shorts are taboo except when taking part in the national sports of wrestling and soccer. An advertisement in Senegal showing a man wearing shorts would draw howls of protest, despite a tropical climate that seems perfect for shorts. There's no inherent universal goodness or badness when it comes to wearing shorts; the differences in culture and the influence of religion produce the differences in perceptions. Clearly, then, ethics are tied into our society's values, and those values vary by society and seem subject to change.

Our ethical decisions are further influenced by our choice of media organizations and, to a lesser extent, the individual characteristics of the mass media channel. For example, newspaper journalists who create composite characters and invent scenes in news stories likely would lose their jobs, but filmmakers do it all the time with movies that are "based on a true story." Both seek to tell the "truth," but traditional newspaper journalists feel a moral obligation to facts, yet filmmakers may feel an obligation to a metaphysical truth in which facts might intrude on larger truths (not to mention the need to entertain). Or we may be in the business of producing sex- and violence-filled messages that would make our grandmothers blush or bring premature knowledge to a 9-year-old, but we are able to live with ourselves through the knowledge of our First Amendment freedoms and the belief that it ultimately is the responsibility of a viewer or parent to decide whether to consume our messages. Or we may be in a public relations job that requires us to spin a message in a way that may not be 100 percent truthful but will make our client look good. To live with ourselves and reduce the uncomfortable cognitive dissonance between our ethics and our actions,[6] we decide whether to stay in our chosen communication field by agreeing with the prevailing standards, to find a different line of work because we cannot live with those standards, to work within the system to change those standards, or live a life of quiet desperation by staying in a field whose standards we don't agree with but are afraid to challenge.

With help from the *Good Morning, Freedonia* case study, we'll spend this chapter thinking about ethics and describing good and bad ways to make ethical decisions. What we won't do is give you an answer, because ethics rarely offers tidy solutions. Well-meaning people can reach different decisions that they can fully justify to themselves and to others. What's important is that we make our decisions only after clear thinking – not just ad hoc (Latin meaning "for this purpose") decisions where we quickly shoot from the hip or rely on the prejudices of history or of moralizing. In this chapter, we will think about the process of thinking, and we will help you identify your ethical standards. We will introduce a systematic way to guide you in thinking – but, ultimately, you must make your own choices.

FOLLOW THE LAW?

When facing an ethical choice, our first response may be to focus on the law. This is particularly true for mass communicators, who revel in the freedom of the First Amendment. Even though "Congress shall make no law … abridging the freedom of speech, or of the press," lawmakers have made plenty of laws that restrict an absolute right to free speech. Speech judged to libel or unfairly invade another person's privacy can lead to multimillion-dollar verdicts, and multiple federal agencies regulate commercial speech. Pornography is generally legal, but porn involving children is illegal, and pornography that fails the Miller Test created by the Supreme Court* is labeled obscene and therefore illegal.

Yet relying on what is legal is not sufficient when it comes to questions of ethics, because a perfectly legal message may not be perfectly ethical. Because of its potential effects on society through its depiction and treatment of women, pornography often is a question of ethics, not law. Plenty of television shows appeal to our base instincts in order to draw as large an audience as possible, but can appealing to the lowest common denominator always be justified? A news story with incorrect facts about a politician or a public figure may not be judged libelous because of the higher burden of proof in a libel case, but the story remains wrong.

Obeying laws seems reasonable, as we can agree that it's generally in society's best interest when people follow the rules. There are times, however, when you can argue like Mr. Bumble (from Chapter 51 of *Oliver Twist* by Charles Dickens) that "the law is a[n] ass – a[n] idiot." Segregation was the law in parts of the United States through the 1960s, but many high-principled people believed Jim Crow laws were unethical and were willing to risk jail, beatings, and death when they followed their ethical beliefs and disobeyed. As a journalist, you may be willing to risk jail by refusing a judge's order to reveal a confidential source. As an advertiser, you may risk a fine by publishing an ad that breaks a content-based rule you believe violates your First Amendment right to free speech. These times are rare, and most of the time we are doing the right thing by obeying the law.

Simply obeying a law, however, does not mean you have made an ethically sound decision. Ethics are not necessarily about law, which can best be described as the agreed-upon bright lines that define the outer limits of acceptable behavior. Take, for example, federal laws that forbid tobacco ads on television or on billboards within 1,000 feet of a public school.[7] Society has decided that in order to protect impressionable children it is reasonable to restrict the free speech rights of companies that make legal products. But some argue that high-sugar, high-fat foods also are bad for children's health, yet no law restricts cereal makers from advertising their products to children. That means the maker of Chocolate Frosted Sugar Bombs (the cereal from the "Calvin and Hobbes" comic strip) could bombard children with ads for a nutrition-free product that tastes like "eating a bowl of Milk Duds."[8]

---

* The Miller Test, created by the Supreme Court's 1973 ruling in the *Miller v. California* lawsuit, says speech is obscene if the average person, "applying contemporary community standards, would find that the work, taken as a whole, appeals to the prurient interest," if it depicts or describes sexual activity or excretory functions (according to state laws) in a "patently offensive way," or if taken as a whole lacks "serious literary, artistic, political or scientific value."

Moreover, there's no law that says the maker of Chocolate Frosted Sugar Bombs could not use bikini-clad models when advertising to children. But cereal companies don't use sex to sell children's cereal – not only because they figure those ads would be ineffective or unethical, but because they also know they could expect a backlash of bad publicity and boycotts by moms and other do-gooders. Kellogg's, McDonald's, General Mills, and others went so far as to stop children-targeted ads for foods that fail to meet their tighter nutritional guidelines. They did so voluntarily, the *New York Times* noted in a June 2007 story,[9] not just because it was the right thing to do but because they faced lawsuits and federal regulation. In short, those food companies could not rely on laws (and ultimately did not want laws) that told them what to do. In reality, laws rarely come into play when we make ethical decisions. It's necessary to consider the applicable laws when making an ethical decision, but it's clearly not sufficient because ethics asks "should I?" and not "is it legal?" Thinking about law does us little good in the case of *Good Morning, Freedonia*, because no law forbids a TV station from blurring the lines between editorial and advertising. A quote attributed to Plato summed it up nicely: "Good people do not need laws to tell them to act responsibly, while bad people will find a way around the laws."

FOLLOW A CODE OF ETHICS?

If laws offer limited help when we must make decisions about ethics, what about codes of ethics? Organizations representing journalists, broadcasters, advertisers, public relations practitioners, bloggers,[10] and the adult entertainment business[11] have published codes of ethics that spell out the minimum expectations and the highest values of their members. Those codes serve as ethical trailheads to newcomers and as a public relations tool to show outsiders that the organization's members take ethics seriously. But as Black, Steele, and Barney point out, "the best codes have built-in limitations"[12] because they cannot anticipate every situation.

In thinking about our *Good Morning, Freedonia* case study, codes may be useful in reminding us that not everyone thinks it's OK to blur the line between editorial and advertising. The American Society of Magazine Editors' ethical guidelines call for editorial integrity "to make sure that the difference between advertising and editorial content is transparent to readers and that there is no advertiser influence or pressure on editorial independence."[13] The Radio Television News Association's code (2000) says journalists should be sure to "[r]ecognize that sponsorship of the news will not be used in any way to determine, restrict, or manipulate content."[14] The Society of Professional Journalists says its members should "[d]istinguish news from advertising and shun hybrids that blur the lines between the two."[15] Still, plenty of magazines blur the line – some even sell the cover to advertisers – and some television stations sell product placement segments inside of newscasts.[16] They do so with only the savviest media consumer knowing that this is taking place, although in some cases federal regulators require broadcasters to make clear that a product placement (or its public relations equivalent, a video news release) is included in a show. Some stations include the disclaimer during the segment; others wait to include it in the closing credits, which raises yet another ethical issue.

The journalism, television news, and magazine codes say that blurring the line is bad, but the codes cannot stop the station from selling product placements in its newscasts. Codes of ethics are voluntary. Media practitioners do not have to join the trade group to practice the trade, and the worst the trade group can do is kick out the transgressors. (Some academics say communication is not a true "profession," like law or medicine, in part because anyone can be a mass communicator in a nation that has no legal barriers to entry.) Codes of ethics, then, ultimately offer limited help when making an ethical decision and are often unenforced and unenforceable when broken. Clearly, then, a better approach is needed than relying on law and codes when making ethics-related decisions.

THINKING ETHICALLY: INTRODUCING THE POTTER BOX

With few exceptions, mass media ethics textbooks[†] borrow a decision-making strategy proposed by Ralph Benajah Potter, Jr., a Presbyterian minister who taught from 1965–2003 at Harvard Divinity School.[17] His doctoral dissertation began as an effort to delineate a Christian position on nuclear weapons, but he found that he could not land on a single justification because multiple "elements of belief were coming together in the establishment of people's concrete decisions about what ought to be done."[18] To work through the ambiguity, he found himself sorting his notes on the topic into four piles,

---

† The three most used media ethics textbooks use the Potter Box to help students manage the decision-making process. *Media ethics: Cases and moral reasoning* (Pearson, 2005) and *Media ethics: Issues and cases* (McGraw-Hill, 2004) both rely heavily on the Potter model. *Ethics in media communications: Cases and controversies* (Thomson Higher Education, 2006) concatenates the Potter model into what author Louis Alva Day calls the "SAD formula" – situation definition; analysis of the situation, including the application of moral theories; the decision, or ethical judgment. Another variation of the Potter Box is the "point of decision" pyramid described by *Contemporary media ethics: A practical guide for students, scholars and professionals* (Marquette, 2006), which builds from a philosophical base to a middle that includes considerations of facts, principles and values, and stakeholders and values, before reaching the point of decision at the top.

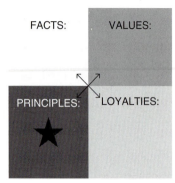

FIGURE 15-1 The Potter Box

and those piles led to a model – soon called the "Potter Box" – that is widely used when a person making a decision wants to systematically consider myriad and conflicting factors. Potter suggests that decision makers should:

- Define the **facts** of the case
- Identify the **values** of the decision maker
- Consider the **ethical principles** of moral philosophy that could be applied
- Balance the decision maker's **loyalties**

when making a decision. The box (Figure 15-1) helps a decision maker balance considerations of the immediate, "real-life" parts of the problem (facts and loyalties) and its more philosophical parts (values and ethical principles).

Although it is useful to start with the facts when working through the box, the box "is not merely a random set of isolated questions, but a linked system" that allows you to move among topics as the need arises.[19] Thinking about the values might lead you to focus on loyalties, which might move you think about principles. And thinking about principles might lead to changes in your definition of the ethical problem, which leads you back to the first part of the box. Eventually, going through the box several times – with a different focus each time – can help you reach a solution.

After working with the Potter Box, it quickly becomes clear that the approach is not a Magic Eight Ball that spits out a single answer. The "right" answer to you might come in Quadrant Three (principles) and Quadrant Four (loyalties) to someone else. Ultimately, well-meaning people will reach different solutions when they have different values or different loyalties. A person using the Potter Box at different times could reach different conclusions about the same topic. It can be a frustrating process – and may have to be done quickly under the duress of deadline – yet the Potter Box is designed not to make the decision but instead to help you organize your thinking as you reach an ethically defensible decision.

Thinking Ethically: Applying the Potter Box

This section of the chapter focuses on the four steps in the Potter Box, providing general insight on each step as well as seeing how the box could be used to make a decision in the *Good Morning, Freedonia* case study. Space limitations do not allow for fuller discussions on each of the steps, so refer to the list of references at the end of the chapter for more insight on the Potter Box's uses.

1. Define the Facts

General insight: Although it may seem easy, determining the facts that should play a part when making a decision can be quite difficult. Now is time to focus on gathering information without prejudging those facts, playing favorites with facts, ignoring facts, or hiding facts. Though it is important to realize that some facts are more important than others, it's also worth remembering that we may not be able to gather all the facts we truly need to make a decision. As former Defense Secretary Donald Rumsfeld explained, "There are things that we don't know. But there are also unknown unknowns. There are things we don't know we don't know."[20] The best we can do is to define the situation as clearly, accurately, and completely as possible, with the understanding that new facts can change our analysis.

Good Morning, Freedonia: A fictional case study by definition must present enough facts to prompt discussion and proposed solutions, but consider other information that might be useful in making a decision. What might your corporate bosses think about the plan to sell part of the show, and what do they think of you in general? Have other stations in Freedonia or in your chain done something similar, and what happened in those instances? Can you order an analysis to determine whether the sales manager would be right in predicting that the show would be profitable in 9 months by selling product placements? Do you know enough about your personnel to be able to predict whether the news director would quit in a sanctimonious huff, or if the sales manager would quit and complain to corporate bosses that you kept him from maximizing revenue, based upon your decision? With the exception of the question about what the corporate bosses might think, none of individual questions would be enough to lead you to a decision but taken altogether could contribute to the decision.

2. Identify the Values

General insight: Like its Latin root meaning "worth," this stage requires thinking about all the people, groups, beliefs, and issues that have significance for the decision maker. Values are important because they ultimately influence our behaviors, as we are rarely comfortable with actions that do not comport with our strongly held attitudes about what is good or bad, right or wrong, and useful or folly.[21] Those values are inculcated from parents, role models, organizations (whether it be churches or street gangs), peers, and society all around us. The values can be seen negatively or positively – Rokeach showed, for example, how socialists valued "freedom" and "equality" highly, communists valued "equality" but not "freedom," and fascists valued neither.[22]

A decision maker's values can be lumped into several categories. A list of values held by media managers might include:

Moral – justice, fairness, truth, honesty, transparency, nonviolence
Logical – consistency of thought, wisdom, inner harmony

Professional – freedom of speech, freedom of the press, the public's right to know, autonomy, quality story-telling, innovative, seeking recognition for good work, maximizing profits, providing "truth" to the public, speaking truth to power, pleasing an audience, pleasing bosses
Personal – salvation, self-respect, mature love, self-control, a comfortable life, a happy life, broadmindedness
Societal – thrift, restraint, personal freedom, personal responsibility, national security
Aesthetic – a world of beauty, imagination, and pleasure[‡]

This list is not exhaustive, as values vary by decision maker. It is clear that values can easily become in conflict with one another. One media ethics writer defines ethical thought as finding ways to "negotiate among conflicting values."[23] Regardless of whether a decision maker is aware of it, values often are the starting place – and the fallback position – when making a decision. The key to the Potter Box is to be able to identify the competing values and, when possible, determine which of the competing values deserve more consideration than others.

Good Morning, Freedonia: The key in this step is identifying which values might be in conflict with one another. If you rose from the news ranks to become station manager, then your values might lie in basic news values related to being credible with an audience and autonomy. You might consider the aesthetics of a newscast that includes product placements. Your personal self-respect might come from delivering a news product that does not blur advertising with editorial content. You might struggle with the moral issue of transparency, as the audience may not understand that the news show contains product placement. If you rose from the sales ranks to become general manager, then your values might be closer to maximizing profits and pleasing bosses. Your personal self-respect might come from creating content that makes it appealing to advertisers. Regardless of your background, you may value the happiness and comfort that come with your high-paying, high-power position in your community.

As stated before, your values are based on your upbringing and world view. How you rank your values depends greatly on what is important to you – and, perhaps, what you are willing to do to keep your job.

[‡] This list of values is compiled in part from Milton Rokeach's list from his values survey and from Christians et al., *Media ethics: Cases and moral reasoning*, pages 25–26. Though Rokeach's list has values listed in sets of terminal (end-states of existence) and instrumental (modes of behavior) values, the chapter's list combined those values into the single set.

3. Consider the Ethical Principles of Moral Philosophy

General insight: The wisdom of many millennia is the focus in this part of the box, which asks decision makers to choose among the many moral philosophies that have both stood the test of time and provide consistency in ethical thought. By relying upon one of these principles, a decision maker can steer clear of moralizing and instead reach a decision that can be both ethically justifiable and ethically consistent.

Louis Hodges, a Duke Divinity School graduate and retired Knight professor of journalism ethics at Washington and Lee University, listed five key values that are central to ethical principles – duty, love, rights, virtue, and utility.[§] These philosophies are contradictory, as they appeal to different values, and one may be better than others given the situation that needs resolving. The approaches can further be categorized by whether they are focused more on the outcome (known as *consequentialist* ethics or *teleological* ethics, from the Greek word meaning "end" or "purpose") or focused more on the idea that some acts are good or bad regardless of the outcome (known as *deontological* ethics, from the Greek word meaning "duty" or "obligation"). As a simple example, deontologists would nearly always tell the truth, because they believe it is wrong to lie, and teleologists would balance the damage of a lie against the possibility that telling the lie is less harmful than the result of not lying.

Though plenty of thinkers have crafted well-defined ethical principles, the ones that Western mass communicators pay closest attention to include those stated by the following men.

Aristotle and Confucius

Aristotle, a student of Plato, offered the "Golden Mean," which states that what is ethical lies between the extremes of excess and deficiency. Confucius, who lived half a world away a century earlier, described a similar ethical principle in *The Doctrine of the Mean*.

Aristotle was influenced by a Greek culture that sought lives of harmony, proportion, and symmetry. As he wrote in *Eudemian Ethics*, "even greatness of spirit must be a middle ground."[24] His *Nicomachean Ethics* described three pillars – a balanced state that leads to good health, a definition of virtue as what falls between two vices, and that your mean will be different from the mean of others.

This last pillar suggests that finding the golden mean is not a simple "divide by two" solution in which the mean is the precise middle. Instead, different

---

[§] Another value, the "ethical egoism" defined by Machiavelli and others that argues people should do what is in their own self-interest, ultimately has flaws because it neither contributes to Pareto Optimality nor provides the consistency that a true moral philosophy would require.

situations require different decisions about where the mean lies. Because of this, the "Golden Mean" approach is a teleological approach that values both virtue and utility.

Jesus Christ

His principle of *agape* has been translated from the Greek to mean "love" or "charity," which is distinct from love for family, the "philia" brotherly love for others, or sexual love. Christ's statement that his followers should "love your neighbor as yourself" (Matthew 22:39) has led to a Judeo-Christian ethic of focusing on the worth and needs of others. This ethical principle focused on love and virtue and can be both deontological (always follow the rule of self-less love for all, especially the weak) and teleological (be willing to focus on outcomes that will best help others).

Immanuel Kant

This eighteenth-century German philosopher is best known for a deontological approach to ethics that values duty above all else. His "Categorical Imperative" requires that people do only what they would want to become a universal law, and it requires that people are treated as an ends unto themselves and not merely a means to an end. Put more simply, it says that you should do only what you would want everyone else on the planet to be able to do – and do not worry about the consequences because higher truths are at stake.

John Stuart Mill

A century after Kant came a different approach from Mill, a London-area philosopher who defined a more practical teleological theory first described by Jeremy Bentham. Their theory of utilitarianism argues that an ethical person will seek the greatest good (or happiness) for the greatest number, or at least the least bad for the fewest number. This appeal to utility requires people to consider all the possible actions, their possible consequences, and to calculate the amount of good or bad that could happen to the fewest or most people. Ethicists have differentiated between "act" utilitarianism, which takes a case-by-case look at a situation, and "rule" utilitarianism, in which people look for the ethical rules that can do the most good or least harm. The problem, of course, is that we cannot always predict accurately which choice will bring the most good or least harm.

In using this approach, a government could justify buying land from an unwilling seller in order to build a road that will help everyone in a community, or a newspaper not printing the name of a rape victim because harm to that victim is worse than the harm to the community in not having the victim's name.

John Rawls

The twentieth-century Harvard philosopher focused on the ethical duty we have to justice. His best-remembered approach requires decision makers to start from an "original position" of ignorance about themselves. They are to reach the fairest and most just decision without knowing what role they play, because reasonable people would reach a decision that protects weaker parties. It is a more complicated approach than the Golden Rule's "do unto others as they would do unto you," but the sentiments are similar. Rawls described his work as deontological in nature, because fairness – especially for society's weak – is more important than producing the greatest good for the greatest number.

A critique of his work comes from feminist theory, which argues that more important than justice is concern about relationships and caring for others.

William David Ross

This Scottish philosopher, who died in 1971, was focused on the binding duties we have toward each other. These seven *prima facie* duties include fidelity (keep your promises; do not lie), reparation (make up for your wrongdoing), gratitude (when possible, repay good), non-malfeasance (do not hurt others), justice, beneficence (work to improve the world), and self-improvement.

Ross acknowledges that his list is incomplete and that items on the list can compete with each other; when this happens, work for balance to make up for the shortcomings. His approach is a deontological one with a focus on duty.

Good Morning, Freedonia: It is clear that not all of the ethical principles mentioned are of equal worth in considering the situation, but the one(s) you choose to focus on can be instrumental in influencing the decision you make. In some instances, two people could use the same theory to justify different decisions. Think about the decision of whether to allow product placement inside of the show through the framework of these philosophies.

Aristotle and Confucius could be used to argue that product placement – if not in news shows, not involving news personnel, not pushy, and limited to well-defined segments – might be justifiable in certain circumstances. One station general manager has made this argument.[25] Or it could be that some of the values stated in the second box – transparency and self-respect, for example – are so overarching that the golden mean has no middle ground.

Kant's "Categorical Imperative" could be used to argue that allowing a news show to include product placements is wrong, because we would not want all news shows to include such ads. The news director would likely rely on this rules-based approach when arguing that the line between commerce and news should never be crossed, and doing so would crassly treat audience members not as news consumers but as an audience that can be manipulated by advertisers regardless of the setting.

John Rawls would ask you to think of yourself as an audience member who may not be aware that the same show uses similar formats to deliver both news and advertising. Rawls would suggest that, at the very least, it would be unethical if the audience is not aware that the show includes product placement.

John Stuart Mill's utilitarian approach is tricky, because of the difficulties in determining what would do the most good or the least harm. The sales manager can argue that the bad that could come from introducing advertising content into the program would be more than made up for by the revenue, and that labeling the advertising content would further limit the downside. The news director can argue that the loss of credibility in the station's news operation could not be offset by the financial gain. Neither has the crystal ball that lets them see into the future, which makes your utility-based decision all the more difficult.

What would Jesus do? It is hard to say, because the principles of agape love seem difficult to apply in this situation. The same goes for Ross's prima facie duties, where a conflict exists between self-improvement (if it can be defined that making a quicker profit is self-improvement) and fidelity (which can be defined as maintaining an obvious wall between news and advertising for viewers).

4. Balance the Decision Maker's Loyalties

General insight: The fourth box asks decision makers to consider to whom they hold duties or obligations. This part of the box helps people identify the numerous and competing people, organizations, and groups to whom allegiances may be held, to consider how those competing interests may be helped or hurt by the decision, and ultimately to rank those loyalties when making a decision.

To whom might we feel the need to be loyal? Day and Christians et al.,[26] list six types of obligations:

1. Yourself. Above all else, you should be able to maintain your integrity and to live with yourself and the decisions you make. At some point, there may be a line we are not willing to cross in order to advance ourselves; Christians et al. remind us that careerism can lead us to "act out of our own self-interest while we claim to be following our conscience."[27]
2. Objects of moral judgment. We should be especially careful to consider the harm we can do to people/groups who are "affected directly by our ethical decisions,"[28] such as children who may be in our audience or people who are the topic of news stories.
3. Financial supporters. The people who ultimately pay our salaries – whether they be subscribers, advertisers, or clients – deserve our attention, and not only because they are the ones who buy our products.
4. Our organization. This not only includes our immediate supervisor or others in our office, but also could include shareholders and other parts of a conglomerate for which we work.

5. Our profession and colleagues. We often make decisions based upon what our peers will think, and we work to uphold the highest expectations of our craft and others who practice it.

6. Society. Though this group seems amorphous, it is instructive to remember that our messages (and our gatekeeping of messages) play a role in setting our society's agenda. We should remember that society is made up of many groups with competing wants, needs, and interests, and that we cannot always predict what impact we will have on those groups and society at large.

As with other elements of the Potter Box, it is easy to see the conflicting loyalties. The task of the Potter Box is to help us identify the stakeholders and determine a potential order of loyalties. How we choose that order often is based on which ethical principle we choose, such as deciding between Kant's rule that we must treat each person as a means unto himself and Mills's understanding that the best we can do sometimes is seek to limit the damage we must do.

Good Morning, Freedonia: The sales manager in this case would argue that our duty to our employer, and indirectly to our advertisers, deserves our top loyalty. The news director would argue that the duty to the audience (and therefore to society) as well as a duty to professionalism would be more important than other loyalties. As station manager, you must balance those competing loyalties with an over-arching duty to yourself as you make the final call.

A Solution? Limits of the Potter Box

The Potter Box is useful in thinking about issues and assigning priorities, but it provides no promise of perfect solutions. As we close the box and the *Good Morning, Freedonia* case study, note that the authors have not recommended a solution. Our hope is to introduce the box and some of the variables that come into play when making a decision.

The box is useful, but profit-centered corporations may move it to the backseat and focus more on the bottom line than on communication ethics. Backus and Ferraris note that "there appears to be no usage of the Potter Box in business communication outside public relations."[29] An ethics textbook used in many business schools[30] includes a similar model that specifically mentions legal requirements and economic outcomes that are not explicitly mentioned in the Potter Box.¶ A media manager must be aware of the economic considerations

---

¶ A search of the *Journal of Mass Media Ethics* mentions the Potter Box in at least 15 articles between 1985 and 2009, yet the Potter Box was not mentioned in articles published by the *Journal of Business Systems Governance & Ethics*, the *Ruffin Series in Business Ethics*, *Business Ethics: A European Review*, *Electronic Journal of Business and Organization Ethics*, and *Business Ethics Quarterly*. It was used once in a 1998 *Journal of Business Ethics* article.

of a decision, of course, but must balance it with larger societal implications in order to make a decision that is truly ethically justifiable.

PRACTICAL PERSPECTIVES ON ETHICS

The manner in which these principles of ethics are applied varies within the media. Some professions, such as journalists, get additional guidance from codes of ethics or professional responsibility created by trade organizations. Others have to rely on a combination of training, personal experience, and good advice to inform their behavior. This section explores specific issues you might address in your professional career.

Ethics and Journalism

Journalists have long been held to a higher standard of ethics and responsibility because of their unique role in a democratic society. The First Amendment to the U.S. Constitution establishes the press as deserving of freedom from interference from the government. But with that freedom comes a higher level of responsibility than most jobs in media. In addition to the legal considerations, there is also a set of practical considerations for high standards of ethics among journalists – ethical behavior helps journalistic organizations maintain their credibility, which is vital for attracting audiences and selling advertising.

The ethical standards expected of journalists have been compiled in codes of ethics created by professional organizations, media outlets, and other organizations from across the globe (Society of Professional Journalists, 2009). A representative code from the Society of Professional Journalists is reproduced in Figure 15-2. This code divides the ethical responsibilities of journalists into four categories: "seek truth and report it," "minimize harm," "act independently," and "be accountable."[31] Within each category, specific standards guide reporters, editors, and others involved in the journalism profession.

Ethics and Entertainment

The creation of entertainment programming, especially for television and the movies, creates ethical challenges that are very different from, but no less challenging than, those for journalism. At first glance, the process of creating and producing entertainment programming might seem to work outside of traditional media ethics considerations. After all, entertainment programming is less serious and usually involves creation of fiction.

From an ethical perspective, the problem is that people can learn as much from entertainment as from informational content. Albert Bandura's social learning theory[32] explores the manner in which people learn behaviors that

Preamble

Members of the Society of Professional Journalists believe that public enlightenment is the forerunner of justice and the foundation of democracy. The duty of the journalist is to further those ends by seeking truth and providing a fair and comprehensive account of events and issues. Conscientious journalists from all media and specialties strive to serve the public with thoroughness and honesty. Professional integrity is the cornerstone of a journalist's credibility. Members of the Society share a dedication to ethical behavior and adopt this code to declare the Society's principles and standards of practice.

Seek Truth and Report It

Journalists should be honest, fair and courageous in gathering, reporting and interpreting information.

Journalists should:

— Test the accuracy of information from all sources and exercise care to avoid inadvertent error. Deliberate distortion is never permissible.
— Diligently seek out subjects of news stories to give them the opportunity to respond to allegations of wrongdoing.
— Identify sources whenever feasible. The public is entitled to as much information as possible on sources' reliability.
— Always question sources' motives before promising anonymity. Clarify conditions attached to any promise made in exchange for information. Keep promises.
— Make certain that headlines, news teases and promotional material, photos, video, audio, graphics, sound bites and quotations do not misrepresent. They should not oversimplify or highlight incidents out of context.
— Never distort the content of news photos or video. Image enhancement for technical clarity is always permissible. Label montages and photo illustrations.
— Avoid misleading re-enactments or staged news events. If re-enactment is necessary to tell a story, label it.
— Avoid undercover or other surreptitious methods of gathering information except when traditional open methods will not yield information vital to the public. Use of such methods should be explained as part of the story.
— Never plagiarize.
— Tell the story of the diversity and magnitude of the human experience boldly, even when it is unpopular to do so.
— Examine their own cultural values and avoid imposing those values on others.
— Avoid stereotyping by race, gender, age, religion, ethnicity, geography, sexual orientation, disability, physical appearance or social status.
— Support the open exchange of views, even views they find repugnant.
— Give voice to the voiceless; official and unofficial sources of information can be equally valid.
— Distinguish between advocacy and news reporting. Analysis and commentary should be labeled and not misrepresent fact or context.
— Distinguish news from advertising and shun hybrids that blur the lines between the two.
— Recognize a special obligation to ensure that the public's business is conducted in the open and that government records are open to inspection.

Minimize Harm

Ethical journalists treat sources, subjects and colleagues as human beings deserving of respect.

Journalists should:

— Show compassion for those who may be affected adversely by news coverage. Use special sensitivity when dealing with children and inexperienced sources or subjects.
— Be sensitive when seeking or using interviews or photographs of those affected by tragedy or grief.
— Recognize that gathering and reporting information may cause harm or discomfort. Pursuit of the news is not a license for arrogance.
— Recognize that private people have a greater right to control information about themselves than do public officials and others who seek power, influence or attention. Only an overriding public need can justify intrusion into anyone's privacy.
— Show good taste. Avoid pandering to lurid curiosity.
— Be cautious about identifying juvenile suspects or victims of sex crimes.
— Be judicious about naming criminal suspects before the formal filing of charges.
— Balance a criminal suspect's fair trial rights with the public's right to be informed.

Act Independently

Journalists should be free of obligation to any interest other than the public's right to know.

Journalists should:

— Avoid conflicts of interest, real or perceived.
— Remain free of associations and activities that may compromise integrity or damage credibility.
— Refuse gifts, favors, fees, free travel and special treatment, and shun secondary employment, political involvement, public office and service in community organizations if they compromise journalistic integrity.
— Disclose unavoidable conflicts.
— Be vigilant and courageous about holding those with power accountable.
— Deny favored treatment to advertisers and special interests and resist their pressure to influence news coverage.
— Be wary of sources offering information for favors or money; avoid bidding for news.

Be Accountable

Journalists are accountable to their readers, listeners, viewers and each other.

Journalists should:

— Clarify and explain news coverage and invite dialogue with the public over journalistic conduct.
— Encourage the public to voice grievances against the news media.
— Admit mistakes and correct them promptly.
— Expose unethical practices of journalists and the news media.
— Abide by the same high standards to which they hold others.

FIGURE 15-2 Society of Professional Journalists code of ethics. *Source: http://www.spj.org/ethicscode.asp*

are modeled by others, including those in the media. Bandura indicated that the likelihood of copying a behavior modeled on the media is a function of people's perceptions of their ability to copy the behavior and the perceived consequences of engaging in the behavior.[33]

Consider this example: The 1993 movie *The Program* included a famous scene where college football players demonstrated their courage by lying on the double-yellow stripe in the middle of a road. A small handful of teens who watched the movie saw lying in the road as a test of their own courage, copying the behaviors they watched in the movie. A Pennsylvania teen died, and at least two others were hurt. The question here is ethical responsibility. The Walt Disney Co. deleted the scene within a month of the movie's opening (New York Times, 1993). The question remains: Do writers and directors have a responsibility to not portray behaviors that could be damaging to audience members?

A more common example is the media's depiction of smoking and drinking. Public health officials have long pressured the media to limit the depiction of smoking and drinking onscreen so that audience members – especially impressionable children – won't copy those behaviors. But in reality, people *do* drink and smoke. Should reality be sanitized to protect the audience?

One consistent answer that media organizations have used is to show the consequences of negative behavior. If criminal behavior is shown, the criminal would be caught and/or punished before the end of the program. One of the authors of this chapter once wanted to add a food fight to a children's television show but was concerned about the likelihood of children copying the behavior. The answer, in applying Bandura's theory, was to follow the 10-second food fight with a 1-minute scene in which the children throwing the food were required to clean up the mess they made. The dramatic point was made, and the final product was more entertaining than the original script.

A separate consideration is the blurring line between entertainment and news. News organizations have long had ethical codes, but those in entertainment don't have that level of guidance. What happens, then, when the two are merged? Is the morning show example from the beginning of the chapter an example that falls under "journalism ethics" or "entertainment ethics"? What about a radio talk show or a comedy news show on cable television?

Ethics and Sales

As discussed earlier in this chapter, many business executives base their ethical decisions on Pareto Optimality – the idea that decisions in business should be guided by what is best for the stockholders. In practice, however, these decisions are not as simple as maximizing short-term profits. Many decisions with short-term benefit can prove damaging or even disastrous in the long term. For example, selling the largest possible advertising schedule to a client may benefit a media organization in the short term, but in the long term, the size and efficiency of the advertising schedule have to match the needs of the business. When businesses invest in advertising, they expect to earn a return on their investment. Those who realize that return on investment are much more likely to continue to invest in advertising, benefitting both the advertiser and the media organization.

Ethics in advertising involve more than attention to the needs and goals of the media organization – it also involves ethical behavior in relation to the audience. Just as a business expects a return on investment from advertising, consumers also expect – and deserve – a fair return on their investment in the products they buy as a result of advertising messages. Media organizations have ethical and legal responsibilities to avoid false or misleading advertising. Some companies will always exist by trying to sell questionable products or services, and it is easy for a media organization to reject responsibility for the messages and to push that responsibility on the advertiser. Such short-term thinking ignores the long-term consequences – if any advertising messages lose credibility with the audience, the credibility of all advertising messages may become questionable in the minds of the consumers.

Ethics and Content Ownership/Distribution

As discussed earlier in this text, media organizations are engaged in the processes of content creation, processing, and distribution. As you might expect, the lucrative role of content management has as many ethical challenges as any other area of communication.

Content owners are consistently faced with the issue of what rights to content they actually acquire when content is created. Trade unions in the entertainment industry have long recognized the role of creative artists (especially writers, performers, and directors) in creating valuable media content, requiring "residual" payments to creative personnel every time content generates new income. For nonunion productions, the content owner must decide or negotiate the rights that are conferred when content is produced "for hire." This issue has become especially problematic as new media have emerged over the past 20 years that enable a content owner to earn additional revenue. The two ethical questions are: (1) Did the original (or subsequent) agreements convey rights to distribute the artists' work in new media? and (2) Does a content owner have an ethical responsibility to share revenue from these new channels with the people who played a role in creating the content?

Most contracts drawn up over the past few decades include wording that addresses the first question, conveying the rights in "any and all media now existing or created in the future." The second question is more complicated – it is easy to state that, because a content owner has purchased or negotiated the rights, that owner deserves *all* the revenue from additional distribution.

But a competing perspective asserts that creative artists should be entitled to a portion of the revenues from their work. This is not a legal issue – as of this writing, the law is clearly on the side of the content owner. But it is an ethical issue that content owners must address.

The ethics of the "processing" of media content are more complicated. Limits of technology used to prevent content from being modified without a great deal of time and effort, but today's digital technology allows content creators and editors to "sample" or modify existing media content (including photos, audio, video, and graphics) to create derivative works. A great example is the iconic poster of Barack Obama that was created during his 2008 presidential campaign, in which an artist (Shepard Fairey) extensively modified and colored an Associated Press photograph of Obama to create a "new" work. A lawsuit over the issue remains in federal court as of this writing.

There are both legal and ethical dimensions to modifying media content to create derivative works. The courts consider a wide variety of issues in deciding legal ownership, including the amount of work taken, how much income was generated from the derivative work, and whether the derivative work is a parody or makes a political point. The ethical issue is much simpler – should you have to get permission from and give credit to a content owner when you take part of their work to create a new work?

ETHICS AND USER-GENERATED CONTENT

From the two-decades-old *America's Funniest Home Videos* to Web sites such as YouTube and Facebook, media organizations are relying on user-generated content. Allowing users to contribute media content has multiple advantages for a media organization, ranging from content that costs much less to produce than the cost of producing original content) to strengthening relationships between users and media organizations. But media organizations must address a number of ethical issues in adding user-generated content to their message mix, including:

- **Ownership of content:** Every time users contribute content, the organization must clearly define the rights that users are conferring to the media organization. These rights are especially important for breaking news items, where members of the public may be more likely to have pictures or video because they were on the scene as the story happened. (It is also important to note that a statement indicating that users confer all rights to your organization when submitting content may not be binding if challenged in court.)
- **Realism of content:** The ability to contribute content also gives members of the public – especially those with a specific agenda to push – an opportunity to falsify content. The motives for faking news range from simple

mischief to complicated agenda setting, but, in all cases, it is the responsibility of the media organization to verify the source and validity of the content.

- **Labeling and editing of content:**   Media organizations have a responsibility to credit the source of content, especially to make it clear that the content came from third parties not affiliated with the organization. Otherwise, for example, consumers might believe a press release was written by your news staff. Given that traditional media are known for their gate-keeping actions, failure to draw clear distinctions can hurt an organization's credibility by making it seem as if the organization has vouched for the content's accuracy.

- **Opinions vs. facts:**   Research has indicated that blogs, which are one of a primary source of user-generated content, contain a disproportionate amount of opinions versus original information.[34] When allowing users – or your own staff – to contribute blogs to your organization's Web site, the site must clarify the responsibility for such content. The question is whether it is ethical for a media organization to make money off someone's work (usually by surrounding this user-generated content with advertising), but then place all of the legal – and financial – responsibility with the submitter.

  Related to this issue is the editing of user comments on Web sites. Many blogs and news sites let readers comment on content but do not edit the comments because, if media organizations edit those contents, they may be liable in cases of libel or privacy invasion. The result can be a free-for-all of name-calling, insults, and lies that are tolerated for the sake of legal troubles.

- **Expanding your reporting base:**   It is possible to use "citizen journalists" and other user-generated content to replace the work of reporters, photographers, editors, and other paid staff for your organization. At first glance, this might seem like an inexpensive source of content. However, there is a high value in professionals trained in their craft as well as ethics and First Amendment law. Any time professional reporters are replaced instead of supplemented by user-generated content, the media organization risks its own standards and introduces a breadth of legal considerations.

SUMMARY

This chapter has explored and applied ethical principles to the management of media organizations. The answers to ethical questions are not simple, and they are rarely obvious. The important lesson from this chapter is that all media executives – in fact, anyone who works in media – should learn and practice a set of ethical standards that will help in making good decisions that protect the organization, the people involved, and the audience. Time spent understanding your own ethical standards, and the standards of your organization and industry, will pay off when deadline decisions must be made.

CASE STUDY 15.1 A PIECE OF ADVICE

The general manager of a local television station that has traditionally placed third or fourth in news needs to make a big move by hiring someone who will bring in big ratings. Extensive research in his market indicates that a well-known anchor (Joe King) on the competitive station is pulling high numbers in terms of recognition and also ranks high when those surveyed are asked whether he is a reason for viewers to watch the news. His contract is coming up in 3 months, and rumor on the street is that this anchor no longer wants to continue working for the competition – he has grown tired of their particular brand of news.

The GM doesn't take any chances and offers this high-profile anchor a package which he gladly accepts. However, the viewers will have to be patient, because Joe King will have to work in an "off-air" position for 1 year as part of his noncompete clause. Before you know it, a full year has passed and a well-planned promotional campaign rolls out announcing that Joe King, everyone's favorite news anchor, is back on the air and better than ever. After the first week on the air, it appears that Joe is going to be just the answer to their rating woes.

Unfortunately, over the next 9 months, ratings are not only flat – they are actually lower in some newscasts. In a move to complement Joe's style of anchoring, the GM also hires an Emmy-award-winning investigative reporter who is aggressively going after a local car dealership, Lee's Automotive. This dealership has had several complaints filed against it for selling used cars financed at higher-than-agreed-upon rates. In addition, some customers claim that they were taken advantage of due to age and physical disabilities. The investigative reporter works with the Attorney General's office to go undercover and get a local expert to view some of the footage and provide comments on how this dealership is cheating customers.

In the meantime, the new anchor, Joe King, receives a phone call from the owner of this car dealership because he has sponsored Joe's charity event every year. In fact, Joe has developed somewhat of a friendship with Michael Lee, the owner of Lee's Automotive. Michael tells Joe about the investigative piece that his news department is conducting and asks that the story be fair and balanced. Joe responds that he does not have anything to do with the story. Michael replies again, "Be sure it is a fair story." Joe tells him he'll call him back, and they exchange a couple of phone calls.

Joe finds out more about the story and is now being asked by people in the sales department if he has spoken to Michael Lee of Lee Automotive. Joe tells them that he has not spoken to Michael.

One day prior to the investigative story's airing, Joe calls Michael and advises him that at this point the best he can do his work with a PR specialist to put a positive spin on the story. In fact, he goes on to tell Michael, "My wife does PR on the side, and she could really help out in this situation." He goes on to tell Michael that some of the salespeople have been asking him if he had spoken to him, and he told them "No," as he wants to keep this between them. Michael agrees and asks about the fees his PR specialist wife charges. Joe replies, "My wife will be fair in her pricing." Joe hangs up feeling like he did the right thing. He ethically cannot provide consultation to Michael and has deflected it to an outside party. Michael, on the other hand, was desperate for help and recorded the entire conversation.

After the story breaks, Lee's Automotive is experiencing a 50 percent drop in business. Mr. Lee hires an attorney and also releases the recorded conversation to the local newspaper which runs a story on the incident. Mr. Lee explains that he felt like he was being forced to use the services of Joe King's wife because of the negative story the station was about to run the next day. He also claims that many of the facts in the story were distorted and not fully explained.

The GM stands by the actions of his anchor and explains that Joe was attempting to help, and it was simply a mistake to recommend his wife.

Assignment

Write a one- to two-page evaluation that includes the following elements along with your personal perspective on this event:

1. If you are president of this television station, do you support the actions taken by the general manager?
2. What ethical issues does this situation project?
3. What steps would you have taken if you were the general manager?
4. If you worked at another TV station, would you cover this story?
5. Go to Poynter's Institute and review the Ethics Codes. Do you see any violations?
6. Did this act violate any FCC rules?

7. What impact would this have with the viewing audience?
8. Do you keep Joe King on as your main anchor? If you keep this employee, do you have him address the viewers? How about other employees?
9. What about Michael Lee? Did he break any laws in recording the conversation? Find out what the laws are in your state. Should you take any action?
10. If you ran a television station, what steps would you take to prevent this from happening?

REFERENCES

1. Reilly, B. & Kyj, M. (1990). Economics and ethics. *Journal of Business Ethics* 9, 693.

2. Hosmer, L. T. (2006). *The ethics of management*, 5th Ed. New York: McGraw Hill/Irwin, 31.

3. Rohmann, C. (1999). *A world of ideas: A dictionary of important theories, concepts, beliefs, and thinkers.* New York: Ballantine Books.

4. Black, J. & Bryant, J. (1995). *Doing ethics in journalism: A handbook with case studies (first edition).* 1993. Greencastle, Ind: *Introduction to mass communication* (4th ed.). New York: McGraw Hill.

5. Christians, C. G. (1997). The ethics of being in a communications context. In *Communication ethics and universal values*, C. Christians and M. Traber (Eds.), 3–23. Thousand Oaks, CA: Sage; Christians, C. G., Rao, S., Ward, S. J. A. & Wasserman, H. (2008). Toward a global media ethics: Theoretical perspectives. *Ecquid novi: African Journalism Studies* 29, 135–172.

6. Festinger, L. (1957). *A theory of cognitive dissonance*. Stanford, CA: Stanford University Press.

7. United States Food and Drug Administration. Saving our children from tobacco. Retrieved May 29, 2009, at www.fda.gov/FDAC/features/896_tob.html.

8. Watterson, B. 1990. *Weirdos from another planet*. Riverside, NJ: Andrews and McMeel, 1990, 43.

9. Martin, A. (June 14, 2007). Kellogg to phase out some food ads to children. *New York Times* national edition, 1.

10. Cyberjournalist.net (2003). A bloggers' code of ethics. Retrieved June 1, 2009, at http://www.cyberjournalist.net/news/000215.php.

11. Free Speech Coalition (2006). Ethics and best practices. Retrieved June 1, 2009, at www.freespeechcoalition.com/FSCview.asp?coid=595&keywords=code+of+ethics.

12. Black, J., Steele, B. & Barney, R. (1993). *Doing ethics in journalism: A handbook with case studies*, Greencastle, IN: Society of Professional Journalists, 8.

13. American Society of Magazine Editors (2008). ASME guidelines for editors and publishers. Retrieved May 29, 2009, at www.magazine.org/asme/asme_guidelines/index.aspx.

14. Radio Television News Directors Association (2000). Code of ethics and professional conduct. Retrieved May 29, 2009, at www.rtnda.org/pages/media_items/code-of-ethics-and-professional-conduct48.php.

15. Society of Professional Journalists (1996). Code of ethics. Retrieved June 4, 2009, at www.spj.org/ethicscode.asp.

16. Schiller, G. (March 16, 2006). Advertisers get piece of local news shows: News lures sponsor. *Hollywood Reporter*. Retrieved June 1, 2009, at www.hollywoodreporter.com/hr/search/article_display.jsp?vnu_content_id=1002197780.
Smith, D. C. (March 3, 2003). Disguising ads as the local news. *Broadcasting and Cable* 40.

17. Harvard Divinity School (2007). Ralph B. Potter Jr. biography. Retrieved June 1, 2009, at www.hds.harvard.edu/faculty/em/potter.cfm.

18. Potter, R. B. (October 1999). The origins and applications of "Potter Boxes." Paper presented at the State of the World Forum, San Francisco, CA, 2.

19. Christians, C. G., Rotzoll, K. B., Fackler, M., McKee, K. B. & Woods, R. H. Jr. (2005). *Media ethics: Cases and moral reasoning.* Boston: Pearson, 6.

20. *Newsweek* (March 10, 2003). Perspective, 21.

21. Rokeach, M. (1973). *The nature of human values.* New York: Free Press.

22. Rokeach, M. (2000). *Understanding human values.* New York: Free Press, 180.

23. Plaisance, P. (2009). *Media ethics: Key principles for responsible practice.* Los Angeles: Sage, 6.

24. Aristotle, *Eudemian Ethics,* 1233a 1.

25. Lawhead, J. (March 10, 2003). Syracuse GM defends magazine show. *Broadcasting and Cable* 40.

26. Day, L. A. (2006). *Ethics in media communications: Cases and controversies.* Belmont, CA: Thomson Higher Education.

27. Christians et al., op. cit.

28. Day, op. cit., 32.

29. Backus, N. & Ferraris, C. (2004). Theory meets practice: Using the Potter Box to teach business communication ethics. Paper presented at the Association for Business Communication annual convention, October, Cambridge, MA.

30. Hosmer, op. cit., vii.

31. Society of Professional Journalists, op. cit.

32. Bandura, A. 1986. *Social foundation of thought and action.* Englewood Cliffs, NJ: Prentice-Hall.

33. New York Times (1993). Disney plans to omit film scene after teen-ager dies imitating it. Retrieved August 21, 2009, from http://www.nytimes.com/1993/10/20/us/disney-plans-to-omit-film-scene-after-teen-ager-dies-imitating-it.html.

34. Roberts, C. & Murley, B. (2005). Biting the hand that feeds: Blogs and second-level agenda setting. Presented at the national Media Convergence Conference, October 2005, Provo, Utah.

Index

411